ETHIOPIAN
REMINISCENCES

Early Days

ETHIOPIAN
REMINISCENCES

Early Days

Richard and Rita Pankhurst

TSEHAI
Publishers & Distributors

MARYMOUNT
INSTITUTE PRESS

Tsehai Publishers
Loyola Marymount University
1 LMU Drive, UH 3012, Los Angeles, CA 90045

www.tsehaipublishers.com
info@tsehaipublishers.com

ISBN: 978-1-59907-059-9 (Paperback)
ISBN: 978-1-59907-070-4 (Hardcover)

First Edition: May 2013

Publisher: Elias Wondimu
Copy Editor: Ellen Hoffs
Layout Design: Tessa Smith
Cover Design: Kerri Blackstone
Design Assistant: Sara Martinez

A catalog record for this book is available from:
Institute of Ethiopian Studies Library at Addis Ababa University
U.S. Library of Congress Catalog Card Number, Washington, DC
British Library Cataloguing in Publication Data

10 9 8 7 6 5 4 3 2 1

Printed in the United States of America

LOS ANGELES | NEW YORK | ADDIS ABABA | JOHANNESBURG

To the memory of
Mengistu Lemma and Afewerk Tekle,
"best men" at our wedding and life-long friends

Contents

Amharic Transcription

In transcribing Amharic words into English the system employed is a departure from that proposed by Stephen Wright, whose contribution to Ethiopian Studies is mentioned in this volume and whose views on this subject will be discussed in our second volume. We have largely followed the system used by Reidulf Molvaer in '*Black Lions: The Creative Lives of Modern Ethiopia's Literary Giants and Pioneers*' (1997), making exceptions for some frequently used names, well established with other spellings.

Introduction

People, knowing that we were long-time residents, often asked us how long we had been in Ethiopia. We would ask in return whether they had ever heard of Lucy, the prehistoric hominid discovered in Eastern Ethiopia in 1974. When, as usual, they replied in the affirmative, we would solemnly tell them that we had been to her wedding.

Our questioners might then ask what it was really like, over fifty years ago, living in Addis Ababa, and travelling about the country. To answer this question we thought that Richard, the scribbler in the family, should write down a reply, so as not to have to repeat it so often. We found, however, that this was easier said than done. Our lives had been intertwined for so long that we often had to depend on our partner for the answer to any question. We therefore plumped for a Joint Autobiography in which we would both have a say—each recalling their separate experiences, while sharing their common ones.

We, the authors of this work, were both born in 1927, a little more than a decade prior to the beginning of World War I, and grew to adolescence and maturity in the immediate post-war world. We both arrived in Ethiopia in 1956, Richard with his mother, Sylvia Pankhurst, in July, and Rita in November.

We left Britain for Ethiopia, with relatively little knowledge of life in the country which lay ahead. Richard, aged eight, had however met *Hakim* Werqneh, the Ethiopian representative in London, in 1935, and had played with his children. On 3 June of the following year, Richard's mother had gone to Waterloo Station to welcome Emperor Hayle-Sillasé into exile, due to the Italian Occupation of Ethiopia. Richard had accompanied her. His mother had by then founded a London-based weekly newspaper in Ethiopia's defence, which she was to edit for twenty years. As he grew older, he began to contribute articles and drawings to the paper. He later made friends with a number of Ethiopian students in England, and briefly visited their country with his mother in 1950-1. He had grown up in an atmosphere in which Ethiopia was of paramount importance.

By contrast, Rita knew scarcely more about Ethiopia than most other Europeans of her time, namely that its Emperor, at the League of Nations in Geneva in 1936, had nobly defended his country against fascist aggression.

Emperor Hayle-Sillasé in exile in Britain, 1936, welcomed by Anthony Eden, British Minister for League of Nations affairs

Rita, who was born in Romania, had travelled in Europe—and through her work, had become interested in Japan. She found Ethiopian civilization very different from that of any country known to her. Though from a relatively wealthy family she was amazed by, and later somewhat critical of, the Ethiopian court ceremonial and the lavish lifestyle of the aristocracy. She soon also became aware of the poverty that led to the numerous beggars in the streets, and joined the Social Service Society, established for their welfare.

From the moment she arrived in Ethiopia, she kept in regular contact with her parents through weekly letters. These were prompted by her desire to allay fears for their daughter, living in a far-away continent about which they knew little, and marrying into a politically active family. The Pankhurst's milieu was very different from her own, in which politics were not discussed. Her letters, written before the advent of electronic communication, constitute a major source for this book. They record our daily life in Ethiopia, as well as some occasional events of national importance.

The reason why the authors came to be in Ethiopia was that Richard's mother, had planned to replace her politically-oriented newspaper, *New Times and Ethiopia News*, with a more substantial culture and development monthly magazine, the *Ethiopia Observer*. At the age of 74, she accepted an invitation from the Emperor to come with her son to live in Ethiopia, and decided to edit her publication from Addis Ababa.

Richard wanted to accompany his mother, who was not in the best of health, and he asked Rita to join them. Sylvia was happy that her son had found a partner and the three of us lived in harmony until she died in 1960.

Our lives, in those first four years, revolved largely around Sylvia's activities. She was travelling and collecting information for the *Observer*; raising funds for the development of the Princess Sehay Hospital, which she had founded; and took an active part in the newly established Social Service Society, one of the first citizens' welfare societies in Ethiopia. To keep in contact with people who could provide information for her articles, she assiduously attended State and other functions, though these tired her. We usually accompanied her.

Soon after arriving in Ethiopia, Rita joined the National Library of Ethiopia. With Richard's support, she organised a series of public lectures which contributed to the growth of Ethiopian consciousness of Africa. She was asked by the Emperor to set up an exhibition at the Palace; and worked, at first with her mother-in-law, in the Social Service Society.

Richard, beside lecturing at the University College of Addis Ababa, assisted his mother with the *Observer*; helped to edit Ethiopia's first Five Year Plan; and wrote his first books on Ethiopia, as well as numerous "learned" and popular articles for the Press.

Richard and Rita, as the years went by, became increasingly involved in Ethiopian academic affairs, with the Institute of Ethiopian Studies and the Kennedy Library respectively. Richard and Rita were destined to live in the country (with breaks in the UK) for the next half-century, far beyond the period covered by this book.

The next decade in Ethiopia witnessed major changes—in our family's life no less than in the annals of the country at large. In December 1960, three months after Sylvia's death, the Imperial Bodyguard staged a *Coup d'État*, which, though abortive, led perhaps inexorably to the Ethiopian Revolution of 1974.

The early 1960s saw the birth of our two children, Alula and Helen. In subsequent years, which lie beyond the scope of this volume, we became increasingly active in Ethiopian academic affairs, Richard as Director of the Institute of Ethiopian Studies and Rita as University Librarian in charge of the newly established Kennedy Library. Seeking to contribute as well as to study our adopted country we involved ourselves in various other activities, most notably the long struggle for the return of the ancient Aksum obelisk looted during the Italian Occupation.

CHAPTER 1

A Changing World

RICHARD

POLITICAL HORIZONS

Though few in Britain realised it at the time, the "international situation", as people then called it, was beginning to deteriorate immeasurably. The era of Fascism had dawned. Mussolini in Italy, Hitler in Germany, Franco in Spain, and would-be dictators in several other European countries were seizing the political initiative all over the continent. Democratic countries and institutions were coming under ruthless and, as many hoped or feared, fatal attack. The principles of Liberty, Equality and Fraternity, which two generations of the Pankhurst family had regarded as embodying the universal aspirations of the human race, were under serious threat—perhaps for the first time since their formulation in the French Revolution of 1789. Fascism seemed everywhere on the ascendant, and was challenged, my parents believed, with far from sufficient resolution.

The world was entering what became known as the Age of Appeasement. It was, for many opponents of dictatorship, a frustrating and seemingly endless nightmare, though in fact it was to last less than a decade: a decade which led on, with the inevitability of a Greek tragedy, to World War II, with all its horrors, followed by a much transformed and scarcely recognisable post-war world. Such was the time in which I grew up, and passed my childhood and early teens.

In Italy, Mussolini had come to power, and, in October 1922, staged his so-called March on Rome. Six years later, when I was one year old, he was responsible for the assassination of the Italian Parliamentary Deputy, Giacomo Matteotti, who will be mentioned again in these pages. In 1932 the dictator ordered his elderly fascist follower, Emilio De Bono, to prepare for the invasion of Ethiopia, then internationally better known as Abyssinia. That aggression, which was to test the then League of Nations to the breaking-point, was entirely unprovoked and involved the use of poison-gas, then outlawed by international convention. The conflict began towards the end of 1935,

Giacomo Matteotti, Italian Parliamentary
Deputy, assassinated by Italian Fascists in 1924,
after their rise to power in 1922

just before my eighth birthday—and was, as we shall see, to have a major influence on my life.

Crucially important events were, meanwhile, also taking place in Germany. Hitler had come to power in 1933, when I was six. He ordered his troops into the demilitarised Rhineland in 1936, and annexed Austria two years later. Also in 1936, the Spanish Civil War had broken out: Italian Fascist and German Nazi "Volunteers"—with their aeroplanes and tanks—were soon gripped in a deadly conflict with the forces of the Spanish Republic. In 1939, Franco finally triumphed. However, that victory was merely a prelude to the ensuing European War, which broke out only five months later.

EARLY DAYS

I was called Richard after my grandfather, my mother's father, Richard Marsden Pankhurst. Much beloved by his children, above all by my mother, he was a late nineteenth century Manchester lawyer, a Republican, and an early member of the Independent Labour Party. My second name, Keir, was given to me in memory of the early twentieth century Labour leader Keir Hardie, who was an intimate friend of my mother's—and of her father's before her. She drew two portraits of Keir Hardie, which are now preserved in the National Portrait Gallery, in London. My third forename, Pethick, was that of Emmeline Pethick-Lawrence, one of my mother's closer Suffragette comrades, who fought with her for Votes for Women, in the years prior to World War I, and will figure in this memoir.

The political events in Europe, as they unfolded, impinged increasingly on my childhood consciousness. My earliest memories are of living in a large old three storey house, long since pulled down, at 3 Charteris Road, Woodford Green, Essex, north-east of London. The house was only five minutes' walk from Woodford Station, itself about an hour's steam train journey from the city centre. In several rooms books on history and literature lined the walls, while a room on the top floor stored an ever increasing pile of back issues of my mother's weekly newspaper *New Times and Ethiopia News* *(NT&EN)*, behind which I and my friends would sometimes hide. In another room there was a mountain of pamphlets and newspapers in many languages and of every political and religious persuasion. They were sent in exchange for *NT&EN,* or in an attempt to influence its editor.

My parents had an extensive, largely unkempt garden, which sported a variety of apple trees on two sides, pear trees on the third, and elsewhere an abundance of raspberry, blackberry, black and red currant, and gooseberry bushes. A venerable old oak tree stood at the back of the garden just beyond our fence. My father, who, when working, often put on a long grey overall coat, prided himself in doing most of the cooking, as well as much of the washing-up. There was also a woman who came in from time to time to do the cleaning, and clothes washing—which latter was then hung up to dry in the kitchen on long poles, with the help of a pulley. At one stage there was a Danish *au pair*, Gurli Jensen, who came to learn English. Sundry European refugees also from time to time helped out in the house.

A third of the building was occupied by tenants, whose rent contributed significantly to meeting household expenses. A gloomy, generally locked, room on the top floor was occupied by an aged, and to me mysterious Englishwoman, Mrs Green, who made a solitary appearance every few months. The first floor was the possession of a couple from the West Indies who ran the local Broadway Music Saloon, and later by a family which seemed to spend most of their daylight hours listening to the entertainment offered by the so-called pirate wireless stations, Radio Normandie and Radio Luxembourg. Our cleaner, who much enjoyed these programmes, spent a disproportionate amount of time "working" on the first floor while listening to them. In those days before central heating much time and effort had, however, to be devoted to carrying up coal or coke and lighting fires, not to mention chimney-sweeping, which was an art or craft in itself.

There were always several domestic animals around: a dog, usually an Airedale, the occasional tortoise, a cat, and a goat, which my father milked and was heart-broken when she died of pneumonia. One of our dogs, to my great distress, was run over by a train while I was being taken in my pram over the nearby Woodford level-crossing. Family lore had it that the animal died, valiantly barking at an oncoming train, to save little Richard. As time went on, some animals got named after historical figures or concepts that I learnt about at school. There was thus a well-built cat called Todtleben, one of the Russians involved in the Crimean War of 1853-6 and which we, schoolboy ignoramuses, referred to as Toddle-Ben. Our Khaki Campbell duck was given the exalted name of Cyclic Quad, i.e. an abbreviation for the geometric term "cyclic quadrilateral". Subsequently, during the war years, I had a dozen chickens or at times ducks. I greatly enjoyed watching the latter jumping happily into whatever bowl of water we provided, and the eagerness with which they washed their feathers. During the World War II

Richard Pankhurst's grandfather, Richard Marsden Pankhurst 1834-1898, a lawyer and early supporter of women's suffrage, and other radical causes

period of rationing I used to present my mother's old Suffragette friend Emmeline Pethick-Lawrence and her MP husband Frederick, with a monthly box of eggs, usually duck eggs, for which we of course never expected nor received payment.

Though living a sheltered life, far away from the catastrophes embroiling more and more of the world, I was beginning to catch glimpses of what was taking place on the Continent of Europe, in Ethiopia, and elsewhere. I learnt relatively little from the Press, for though my parents took the *Manchester Guardian*—now the *Guardian*, as well as *The Times*, the front pages of those broadsheets, like those of other great newspapers of the day, were scarcely designed to catch a child's attention. The front page was devoted to boring advertisements, while news items, introduced with only small headings, were relegated to the inner pages. My parents, moreover, did not possess a radio until around 1935, and television was still unheard of.

My growing awareness of international events therefore resulted mainly from hearing my parents talking about them, for the most part with visitors. These included a wide variety of refugees, from Italy, Germany, Austria, Hungary, Poland and Spain, but later, as a result of the Italian invasion of Ethiopia, from that country itself, as well as from its supporters. Some of the latter came from the West Indies and many parts of Africa: Kenya, the Gold Coast (later Ghana), Nigeria, Egypt, and South Africa, as well as Austria, Hungary, France, Belgium, and Sweden.

Painting by Sylvia of a little boy when in Venice on a scholarship from the Manchester School of Art, 1902

MY PARENTS

My parents were old-style libertarian socialists. They were also committed anti-fascists, anti-racists and anti-colonialists. So, by and large, were many if not most of their friends, not a few of whom I met—or heard talking—as a child. Following the practice of many who shared their political and philosophical point of view, and anticipating later more widespread practice, they on principle never married.

I was influenced in one way or another by both parents, though more by my mother, whose surname I bore. Her greater influence largely resulted from the fact that she outlived my father by six years, and that was the time when my life and career took shape. It was in particular her involvement with far-off Ethiopia, the Land of Prester John and the only country in Africa to survive the European Scramble, i.e. the colonial expansion of the European Powers in Africa, which caused me to become fascinated by that country in which, as we shall see, I was to spend most of my working life.

My mother, Estelle Sylvia Pankhurst (who made little or no use of her first forename), was born into a politically active family in Manchester in 1882. The second of three sisters, daughters of the Manchester lawyer Richard Marsden Pankhurst, and his wife Emmeline Pankhurst, the founder of the Women's Social and Political Union (WSPU), my mother was by training an artist. Much of her early life was connected with the WSPU. Established in Manchester in 1903, it soon extended its activities to London and the rest of Britain. It was the organisation which launched the militant Suffragette movement, and played a unique role in winning British women the Parliamentary vote. My mother, like other Suffragettes, was often arrested, and

Mosaic of St. Mark, copied by Sylvia

responded by carrying out frequent hunger, thirst and sleep strikes and was forcibly fed. She was frequently arrested under the so-called Cat and Mouse Act, according to which a prisoner was released when her health was seriously endangered by a hunger strike, only to be re-arrested when she was seen to have recovered. In the course of the struggle she went on lecture tours to the European Continent and to the United States. She later gravitated to the East End, the poorer, working-class area of London, where, independently of her more conservative mother and sister Christabel, she founded the East London Federation of the Suffragettes. She edited its weekly newspaper *The Women's Dreadnaught*, which was later renamed *The Workers' Dreadnaught*. An enthusiastic supporter of the Russian Revolution of 1917 she later travelled to Russia, where she met—and disputed with—Lenin. She left an account of her visit in her book *Soviet Russia as I Saw It*, and was criticised in the Russian leader's polemic *Left-Wing Communism: An Infantile Disorder*.

After Votes for Women were won in Britain, and in the years of my infancy and childhood, my mother devoted much of her time to writing. She chronicled the Suffragette struggle, and her own involvement in it, as well as her political and social work in the East End, in two semi-autobiographical works: *The Suffragette Movement* and *The Home Front*. She also produced a brief biography of her mother Emmeline; a collection of poems entitled *Writ on Cold Slate*; a survey of maternity problems in Britain; a plea for an international language (in which she favoured a Latin-based artificial language called Interlingua); and a history of India. Long interested in poetry, she also collaborated with a London-based Romanian scholar G. Stefanovici in

Richard Pankhurst's grandmother, the Suffragette leader, Emmeline Pankhurst,
being arrested while agitating for women's voting rights, 1908

translating the poems of Romania's national poet Mihai Eminescu; and began work on an unfinished history of the European Socialist movement, as she had seen it, entitled *In the Red Twilight*.

For part of this time she lived in East Marden, near the Welsh frontier, where I was enrolled as a day-boy in an experimental school run by Dora Russell, wife of philosopher Bertrand Russell. She asserts in her autobiography that I was "a very determined little boy", and "the only male who succeeded in bullying his intrepid mother."

My mother's writing did not by any means constitute the end of her political activity, but only a temporary reduction in them. Visiting Bologna in northern Italy in 1919 she had seen Fascist *squadristi*, or thugs, beating up their opponents. This had turned her overnight into an anti-fascist. She

Richard's mother, Estelle Sylvia Pankhurst, contemporary portrait, ca 1945

held that Italy was the first victim of Fascism, but that, because of its militaristic and chauvinistic character, there would soon be many more.

Though a loving parent, she was as I remember her, always busy in one good cause or another. She was, however, more interested in the current struggle in which she was at that time involved, than in recalling the campaigns of the past. She was therefore not prone to reminiscing for its own sake. Some of my earliest memories are nevertheless of her discussing the Suffragette movement with former colleagues: among them Norah Smythe, who on occasion visited us in Woodford, as well as Maude Joachim, Emmeline Pethick-Lawrence, and Millie and Fanny Gliksten, most of whom also figure extensively in her writings.

My father, Silvio Erasmus Corio, who was born in Piedmont, in northern Italy, was by profession a printer-cum-journalist. A Socialist, and the son of a keen supporter of the *Risorgimento*, or Struggle for Italian Independence and Unity, he believed, like most left-wing Italians of his generation, in Anarchism rather than Communism. He was thus a disciple of the Russian Prince Piotr Kropotkin, and the Italian Enrico Malatesta, whom he knew personally, rather than of Karl Marx, who then had little following in Italy. Italian Anarchists tended to accept the idea of political assassination. One of those they had assassinated was King Umberto I of Italy, who is known to Ethiopian historians as the Italian monarch responsible for the earlier invasion of their country, and died at Monza in 1900. My father claimed that those in the know declared that the designated assassin had lost his nerve at the last moment, and that it was a companion of the latter who actually carried out the deed.

My father's political beliefs and support of the nascent Italian trade union movement led him into exile. He travelled first to Paris and later to London, where over the years he wrote extensively for the Italian emigré press. He also interpreted or served as a guide for Italian Socialists visiting England, among them Malatesta, Modigliani, Serrati and the Treves brothers. He also assisted the British author Francis McCullagh with the latter's book *Italy's War for a Desert*. This today largely forgotten work constitutes a well-documented critique of Italy's ruthless invasion of Libya in 1912.

Richard's father, Silvio Erasmus Corio, Italian refugee in England, ca 1935

Towards the end of World War I my father met my mother, and was involved in the printing of her book *Soviet Russia as I Saw It*. He later also assisted her in the production of a short-lived cultural journal, entitled *Germinal*, and was instrumental, as we shall see, in her founding an anti-fascist organisation, the Women's International Matteotti Committee.

Princess Sehay Hayle-Sillasé, the Emperor's youngest daughter, ca 1933

At the time of Fascist Italy's invasion of Ethiopia in 1935-6 he urged her to publish a newspaper in that country's' defence, found a suitable printer, and acted as unofficial co-editor. He coined the phrase "Fascism Means War!", which was frequently employed in the paper. He was later also involved, as shown in a later chapter, in proposing the founding of Ethiopia's first teaching hospital, which was named after Emperor Hayle-Sillasé's daughter, Princess Sehay, a trained nurse.

An habitué of the British Museum Reading Room—I remember the huge piles of his Reader's Book Application forms on our mantelpiece in Woodford—he was fascinated by comparative linguistics. He accodingly frequented second hand book-shops and, though never rich, purchased a sizeable collection of dictionaries of almost every language under the sun.

CARLO ROSSELLI AND THE WOMEN'S INTERNATIONAL MATTEOTTI COMMITTEE

One of my earliest memories of my parents' involvement in the international struggles of the day dates back to 1934 when I was close on seven years old. Coming down from my bedroom one morning I saw, to my great surprise, our large round mahogany sitting-room table covered with innumerable shining objects, like knives, of different shapes and sizes.

The origin of this strange display lay, as I later learnt, in Giacomo Matteotti's assassination ten years earlier. Subsequently, in 1932, my father received disturbing news from Paris. It came in a letter from Carlo Rosselli, the leader of the Italian émigré democratic movement *Giustizia e Libertà* ("Justice and Liberty"). He reported that Matteotti's widow, Velia, and her two sons were being persecuted. Their house was under constant police surveillance.

Carlo Rosselli, leader of the Italian *Giustizia e Libertà* movement, which opposed the Italian invasion of Ethiopia, assassinated in 1937

A search-light was directed on the building all night to check on, or deter, visitors. The Matteotti boys were forbidden from using their father's name, and one had been obliged to give the Fascist salute to a photograph of the Dictator who had ordered their father's death. Matteotti's grave was moreover frequently vandalised.

Carlo Rosselli further reported that an Italian physician, Dr Mario Germani, who had dared to visit Velia, had been exiled to the then crowded Mediterranean penal island of Ponza. It was on this island that the Ethiopian Emperor Hayle-Sillasé's cousin *Ras* Imru was imprisoned only a few years later, and where Mussolini, by a strange twist of fate, was himself detained, after his fall from power.

One of the prisoners with Dr Germani was a young man called Max Salvadori, the future professor of that name, who had been arrested for clandestine activity on behalf of *Giustizia e Libertà*.

My mother meanwhile, shocked by Rosselli's report, began phoning and writing to her friends, and before long founded a Women's International Matteotti Committee to agitate against Velia's persecution, and to draw attention to the totalitarian character of the Fascist regime. The committee gained the support of a galaxy of men and women of good will. They included Bertrand Russell, whose wife's school I had attended; the socialist political scientist Harold Laski, under whom I was later to study; her old fellow Suffragette comrade Emmeline Pethick-Lawrence; and George Lansbury, the then pacifist leader of the Labour Party. By contrast, the renowned playwright George Bernard Shaw, displayed no interest in Matteotti or the fate of his wife and family. This led to a polemical exchange letters between my mother and the supposedly progressive "GBS".

Despite Fascist censorship, news of the Matteotti Committee duly reached Italy. One of those who heard about it was Max Salvadori's English mother, Giacinthia Salvadori, who succeeded in visiting her son on Ponza. There she learnt that the island, which housed some 300 deportees, had no doctor except Dr. Germani, and that he lacked the surgical equipment with which to practice. She therefore appealed for such instruments as she put it as "an act of charity towards those that suffer that their country may again be free."

My mother responded to this appeal by raising funds for the equipment requested, which were duly displayed on our sitting-room table prior to their dispatch to Italy—hence my childhood memory.

The instruments, I may add, never served their intended purpose. Despite written assurances from the Italian Embassy in London, they were confiscated by the Fascist authorities in Italy, and failed to reach poor Dr. Germani.

Another of my early memories was of Carlo Rosselli himself. A close friend of my parents, I recall him visiting our house one summer, and spending a day in our garden, where my father had erected some kind of wooden summer house. Later, I learnt more of Rosselli's life, notably his escape in 1929 from Lipari, another of Mussolini's penal islands. Located off the Sicilian coast, it had housed 500 political prisoners, and was so closely guarded that escape seemed impossible. Rosselli and two fellow detainees, Francesco Nitti and Emilio Lussu, nevertheless succeeded in escaping to France on a steam-boat. As a child I heard with excitement that whenever the escapees refilled the boat's engine with petrol, they cut holes in the oil can, so that it would sink without indicating the escapees' route to the pursuers.

Rosselli was later to participate in the Spanish Civil War, in which he was wounded. Referring to his ambition to overthrow Mussolini, he coined the famous would-be prophetic slogan *Oggi in Spagna; domani in Italia*, "Today in Spain; Tomorrow in Italy."

ROMANIA AND WHITEWAY

Another of my childhood memories sprang from the fact that my mother had, as we have seen, translated poetry of the Romanian national poet Mihai Eminescu. She and other translators were unexpectedly invited to the unveiling of a monument to the poet, to be erected at Constanța in a fine location overlooking the Black Sea, and it was decided that my father and I should accompany her. The journey, in those days before flying became common, was a long one, by train. The easiest route would have been via northern Italy. There was, however, a serious danger that my father, whose Italian passport had been withdrawn by the Italian Embassy, would have been arrested on entering his native country. Therefore we had to travel instead through Germany, and change trains in Berlin.

Travelling through the newly established Nazi Reich was an experience. When dusk fell my parents put me to bed on one of the carriage seats, and to help me sleep tore out a page from the London *Times*, and affixed it to the ceiling-lamp to shade me from the light. They hadn't reckoned, however, with the frontier guards, who, on entering the compartment, immediately caught sight of the "seditious" foreign newspaper, and snatched it away.

We passed through the German capital in the immediate aftermath of Hindenburg's funeral in early August, 1934. I recall the long Nazi flags with black borders, hanging down from the buildings in many of the principal streets. One other incident, which my mother later recalled, was that when we went to the grocers to purchase supplies for the long journey ahead, my father paid, but the shopkeeper gave *her* the heavy shopping bag to carry. This she saw as symbolic of the status of women in the new Reich.

Romania was an exciting place for seven-year-old Richard, who, people assumed, was named not after his grandfather, Richard Marsden Pankhurst, but after the Crusader, Richard the Lionheart. Blessed with bright sunshine—we were coming, it should be recalled, from rainy England, there were many unusual things to admire: the ever-changing countryside, with its mountains, rivers and plains, and the so-called Black Sea, which seemed to me bright blue; the colourful and attractively embroidered peasants' costumes; the painted Byzantine-style churches (from my childish point of view we visited too many), most notably, the remarkable church of Curtea de Argeş with its gold decoration and painted domes; railway stations, rendered beautiful by colourful flower-beds—a practice then unknown in Britain which caused my mother to write about it in the local Woodford press; the warm beach at Constanţa before the subsequent mass tourism at Mammaya and elsewhere; newspapers illustrated with coloured photographs which did not become common in Britain for many a year; coins bearing the effigy of a boy king—King Michael, who, as evident from the currency then in circulation, had, curiously both succeeded and preceeded, his father, King Carol; and the uniforms of the latter's palace guards, the colours of which seemed to change every day, and who, every now and then, delighted him by playing the bugle. No less amazing to the little visitor was the swimming pool at the Lido Hotel with, marvel of marvels, artificial waves, which almost hurled him to the edge of the pool. Punctuality on the journey, however, was not a strong point, and I soon distinguished three types of time: "Time by the clock, Mummy's time, and Romanian time."

While in Romania I was befriended by a Romanian boy, Arcadiu Petrescu, nicknamed Dudu, who was my elder by a couple of years. He was the son of a judge, the man in charge of the Eminescu celebrations. When I returned to Britain, Dudu and I developed into "pen-pals", and continued as such into the post-war Romanian Communist era, when, wishing

Richard's Romanian pen-friend, Arcadiu (Dudu) Petrescu, ca 1934

to avoid the attentions of the police, he chose to post his letters during visits to neighbouring countries. By then a prominent neurologist, as well as an amateur historian of Eminescu, he attended many international conferences in his field.

It was sad to learn, long afterwards, that the venerable Romanian scholar Nicolae Jorga, whom we had met—and whom I remember to this day, was subsequently murdered by the pro-Fascist Romanian Iron Guard.

We had cause to remember Romania in one other context. That was when Emperor Hayle-Sillasé delivered his famous address to the League of Nations on 30 June 1936, and Italian Fascist journalists sought noisily to disrupt the proceedings. They were immediately expelled from the hall by the chairman, the Romanian Foreign Minister, Nicolae Titulescu, who ordered *À la porte les sauvages!* (Out with the savages!). For this he was dismissed from all government service, and went into exile, without ever returning to his native land. Rita and I, as residents of Addis Ababa, were later involved in a movement to have a street in the Ethiopian capital named in Titulescu's honour.

A visit to Whiteway, a Utopian colony in the beautiful Cotswold Hills of central England, left less impression on my youthful self. It was only a decade later, when studying the history of Utopian Socialism, that I saw the philosophical significance of the project. Much later still I learnt of the travels of one of Whiteway's most enterprising residents, the Belgian traveller Gaspar Marin. Journeying far and wide outside Europe,

Stone Bomb monument erected in 1935 by Sylvia in Woodford, in protest against aerial warfare, often visited by Pacifists and anti-war demonstrators, among them Sylvia Ayling, a Woodford pacifist. It was re-dedicated in 1936.

he wrote a diary of his travels, the Ethiopian portion of which I was subsequently to edit. Marin also recorded the reminiscences of Ibrahim Isma'il, a Somali seaman in Britain. Impressed by this autobiography, the first of its kind, I also published the text, until then unknown to the world of scholarship, in the 1977 volume of the Italian journal *Africa*.

THE STONE BOMB

My mother expressed her pacifist, humanitarian and anti-imperialist views in the early 1930s when she erected Britain's first, and as far as I know, only, anti-war monument on a piece of land which she owned at Woodford and on which we had formerly resided, before we moved to Charteris Road. The monument, which took the shape of a bomb, was designed by a British sculptor Eric Benfield, and unveiled by Phillip Zaphiro, a Greek attached to the Ethiopian Legation in London. Still extant, it features from time to time in anti-war demonstrations of one kind or another. It took the form of a bomb and came to be popularly known as the Stone Bomb. The sculpture was dedicated, ironically, to the British delegation to the League of Nations, which had "upheld the right to use bombing planes" on the grounds that the tribesmen of northern India needed to be bombed to keep them in order.

THE ITALO-ETHIOPIAN WAR

Fascist Italy's invasion of Ethiopia in 1935-6 was a major turning-point, not only in the history of the two countries involved, but also in that of the League of Nations.

The Italo-Ethiopian War impinged on the British public's attitude to Fascism and world affairs. It was likewise to have had a decisive effect on my life. To explain this one must recall that by the winter of 1934 my parents were convinced that Mussolini was preparing to invade Ethiopia. The build-up of Italian forces and the development of roads, airports and harbour facilities in the two adjacent Italian colonies, of Eritrea and Somalia, made this abundantly clear. So did the Wal Wal "incident" of 5 December 1934, a clash of arms which followed the illegal penetration of Italian colonial troops far into Ethiopian territory, and was used by Mussolini as a pretext for war.

My parents, as staunch anti-fascists and anti-colonialists, were both naturally, opposed to the anticipated invasion of Africa's last independent state. Neither of them had actually visited it, or indeed travelled anywhere on the African continent: nor, for that matter, had Mussolini himself. My father, as a conscript in the Italian army had, however, heard about the country from older Italian soldiers who had participated in the earlier Italian invasion of Ethiopia, in 1895-6. Some of them had been captured after the Ethiopian Emperor Menilek's resounding victory at the Battle of Adwa. Sharing the opposition to colonialism, widespread in the Italian Left, he recalled that his friends among the returning troops told of the existence of a well organized Ethiopian state, with long historical traditions and a vibrant culture, very different from the "country of barbarism" conjured up in Fascist propaganda.

My mother saw the Ethiopians as victims of what she considered an evil creed. As a student of art, she was moreover conscious of the high quality of Ethiopian manuscript illustrations, which she had seen in the then British Museum (later Library), and which have been described as "African art in a Byzantine setting." Long afterwards I studied and wrote about such work in some depth.

Already engaged in the international struggle against Italian Fascism, my parents rushed to Ethiopia's defence. My mother wrote numerous letters to the British and world press, drawing attention to the Duce's expansionist plans. My father likewise wrote to the principal Italian anti-fascist refugees in Britain, France, the United States and Mexico, and to the Italian emigré press. He ridiculed Mussolini's argument that the conquest of Ethiopia would bring prosperity to the starving peasantry of southern

Photograph of the Emperor in Bath, taken by Richard as an eight year old boy with a Brownie Camera

Italy, and urged his compatriots to reject Mussolini's bellicose propaganda, and instead to support Ethiopia in the struggle against the Fascist dictatorship.

NEW TIMES AND ETHIOPIA NEWS

Faced with the opening of hostilities, the Fascist use of poison-gas, and the imposition of abortive League of Nations Sanctions, my parents realised that well-meaning letters to the press were inadequate, and accordingly founded a weekly newspaper of their own in Ethiopia's defence. Entitled *New Times and Ethiopia News*, and often referred to for short as *NT&EN*, it was, as its headline often proclaimed, an Anti-fascist weekly. The first issue was on sale in London on the day Emperor Hayle-Sillasé arrived in Britain as an exile.

My mother, as we have seen, was a member of the London crowd which gathered to welcome him on his arrival at Waterloo station on 3 June 1936, and I was there too. I met him again some weeks later, when my parents travelled by train and taxi to "Fairfield", his residence in Bath in the west of England. His house, contrary to some reports, was by no means sumptuous. After spending a night in a Bed and Breakfast establishment run by a Mrs Herring (who explained to me at great length that she was

Tapestry by Berit Sahlström based on a photograph by Richard of his mother with the Emperor, 1936.

not a fish!), we paid our visit to the royal exile. At the end of the interview, I chanced upon interviewer and interviewee in the garden. With my small Brownie box camera, I took a photograph of him, and one of him with my mother.

Dignified as ever in his bearing, he wore traditional Ethiopian dress. These were some of the first photos I ever took. The photograph was long afterwards developed as a tapestry by the Swedish artist, Berit Sahlström, wife of the Ethiopian-Eritrean historian Tekeste Negash. Sadly, I never became a photographer. My name was however included in a list of contributors to the newspaper presented to the Emperor as a scroll. This so impressed the local printers in nearby Walthamstow that they reproduced it on incredibly bright yellow paper.

NT&EN supported not only Ethiopia, its principal *raison d'être*, but also the other "victim nations", as my mother chose to term them: China, Spain, Austria, Albania, Czechoslovakia, and Poland. Officially edited by my mother, the paper was virtually co-edited by my father, who wrote many articles under the *noms de plume* Crastinus and Luce. He also spent one or two days each week at the printers, deciding on which pages the various articles should appear. Those were the days before the introduction of computer-printing; I often accompanied him, and acquired a love for the smell of printers' ink.

Some of the earliest articles in the paper, many couched in eloquent but plaintive mood, were written by *Hakim* Werqneh, the Ethiopian Minister, or in effect Ambassador, in London. He had a remarkable history. Believed, incorrectly, to have been an orphan, at the time of the British military expedition against the Ethiopian Emperor Tewodros II at Meqdela in 1868, he had been taken to India by the returning troops and had been given an English name. He had subsequently studied medicine and surgery in Scotland, and eventually returned to his native land as its first foreign trained physician, but was later appointed Ethiopian envoy to Britain. The rank is now equivalent to "Ambassador", a term not used at that time. His articles in *NT&EN* were signed: "Dr Charles Werkineh Martin". A jovial and highly Anglicised diplomat, and a member of the Indian Rationalist Society, he became a

Hakim Werkineh aka Dr Martin, Ethiopian Minister in London, 1935-6

close friend of our family, and together with his children, often visited our house. A fully qualified doctor, he on several occasions gave me medical advice, and prescriptions, for childhood illnesses. I later visited him in his house in Addis Ababa, and will always

Amanuél Abraham, Hakim Werqneh's Secretary in London at an *NT&EN* Garden Party, 1934, photo Richard Pankhurst

remember his dignity, independence of mind, and sense of purpose.

Another visitor to our house at that time was Dr. Martin's secretary Amanuél Abraham, an Ethiopian Protestant (and later himself an Ambassador to Britain and Italy). I remember once showing him my most recent prized acquisition, the Khaki Campbell duck, Cyclic Quad. Since birds with webbed-feet are not highly regarded in traditional Ethiopian culture, he may not have shared my quirky admiration for this creature.

Yet another visitor early in the Italian Occupation was David Hall, an Ethiopian functionary of partial German descent. A soft-spoken man, he came to Woodford, in some secrecy, to tell my mother of his hope that Hitler, anxious to establish his superiority over his fellow dictator Mussolini, might be persuaded to dispatch arms for Ethiopia. My mother, preoccupied with what she considered the evils of the Nazi regime, and the official friendship between the two totalitarian states, failed to appreciate the possibility of German support for Ethiopia, which in any case, was soon suspended.

My younger Ethiopian friends at this time included Mikaél and Gebriél Tédros, sons of Tesfa-Yohannis Tédros, an Eritrean restaurateur settled in London. They were keen supporters of *NT&EN* and my friendly competitors in selling publications and raffle-tickets for pro-Ethiopian fund-raising

My mother succeeded meanwhile in making contact with the Ethiopian Patriots, who continued to resist the invader after the Emperor's departure from his country early in May 1936. She published almost weekly reports on their activities. A few copies of *NT&EN*, printed in the Ethiopian language Amharic, were smuggled into Italian-occupied Ethiopia. Many years later, when I was Director of the Institute of Ethiopian Studies in Addis Ababa, a Patriot from a remote part of Gojjam in the north-west of Ethiopia, presented the Institute library with a dog-eared and much folded copy he had received during the occupation. My parents were also involved with Carlo Rosselli and *Hakim* Werqneh in smuggling anti-fascist literature to the Italians in Ethiopia. This took the form of miniature pamphlets written in Italian on wafer-thin rice paper.

Many articles on Ethiopia's patriotic resistance, which continued throughout the occupation, were contributed by *NT&EN*'s Jibuti (Djibouti) correspondent, *Wezir* Ali Baig, greatly admired by mother, who corresponded with him constantly until his death. He had a few years earlier worked as a stringer for the pro-Italian novelist Evelyn Waugh. Much of Wezir's information was collected for him by the patriotic *Lij* Andargachew Mesay, the emigré Ethiopian consul in Jibuti, who was long afterwards to deliver a moving oration at my mother's funeral.

My mother wrote a weekly editorial for *NT&EN* on international affairs, as well as many other articles of topical interest. These included two long essays: "Fascism as It Is" and "How Hitler Rose to Power", which were serialised over many months. Waking in the morning, and going down for breakfast, I would often find her still writing at her desk, the table scattered with discarded drafts of her articles. It was also her custom to

Young Ethiopian Patriots during the Italian Occupation, photo Arnold Wienholt, ca 1940

reply to the morning's post as soon as it arrived, by dictating to a secretary, who typed the letters in our house. (My mother, contrary to report, never typed). In those far-off days there were several posts a day, so that a letter posted early in the morning could often be answered by a reply received later the same day. I, too, have throughout my life tried to answer letters immediately, before turning to other matters and continue to do so with internet communications.

The newspaper also carried articles from other writers. One of the best known was Nancy Cunard, the anti-racist daughter of the shipping magnate of that name. The editor of the mammoth volume *Negro,* she wrote for the *NT&EN* on the fate of the defeated Spanish Republican soldiers who had found refuge in France. Timely articles were also contributed by other writers, among them the Hungarian, Béla Menczer, the Austrian Ruth Schultz-Gaevernitz, and several Romanians.

The *NT&EN*, which was dispatched to numerous Members of Parliament and "leaders of opinion", also raised funds for Dr. Martin's Fund of Mercy (for Ethiopian refugees), to which end my mother held a series of fund-raising bazaars and fêtes, concerts and film shows. Though little more than nine years old, I was one of the keenest supporters of such events and assisted in selling sundry programmes, raffle-tickets and the like.

Title page of Hiob Ludolf's 17th century *New History of Ethiopia*, which Richard copied out weekly for inclusion in *NT&EN*.

Hakim Werqneh's eldest sons, Theodore and Bejamin, killed during the Fascist Occupation, 1937

Fundraising events in the years which followed were frequently attended by the Emperor, who would often formally open the proceedings.

As I grew older I became more involved in *NT&EN's* production. As a schoolboy I thus copied out for the printer the entire text of the late 17th century English translation of the German scholar Hiob Ludolf 's *New History of Ethiopia*, which was serialised weekly for many months. I also drew most of the maps reproduced in the paper, but could not, I fear, be restrained from decorating them with large lions, many resembling childishly conceived pussy-cats rather than the king of beasts.

The period after 1936 was fraught with many international difficulties, about which I was becoming increasingly aware. My consciousness of what was taking place on the Continent of Europe was intensified by meeting refugees, some of whom stayed in our house, often for long periods of time. They came mainly from Italy, Germany, Austria and Spain, and told heart-breaking stories. Such asylum-seekers included many Jews from Germany and Austria. Among them were Edna Schmosch whom I still remember, and there were also two young Basque women from Spain, plus an occasional Italian. My special childhood friend was a Russian girl called Diana Petroff, whose parents my mother

Hakim Werqneh's children in England, ca 1935

Hakim Werqneh's youngest son, David and daughter Leah, ca 1935

had met many years earlier in Moscow, and had later managed to get her into the well known progressive school Dartington Hall. Having passed through a near famine situation, she had at times to be coaxed with great difficulty to eat—I became skilled at that!—though on one occasion she caused some consternation at her school by consuming a whole blancmange—"pink death" as we school-children used to call it—intended for many students.

Awareness of the Fascist Menace, as people then called it, was intensified by often terrible news of the day. An attempt in Addis Ababa on the life of Rodolfo Graziani, the Fascist Viceroy of Ethiopia on 19 February 1937, was followed by a three day massacre, in which the Italian Blackshirts shot, burnt or beat to death thousands of innocent Ethiopian men, women and children. Those killed included

Ras Desta Damtew, who was executed after capture, 1937

Theodore and Benjamin Martin, the eldest sons of Dr Martin. I had never met them as they had rushed off to serve their country before I knew the Martin family, but, knowing their younger brothers John and Charlie and their sister Leah, all of them around my own age, brought their loss vividly home to me.

Later that year I learnt the stark news of the assassination of someone I had met personally: Carlo Rosselli. He was killed in France by French Fascists, reportedly on Mussolini's orders, virtually on the anniversary of Matteotti's assassination a decade earlier.

My parents were deeply shocked by both events as well as by the execution of *Ras* Desta. My mother helped to organise a Requiem Mass at St George's Church in Hart

Memorial service for *Ras* Desta and victims of the Graziani massacre, right to left, the Emperor, *Ras* Kasa Haylu, Hakim Werkneh, Hiruy Welde-Sillasé, 1937

Richard reading *NT&EN*,
ca 1937

Street, Bloomsbury, for those killed in Addis Ababa, while my father, mourning Carlo Rosselli's death, wrote an article in *NT&EN*, entitled "Letter to a Dead Man who is Alive." The newspaper adopted Rosselli's symbol of a fiery Sword of Justice, and I, as artist in residence, helped to design this as part of the paper's logo. I also read in *NT&EN* of the bombing of Guernica in Spain, as well as the destruction in Catalonia of several schools, tragic photographs of which were graphically reproduced.

Such distant events were soon to be followed by others nearer home.

Throughout this time my mother was advising refugees on how to enter and remain in Britain, and carried on an extensive correspondence on these matters. Since a would-be immigrant could not be deported so long as his or her case was under official review she utilized an unofficial rota of members of Parliament willing to ask appropriate, delaying questions.

TIME OUT OF SCHOOL

My parents, as I remember, had little time—or money—to go up to London for many concerts. They had, however, what we would now consider a very antiquated gramophone, and a small library of 78 records. These included recordings of arias from popular Italian operas, sung among others by such renowned figures as Enrico Caruso and Feodor Chaliapin, as well as items of political or anti-fascist interest. Among the latter I recall the Ethiopian National Anthem with that of Afghanistan on the reverse; music conducted by the Italian conductor, Arturo Toscanini, who was acclaimed in Woodford for refusing to conduct the Fascist song *Giovinezza*; and, one of my favourites, the Spanish Republican anthem *Inno de Riego* which had the Italian Red Flag, *Bandiera Rossa*, on the reverse.

My father was reluctant to teach me Italian. This was because he had seen young Italian-speakers seduced, as he thought, by Fascist propaganda. He was irritated to hear younger Italians abandon the traditional polite form of address *lei*, in favour of the supposedly more egalitarian *voi*, popularised by Mussolini.

Paradoxically he was a great devotee of Italian poetry, and delighted in reciting Dante and other Italian poets to me—even though I could scarcely understand them. I still recall him reading Giosuè Carducci's ironic piece about an imaginary guillotine, operated by a steam-engine in China, which in three hours could supposedly decapitate a hundred thousand heads placed in a row. One of my treasured possessions is my father's tiny red leather-bound volume of Carducci's poems, published in Florence in 1882, which begins:

Hanno fatto nella Cina
Una macchina a vapore…
Questa macchina in tre ore
Fa la testa a cento mila
Messi in fila.

As far as theatre was concerned, my mother, who spent such free time as she allowed herself reading English poetry, took me to Shakespeare performances at the Old Vic. Many of these were produced by Donald Wolfit, whom she deemed the greatest of the then Shakespearian actors. He was later to support some of her pro-Ethiopian activities, and on one occasion gave a performance in Addis Ababa under British Council auspices. He subsequently complained that it was difficult to recite Shakespeare at the Ethiopian capital's high altitude, for, finding himself short of oxygen, he was obliged to breathe much faster than usual, with the result that the bard's words tumbled out of control. We also went on a few occasions to the Yiddish Theatre in the East End.

My father would on occasion take me to the old Caledonian Road "cattle market", where seemingly innumerable second-hand articles were on sale, on open stalls, for a few shillings or pence. My mother would never go near the market. She said it reminded her of the misery of many destitute families she had known in the East End, of London, who had been obliged to sell all their property in order to survive. Oblivious of such tragedies, over the years I bought several fascinating items. They included two or three small Hindu bronze sculptures and a few wireless crystal set radios, which one listened to with head-phones. I was a great fan of such instruments, and constructed a few of my own. I would listen to one or other of them after being put to sleep—in a then rather novel type of bed which folded up when not in use. I was thrilled one night to hear the news that the invaders somewhere in Ethiopia had been attacked by a group of crocodiles.

I had three other hobbies: growing exotic cacti, in pots; photography, for which I had a dark room; and stamp-collecting. I specialised mainly in Ethiopian and Spanish stamps and recall my childhood admiration of the wild animals on the one, and the huge sailing ships on the other. I also had a sizeable collection of British Penny-Black stamps, given to me by an old Suffragette friend of my mother's, Miss Isabel Seymour, a descendant of a family once related to British royalty. Letters from the aforesaid Jibuti correspondent *Wezir* Ali Baig led meanwhile to the arrival of wonderfully large stamps from that French Protectorate.

I spent several weekends over the years at the house of another of my mother's friends, the Quaker philanthropist Miss Isabel Fry, who lived at Church House, near Aylesbury, in Buckinghamshire. A great supporter of *NT&EN*, and subsequently the Honorary Treasurer of the Princess Sehay Hospital in Addis Ababa, she had many international and humanitarian interests. My fellow guests on several occasions included young Jewish children who had just arrived from Germany or

Czechoslovakia on the *Kindertransport* which rescued them from central Europe on the eve of World War II. On another occasion Miss Fry, a highly self-disciplined woman, invited two aristocratic Ethiopian youngsters to dinner. Unaccustomed to the tyranny of the clock, they failed to appear at the appointed hour. After five minutes or so Miss Fry's very prominent jet black eyebrows rose, and a quarter of an hour later one of the culprits caused something of a stir by allowing his bath to overflow, as evident from the water pouring onto the dining room table. I do not think that they were invited again.

WORLD WAR II

In Woodford the first months of the European war, in the autumn of 1939, were quiet. My parents, who had opposed Mr Chamberlain's Munich agreement surrendering Czechoslovakia to Germany, and the Ribbentropp-Molotov agreement giving Hitler a free hand to the East, fully supported the Allied war against the Nazis. My mother, recalling the suffering she had witnessed in the East End during the First World War, founded a Women's War Emergency Council with the help of sundry local worthies. It advocated the need to learn the lessons of the previous conflagration by introducing price-control and rationing. She also involved herself in humanitarian work: I recall the arrival by post at our house of innumerable parcels of old clothes for distribution to evacuated children, as well as the disappearance from our kitchen of the pots and pans which she took round to a local Government centre collecting metal for the manufacture of Spitfires, Hurricanes and other aircraft.

Unlike many youngsters of my age I was not myself evacuated. I was then attending Chigwell Public School, where I remember that one of the teachers had visited Germany for the Berlin 1936 Olympics, and was a great enthusiast of Adolf Hitler.

One schoolboy prank at Chigwell which was sometimes proposed—and I did not appreciate—sprang from the idea that since pancakes were traditionally tossed from a frying pan on Shrove Tuesday, schoolboy Pankhurst should similarly be hurled into the air on that day. It was fortunate, however, that the principal bully boy's parents were supporters of the League

Richard as a young schoolboy, ca 1936

of Nations, and hence pro-Ethiopian. He therefore stood by me and restrained the pranksters.

Going to Chigwell had necessitated a longish and sometimes unpredictable journey by LNER steam-train. To obviate this, during the anticipated wartime difficulties, I was moved to Bancroft School, on the Woodford High Road (not far from the Stone Bomb!), which could be reached on foot in half an hour's brisk walk. I attended this school until the end of the war. It was there that I was introduced to Shakespeare's *Hamlet*, which was to remain with me throughout my life, and developed a fascination with French history from Napoleon the Great to, as we liked to say, Napoleon the Little.

Another wartime change related to our diet in what came to be known as an age of rationing. We had until then been Vegetarians—I firmly so. I recall the irritation with which I refused to listen to our doctor's advice that I, being of a supposedly weak constitution, should eat "tasty fishie, fishie." However, in view of wartime difficulties, and the need for simplicity, my parents decided when necessary to eat meat. Not for the first, or last, time, were considerations of animal welfare avowedly subordinated to those of humans. However, we continued to eat Allinson's wholemeal brown bread.

This period witnessed the rationing of basic foodstuffs, as well as clothing, and, of particular interest to a twelve or thirteen year old, sweets. Having his parents' two rations as well as his own, he was however scarcely deprived, the more so as a kindly old proprietor of a nearby sweetshop declared himself a supporter of "the movement"—whatever that was I no longer remember—and never allowed us to leave this premises empty-handed.

After some months it became apparent that Woodford lay directly on the German Luftwaffe's flight path to London. We were conscious of this one Sunday, when I went with my parents to spend the day in the centre of London—and saw an unprecedented display of the German air force flying over the town. That night, heavy bombing began in earnest. Taking our old steam-train from Liverpool Street station to Woodford—in those days before the line's electrification—we were obliged to spend the night at the next station, Bethnal Green. There I was put to bed on an immense and dusty pile of railway records, four or more feet high dating back many decades. Later as a student of economic history at the London School of Economics I wished that I had had the time to study them, for they would have constituted the basis of fascinating research in transport history: but that was not to be. We later learnt that the friendly Italian anti-fascist restaurateur in Charing Cross Road in whose premises we had dined, was killed that night in enemy bombing.

At home in our garden in Woodford, we had two corrugated iron Anderson air-raid shelters, covered with unusually thick turf. They were so called after a former Home Secretary. People normally had only one such shelter, but we had been allocated a second for our tenants, who subsequently left, and no one had the energy to dig it up. In the next few years it became our practice, at nightfall, for me to go to bed in one shelter, while my parents wrote in the house until the bombing became heavy, whereupon they would rush to the second shelter for the night. Inconvenient as this was, it bore no comparison to the nocturnal life of so many Londoners who spent their nights on Underground train platforms. Travelling home of an evening we would see them preparing their beds for the nightly ordeal.

By day we youngsters would look out for newly bombed buildings, collect shrapnel, and admire a fellow schoolboy who, I am sad to say, was the proud owner of an unexploded German incendiary bomb—so bright and shiny. I also helped to ensure that the black-out regulations in the house were strictly followed, and befriended our local Air Raid Warden, Monsieur Lek, a Belgian refugee.

Later in the war, we saw the small engine-operated V1s, popularly known as Doodle-Bugs, or Hitler's Secret Weapons, flying over us, and emitting smoke, on their route towards London. They also came by night, when we saw them as fiery blobs in the dark sky. As soon as their engines stopped, we had to rush for shelter—for on falling to the ground they would explode, wreaking serious damage to life and limb. More awesome were the subsequent V2 rockets, which crashed down without any warning. On this account the destruction they produced was at first popularly attributed to rather mysterious gas pipe explosions.

Attacks by V1s and V2s continued to very near the end of the European war. It was with an intense feeling of relief, almost of liberation, when we realised that they had come to an end: that one could live one's life without the constant threat of death, and at last sleep undisturbed at night.

The war was at first politically a curious time for my mother and her newspaper. Her continued support of Ethiopia, and her opposition to Italian Fascism, displeased the British Foreign Office. It did not want to see anything published that might offend Mussolini, and conceivably draw him into the war on Hitler's side. She feared, as she wrote at the time to the Emperor and to her Parliamentary friends, that she might be prevented from publishing her anti-fascist views. The British Ministry of Information (situated in what is now London University's Senate House) and Censorship authorities prohibited her from dispatching her newspaper to neutral countries, which officially included Italy, but permitted her to write what she liked, and to continue publishing her paper.

Mussolini's entry into the European war, on 10 June 1940, however, brought about an immediate change. The Foreign Office, for the time being at least, approved of my mother's anti-fascist stance, and my father was invited to give an Italian broadcast on the BBC. It was introduced by the music of the *Inno di Garibaldi*, which had inspired Italians fighting for independence and unity two generations or so earlier.

I recall the excitement on the evening we heard over the radio the historic news that "Signor Mussolini" (the BBC still adopted polite protocol when referring to the Dictator) had declared war on Britain and France. A dinner party was in progress, attended by a number of Italian refugees. They burst into cheers, for they realised that Mussolini's declaration of war ensured that their long years of waiting were at last drawing to an end. They were convinced, as my father observed in an article in

NT&EN, written in both English and Italian, that the Italian and German Dictators would assuredly fall together.

The Emperor, Dr Martin and other Ethiopians in exile took a similar view, concluding that this was the time to redouble their struggle for independence, by collaborating with the British in the war against the common enemy in East Africa. Hayle-Sillasé was shortly afterwards flown by the British to Sudan to begin the Ethiopian Liberation Campaign, which led to the collapse of Italian rule in East Africa ten months later, and to his triumphant return to Addis Ababa in May 1941.

Mussolini's declaration of war also led to some rethinking nearer afield. On hearing the news our next door neighbour, a retired pro-fascist British army officer who had visited Italy and been received by the Duce and the Pope, changed his views overnight. He crossed our road in Woodford, to tell my father that he (the officer) had previously thought that she had been "barking up the wrong tree", but was now convinced that she had been right after all.

At around this time my mother, who was on the German list of persons to be arrested in the event of a Nazi occupation of Britain, received two postal threats on her life. One was from a fanatical British pro-Nazi sympathiser in Depford, Kent; and the other from an Italian Fascist, who was believed to have been employed in Soho, London's Italian restaurant quarter. However, our household, as far as I remember, paid little attention to such warnings. In those days our back door was scarcely ever locked.

While at school I joined the Air Training Corps (ATC); was given a somewhat badly-fitting grey-blue uniform; learnt to recognise Spitfires, Hurricanes, and other fighter and bomber warplanes, both British and German; and became fairly proficient in tapping out the Morse code. I also spent several weekends at various RAF bases, where I was instructed how to rotate an anti-aircraft gun—a skill which, as things turned out, I was never required to use.

My mother meanwhile continued to publish her paper. After Mussolini's entry in the European war she demanded that Britain should recognise Ethiopia as an Ally, with the same status as European Allies, such as France or Belgium, which were under German occupation. In the months and years that followed, she defended Ethiopia not only against the Italians, who had first invaded the country, but also against its British liberators. Supported by several British leaders, most notably Colonel Josiah Wedgwood MP she did battle with some British colonial officials and others who proposed dismantling the country politically, or the imposition of control virtually tantamount to that of a Protectorate.

One of her chief political allies in this struggle was Colonel Orde Wingate, who had served in 1941 as the Emperor's commander in the Liberation Campaign. A keen advocate of Ethiopian independence he differed radically from many British officers who wanted to place the country under some form of colonial protection. He had for that reason been suddenly recalled from Addis Ababa without the opportunity of even saying good-bye to the Emperor. My mother learnt by chance of Wingate's presence in London, for he was then residing in a Hill Street flat, off Park Lane, in a building

The Emperor with British Field Commander, Colonel Orde Wingate, 1941

occupied by her friend and former Suffragette, Millie Gliksten, who thirty years earlier had secretly provided her with accommodation when she was hiding under the Cat and Mouse Act.

The result was that one afternoon that week I went with my mother to visit Wingate in his flat, where he gave us a vivid account of the campaign he had just fought in Ethiopia. I was much impressed by his pent-up energy, which, as he walked backwards and forwards in his small room, reminded me of a lion or tiger in the zoo at feeding time. He also told us of an idea he had of launching a Lawrence of Arabia type attack on the Italians in Libya from the South. Wishing to document the important contribution which the Ethiopian Patriots had made, he lent my mother a copy of his official campaign report. However, fearing that he was under official investigation on account of his pro-Ethiopian stance, which ran contrary to that of British officialdom, he phoned my mother on the following day asking her to return the document. His wife Lorna accordingly came to our house by train to collect it, and I was sent to copy the map in his report, while the two women enjoyed a leisurely tea. On the previous day he had informed us in confidence that, after the War, he intended to stand as a Labour Parliamentary candidate but this was not to be, as he was killed in an untoward aeroplane crash in Burma on 24 March 1944.

The Emperor's youngest daughter, Princess Sehay, whom I vividly remember as a vvivacious, widely admired and dedicated young woman, had trained in London during the war at Great Ormond Street Hospital and Guy's Hospital, but died on 17 August 1942 after complications arising from childbirth. She had trained in Britain as a qualified nurse, had served in London hospitals during the German bombing of the city, and was generally much respected. She had hoped, on returning to her own country, to found a modern hospital and other up-to-date medical facilities, but had been prevented by her premature death. This led my mother to launch a campaign to realise Sehay's ambition. A Princess Sehay Tsahay [sic] Memorial Hospital Council was duly established, with a galaxy of distinguished members, including King George's personal physician Lord Horder. Innumerable fundraising activities for the hospital were duly organised—in which I humbly participated. *Ras* Imru Hayle-Sillasé, a prominent Ethiopian nobleman, served as chair of the Addis Ababa` hospital committee. The Hospital, Ethiopia's first teaching hospital,

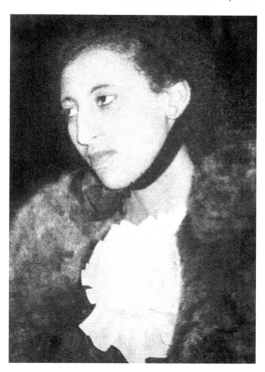

Princess Sehay while in exile in England. She interpreted for the Emperor on important occasions and often acted as a spokesperson in defence of Ethiopia, ca 1939

was duly completed, and many years later our son Alula was to be treated there.

The British General Election of 1945, which Wingate had anticipated, was a stirring moment. The size of the electoral defeat of the Conservatives, and of the Labour victory, in those days before Gallup Polls, was a great surprise. It seemed a dramatic break with the past, particularly with the widely discredited policy of Appeasement, and the opening of a new, and internationally more just world, in which our Indian friends would soon be gaining their independence.

Woodford, where we lived, was Prime Minister Winston Churchill's staunchly Conservative constituency. The Labour and Liberal Parties decided not to oppose the victorious wartime leader on the dubious

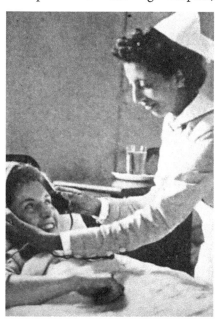

Princess Sehay as a nurse in London, 1941

Sylvia Pankhurst fund-raising for the Princess Sehay Memorial Hospital in London's Bedford College 1945. Left to right Isabel Fry, Treasurer, Brigadier G.S. Parkinson and Cannon A. Douglas, Richard in the background

Later fund-raising event at Bedford College, London 1953, left to right, Counsellor Birhanu Tesemma, Mrs Ivy Tims, Princess Rosalie Viazemski, Miss Ellené Imru, Siyyum Arero, Ethiopian student, Sylvia, Mr Peter Freeman MP

Richard's LSE Indian friends, centre Mehr Fardoonji, 1946

argument that one could vote for them without opposing him. My mother however felt very strongly that he should be opposed, and though not wishing to stand herself, encouraged an ex-RAF officer called Clements to do so. When he however decided not to enter the electoral struggle she earned some publicity for an alternative candidate by announcing that she was giving him her support. He was a hitherto totally unknown figure, by name Mr Hancock, who called himself the Man with a Plan.

One of the results of the Election was that she now had a dozen or so friends among the newly elected Labour MPs and an indirect consequence for me was that it became easy to obtain visitor's tickets to attend Parliamentary debates. These in those days were more interesting to follow than today in that proceedings in the House were not yet broadcast, let alone televised.

Evidence that the world was beginning to change was provided in the following year by the long-awaited grant of Indian independence. But in Africa the winds of change had still to blow.

The future of the former Italian colonies of Eritrea, Somalia and Libya, lost as a result of the Fascist collapse in 1941, and resolved only after the dispatch of two international commissions of inquiry, took well over a decade to bring to an end. My mother was intimately involved in this on-going struggle, writing a small library on the ex-colonies. In addition to innumerable historical and other articles for *NT&EN* and other publications she wrote *Ex-Italian Somaliland* (1951, reprinted 1969); *Eritrea on the Eve: The Past and Future of Italy's "first-born" colony; Ethiopia's Ancient Sea Province* (1952); *Why Are We Destroying the Eritrean Ports?* (1952); and *Ethiopia and Eritrea: The Last Ten Years of the Reunion Struggle* (1953).

While working on the latter book she was recovering from a serious attack of coronary thrombosis which her doctor first expected to be fatal. I therefore helped her to bring her manuscript together. For this reason she placed my name on the title page as co-author, but I was really little more than her amanuensis.

RITA

FAMILY BACKGROUND

I was born on 5 July 1927, in the old university city of Iaşi, the capital of the Province of Moldavia, in north-eastern Romania. My only sibling was my brother Andrei, older than me by four years. The age gap between us was too big for us to play together on equal terms, but was apparently not big enough for him to feel protectively about me. My early recollection was that he enjoyed teasing me. In adolescence and early adult life our paths seldom crossed and it was only while my husband and I lived in London in "exile" from Ethiopia in the late seventies and early eighties, that Andrei and I found common ground and began to see each other regularly.

I did not know my father's parents well for they lived in the capital, Bucharest, in the far south of the country. But before leaving for England in February 1938, I stayed with them for some weeks. My grandfather, Moritz Einhorn, had a shoe shop. The Einhorns lived in a small apartment together with their youngest son Bruno, who was employed by Shell. The walls in his room

Rita's paternal grandmother "Omama" Ida and her youngest son, Bruno, in party dress, Bruno as a girl, ca 1925

were covered with his excellent cartoons, which fascinated me. He had also enjoyed sailing on a small artificial lake in Bucharest. This stood him in good stead when, during the Second World War, he escaped from Romania to Israel on a small sailing boat with a few friends, none of whom had the least notion of sailing.

In the flat there was an upright piano on which my grandmother, "Omama" Ida, as we called her, would play. Two of her sons, my father and the middle brother, Fred, inherited an interest in classical music and Fred also composed.

The Einhorns: Rita's father Alex, grandmother Ida, uncle Bruno, mother Lotte and grandfather Moritz, ca 1930

My father's ambition had been to become a violinist, but his father wished him to go into the shoe trade and sent him to London to study commercial subjects. This he dutifully did and became quite quickly successful in business, though he spent much of his time at concerts and recitals, and at the opera.

Omama Ida, as we called her, was tall and generously built. Her pleasure was to serve each member of the family with the food he/she liked best, so that there were often quite a number of separate little dishes on the table. She was of a cheerful disposition, but by the time I came to Bucharest, she was already unwell, probably with angina. I slept on a couch at the bottom of their bed and occasionally woke up to hear her groan.

My maternal grandparents lived in Iași. My grandfather, Moritz Wachtel, was a banker and industrialist who died of cancer soon after my birth. He must have become an important figure in the Jewish community as I found a reel of film of his funeral and a photograph of a grand commemorative dinner. I gave these, together with records of the Jewish Hospital in Iași, which he supported, to the Jewish Diaspora Museum in Tel Aviv. The curator was very pleased. He said that there were many Romanian Jews in Israel, but there was a paucity of records about their lives in Romania.

Rita's maternal grandparents, Betty and Moritz Wachtel, ca 1925

After coming to Iași and marrying my mother, my father, Alexander Einhorn, was taken into the bank (Banca Moldova). It went into liquidation and my father ventured into industrial projects. He part-owned a factory making rope out of jute, which, he used to say (according to my brother), supplied the British Navy. Andrei told me that our father also had an interest in a sugar factory in Iţcani, and was involved in "Ţesătura", a cotton cloth factory in Iaşi.

Throughout his life he had the gift of understanding and being happy with children. We benefited from his attention and ability to entertain us, as did our children. He had a great sense of humour and also enjoyed good company, old and young. A great lover of classical music, his decision to emigrate with his family to England, was not entirely unrelated to its musical cornucopia. In later life he came to know many figures in the musical world and, in his seventies, developed a particular friendship with Friedelind Wagner, the granddaughter of the composer. At my father's funeral ceremony we played a recording of *In Paradisum* from Fauré's Requiem.

My grandmother, on my mother's side, "Omama" Betty, outlived her husband by many years. My mother recounts that, on an occasion when, in their youth, my grandmother and her sister were sitting at a first floor window during a holiday in Vienna, they overheard some young gallants below regretting that the attractive young ladies at the window were wearing wigs (as was expected of Jewish women in less progressive Romania at that time). My grandmother apparently removed her wig and never again wore one. When in old age Omama Betty came to live with us in London she asked my mother why she did not follow the Jewish dietary laws. My mother said she would do so if her mother returned to wearing a wig. My mother also told me that, as an early teenager, Omama Betty gave her consent to be married in exchange for a black dress. She was pregnant with my mother, her third child, at the wedding of her eldest daughter. This has caused a geological fault in the family as aunts and cousins who should have been a generation apart were often of the same age.

Omama Betty came from Lithuania and spoke Yiddish and German. Her Yiddish was wonderfully pithy and although I never spoke the language, I absorbed odd Yiddish words and phrases first heard from her, such as *Deine Zures möcht ich haben* (I wish I had your worries). Sayings in German and Yiddish first heard from her, well up quite unexpectedly from my memory. About a man who could not sit still, she would say '*Er hat Stecknadeln im Popo* (He has pins in his bum). On a higher plane she had two favourites, both difficult to translate because they are so concise. One applied to someone who was likely to move things carelessly, but it was also used inappropriately by us as children because it struck us as funny. It was *Vorsicht ist die Mutter der Porzellankiste* (Careful handling is the mother of the china crate). And *probieren ist über studieren* (Trying something out is better than studying it).

She kept kosher and I remember marvelling at the extent of the crockery in her kitchen. We would celebrate Jewish festivals in her apartment, as my parents were not religious. My mother used to tell me not to tell my grandmother if we had had ham or other pork for lunch prior to seeing her. This was quite a burden for me, and I dreaded being asked by Omama what we had eaten. I remember us eating the forbidden ham on buttered *Matzes*, the unleavened bread eaten by Jews in commemoration of the Jewish exodus from Egypt. Fortunately she never asked us, probably because she knew. The festival I remember best is when we used to pretend we were the children of Israel coming out of Egypt. We used to walk round and round her dining-room table and when our journey came to an end (if I am not getting the festivals muddled up) we used to eat delicious *Hummentaschen*, sticky, sweet samosas filled with nuts and coated with caramellised sugar.

Omama was much taken with my father, who was tall and handsome, and quite slim in the early years of his marriage. He had curly hair and did his best to smooth it out, not always successfully. To his embarrassment, Omama was overheard congratulating him on his lovely curly hair.

She had survived the Second World War with the help of food parcels, which my mother was for ever sending to our relatives and friends in Romania. Omama's first experience of air travel, which she much enjoyed, was when she left Romania for Israel in her late eighties, before joining us in London. Always neatly dressed, she took care of her appearance. When, aged ninety, my mother took her to the dentist, she whispered: "Tell him I am eighty-nine"!

MY PARENTS

My mother Charlotte, known as "Lotte", had to make do with the fact that her oldest sibling, was old enough to be her mother and even her other sister was twelve years older than she was. Lotte was a rebellious child, once climbing on the roof to get her own way about some matter that I can no longer recall. She was sent to finishing school in Switzerland and made some life-long friends there. Among the accomplishments expected of the young boarders was to be able to draw and paint. Both my brother and I have competent watercolours she made at the time. She had wanted to become an interior designer, but at that time it was considered unsuitable for a banker's wife to have a career; however, gardening and flower arrangement, as well as the designing and arrangement of the interiors of the houses she lived in, became outlets for her creativity.

She was a wonderful gardener, and I remember many details of our garden in Romania. There were two lawns at the back of the house, the further one being some half a metre higher. In the middle of the upper one was a magnificent walnut tree, from the unripe walnuts of which our cook made a marvellous green preserve. Between the two lawns my mother had created a splendid rockery of cacti and alpine flowers. Around the edges of the lawns there were peach, apricot and sour cherry trees and in the corner were the soft fruit bushes. Near the front gate rose a magnificent silver pine. I have a vivid memory of it, heavily laden with snow. Long afterwards, when Richard and I were in Iași during Ceaucescu's regime we looked in vain for the house, which had been pulled down to make way for some flats. I was particularly disappointed to find that the silver pine was no longer there.

My brother has added the following reminiscence: "To the right of the garden, just past the tree you mentioned, there was a recess into the neighbour's garden where

Portrait of Rita's mother, Charlotte, 1937

stood a two-storey building some 15 metres square. The top floor was where the pigeons congregated. The ground floor had a large entrance leading to a mighty staircase that led down into the basement. Here in a kind of sandbank, grew celery, carrots, potatoes and other vegetables, all in leaf, the leaves white in the absence of sunlight." I wonder whether in fact this was a winter storage system rather than a vegetable garden. "Opposite", Andrei continues, "pickles were kept in large barrels some 3-4 feet high. There were *gogonele*—pickled small green tomatoes; *ardei*—large pimentos of different colours, grilled, peeled and marinated in olive oil; large gherkins in a sweet pickle; and, the favourite, a large whole green water melon. These were sliced one inch thick. The skin kept its green colour, and the inside, its vivid bright red. The melon, just like the pimento, were deliciously mild." Having read this description of Andrei's memories, the reader will not be surprised to learn that he chose a famous catering school at Lausanne, Switzerland, for his further studies, and became a hotel manager.

My mother was always elegantly, but never flamboyantly, dressed. I remember that the dressmaker who came to the house to fit mother's new clothes, had to spend much time ensuring that the hemline of the dress was perfectly straight. Later, when we were in Bucharest before leaving Romania, mother took me shopping to *Galeries Lafayette*, a branch of the French department store of that name. It astonished me by its size and glamour. Its lift, the first I ever used, and never forgot, had cut-glass walls slowly revealing, as we went up, the whole ground floor of the store glittering below us.

Throughout her married life my mother wore her hair neatly parted in the middle and pulled over the ears into a bun, in the style made famous by the Duchess of Windsor. Like my grandmother, my mother was not tall, but she had a dignified and quiet presence that was much admired. Also like her mother, my mother was very forthright. One of her nicknames was *Tante Patcherke*, which could be translated as Aunt "lacking diplomatic skills." One much remembered incident contrasts her straightforward approach to that of my more diplomatic father; shortly before he came home one afternoon my mother had told Andrei to pick up a handkerchief that had fallen on the floor. Andrei replied that he could not see it. The confrontation continued until my father appeared. When informed of the situation he asked Andrei to pick up the handkerchief without seeing it, whereupon Andrei promptly did so.

My mother also had a practical streak and dealt efficiently with household matters. On one occasion at a ladies' dinner party at home, a mouse made its appearance. All the women guests screamed and leapt onto their chairs. My mother coolly caught the mouse and removed it. An artist shortly afterwards, hearing about it, drew a cartoon of the event in which my mother figures as a cat catching mice. She never liked this cartoon, but I am pleased to have it in my possession.

My parents both loved music. They had acquired a Bechstein grand piano and would play transcriptions for four hands of a range of classical music. I recall falling asleep to music drifting through from the conservatory. There was a vibrant social life in which my parents participated, with fancy dress balls to raise money for various causes.

Caricature by an artist who heard that Rita's mother had caught a mouse at a dinner party, ca 1933

The costumes were of course home-made. There was also much entertainment at our house. I used to look forward to such occasions, as a trolley of aperitifs usually preceded the dinners. I would be expected to make an appearance, properly dressed, and could then nosh from the trolley, replete with olives, salami, pastrame, caviare and other delights.

Mealtimes in the family were also memorable. We had a wonderful cook who produced a great variety of dishes to my mother's high standards. The only dish both Andrei and I heartily disliked was one in which spinach predominated. If we kept an especially favoured morsel of something else on our plate to savour at the end, my father would distract us and then remove the plate. Eventually we were careful not to give him this opportunity.

LIFE IN IAŞI

In my mind our house was a palatial building, but it was probably only a typical residence of the better-off bourgeoisie of that time and place.

One entered by a vestibule furnished with beautifully carved Romanian peasant furniture. A small octagonal table that I greatly treasure was part of that furniture set. The table accompanied me to Oxford and subsequently to Addis Ababa, where it still stands, surviving the attentions of our children and grandchildren.

The reception room also had a Romanian flavour with a couch covered in Romanian carpets and cushions. Two huge glass-fronted bookcases, with brass handles stood on either side of the entrance. The books, mostly paperbacks bound to order, were mainly novels in French, German and Romanian, and translations from English.

Other sections of the library contained books about Romania as well as musical scores and books about music.

Andrei inherited the bookcases and kept them in pristine condition. He was also proud of retaining, through his various peregrinations, one of our father's upright armchairs, together with photographic evidence of their original site. My mother's desk, made to her design, was also inherited by my brother. It had brass fittings matching those of the book cases, but its special feature was a shelf on which she nurtured her cacti. On the walls were several paintings by Grigorescu and other famous Romanian painters. The main features of the salon were the Bechstein grand piano and the profusion of plants in the alcove. There was also an almost life-size statue on a marble pedestal, the subject of many jokes. It represented a maiden being wooed by a swain, and was from some well-known porcelain factory. My mother detested it, but perhaps because it was a valuable wedding gift, it accompanied us to London and stood romantically in our drawing room.

The dining room was sombre-looking, as the furniture was dark and heavy. A display-case contained my mother's collection of fine porcelain cups from famous European porcelain factories. I inherited the cups and kept them wrapped in tissue paper for many years until I decided to risk using them.

Behind the whole length of one of the walls there ran a pantry/larder, kept locked, where food was stocked, or more accurately, "stockpiled." My mother had inherited a "siege mentality" from her mother, so that there were considerable stocks of dry food of all kinds. I inherited something of this failing, for which, later, I was teased by Richard, and even later, by my children.

The kitchen was large, and had a wood-fed stove, and great iron pots and pans. Our cook herself was of ample proportions, like all good cooks. I do not know how she managed to provide meals for the four of us plus the governess, often twice a day, six or seven days a week, with complicated dishes, often comprising three courses. This is not to speak of having to cater for all the guests who came for normal lunches, afternoon bridge occasions, dinners and parties.

Electric fridges had not yet made an appearance: ice came to the house in long rectangular ice blocks brought by horse and cart. Ice cream was made in wooden pails, which had some turning mechanism operated by hand. It took hours of churning to produce the ice cream that would be consumed in minutes. Newly made jam would be decanted from large pots under the vine-covered trellis outside the kitchen. Much else was home-made. Beyond the kitchen were the bedrooms of the maid and manservant.

Though the rooms were centrally heated, the children's nursery and school room had a floor-to-ceiling tiled Russian style stove fuelled by logs. I had to wash in my bedroom with luke-warm water, standing in a little rubbery tub with low floppy sides. I have a faint recollection that my father had to be called on one occasion to find a way of making me accept this form of washing on a winter morning. In a windowless little room leading to the kitchen the seamstress would sow and mend, with a foot-propelled Singer sewing machine. She would endlessly fashion and embroider table linen and all sorts of little mats, under a single electric light bulb. At night our dachshunds slept there.

From our children's school room a double door led to a terrace overlooking the garden. Because it was a cool area, ice cream was made there. In May 1936, in the garden, below the terrace we celebrated Andrei's Bar Mitzvah, in the presence of a large circle of family and friends. He managed to get through the Hebrew he had had to learn for the occasion. Not long after this event my father took him to England for education. I heard Andrei say, many years later, that his departure was hastened by his having had a fight at school with the son of a prominent local Fascist.

My interest in food started early. It is reported that, at the age when propulsion takes place on all fours, I found my way to the sideboard where the sugar bowl was kept, crammed my mouth with sugar lumps, took a few more in one hand and, thus satisfied, backed away. One result of my gluttony was

Moni, Rita and their uncle Bruno in the gym area of the garden in Iaşi, ca 1934

that I was, and remained, like Omama Ida, on the generous side. This encouraged my parents to create a gym area in the corner of the garden where we were urged to climb a ladder fixed to the wall and do other exercises under the watchful eye of an instructor.

We had a loving and good-natured German-speaking nanny called Toni, who also did some sewing and embroidery. Her Russian husband was not always sober. I saw where she lived only once, after heavy rains, when the flood waters had entered her house. Comprising only two rooms, it was situated in a poor, low-lying quarter of the town. I was shocked to see how unlike our own house it was. Toni had taught me to do cross-stitch and embroider in the geometric Romanian style. I embroidered with blue and black thread a Romanian baby's dress in very thin white cotton, and kept it religiously for the possible birth of a daughter and a granddaughter. However, being of a forgetful disposition, I was able to find it only *between*, but not *at* the appropriate time for, these events. I do not believe my daughter Helen ever embroidered a garment. I would be surprised if, with all the other calls on today's children's time, my granddaughters ever will.

When I found myself in Iaşi with Richard in 1968, we visited Toni's family. The Communist regime had been kind to her, and she and her family had been assigned a small flat in one of the new workers' housing estates. She called upon her grandson to show us round the town. I asked him to take us to the famous 17th century Monastery of the *Trei Ierachi* (Three Hierachs of the Romanian Eastern Orthodox Church) , with its beautifully carved external columns. Our little guide had no idea where it was, but he did show us with pride the Consomol (Communist Youth League) "palace."

My cousin Moni, who was a year older than I, came from Bucharest to stay with us when I was eight or nine. There had been intermarriages between my father's and my mother's families at several levels. In one instance my father's brother Fred had married my mother's eldest sister's daughter, Thea, and Moni had been the offspring of this marriage. Moni was thus my cousin on my father's side and the daughter of my cousin on my mother's side. Sadly, the marriage of her parents had broken up; her father had re-married and her mother had committed suicide. Moni must have suffered severely from these events. When Moni came to live with us, I was in primary school. She told me that, on one occasion, I was angry with her when she came up with better test results. My own memory has conveniently forgotten this incident. Apart from that we were good friends.

I remember little of my four years in primary school, perhaps because the teacher was not inspiring. We had to wear black smocks, a white collar and a red bow. Although the uniform was supposed to obliterate distinctions between rich and poor, the quality of the materials used varied widely according to the income of the parents. I remember only two incidents. One was when the teacher made it clear that we had to bring her a present for some occasion or other, and I was worried that the present I would be bringing would not please her. I believe it was a handbag. The other incident was hearing a boy jeering at another one for being Jewish.

We saw much of our relative, Rodica (Dudu), a slim and pretty girl whose parents lived further up Copoul, the hill on which our houses stood. Her grandmother was my mother's sister, but, because of the "geological fault'" in the family, it was her mother who was my cousin. Rodica escaped from Romania by paying a man to enter into a

fake marriage with her. She subsequently settled in Paris with a genuine husband and had two children.

Above our house on the hill there was a little park where we often walked, and beyond that were the cavalry barracks. We were aware of it only at their meal times when we would hear the trumpet call, to the words we had learnt: *Lingura și strachina, mämäliga'e gata* (Bring spoon and bowl, the *mämäliga*'s ready). *Mämäliga* was the maize meal which formed the basis of the peasant diet.

It was customary in the 1930s for wealthy Romanians to have governesses for their children. My parents wanted us to speak French and German as well as Romanian. To this end we had French- and German-speaking governesses alternately, already before we went to primary school, aged seven. I remember little about most of these, except an English one who had a white poodle

Rita with her brother Andrei before he set out for primary school, ca 1931 and a Swiss one, who was a naturist and liked to go barefoot in the forest above the chalet we rented in the Carpathian Mountains during the summer. Dudu reminded me recently that one governess we all disliked passed too closely in front of our Alsatian and was bitten by it in her posterior, to the unkind delight of the various children who saw the incident. Andrei has a much better recollection of some of our governesses, with whom he would carry on mild flirtations.

However, there was one governess who was very important in my childhood. She was Frau (Mrs) Jacobi, a German refugee. She was not Jewish, although her husband, who appeared from time to time, was. I used to wake up every morning to the sound of her washing her hair in the washbasin in the room we shared. She told me

Portrait of Rita, ca 1932

that she got into the habit when she and her husband lived in Mexico. She was not only a wonderful teacher but also a poet. Among many other things I learned from her was to appreciate German poetry, some of which I can recite to this day. I recall looking with her at the page-size illustrations of the German children's tale, *Struwelpeter*, and learning the words that, I think, rhymed. Under her guidance I also enjoyed making coloured crayon maps of different parts of the world.

I loved Frau Jacobi. One day when my mother was putting on make-up in her dressing room, and somehow we came to talk about beauty, I declared categorically that Frau Jacobi was the most beautiful woman I knew. My mother could not resist a smile, as Frau Jacobi was not beautiful by any standard. She was tall and thin, with a face that faintly reminded one of a camel's. It was crowned by a crop of thick straight blond hair that made her head look like a miniature haystack. Sadly I heard much later that she had committed suicide in Argentina. Perhaps my parents felt I was too young at the time to cope with her death.

I remember well the winters and summers in Romania. In mid-winter our tennis court would be doused with water in the evening, ready for skating on the next day. I used to go shopping with my mother and our two miniature dachshunds on one divided lead. We would go to Pogor, the best grocer in town for our salami etc, and

Frau Jacobi and her husband in London, left on their way to Argentina, visiting Rita, right with her mother and brother, ca 1938

end up at the best pastry shop, Zamfirescu. My hope was to be offered a bonbon there, and this usually happened. We were in fur coats with fur hats and muffs, and when it was very cold we would go by horse-drawn sleigh. Bells were attached to the harness, to alert pedestrians and other sleighs to our presence, as the sleigh travelled rather

Rita and her mother with dachshunds, shopping in Iași, ca 1938

silently over the snow. We possessed a thick rug lined with mink, for travel in the sleigh when it was really cold. It came with us to England and ended its days as a camping rug in Ethiopia.

My father had the belief, common among Jews, that it was not a good idea for them to be conspicuous, and was not happy that we paraded in expensive furs and with two, not one, unusual dogs on the leash. I was conscious at an early age that being Jewish marked one out from the Romanians around us, who were Orthodox Christians. This consciousness of who was, and who was not a Jew, remained with me for a very long time, though it eventually became very faint. I did, however, retain a certain reserve about being in any way conspicuous.

Rita's mother at the window of the chalet in Borsec, Transylvania, where the children spent part of their summer holidays, ca 1936

Andrei and I, later joined by Moni, spent the summer holidays partly in the mountains and partly by the seaside. To get to Borsec in the Carpathians was a full day's journey by car. Our driver Nicu would regularly swear at the drivers of hay carts that ambled all over the road. If a priest or a black cat crossed the road in front of the car he would cross himself and stop for a couple of minutes. We children were often carsick. We would stop at Sibiu to buy the salami for which the town was famous, and end up at the wooden, steep-roofed chalet of a hunter friend of my mother's, where we stayed for a month or so. It was up above the village, on the edge of the woods where we would pick wild strawberries. From its windows there was a lovely view of the Ceahlău Mountain range. We ate at a German pension further down the hill and visited the village where Hungarian gypsies sold their craftwork. On occasion my parents would hold a small party in the chalet and I could hear the gramophone playing popular Romanian music. It is alleged that on one occasion I stood up in my cot, rattling its sides and shouting *Vreau Cotnar*, "I want *Cotnar*," a well known Romanian wine. The grown-ups would go on hiking expeditions while we children enjoyed the nearby woods.

After the mountains, we decamped to Eforia, a pretty little Black Sea resort near Mamaia. It had whitewashed houses, mainly hotels and pensions, with dark blue shutters, and was patronised by several families and friends from Iaşi. We children would be sent down to the beach to sunbathe in the early mornings so as to benefit from the ultra-violet sunrays. We then had swimming lessons, or joined the adults at the beach, where Turkish vendors would offer hot pasties and cool sour milk. There followed long drawn-out lunches with Dudu, who never had much of an appetite, as she steadily munched each mouthful, to delay having to accept the next one. In the hot early afternoons we would sleep. I remember the bright light filtering through the shutters as I rested. In the late afternoon our governess would take us for walks to the mud baths or to the market where watermelons were on sale. We would eat freshly roasted corn on the cob sold on the promenade above the cliffs. Occasionally, after dark on moonlit nights, we could see dolphins leaping over the water.

By coincidence in mid-August 1934, Richard and his parents were in Constanţa, as he relates earlier in this chapter. This was only some 20 kilometres (km.) from Eforia, further south along the Black Sea, where, at that time, I was learning to swim. Twenty years, however, were to pass before we met.

From time to time, my parents would go to other parts of Europe, mainly to Vienna. They came back with the latest gadgets, of which I remember two. One was the most useless of all the ones I later came across, though it was popular at home. It was a metal egg-topper that operated like scissors. It came into regular use for topping boiled eggs when our children were small, so much so that, confronted with a boiled egg elsewhere they were at a loss as to how to open it. The other, also of metal, was a crumb remover. I have seen many attractive such implements since then, but none of them were as efficient. The one my parents brought could be unscrewed so that the brushes could be properly cleaned. The brushes themselves were fine and closely packed, so that one sweep took away all crumbs in their path. Both utensils are still in working condition after many decades of use.

As Hitler rose to power my father saw the forthcoming danger for Jews in Europe and decided to emigrate. He and my mother visited Israel, but felt they did not wish to live there. The second option was England where my father had studied, and had had some success in business. He was impressed by the British way of life and thought he could make a good living as a merchant in the City of London. Nor was he unmindful of the rich musical scene in that city. He therefore took Andrei to England in October 1936 (in a specially made knickerbocker suit). Andrei remembers that they travelled in the Orient Express via Budapest, and that they spent the afternoon on the island in the Danube facing the castle. My father left him in Cambridge, selected because it was envisaged that Andrei could enter the British education system, after first staying with an English family, the Mantells. Mrs Mantell was the sister of an Englishwoman who had married my mother's nephew, Fred Dinermann. Having spent some two months with the family and having had some English lessons from Mr Mantell, Andrei was accepted at St. Faith's, Cambridge, the preparatory school for the Leys Public School, to which he later progressed.

In February 1938, after a short stay in Bucharest with my paternal grandparents, we followed. My parents' friends in Romania, were surprised at my father's decision, as they could not see any threat to their lives; however, events proved him only too right.

THE PERSE SCHOOL IN CAMBRIDGE

I had already travelled overnight by sleeper before taking the train across Europe on our way out of Romania in February 1938. Some months before we left, I had enjoyed my first night sleeping on a train. I was put on one at Iaşi and enjoyed the overnight ride to Bucharest. As a child, ever since that journey, I had always enjoyed exploring the various brass fittings, the tiny washbasins, the ladder to the upper bunk and the irregular motion of the moving and stopping night train. I was reminded of it when my father visited us in Ethiopia. On his birthday we took the night train to Dire Dawa— the only railroad line in Ethiopia which reached Addis Ababa from Jibuti in 1917.

It was a rather rough crossing to Dover, my first on a ship. Remembering our slow and dusty summer journeys by car from Iaşi into the Carpathian Mountains, I concluded that trains were a greatly superior form of transport, both to ships and automobiles. I have a sneaking feeling that I would still enjoy that form of travel were the opportunity to arise today.

To introduce me to good spoken English my parents, curiously, picked on a young Canadian woman. She took me round the sights of London. As she spoke a smattering of French we resorted to that language in emergencies, but at the age of ten I was still young enough to pick up (Canadian) English from her, fairly rapidly. I do not remember what monuments she took me to see during the months we spent together, but I recall her home, which was a tiny flat with a minute kitchen. What struck me was that, despite the lack of space, she kept strictly to the kosher rules of separating meat-based and milk-based dishes, so that there were two parallel sets of crockery, pots and pans, etc. even in her little flat.

At the beginning of the summer term I entered the Perse School for Girls in Cambridge. That town was chosen because Andrei was already at school there, and my parents expected that the Mantells would keep an eye, first on him, and later on us both. Also taken into account was that Cambridge was an ancient university town, and that it was not far from London, where they intended to live.

The Perse was a Direct Grant school, which meant that it was funded partly by government grant and partly by fee-paying parents. Such schools were well regarded, and the Perse had a particularly high reputation. A few girls from poorer families received scholarships, and although the teachers tried to obscure the distinction between fee-paying and non-fee-paying pupils, we soon became aware that there was this difference.

The school had no boarding facilities, but there was an informal arrangement with the owner of a boarding house further along the opposite side of Panton Street, named La Ruche (The Beehive). It was run by Mademoiselle Malandain, one of the school's French teachers, an energetic and hot-tempered French woman from Normandy who took in about twenty Perse School pupils of all ages for the duration of the three terms of the school year. We slept in four dormitories of unequal size on the first and second floors, and shared one bathroom in which we had a bath once a week. We ate in one of the ground floor rooms and did our homework, read or chatted in another, the third room being her private salon. There was also an extension at ground floor level, large enough to accommodate us for tea, or to serve as a homework area. Above it was a glass-walled enclosure where her French assistant slept, in no great comfort, as her "room"' was hot in summer and very cold in winter. This may have been one reason why the assistants did not usually remain for more than one year.

In the thirties, central heating was not the norm in English houses and double glazing had not yet been invented. During my first winter at La Ruche, I longed for the great pipes of central heating and the double sets of windows that kept us warm at home in Iaşi. The downstairs rooms had open fireplaces burning coal. Early lessons in sharing scarce resources came through protests against those who hogged the fire. It was sitting round the fire that I read many an English novel, in small, tightly printed volumes bound in dark imitation leather.

There was no heating in the bedrooms and I remember getting into bed with ice-cold feet, pulling the blankets round my ears, and waiting until I gradually warmed up. Many of us suffered from chillblains. Although we were supposed to be quiet once in bed, we naturally carried on whispered conversations till we fell asleep. On one occasion we were talking about our parents, and when it came to the turn of one girl who had said little, she told us in a quiet voice that her parents were divorced. This was received with silent consternation and no one spoke for some time.

The school building, in Panton Street, was two storeys high and did not fail to impress me. Though there was an imposing black door for visitors, we entered through a small gate at the side of the building. I was put in the Lower Third in a dark room with each desk and chair forming a single unit. The school uniform, in the cold months comprised a white blouse, striped navy and pale blue tie, navy blazer and serge skirt, long socks and navy, laced shoes. In summer we wore pale blue cotton dresses. We could choose from two or three patterns superimposed on the blue background. I liked these uniforms that were a great improvement on the black smocks of my Romanian primary school.

In the morning we assembled in the School Hall for prayers. I followed the "lessons", i.e. the readings from the Authorised English Bible, in a Romanian translation. I do not know how this Romanian Bible came into my possession, but it made the lessons a linguistic, as well as a Biblical exercise. It helped me to keep up the language. The other, more important factor that helped maintain my Romanian was the letter we were expected to write to our parents every Sunday. At this stage I also spoke Romanian at home during the holidays, though English gradually supplanted Romanian in family conversations. I could also speak Romanian with Andrei. The Leys School, the Public School he attended, was only two streets away from La Ruche and I used to meet him at lunchtime at some point between his school and mine. He would come on his bicycle, and we would exchange news from home, soon speaking to each other in English.

Presiding over Morning Prayers was our headmistress, Miss Cattley, who took naturally to her position of authority. She wore her beautiful auburn hair in a bun at the nape of the neck. What we did not know at the time was that she made every effort to accommodate the children of refugees from Europe. She also employed Trude Falk, a young Jewish educational psychologist from Vienna, as a French teacher. She was by no means a native speaker of French and had no experience of teaching. Perhaps for these reasons, we used to tease her. She later found a job in her field of expertise and I developed a friendship with her that continues to this day. In June 2011 we celebrated her 100th birthday.

From the beginning I loved singing the hymns. When prayers were finished, the Orthodox Jewish girls who had not participated in the prayers came in and climbed the steps to the platform to hear the school announcements. I was glad not to have to parade so conspicuously with these girls.

Miss Cattley, Headmistress of the Perse Girls School, Cambridge, which Rita attended 1938-1945

I must have made rapid progress with my English as I was promoted to the next class at the end of the school year. This is not surprising. Although we were expected to speak French with Mademoiselle Malandain we spoke English among ourselves and I had to choose between speaking English or remaining silent. The worst of my early days at La Ruche was not my lack of English but my ignorance about horses, the favourite topic of conversation. Several years later one of my friends at La Ruche who was a weekly boarder, invited me to her home one weekend. She lived in the country outside Cambridge and her family kept horses. Before I could think of a way of avoiding it I found myself propelled onto a horse. I hung on tightly and managed not to fall off. However, I remained fearful of the creatures all my life. Having safely survived the ride I was taken round the stables. My friend breathed in the stable smell and confessed that she would like to find a way of making perfume out of it.

In the summer of 1939 a young Jewish woman, Renate Klapper, "Ray", arrived in England from Berlin. She was barely out of school, and had been in one of the last *Kindertransport* convoys bringing Jewish children out of Germany. Faintly related to us, she became part of our family. As a refugee she had to enter specified professions in which there was a shortage of labour. She chose nursing. She spent her free days and holidays with us as she moved up the nursing ladder, eventually becoming a sister tutor in midwifery.

WAR YEARS

I was twelve-years old during the summer vacation of the year following our arrival in Britain when the war broke out. Like everyone who experienced that event, I remember the announcement on the radio, on the morning of the third of September,

1939. We had had physical evidence that war was approaching because on Hampstead Heath, which extended directly beyond our garden, barrage balloons, held down by metal cables, had been positioned, to destroy low-flying enemy aeroplanes. We could see these large, silvery grey silky objects floating above us in a bright sky. As Neville Chamberlain spoke, I was aware of the solemn, anxious looks on the faces of my parents, and knew that things would change for all of us. Some changes took place forthwith; others came about gradually. An immediate black-out was ordered and soon air raid wardens began to patrol the streets, ensuring that not a chink of light was visible from outside. A little later an anti-aircraft battery was established on the Heath. It was so close to the house that Andrei remembers hearing the officer give the order: so many degrees-fire-cease fire etc. He would collect shrapnel from the artillery they fired which had landed in our garden.

We lived—of course with a Dachshund, but only with one, called Bobby, like all his successors—in a large house in Hampstead at 11 Constable Close, NW 11.(My father considered 11 his lucky number, as he had lived at 11 Warwick Avenue during his first stay in England. My husband and I later lived at 22 Lawn Road in London, so that I have inherited a liking for 11 and its multiples). Citizens were encouraged to dig air raid shelters in their gardens. My mother preferred the option of reinforcing one room with additional wooden beams, building a brick wall in the garden about one foot beyond the windows, and taping them to prevent broken glass from flying in. The room passed inspection and we were thus able to spend much more comfortable nights in that room than we would have done, had my mother opted for the tin-roofed underground earth shelters in which most people who had gardens passed the nights when there were air raids. When the air raid warning sirens went, Bobby would waddle obediently into the protected room ahead of us.

A regular activity, carried on by my mother, was the dispatch of parcels of food to relatives and friends in Romania. They derived income from the sale of the contents, especially from Nescafé, which was much prized, as other coffee was not available. Our nanny Toni told us years later what an enormous difference the parcels had made to her life during the war.

Between terms and during the summer vacation Andrei and I, and Ray when she was free, would go home to London. One highlight for me was hearing Myra Hess give a piano recital at the National Gallery. It was part of a series of recitals given at lunchtime, to avoid audiences having to travel during the black-out.

Throughout the war, I was, for most of the time, at school in Cambridge. As the town was small and had few industries, it was not a major target for the German bombers. However, we had all been issued with gas masks, had to learn how to wear them and were expected to keep them with us at all times. When in November 1940 Romania came into the war on the German side I had to register as an "enemy alien" in Cambridge, and had to report to the police station every week.

Melle Malandain put bunks in the musty basement of the boarding house, and we slept there when the sirens went, but after some time the inspectors came and decided that the basement was not a good enough shelter. We had instead to run across the road in our nightclothes to the reinforced shelter in a room at the school. This procedure woke us up completely. Most of the time, luckily for us, the bombers flew over without dropping their load. On one occasion, however, several of us heard the whistle of bombs dropping on the town.

In 1940, as the bombing of London intensified, my parents decided to move to Oldham, an industrial town near Manchester, in the Northwest of England. My father bought a silkscreen printing business housed in a typical industrial "mill", i.e. a brick building of several stories where various industrial processes were carried on. As they settled down in a Manchester hotel in preparation for moving to Oldham the next day, the *Blitzkrieg*, i.e. Lightning War, or *Blitz* for short, moved with them. It was the first time Manchester was bombed. My mother was so tired from the exertions of the move from London that she refused to go down to the shelter and survived the night in her bed.

The silk-screen business included one or two designers; the workers who etched the silk screens, one per colour, to allow the paint to reach the material; and the screen operators, who poured one colour of paint into each frame and then moved the frames along the tables that stretched the length of the building. When the designers made a new design, often multicoloured and gaudy, a trial print run would be made. My father would show it to my mother. If she reacted with horror he had the necessary indication that the design would sell well. Visiting the mill gave me my first sight of a factory. It was an austere structure several storeys high. The silk-screen area had windows on all sides, so that it was well ventilated, but I remember that the floor was uneven and caked with paint. Conditions must have been worse in the manufacturing sector.

Andrei, when at home for vacations, was expected to fire-watch at the mill, for which he was paid seven shillings and six pence per night. He told me that, on his first night on duty, he asked the warden from which direction the enemy planes were likely to come. "Never mind the planes, mate," he yelled at Andrei, "just watch the pigs in the yard below." The mill workers were allowed to keep two pigs in the yard to slaughter for Christmas, but they had to be carefully guarded until that time.

As soon as my parents arrived at their new residence, to their surprise, the neighbours promptly offered them tea. With that began their induction into North of England life. Prior to their moving to Oldham their circle comprised friends and relatives from continental Europe. In Oldham there were none, but they made lifelong English friends. These included the Director of Education and the Director of Health of Oldham, and the brother of William Walton the composer. This brother was a music teacher, and I took lessons from him.

My father was encouraged to join the Manchester Pedestrian Club. Members walked briskly every Saturday into the nearby Lancashire and Yorkshire countryside and, several times a year, ventured further on week-end expeditions. It gave my father a taste for walking—which he passed on to me—and he made several good friends, as well as keeping fit in an enjoyable way. He continued to join in the week-end walks after we moved to London, as did my brother. It was, of course, in those days, a men-only association.

When Romania entered the war my parents' radio was taken away, but in due course it was returned. We used to listen to the King's Christmas speech on it. Among our friends who were invited to the Christmas dinner, there was one ultra patriotic woman. When the strains of the National Anthem entered our drawing room, where we were all comfortably seated, she promptly rose to her feet, and so, willy-nilly, did all of us. We gradually got accustomed to the strange Christmas mores of the British. After the meal there were "games." The Director of Education would dress up as a fairy or as a ballerina and romp around the house, while we would have to guess what was happening. Discussing the state of health of the factory workers, the doctor who was Director of Health informed us that the more scrubbed the traditional yellow stone of the doorstep, the more he worried about the hygiene inside.

On my first holiday visit to our Oldham house, I woke up and looked out of the bay windows of my room. It overlooked part of the industrial valley that lay around Manchester. I could see many tall factory chimneys. The sky was blue. I looked several times later that day and saw a thick pall of brown smoke gradually polluting the entire valley.

The highlight of school holidays was going to the Hallé Orchestra concerts conducted by John Barbirolli. It was through these concerts that I first learned the repertoire of classical orchestral music. I remember being thrilled by Jacqueline Du Pré playing the Elgar Cello Concerto with the orchestra at the Manchester Bellevue Hall.

Many foodstuffs were rationed, including meat, eggs, butter and sugar. Each person was issued with a ration card, and consequently there was a black market in rationed goods. In Oldham my mother kept chickens for a while but they did not oblige much with eggs, and the experiment was given up. Every autumn we would store apples on a shelf in the pantry for consumption in the winter. Each apple had to be turned regularly, so as not to rot. It was a futile exercise, as most of them did go bad, and the ones that did not, tasted as though they had rotted. At some time powdered eggs arrived from America. One could make scrambled eggs that had a faint resemblance to the real thing. My father became enthusiastic about the Lancashire speciality, Cheese and Onion Pie, which our house-keeper would prepare for us. It never appealed to my mother.

Our Bobby was still with us. Dachshunds were considered German dogs and on one occasion a passer-by observed, with Northern England sense of humour, that Bobby was "as low as Hitler." However, a young friend of my parents who would come to stay, when on leave from the Royal Air Force, envied Bobby his luck. The airman once remarked that he wished he could take the place of Bobby, and do nothing but eat, sleep and go for walks, at the risk of being insulted. Bobby was on the fat side. My father could not resist feeding him at the table. "Bread and butter", he would say to the dog, whereupon my mother, outraged, would express her irritation with this waste of precious butter, whereupon my father would reply: "I am not giving him butter—only telling him that there was some on the bread."

My mother was elegance personified, like many of her Romanian contemporaries who could afford it. She wore well-cut clothes in subdued colours. She was not too happy with my inattention to clothes and appearance. In wartime there was a limited choice of dresses in the shops and the ones that were larger round the waist than was the norm for young girls, were intended for older women. We used to have difficulty in finding clothes that did not look dowdy on me.

In Cambridge, we were well looked after by Mlle Malandain, who was a good cook. We continued to have enough good food to eat, though I had some trouble with suet pudding, which, I discovered, was made from rendered animal fat. It was served with custard, and this reduced the unpleasant taste. Parents were encouraged to augment our diet with a mix of cod liver oil and malt, with different brand names. The brown, sticky mixture came in large bottles that were kept in a cupboard. After lunch several of us would troop to the cupboard and take a spoonful from our own bottle. Although sweet, the stuff was far from delicious.

Winston Churchill's famous defiant speech in the summer of 1940: "We shall fight on the beaches…we shall never surrender," was another occasion I remember. Mlle Malandain had encouraged us to paint the wall separating our back yard from that of the adjacent house and the joint effort was colourful if not outstanding artistically. When weather permitted we used to eat outside, under a Laburnum tree, protected by our wall on one side and the back of the house on another. The speech came on the radio after lunch and once again the faces of the staff and older girls indicated to me that the situation was grim.

As more soldiers were mobilised, an agricultural labour shortage developed and on a number of occasions lorries would take us to the fields to pick potatoes, and, what was more interesting, strawberries. Later, when I was in the upper classes of the school, we had some kind of military duties. I do not remember anything about these, but a photograph shows me wearing a white blouse with three stripes on my arm. The only duty I remember was serving tea in a soldiers' canteen once a week and I did not enjoy being eyed by them as I carried the trays.

Despite the war, normal school life continued in parallel. We played tennis on the school courts, and walked to our sports fields that led to the Cam River. Being on the plump side, I was never very good at games. My greatest sports achievement was to be selected once for the school's third hockey team. I did like swimming in the river, despite the fact that the water was cold, and ever since I have enjoyed swimming even in British coastal waters. Alas, I do not believe that many would swim in the no doubt polluted Cam these days, although my grandchildren have been known to do so.

Weekends at La Ruche were relaxed. The weekly boarders were gone, so that there was more room for those of us who stayed. On Saturdays we would visit the market stalls of fruit and vegetables, clothes and knickknacks displayed in the square outside the Town Hall. There was also a Milk Bar among the shops facing the square. Here we made the acquaintance of a new drink, the Milk Shake. We could choose from a variety of flavours and enjoyed them all in turn.

Rita as a schoolgirl in war-time "duty uniform", with her mother, ca 1941

Of course we had to go to church on Sundays. We usually walked to the Holy Trinity, in "crocodile" lines, i.e. two by two. There were some four hymns to look forward to, and towards the end of my school life I began to appreciate the sermons pronounced by well-known Cambridge clerics. On occasion we went to King's College Chapel. This was always a treat for us to hear the wonderful sound of the choirboys singing, especially when they were preparing for their Christmas service, which was always broadcast live on Christmas Eve.

On Sunday afternoons I would walk to the Mantells, who lived only a few streets away in a small terraced house. Since Mrs Mantell's sister married a relative of ours, I was expected to consider her and her husband as my guardians. They were working people, and were probably as reluctant to share their Sunday family afternoons with me as I was to trail to their house and consume their tea and biscuits amid humdrum conversation. As time passed I went to visit them less and less. For my parents, however, it was important to know that the Mantells would take care of us in an emergency.

We often went for walks in the Botanical Gardens at the end of Panton Street. It had beautiful exotic trees and a lake where we could admire the ducks and other water birds. Sometimes Mlle Malandain would take us for a picnic to the Gog Magog Hills in her ancient car. We would wander in the beech woods and in season, collected beechnuts. Occasionally my parents would come to see Andrei and me, and we would look at some colleges, or punt on the river.

One or two of us were permitted to go to chamber music concerts in town, but this was sometimes dependent on Melle Malandain's mood. She liked contradicting us, and we discovered that we could obtain her permission by suggesting that we should not go. There were a series of chamber music concerts throughout term time. I listened for the first time to many a quartet by Mozart, Haydn and Beethoven. At home, too there was always classical music. There were recordings on 78s, then 33s; then came the mechanism whereby the records dropped down automatically. My father was particularly fond of Brahms and Elgar, but we listened to the full range of chamber, orchestral and choral music. At that time "early music'" was not yet well known. My father also took me to concerts in my early teens, so that concert-going became part of my life. I also had piano and recorder lessons, but never applied myself sufficiently to continue after school.

I liked school, and life at La Ruche. One of my early surprises was being confronted with written French. Although I could speak it fluently, I had never written it. Having no grammar I was amazed to discover that the same sound would sometimes be written in French with an *accent aigu*, as in *il a joué* (he played, past perfect) and at other times was disguised as *ait*, as in *il jouait* (he played, past imperfect) or '*et*' as in *jouet*. As I became acquainted with the idiosyncrasies of English, this same problem in the latter language did not bother me.

My favourite subject was music. Miss Wood was a dedicated music teacher. In those days children learnt folk songs, but she also introduced us to classical music, and gave us musical appreciation and history lessons. My father was delighted with my little notebook about the lives and works of Bach and Handel, Beethoven and Chopin and other composers. Under Miss Wood's influence, and that of my musical parents I chose music as one of my subject at Higher Certificate level.

We had a dedicated history teacher, Miss Ayles, a tall, thin woman who took great strides across the space in front of the blackboard on which she brought to life the great battles of English history. There was also Miss Fezackerley, the German teacher, who taught us in the last year of school about the German Romantic poets and what Romanticism stood for. The most distinguished teacher, however, was Mlle Barthès, who taught French. She had an aristocratic air about her, dressed as she often was in a long cape, and holding a pince-nez to her eyes. The maths and sciences left me cold. When my parents first visited the Perse they were most impressed by the laboratories, in one of which a fish was being dissected. Despite my father's desire to see me as a scientist, I leaned firmly towards languages and music, and was quite unable to draw. It was assumed that each of us would develop at least one "crush" on a teacher. I chose to have one on Miss Coke, who taught us Latin. No one else had a crush on her, as she was rather gauche and shy.

In my last year at school I lived as a paying guest in the house of the Deputy Headmaster of the Leys School, Mr Stirland, who had two daughters, Betty and Jane, both of whom were at the Perse. We rode to and from school on our bicycles, the most general means of transportation in Cambridge. The Stirlands were Quakers. They wore plain clothes, ate , to my palate, rather bland food, and spoke quietly to one another. In their house I learnt to appreciate the sharp taste of Marmite, which improved the daily bread and butter. Jane and I enjoyed playing music together, one of us on the upright piano and the other on the recorder. There was an air of gentle tolerance in the house, and I was never told off for doing anything they did not approve of.

In the sixth form we had taken the Higher School Leaving Certificate (for me the subjects were French, German, English and Music) and many of us then sat for the University Entrance examinations for Oxford, Cambridge and London (Bedford College). Bedford offered me a scholarship; Cambridge an Exhibition—a lower form of scholarship—and Oxford was willing simply to accept me. I learned later that Latin, which was compulsory for entry into Oxford and Cambridge, had been my Achilles Heel. Because it was so like Romanian, I had managed to get by on that basis, but had not bothered to study it properly. Had I been more diligent I would probably have been offered at least an exhibition by Oxford University. As my parents could afford it, I chose "The other place", as I had already spent six years in Cambridge, and I knew that Oxford and Cambridge were the most prestigious of the English universities.

ABIDING FRIENDSHIPS

I made several life-long friends during my years at the Perse. My closest friend and classmate was Laura Pettoello. Her father, an early refugee from Fascism, taught Italian at Cambridge University and spent his life in retirement working in his extensive library. Years later, after his death, Richard found among his own father's papers, a letter from Pettoello announcing the birth of his daughter, Laura. The two halves of this autobiography thus came momentarily together.

Laura's elder brother and only sibling, was at the Leys, though he did not circulate in the same orbit as Andrei. Her mother was a friendly soul with a big smile who always welcomed me warmly and gave us tea. This did not prevent her and Laura from shouting at each other in Italian as soon as a disagreement arose between them. I used to go to her house after school and we would discuss what we had learnt at home or in class. Laura was very well read and had an interest in art. She would fetch some great art book from her father's library and we would squat on the floor looking at the pictures. She was, and always remained, opinionated. Once she had pronounced some judgment on a book or person, that was the end of it. I admired her decisiveness, as I was too ignorant and unsure of myself to make any such pronouncements. She and I were near the top of the class, she usually being nearer than I. She will appear again later in this account of my life.

Also in my cohort was a French girl, Marianne Weil, a member of a distinguished family of French scientists. As her mother was Jewish, she and Marianne fled to England. Her mother, who was herself a scientist, found work in one of Cambridge University's laboratories. Marianne was shorter and rounder than I was. She was jolly and good fun to be with. We got on famously and I would go to her house after school. As you can by now expect, I remember best that she introduced me to peanut butter, a brand new delicacy that had arrived for her and her mother from friends in America. She, too, will make an appearance in later chapters.

Another boarder at La Ruche became my closest friend in later life. Judy Grey was one year ahead of me at school, and left La Ruche one year earlier to join a school of Architecture in London. She used to amaze me by her unselfishness in our daily common life. At tea-time when there were only one or two chocolate biscuits among many less interesting ones on the plate she would invariably leave the best ones for others. She used to take me to the lovely village of Great Shelford, where her nanny lived and we enjoyed talking about art and architecture. Years later she married an artist who was a Communist, and through them I became aware of the worldview of left-wing intellectuals in Britain. By some good fortune we have lived near each other since the 1950s, though for many years we met only when I was in London on vacation, or when we temporarily left Ethiopia from 1976 to 1987, and when she visited us in Addis Ababa after the death of her son.

Also at La Ruche was another boarder, Ann Bickley, who became my companion at innumerable concerts in later life. She organised these on our behalf. As she had a liking for Handel and Shostakovich, I also developed an appreciation for these composers, so different from each other.

My school days came to an end in May 1945. On VE (Victory in Europe) Day, I travelled by train, as usual, from Cambridge to Oldham. The journey involved three changes, at Bletchley, Crewe and Stockport, so that there was much waiting around for the connection. In the platform tearooms there would be a woman, usually on the sturdy side, serving almost black tea out of a huge aluminium teapot. To this, one added generous quantities of milk and sugar. Ever since those days I have had a hankering after that kind of railway tea. One would arrive, after sitting in compartments full of soldiers, looking the worse for the soot emanating from the train's steam engine.

The next day I was invited to join Andrei and a group of his friends who were going to celebrate in a public house. I was not yet eighteen and this was my first outing to a pub. I did not take to the dim light, smoky air, beery smell and loud simultaneous conversations. I was also surprised that there was nothing to eat. When it came to my turn to order a drink I had no idea what to say. Someone suggested a "Bloody Mary" (Gin and Tomato juice). This remained my standard drink in pubs, not because I liked it, but because it sounded grown up and I was not sure what were the appropriate alternatives. My anxiety at being in a pub has never completely left me, despite the fact that English pubs have been dramatically transformed. Nowadays, when in London, we have been seen at the White Horse pub, below Hampstead Heath, eating Thai food.

CHAPTER 2

Coming of Age

RICHARD

LONDON SCHOOL OF ECONOMICS

The end of the European war coincided with the termination of my schooling. This opened the question of prospective University studies. Entrance to University in Britain was then particularly difficult as service men and women had just been demobilised, and were pouring into the institutions of higher learning, with the result that there was little room for the normal intake of school-leavers. Bancroft School, suffering from the general malaise of the war, had, moreover, done little to prepare us for tertiary education, or to advise us as to careers. My mother at this point asked the advice of one of her old supporters in the East End, Frida Laski, the wife of Professor Harold Laski. He was a renowned Political Scientist at the London School of Economics (LSE) and a prominent member of the Labour Party. As we have seen in Chapter 1, he had earlier supported the Women's International Matteotti Committee.

Frida, on being approached, immediately invited me to visit her husband, which I duly did. After interrogating me closely on my scholarly interests, and my then very uncertain ambitions for the future, he asked me to write him an historical essay on a subject of my choice. I wrote on the Chartist Movement in Britain in the 1840s. On reading it he criticised what he considered some of my too enthusiastic passages, with the comment, "No flowers by request!" However, he seemed to have liked the essay as a whole, and urged me to apply to LSE. He explained the School's then uniquely important role in economics and the social sciences, by enumerating the internationally famous scholars then on its teaching staff: "You've got Tawney [the historian]; you've got Beales [the economic historian]; you've got Ginsberg [the philosopher] ...", etc. He did not add, "You've got Laski."

My choice was thus made. I at once applied for entry to LSE, and was accepted. The school, which then had a considerable number of non-European students, had a largely undeserved reputation of being a hot-bed of "Reds." One of my fellow students,

Harold Laski, political scientist, 1893-1950.

the economic historian Walter Stern, on travelling past it on a bus, once heard a passenger referring to it as "that bloody place, which should be closed down."

Going to LSE straight from secondary school seemed in a sense an overnight transition from childhood to adulthood. It was the more challenging in that the vast majority of students were ex-service men and women with an infinitely wider knowledge of life than we raw youths could ever dream of. Many of our student friends had fought in the British armed forces in one or other theatre of war. Other students had different stories to tell. One of our friends, Arthur Lerner, brother of a famous American economist, had fought in the Spanish Civil War. Captured by Franco's forces, he had been ordered to fill in a political questionnaire; and in reply to the question "What do you think of the Soviet Union?" he had replied, ambiguously: "It is a large country."

Val Sherman, another student, had written for the Yugoslav Communist newspaper *Borba*, and when Tito quarreled with Stalin, surprised us all by his ardent support of the Yugoslav position. Yet another student familiar with the Eastern Bloc, including Romania, was the geographer Geoffrey Last, who, with his wife Margaret, went to that country as a volunteer to build a railway. He had encountered some difficulty in postwar Europe, I forget what, which had caused him to travel by train across Yugoslavia with a receipt from the tailors Moss Bros., instead of a ticket. He was later to become Headmaster of the Medhané Alem Secondary School in Addis Ababa, and will appear in later chapters. Very different was the reaction of one Comrade B…, an enthusiastic Communist convert, who declared that on the day he received his Party card, he understood his "role in world history."

Another fellow student was John Stonehouse, a prominent member of the LSE Lab Soc, or Labour Society, who impressed us all by his great personal ambition, which led him within a few years to become a Minister of Defence. Sadly he later acquired notoriety by disappearing, supposedly having been drowned at sea, apparently to claim life insurance. There was also Louis Haber, a Pole who was widely travelled and well read, often referred to as "the Russian", who prefixed almost any observation he made with the words: "where I come from." He was my particular friend, who regaled us students with the fruit of his extensive knowledge of European and world history. One of his favourite stories, relating to Stalin's purges, was of a Soviet scholar who was accused of being a Japanese spy. At his trial the defence argued that the accused was involved in Byzantine Studies, and pointed out that Byzantium was in the West of the Soviet Union, whereas Japan lay to the East. The judge then allegedly dismissed this argument as irrelevant, declaring: "East, West, same thing." Louis is today known in Ethiopia by English-speaking students for his translations from French of several Ethiopian medieval royal chronicles, which we persuaded him to make and we later published in *Ethiopia Observer*.

Race—and colour—often impinged on overseas student consciousness. There were the inevitable stories of "coloured students" who responded to advertisements of accommodation from English landladies, only to be told on arrival that the room(s) in question had "just been let." Then there was the case of three Sudanese students, two dark and one light, enrolled at a British provincial university—I forget which. Students were expected to share rooms each made up for two inmates. The university authorities, faced by the differences in Sudanese pigmentation, allocated the two darker young men to one room, while his paler compatriot shared with an ordinary resident English student.

Colour, as I myself experienced, was sometimes a source of innocent confusion. LSE at one time had two first-year Sudanese students: Abdel Rahman Mirghani and Ali Sahlool. The first was of typically brown Sudanese complexion, while his compatriot was much lighter, more like an Egyptian. Word in student circles had it that the two, very strangely, came from the same country. Abdel Rahman was a friend of mine, who was often seen going with me to lunch, or to a lecture. Many students therefore jumped to the conclusion that I was the "white" Sudanese about whom they had heard.

Students had, however to contend on occasion with outright racism. One of our friends who did so successfully was an Englishman, Chris Scott, who was married to an African-American woman called Wilma. When confronted with the old question, "What would you do if your daughter married a Negro?" he replied, "My daughter is a Negro." This brought the discussion to a close.

The school was for many of us an exciting experience. We were exposed to most of the distinguished scholars Laski had enumerated. A few of us were likewise inspired by the school's motto emphasising the need to "understand the causes of things." This led me to specialise in Economic History, which I hoped, falsely as it turned out, would help me better understand the world in which we lived. We were all up to a point Marxists in that we felt that the traditional history we had read at school had tended to concentrate too much on the individuals and paid insufficient attention to economic factors.

DISCOVERING POLITICIS

LSE also introduced us to political activism of all kinds. From Laski we heard innumerable anecdotes of political events in which he had, or claimed to have had, inside knowledge. From our fellow students from various parts of the then British Empire, in Africa as well as India, we learnt the exciting story of their on-going struggles for independence and self-determination.

We were also confronted with a wide range of political, religious, and cultural societies, which held meetings, and displayed posters for all to see. I joined two societies, or "Socs," as they were called: the Lab[our] Soc and the Soc[ialist] Soc. For several years I also operated a virtually non-functional Middle East Soc., founded by Val Sherman, which enabled me to display copies of *NT&EN.* on our notice-board. Such societies canvassed a wide range of political and other ideas, which were the more intriguing to us youngsters in that we had scarcely been exposed to political controversy. In wartime Britain it had gone into virtual hibernation.

The Students' Union, to the Council of which I was later elected, involved itself continuously in contemporary political and social affairs. It supported anti-colonial and anti-*apartheid* movements, and assisted the unionisation of hitherto non-unionised hotel workers, by picketing the Ivanhoe and several nearby hotels. At the first meeting I attended I heard a report by Kari Polanyi, daughter of the noted sociologist and historian Karl Polanyi, whose book, *The Great Transformation* I read with fascination. She was speaking most inspiringly on the Union's previous year's activities. Kari's mother Ilona Duczynska, had been a Hungarian opposed to her country's involvement in the First World War. Feeling that the situation demanded resolute action she decided to assassinate the principal exponent of a war policy, Prime Minister Istvàn Tiszà. She accordingly took a pistol from a friend's drawer, but was deterred from action by the news that her intended victim had resigned from the government.

We were exposed to many stimulating lectures, most notably those of Laski himself. Day students, when tired, would often go to his evening lectures for relaxation, and would avidly read his *Grammar of Politics* and other writings, among them, his *Reflections on the Revolution of Our Time.* Long before the modern Era of Terrorism, he was quoted as declaring that "if the people can't get what they want by peaceful means, they will get it by violent revolution." One of his students, my Sudanese friend Mohamed Osman Yassein, a long time bureaucrat, later confided to me that he had learnt from Laski that civil servants should truly be the humble servants of the public, and not, as so often was the case, its arrogant masters.

On one occasion Bertrand Russell, then a great advocate of coexistence between the two great superpowers, came to the School to argue that the West should avoid involving itself in the affairs of the Eastern Block, while the Soviet Union should accept the West's paramountcy in Africa and Asia. My Ethiopian friend Mengistu Lemma, sitting at the back of the hall, thereupon rose to protest that the Great Man was bartering away the independence of the Third World. Bertrand Russell was somewhat disconcerted by this intervention, but took Mengistu's comment in his stride.

The philosopher Karl Popper was also a source of some controversy. Some students who attended his lectures found them opinionated and dogmatic. This led to growing frustration which several students privately drew to his attention. He accordingly announced that he would devote one whole period to questions and discussion. The proposed session was, however, postponed from week to week. When it eventually arrived, a student, as expected, made his point, but the Professor declared that the young man had failed to understand the issue at hand, after which he spent the rest of the period summing up his position. The anticipated dialogue, or meeting of minds, never materialised.

Much of our time was spent, to my mind very boringly, on studying the principles of economics, with all the drawing of supply and demand curves which that entailed. By specializing in history I escaped from them, and scarcely mentioned them when I later attempted to teach the "dismal science" in Ethiopia.

ETHIOPIAN STUDENTS AND DIPLOMATS IN BRITAIN

Ethiopia's liberation from Italian Fascist rule in 1941 was followed by the re-opening of the country's pre-war schools, and the founding of many new ones. There was an almost unquenchable thirst for education in the newly liberated land, with the result that youngsters of the post-war generation, mainly boys, rushed to attend school.

Students, whose lives had been disrupted by the enemy occupation, during which most educational establishments for so-called "natives" were closed, entered school whenever they could, and advanced rapidly from primary to secondary school, whenever possible jumping one or more classes. By the late 1940s and early 1950s many students were ready for tertiary education, which was not yet available in the country. Batches of young Ethiopian men and women were therefore sent abroad for study, at first mainly to Britain, but before long, also to North America and the Middle East. Students, after the end of the war, were likewise sent to France and other newly liberated European countries.

Ethiopian students in England, left to right, seated: Mikaél Imru, Indalcachew Mekonnin, Amha Aberra Kasa, Gennet Efrem and Zewdé Gebre-Sillasé. Standing: including: Daniél Abbebe, Girma Atnaf-Segged, Bereket-ab Habte-Sillasé, Siyyum Sebhat, Mimi Welde-Mariyam, Mengistu Lemma, Almaz Fasika, Debbebe Habte-Yohannis, Richard Pankhurst, Atnafu Mengistu, Zewdé Hayle-Mariyam, William Barnett, Afewerk Tekle, Gétahun Hayle-Mariyam, Mary Taddese, Werqu Habte-Weld, Jarra Mesfin, Petros Be'imnet, Oxford, 1949

The advent of Ethiopian students in Britain was a notable event in my life, no less than theirs. Until that time I had very few Ethiopian friends, for there were not many Ethiopians of my own age in the country. The younger Ethiopians in Britain then numbered little more than a dozen. They comprised the Emperor's son, Prince Sahle-Sillasé, and grandchildren, Seble, Hirut, Sophia and Iskinder Desta; Dr Martin's children, Yohannes, Charlie, David and Leah; and the afore-mentioned Gebriél and Michaél Tédros. However, the number of young Ethiopians in Britain increased greatly in the late 1940s and 1950s, when a sizeable band of students made their appearance. Some were enrolled in secondary schools; others in colleges and universities.

The first handful of Ethiopian students to go to University in Britain went to Oxford. Four in number, they belonged to noble families, and, unlike most of their contemporaries, had spent their exile years in Jerusalem where education was available. Very different in character and personality, they all four became my friends and were destined to play an important role on returning to their country.

Lij Indalkachew Mekonnin, who was attached to Oriel College, was the son of the then Ethiopian Prime Minister, *Bittwedded* Mekonnin Indalkachew, and successively held a number of major posts in Ethiopian Government. A student contributor to *NT&EN*, he was later, at one time or another, Vice-Minister of Education (the Emperor holding the Ministerial post), Ambassador to Britain, and finally, Prime Minister. A young man of considerable ambition, he applied for the post of Secretary-General of the United Nations, but failed to be elected, and perished, sadly, in the Ethiopian Revolution of 1974.

Dejazmach Zewdé Gebre-Sillasé, who attended St. Anthony's College, had the distinction of being the grandson of Emperor Yohannis IV, who had died in 1889, fighting the Sudanese Dervishes—the last crowned head in the world to die in battle. Zewdé, who had been a provincial governor before arriving in Oxford—hence his title of *Dejazmach*—was regarded as a man of immense wisdom. Already as a student at the Hayle-Sillasé Secondary School in Addis Ababa he was a great help to the School Director. Tradition has it that on one occasion two students had a quarrel, which came to the attention of the Headmaster. *Dejazmach,* a prefect, was called to translate. "Well, sir'," he explained, "This boy asked the other boy where his father was"—this being traditionally a great insult in Ethiopia—"Well, and what happened then?," asked the Headmaster unimpressed. "Well, sir," *Dejazmach* replied. "The other boy asked this boy to eat earth"—another great insult—but missed by the poor headmaster! On subsequently returning to Ethiopia, *Dejazmach* held numerous Government positions, but later went back to Oxford where he worked for a doctorate—and where we often visited him. His thesis on the life of Emperor Yohannis, a work of rare distinction, was duly published by Oxford University Press.

Lij Mikaél Imru, who was enrolled in Exeter College, where I used to see him, was the son of *Ras* Imru Hayle-Sillasé, one of the four major Rases, or commanders, who had fought against the Italian invasion from Eritrea in 1935-6. The *Ras* was later captured, and imprisoned on the Italian island of Lipari. After Ethiopia's liberation he returned to his native land, held several ambassadorial positions, and was renowned, almost revered, as a liberal aristocrat.

On one occasion Mikaél invited me to the Cole Society, named after the Guild Socialist Professor G.D.H. Cole. We were to go to the latter's study, to listen to him reading a play about the famous British General Strike of 1926. While waiting for the performance to begin I looked at the book-shelves, and soon realised that all the works on them had been written by the good Professor, and that the bound volumes of periodicals, too, likewise all contained articles by him. When, at the end of the afternoon, I naively asked him who had written the play, he replied: "Me, of course!"

Mikaél, curiously enough, had a double: an Afro-Carribean student at LSE called Peter Farquhar, who was his spitting image. A group of students wanted to nominate Peter to a post on the Student Union Council, but, at the last moment found that they did not have the required photograph. Remembering that a photo of Mikaél had appeared in *NT&EN*, to advertise a lecture he was about to give, we submitted it in lieu of Peter's. No one ever spotted the difference and he was duly elected.

On another occasion I was talking to Peter in the foyer of LSE, when Mimi Welde-Mariyam and two other Ethiopian women students, catching sight of Peter and mistaking him for Mikaél, rushed up, and, to his surprise and embarrassment, kissed him on both cheeks, in the traditional Ethiopian manner.

The fourth Ethiopian student in Oxford was *Lij* Amha Aberra Kasa, who joined Brazenose College, and was also destined for high office. The grandson of the venerable *Ras* Kasa Haylu, who was as close to the Ethiopian imperial line as the Emperor himself, Amha was as pale in complexion as any south European. His family had suffered terribly from the invasion, three of his uncles having been shot by the Italians in cold blood. Amha's post-war responsibilities included organising his country's first General Election based on universal adult suffrage. Women, to my mother's great satisfaction, voted and were elected to the Ethiopian Parliament in terms of full equality with men—a right which had taken the Suffragettes and others so long to achieve in Britain only a generation or two earlier. One of the Ethiopian women elected was *Weyzero* Siniddu Gebru, who became a close family friend: her husband, Major Aseffa Lemma, was my mother's guide during her first visit to Ethiopia in 1943-44 and gave me my first fountain pen!

Recalling the above "Oxford Four" and their fate in the subsequent Ethiopian Revolution of 1974, one may say that their different paths symbolised the varied fate of the country's post-war educated class. Indalkachew rose to the position of Prime Minister, but was shortly afterwards executed. Zewdé, became Minister of Foreign Affairs, but resigned while attending a meeting of the United Nations Assembly, after which he remained in exile abroad for many years. Mikaél became Indalkachew's successor as Prime Minister, and acted for a time as senior adviser to the *Derg*, or Military Committee then in power, after which he withdrew from government service. Amha was kept in detention for a number of years, after which he went into exile, and never returned.

Dejazmach Zewdé Gebre-Sillasé as Ethiopian Foreign Minister, ca 1975

Another Ethiopian student friend was Asrat Welde-Yes, who studied medicine and surgery in Edinburgh—where he developed a strong Scottish accent. A dedicated and hard-working young man, he kindly checked historical references for me during my doctoral studies. He subsequently became Director of the Princess Sehay Hospital, which my mother had done much to found, and collaborated with her in the hospital's development. As his country's Number 1 surgeon and a true professional he treated over a long career an incredibly large number of patients. He once met an American surgeon who called him a Millionaire. When Asrat asked why he had been so described the visitor replied that he had seen from Asrat's curriculum that the latter had carried out four times as many operations as himself, and that since he had a quarter of a million dollars, Asrat must have a million. Asrat, who lived in a rented house, and had virtually no savings, was not impressed. Ours was an enduring association. He later operated on our son's tonsils. Not one to mince his words, after the fall of the *Derg*, he became an opposition politician, was arrested and died a few months after he left detention.

Very different in his character and ambitions, but no less a good friend throughout his life, was a student dispatched to Britain by the then State Bank of Ethiopia: Debbebe Habte-Yohannis. On arriving in England he almost immediately conceived the idea, eventually to be realised, of breaking with Ethiopia's tradition of exclusively state banks, by establishing the country's first private bank. He came to breakfast with us one Sunday morning in Addis Ababa with the idea of enrolling us as founder members of the Addis Ababa Bank he was establishing and was so persuasive that in this, as in so much else, he succeeded.

Mention should also be made of another student friend of this time, Bereket-ab Habte-Sillasé, who came from the former Italian colony of Eritrea, but was considered as Ethiopian as any other student. A young man of wit and intelligence, he studied law, and was most active in the Ethiopian students' association in Britain. He was subsequently involved in drafting the constitution of independent Eritrea. Much later he confessed, in a mood of nostalgia, that he had succeeded in becoming *persona non grata* in both Eritrea and Ethiopia.

There were, at this time, also several distinguished Ethiopian women students in Britain. Foremost among them was Mary Taddesse. Insisting on using that form of her first name, rather than its Ethiopian equivalent, Mariyam, she came from a prominent Roman Catholic family closely associated with the Ethiopian government. She was a student in England when the Emperor came on a state visit, and was enrolled to help with public relations for the event, in which I, a fellow student, assisted her. She subsequently rose to Vice-Ministerial status, in the Ethiopian Ministry of Education, and married a member of the Emperor's then newly instituted Private Cabinet. One of her children once asked her who was "higher: Mummy or Daddy?"

Employees of the State Bank of Ethiopia, sent for training in Europe, left, Siyyum Sebhat, right, Debbebe Habte-Yohannis, ca 1958

Another notable woman student, at LSE, was Yeweynishet Beshahwered, the daughter of a pre-war American-educated intellectual killed by the Italians in February 1937, immediately following the attempt on the life of the Fascist Viceroy Rodolfo Graziani. Yeweynishet, to anticipate my story, was later to share at least two of our interests. She worked with my mother and Rita in Ethiopia's post-war Social Service Society, and later with us in the Society of Friends of the Institute of Ethiopian Studies. Small in build she was described by our Sri Lankan fellow student Raja Indra as the "Pocket edition."

Most Ethiopian students at the time I am describing—the late 1940s and early 1950s—were looked after

Mary Taddese and Werqu Habte-Weld broadcasting on BBC in Amharic on the occasion of the Emperor's visit to Britain, 1954

Meeting of Ethiopian students in England, seated with Sylvia, front row, Committee members including Mikaél Imru, Mary Taddese, Gétachew Beqqele, Amha Aberra Kasa and Zewdé Gebre-Sillasé, Richard in back row, Leicester, 1950

by the Ethiopian Legation, where an Englishwoman, Mrs Holland, was appointed Educational Adviser. My mother was called upon to be the honorary guardian of six other students; two of the Emperor's grandsons, though not of the imperial line: the brothers Merid and Samson Beyyene, whose father had been executed by the fascists, and a grandson of the Empress, Mengesha Yilma, as well as three girls: Almaz Fasika, the daughter of a prominent pre-war French-educated intellectual, and two sisters, Tayyech and Hanna Beyyene.

Richard's tea party for Ethiopian Students at LSE, at which they founded the Society of Ethiopian Students in Britain. From left, Rev. A.P. Hamilton, (Sudan), Mengistu Lemma, Alemayehu Welde- Sillasé, Debbebe Habte-Yohannis, Taddese Mogese; from right Dereje Hayle-Mariyam, Zewdé Hayle-Mariyam, Christmas 1948

The first students to arrive in Britain sprang from the royal family or aristocracy, but they were soon outnumbered by children of less privileged classes, including both the peasantry and the priesthood.

I soon came to know virtually all the Ethiopian students in Britain, and developed life-long friendships with many of them. Not a few came to our house, in far-away Woodford, or joined me on walks in nearby Epping Forest, but before long we decided to organise a more accessible gathering place. To that end I invited all the Ethiopian students I could trace to a tea party at LSE at Christmas 1948, where there were speeches, notably by Mengistu Lemma and Almaz Fasika, as well as by my mother's Labour and pacifist parliamentary friend, Reginald Sorensen

Abbebe Retta, Minister of Public Health, and sometime Ambassador in London, ca 1950

MP. As reported in *NT&EN*, it was on this occasion that the students founded the Society of Ethiopian Students in Britain, which thereafter held Christmas and other gatherings in various parts of the country. I attended most of these gatherings, at least in the first few years. Before long the Society established a little journal of its own, *The Lion Cub*, to which I occasionally contributed articles. Several Ethiopian students, for their part, wrote articles for *NT&EN*.

I met many other Ethiopians in this period. One of the most impressive was Abbebe Retta, a pre-World War II student in Scotland, who later joined the Ethiopian government service and was appointed Ambassador to the UK. A confirmed patriot he wrote anonymously in *New Times and Ethiopia News,* as an "Ethiopian correspondent" immediately after the country's liberation, to denounce proposals to curtail Ethiopia's independence. A scholar no less than a Minister and diplomat he roamed the London bookshops in quest of second-hand books about his country, and built up an important personal library—which was unfortunately dispersed after the Revolution. In the course of his researches he chanced upon the German scholar Enno Littmann's edition of a then little-known philosophical work in Ge'ez, Ethiopia's classical language, reportedly written by a seventeenth century Ethiopian rationalist called Zera-Yaqob. Much taken by this text, which pre-dated European rationalism, and even in the twentieth century Ethiopian context might have been considered risqué, he translated it into English and submitted it to my mother, who serialized it anonymously over several months in her newspaper. Neither she, who quoted from it in her mammoth book *Ethiopia: A*

Birhanu Tesemma, left, and his wife Edith with Tanzanian leader Julius Nyerere, ca 1958

Cultural History, nor Abbebe Retta himself, were then aware that several scholars (for the most part foreigners rather than Ethiopians) believed that the original Ge'ez text was in fact a fake produced by the nineteenth century Italian priest Justin d'Urbino.

A good friend of ours in those days was a dedicated member of the Ethiopian Legation staff, Zewdé Gebre-Hiywet, the future Lord Mayor of Addis Ababa. He most kindly taught me the Amharic characters and a vocabulary of a few hundred words. Later he was transferred to Sweden, where, too, there was an Ethiopian legation. During my school holidays he invited me to stay with him. I recall that he drove me, with his wife and children, on an excursion outside Stockholm. Having stopped at one point, we were approached by a passer-by who asked where we had come from. Zewdé replied, with a smile: "From Stockholm." The people who stood listening, expressed surprise, and the enquirer, shaking his head, said he had never seen people looking like us in their capital.

Another Ethiopian functionary I met at this time, who became a close friend, was Birhanu Tesemma. He served in his country's London Embassy, and had a German wife, Edith. An exile in Kenya during the Italian Occupation, he had long corresponded with my mother, and was later to hold a number of other diplomatic posts. The first of these was that of Ethiopian Consul in Kenya, an important position through which he was to befriend the rising African nationalists on the eve of their country's independence, and later introduced them to us. On subsequently becoming an Ethiopian Senator he was active in demanding the return of the Aksum obelisk looted by Mussolini in 1937—a cause which some of us were later to make our own.

EARLY JOURNALISTIC EFFORTS

Before long I was writing frequent articles in *NT&EN*. My historical studies at LSE inspired me to produce a long serialised article on the ending of slavery in the United States and the subsequent period of "reconstruction."

With an English fellow student, Tony Godden, I also visited much of the European continent from which we in Britain had sadly been totally isolated during the war years. This journey took me *inter alia* to Ciasso, on the Swiss-Italian frontier, where a local physician, Dr Martini Martinolo, an enthusiastic reader of *NT&EN*, offered me and my English fellow student, hospitality. These travels encouraged me to write a series of impressionistic articles entitled "Continental Vistas."

The increasing anti-colonial struggle in Africa, to which we were exposed as LSE students, later caused me to write several theoretical critiques of colonialism. In them I argued against the then prevalent colonialist argument that the nationalist movements in contemporary Africa had been created by a tiny proportion of the population, the so-called intelligentsia, who were "unrepresentative" of their countries. I contended that, on the contrary, when it came to the crunch, the masses would support the educated "natives", and reject the pretensions of their colonial rulers. I also wrote two long serialised historical articles on Ethiopia's neighbours, Kenya and Uganda. The first chronicled the assumption of power by a small minority of White Settlers, and argued that the Mau Mau rebellion of the land-hungry Kikuyu people, which was then taking place, was a just response to selfish and repressive policies of the settlers. As Laski had put it, "If the people can't get what they want by peaceful means...." The articles on Uganda drew attention *inter alia* to the role of the European missionaries as a divisive force which contributed towards European colonial penetration.

My Kenya articles interested Dr K.D. Kumria, an Indian physician and editor of the London magazine *Africa and the Colonial World*, who reprinted them as a book, entitled *Kenya: The History of Two Nations*. It had an Introduction by Frida Laski, and was duly banned in Kenya. I also reproduced the substance of this work as a series of articles for the British railway workers' newspaper in London.

Later, I seized the opportunity of some free days at LSE to burrow in its gloomy library basement. There I consulted old 19th century British newspapers, and wrote a long article on how the news of Ethiopia's historic victory over the Italians at the Battle of Adwa in 1896 was received by the London *Times*. The article was much later widely used in Ethiopia when the country in 1996 came to celebrate the centenary of the famous battle.

I also wrote an obituary of my father, whose health had been deteriorating during that year. In this article I included personal memories which supplement the story of his life in the Italian Dictionary of National Biography.

AFRICAN VISITORS

During these years visitors to our house in Woodford included many Africans struggling for the independence of their countries, or, through Pan-Africanism, that of their continent as a whole. The most famous such visitor was the future President of Kenya, Jomo Kenyatta, who had rallied to Ethiopia's support in 1935 at the time of the Italian Fascist invasion. Then living in London, and the author of the classic book *Facing Mount Kenya*, he at that time founded a Society of African Friends of Abyssinia, and often spoke at my mother's meetings.

Kenyatta was, however, overshadowed in my youthful mind by a more demonstrative friend who often accompanied him. This was the much travelled Pan-African intellectual and entrepreneur, G.T.N. Griffiths, from British Guiana, who showed his sympathy with the cause by adopting the Ethiopian name T.R. Makonnen. Toward the end of the war he ran a restaurant in Manchester, which attracted the patronage of many African American soldiers. This enabled him to help finance the Pan-African movement in Britain, and to assist in the publication of the British journal *PanAfrica*, as well as to subsidize a pamphlet published by my mother on *Italy's War Crimes in Ethiopia*. He took his Ethiopian persona so seriously that I remember one public meeting at which he placed his hands in his waistcoat pockets, and, urging the need for a more resolute policy, declared, "We of the Tigray...." Mekonnin, then my particular friend, once gave me a weighty tome on the history of the Paris Commune of 1870, which I still treasure.

Other Pan-Africanist visitors included the renowned Afro-Carribean journalist George Padmore—who was later to visit us in Addis Ababa; and the Back to Africa leader Marcus Garvey's ex-wife Amy Garvey, who had also been active in the Society of African Friends of Abyssinia. We still own an attractive little Benin bronze statue which she gave to my mother, long ago.

A later visitor to Woodford was the South African author Peter Abrahams. Coming from the country of *apartheid*, he developed a warm affection for independent Ethiopia, became a keen supporter of the reunion of Ethiopia and Eritrea, and wrote several popular articles for *NT&EN*.

Subsequently, during the Mau Mau Emergency in Kenya, I came to know the Kenya African leader Mbiyu Koinange. I first met him at a meeting organised by the Movement for Colonial Freedom, founded by the veteran British Labour leader, Fenner Brockway MP. My mother incidentally had befriended him, in his youth several decades earlier, when he was a Conscientious Objector, refusing to join the British army during World War I.

Mbiyu was a brilliant public speaker, much admired by the Ethiopian students in Britain, who, identifying themselves with his country and its struggle, were much moved by his eloquence. Visiting him often in his house in Winchester Road, near Swiss Cottage, I learnt much, albeit second hand, about his country. Reminiscing, he recalled his student days in America where he had debated with a high Italian colonial official about Mussolini's invasion of Ethiopia. Mbiyu later visited us in Woodford, and participated in several of my mother's meetings, one of which, a fund-raising event for the Princess Sehay Hospital, he chaired. He and my wife's father, Alexander Eldon had a particularly warm relationship. Mbiyu claimed that the latter, though much younger than he, would be regarded as his father in Kikuyu tradition.

There were of course also innumerable British visitors to Woodford. Some of those I remember best included Aburn Webster, a prominent Woodford Liberal, who wrote frequently for *NT&EN* and invited us every Christmas to the reenactment of the Nativity story, in which he played the part of one of the Three Wise Men; Francis Beaufort-Palmer, another committed Liberal, and supporter of many international just causes, who, after attending one of my mother's meetings, would come home with us, and when his visit was unexpected, would often bring what I then considered a great delicacy: fish and chips, bought wrapped, as was traditional, in an old newspaper; Mary Downs, a dynamic, and politically much-committed, teacher from Wales, who spoke most eloquently at many meetings on Ethiopia, Spain, and Appeasement generally; and John Mack, a local Woodford railway worker, who loyally attended all such gatherings after distributing leaflets announcing them.

AFEWERK TEKLE, MENGISTU LEMMA AND HABTE-AB BAYRU

Many of my student days were spent with Ethiopian students in London. One of them, destined to become Ethiopia's leading artist, was Afewerk Tekle. Our first meeting took place at London Airport. It was a holiday, so when he and a fellow student Aseffa Taddese landed, there was nobody from the Ethiopian Legation to receive them. They had come straight from the Hayle-Silassé Secondary School in Addis Ababa, without any money, and did not know what to do. One of the British Airlines ground hostesses (Ethiopian Airlines in those days did not yet fly direct to London) asked Afewerk whether he knew anyone in England. After thinking a moment or two he remembered that my mother had visited his school some months earlier, and, because his schoolboy sketches were promising, he had been introduced to her. The airlines staff duly looked up her name in the London Telephone Directory, after which they phoned her, to tell her of the two stranded Ethiopian schoolboys. The upshot was that she asked me to go to the airport, and bring them home, which I did.

When it came to quartering them for the night my mother phoned Mr and Mrs Tribe, the kindly neighbours of one of my school friends. They kindly agreed to put the young Ethiopians up until the question of their accommodation was settled. Afewerk, because of the nobility of his manners, was a "great hit" with the Tribe family, which included three very fashionable young women: Cynthia, Pauline and a third whose name I now forget. Their admiration of their Ethiopian guest knew no bounds, and, having heard of the Ethiopian *empire,* were soon whisperingly referring to him as "the Prince". This imaginary title spread among Woodford residents "in the know."

Afewerk was soon afterwards admitted to Leighton Park Grammar School. Almost on the first day the teacher was writing something on the blackboard, with his back to the students, when one of them gets out his catapult and despatches a pellet which hits

Richard's hands. A drawing on scraperboard by Afewerk Tekle 1948

the teacher on the head, Afewerk, who, like all Ethiopian pupils at that time, revered their teachers, was deeply shocked, and, not sharing the British schoolboy dislike of "sneaks", rises from his desk, and pointing at the boy with the catapult, cries out, "Sir, it was this boy who did it! I saw him do it!"

My mother, who subscribed to a press cuttings service on Ethiopia, was surprised, one day, to read that an Ethiopian student with a name similar to Afewerk, had won a prize for ball-room dancing. Shortly after this she noticed that Afewerk was wearing a fine gold watch. Putting two and two together she realised that it was he who had won the prize. She suggested to him that he was wasting his time. She had by then persuaded the Ethiopian government to permit him to study art instead of becoming a mining engineer.

He became a close friend of the family, my mother, as a former artist, being particularly interested in his work. He later produced cartoons for *NT&EN*, and a picture of my hands on Scraperboard, which I still own. He was subsequently to be one of the two best men at our marriage, which took place in Ethiopia in 1957, and has remained a dear friend to this day.

Two other notable Ethiopian student friends were at LSE with me. One was the above-mentioned Mengistu Lemma, who had challenged Bertrand Russell. The son of Aleqa Lemma, a famous, and learned, Ethiopian priest, Mengistu had studied traditional Ethiopian *qené*, or poetry, which was then little known in the West. A great enthusiast of traditional classical Ethiopian culture he provided my mother with information on the subject, which she later included in her book *Ethiopia: A Cultural History*. On

Portrait of *Aleqa* Lemma, father of Mengistu Lemma, by Afewerk Tekle, 1965

returning home, he was to emerge as his country's greatest playwright, sometimes described as Ethiopia's latter-day Molière. Mengistu, with whom I spent many hours, was an active member of the Ethiopian Students' Society in Britain, wrote frequently in *The Lion Cub*, and played an important role in Ethiopian student thinking. He argued that Ethiopia should seek to be classed not just in relation to neighbouring African countries, but should aim high, and be compared with the most advanced countries of the world. Though a master of *qiné*, the classical poetry composed by Ethiopian church scholars, he argued that it should be traditional in form, but progressive in content.

Mengistu was also a constant source of entertainment. On one occasion he regaled us with the story of a visit to a London dentist, who happened to be a Roman Catholic. The Pope had just enunciated a new dogma on the Immaculate Birth of the Virgin Mary; the dentist, having placed the patient in the dental chair, asks "You do believe in the new doctrine, don't you?" Mengistu observed that, with the dental pincers threateningly in his mouth, he had no option but quickly to agree to the Papal tenet.

While in England he produced a theatrical sketch for his fellow Ethiopian students. Centred on a burning issue with which he and others had been obliged to contend, it featured a debate between a traditional Ethopian church scholar, who believed that the world was flat, and unmoving, and a European scholar, who held that it revolved round the sun. Neither protagonist yielded and instead, they resorted to alcoholic enlightenment. In the concluding scene they are both drunk, sprawled under the

Habte-ab wrestling in jest with Richard, Hyde Park, London, ca 1950

table. The Ethiopian priest dizzily exclaims, "You are right: the world is going round and round!"

Mengistu at another time developed tuberculosis and was admitted to a British hospital at Ascot. During his prolonged stay there, he struck up a friendly conversation with the nurses, who had never seen a "coloured" person, let alone an Ethiopian before. (Those were the days before extensive Afro-Carribean immigration to Britain, which I witnessed when sailing across the English Channel). Though the son of a notable Ethiopian priest, he sought to entertain the nurses by telling them that he lived in the jungle, was a Muslim, and had no less than four wives. Some days after this, chance had it that four Ethiopian women students, led by Mary Taddesse, came to visit him. The nurses excitedly rushed to his bed, crying out, "'Mr Lemma, Mr Lemma, your wives have come! Which one do you want to see first?" Mengistu had of course no idea as to the visitors' identity, but, quick as a shot, replied, "Tell Number One to come first!" The visitors kissed Mengistu as the nurses watched. Although, kissing is a common greeting among Ethiopians, in the nurses' eyes there was no doubt that these were his wives.

Another Ethiopian LSE friend was Habte-ab Bayru, whose brother Tedla Bayru was for many years head in Eritrea of the then popular Unionist Party, which demanded unity with Ethiopia. Not long after Habte-ab's arrival in London we learnt that a British-Italian Society was promoting the return to Italy of its former colonies.

To further the restitution of Italian rule an inaugural address was to be given on 31 July 1948 in a Queen Anne Street basement by an elderly Italian colonial official, Colonel B. Valentino Vecchi.

Habte-ab, my mother and I decided to attend. The audience was pitifully small, but the chairman announced that the gathering was important as it would launch a movement for Italy's return

Bust of the Eritrean Unionist leader, *Dejazmach* Tedla Bairu by Afewerk Tekle, ca 1948

Demonstration outside the House of Commons against the proposed return to Italy of her former colonies;
left, Mrs M.A. Cotton, Sylvia Pankhurst, Mrs Florance Tédros, Madame Anderson, Mrs Kerrie, June 1948

to her former colonies. The Chairman, Hugh Williams, announced that the representatives of *The Times* and the BBC were present. The speaker, an officious military officer, then held forth at considerable length in Italian, with which the Chairman, and much of the audience, were unfamiliar. The speaker claimed that Italy had been an impressive and benevolent colonial ruler, and that its return to Africa would be important as it would solve Italy's permanent unemployment problem. Half a million Italians, he declared, would be enabled to emigrate to her colonies.

The chairman then called for questions, whereupon my mother visibly displeased the speaker by recalling that the Italian colonies had been used as bases for the invasion of Ethiopia in 1935-6. Habte-ab, speaking in perfect Italian, thereupon created further anger by questioning the Colonel's claim that Italy had been interested in the welfare of the "native" people. To that end he recalled the Graziani massacre of February 1937, in which thousands of innocent Ethiopians had been killed, and suggested that the audience should view a film on Italy's misgovernment of the colonies then showing in London. I next asked a question in similar vein, which was testily disallowed by the Chairman. An Italian anti-fascist refugee in the audience then challenged the suggestion that the poor Italian colonies could support 500,000 immigrants, while an Englishman declared that his compatriots, who had fought to liberate Ethiopia and the former Italian colonies, would not agree to see them returned to their former oppressor, the more so as the British public was proud of having given India her freedom. Interest in the meeting then visibly flagged, whereupon I proceeded to distribute copies of a pamphlet entitled *Italy's War Crimes in Ethiopia,* which my mother had then recently published. This action much displeased the Colonel's friends who, seizing me by the arms, promptly conducted me from the room, whereupon the meeting broke up in some disorder. Nothing more was heard of the Society's proposed initiative on the future of the Italian colonial empire.

Not all our life at LSE was of course involved with Ethiopia. Our studies at the School coincided with the Korean War, which induced many protest meetings in London. Habte-ab and I, as devoted readers of the Left-Wing *New Statesman,* decided one evening to attend one such gathering to be held just over the road from the School in the Kingsway Hall. It was a bitterly cold, dark night, and we walked there shivering. Habte-ab was wearing a black Ethiopian burnouse, or black woollen cloak, I had given him. It almost completely enveloped him, so that only his nose and eyes were visible.

As we waited for the speaker to begin, my neighbour, an elderly Englishwoman, who was an enthusiastic if somewhat uninformed anti-war protester, nudged me, and asked me in a whisper whether Habte-ab was a Korean. When I replied in the negative her interest in him speedily evaporated.

One other night Habte-ab and I planned to go to the cinema. London was then suffering from one of its worst fogs, popularly likened to "Pea Soups." All London buses had stopped functioning—and we had an acrid feeling in our throats. Deciding to walk to our destination we were obliged to hold hands as otherwise we would literally have lost each other. Thanks to Government regulations, notably the banning of coal and wood fires, such fogs are now fortunately things of the past.

POSTGRADUATE STUDIES

Having passed my BSc. (Econ.) exam at LSE, and being much devoted to research, I decided to continue my studies at LSE by working for a Ph.D. That degree was in those days considered far less important than it is at present, and relatively few students in Britain (as opposed to the United States) then studied for it. Looking around for a possible thesis subject acceptable in LSE's History Department to which I felt wedded, and after some consultation with Laski, I opted to work on the early nineteenth century Irish writer William Thompson. Then largely forgotten, he was the most important of the early British pre-Marxist Socialists, and a devoted supporter of Robert Owen, founder of the Co-operative Movement in England. I carried out my research under the supervision of Laski, until he died some months later, and the illustrious economic historian H.L. Beales.

Thompson was interesting in that he attempted to deal with what I considered one of the fundamental problems of our time: how to bridge the gap between Liberalism and Liberty on the one hand and Equality and Socialism on the other. Thompson, writing initially as a follower of the British philosopher Jeremy Bentham, one of the founders of Utilitarianism, accepted the validity of the latter's goal of the Greatest Good of the Greatest Number, but gave it a new corollary. In his *Inquiry into the Principles of the Distribution of Wealth,* published in London in 1824, he argued that a small unit of wealth transferred from a rich man to a poor man would give more happiness to the latter than it reduced that of the former—and so on *ad infinitum.* From this followed the revolutionary conclusion that happiness in economic terms would be maximised by equality.

Thompson also interested me as a social thinker in that he was the author of an *Appeal of One Half the Human Race,* the earliest work expressly written to demand the political enfranchisement of women. He produced it in 1825 in association with his close associate Anna Wheeler, an early feminist. I duly published the fruit of my researches in a book entitled *William Thompson: Britain's Pioneer Socialist, Feminist and Co-operator,* which appeared in 1954. I also wrote the first article ever published on Anna Wheeler, in the London-based *Political Quarterly*—and was later to write an *Introduction* to the 1993 reprint of Thompson's *Appeal.*

I found the study of Thompson interesting also in that it led me to read virtually all his early nineteenth century British and French contemporary social thinkers, as well as later writers who inherited, or did battle with, their ideas. I was likewise much taken by the benevolent thinking of Robert Owen and some of his followers, who introduced me, through their polemics, to the need for systematic rationalist thinking. I also saw much truth in Owen's observation, which I still often quote, that "If any of the evils of this world prove to be irremovable, they will be accepted as inevitable, and childish unavailing complaints will cease to be heard." Recalling this passage in various contexts, and taking it as a guiding principle ("Don't cry over spilt milk"), I noted that it also received reflective attention in Polanyi's *Origin of Our Times.*

Research on Thompson and Owen brought me, for good measure, into contact with the writings of the French Saint Simonians and more particularly their followers in Britain. I was impressed by their breadth of vision, the depth of their critique of contemporary society, and their ability to envisage social systems entirely different from our own, as well as their supreme, almost arrogant, confidence in the correctness—and historical inevitability—of their mission. I made all this the subject of my book *The Saint Simonians, Mill and Carlyle.*

Interest in the Saint Simonians for me extended from Europe to Africa and the East. Believing that God was androgynous, i.e. female as well as male, they persuaded themselves, with reckless self-confidence, that Christ, who was male, would be followed by a Female Messiah. They sought to find her in 1830, "the Year of the Woman", as they chose to term it. Their self-appointed task, ridiculous as it now seems, was to discover their Female Messiah in a harem of the East. Many of them, realising the impracticability, if not absurdity of their mission, later turned their attention to economic development in Egypt and elsewhere in the East. Two of their number, Edmond Combes and Maurice Tamisier, subsequently made their way to Ethiopia, as as I related long afterwards at an International Conference of Ethiopian Studies, held in Addis Ababa in 1966.

I had, meanwhile, rounded off my study of early socialism in Britain by publishing an article on Fourierism in that country. It was published in the *International Review of Social History* by the Amsterdam-based Institute for Social History. Little did I then know that only four years later, I would, after my mother's death, be depositing her papers in the Institute's great archives—which had almost miraculously survived the Nazi invasion and occupation of the Netherlands.

By then increasingly interested in Ethiopia, for reasons which are by now apparent, I enrolled in London as a part-time student at the School of Oriental and African Studies, SOAS. Having been introduced to the Amharic script by *Ato* Zewdé Gebre-Hiywet, I studied the language a little under Dr R.C. Abraham, a notable Australian linguist of African languages. His understanding of Amharic was still incomplete, as evident from the fact that he would frequently ask us to make corrections to the first edition of his textbook. After his weekly class with me, he would make his way to London's East End to collect linguistic information from Somali sea-men. He was soon regarded as an expert on their language, and not long afterwards wrote an introductory textbook on it. He once told me that it was very easy to learn languages "as soon as one knew twelve." Not reaching that score, I never found language learning that easy.

FIRST VISIT TO ETHIOPIA AND SUDAN

In the autumn of 1950, I paid my first visit to Ethiopia in the company of my mother, for whom it was her second visit. Travelling to the country earlier, in 1943, to inspect proposed sites for the Princess Sehay Memorial Hospital, she had tried to take me with her. The European War was then, however, still in progress, and shipping space was at a premium. The British Government had recognised the political importance of the Sehay Hospital in Addis Ababa—the more so as the Russians were also establishing one in the city. She was therefore given authority to sail through the Mediterranean, but I was refused this courtesy—though she had argued that I could help her by holding the tape-measure to measure walls, etc. Her visit later irritated several Foreign Office and War Office officials, who were much displeased by her public espousal of the cause of Pan-Ethiopian Eritrean nationalism, as well as by her insistence that Britain should withdraw from the Ogaden, a region in south-east Ethiopia, then under enforced British military occupation.

My first journey outside Europe, to what we now call the Third World, was a source of great interest and excitement. I caught brief glimpses of an unfamiliar civilisation, with an entirely different culture, customs and institutions.

Addis Ababa in those days seemed little more than an extensive village, or more correctly, groups of villages. Very different from the urban agglomeration it has since become, it possessed few modern buildings. A significant proportion of those which existed had been built during the Italian Occupation, only a decade or so earlier. Such structures have long since been overshadowed by the multi-storey buildings of the post-Liberation period, which began to spring up around 1963. At the time of my visit the capital was dominated by innumerable eucalyptus trees, which made it, as earlier travellers had noted, a "forest capital." The smell of these trees, which originally

Sylvia arriving at Addis Ababa airport on her second visit to Ethiopia 1950-51with Richard.

Sylvia, on her first visit to Ethiopia, welcomed at Addis Ababa Airport by the Minister of the Pen,
Teferra-Werq Kidane-Weld, 1943

came from Australia and were introduced in Menilek's day, permeated the capital to an
extent unimaginable today.

We stayed in a Government guest-house named after the early Shewan King Sahle-
Sillasé. It was one of several villas situated in the spacious grounds of the former Italian
Embassy, which had been seized as enemy property in 1941 at the end of the war, and
had not yet been returned to Italy.

It was a great pleasure to meet some of my Ethiopian student friends, who had
just returned from Britain, and were beginning to take up jobs, mainly in Ethiopian

Sylvia, on her first visit to Ethiopia, laying a wreath at the Liberation Monument in Arat Kilo 1943

government service. Those working in the then State Bank of Ethiopia speedily changed my few pounds Sterling into what were then known as Ethiopian dollars, a name later Ethiopianised to the indigenous *birr*, the Amharic word for silver. Other returnees took me to their favourite restaurants and cafés, and some, most notably Siyyum Sebhat, tried to introduce me to the intricacies and mysteries of Ethiopian government and politics.

Our visit, which I described in *NT&EN*, also took us to the *Hager Fiqr* (Love of Country) Theatre, where we listened to many songs expressing strong patriotic feelings. We also inspected a number of newly established schools, where the students displayed an almost unquenchable thirst for study, and seemed interested in my very rudimentary eye-witness account of education in Britain as I had encountered it.

We also visited Gonder, the old seventeenth and eighteenth century capital, the history of which I was long afterwards to chronicle in my two-volume *History of Ethiopian Towns*; and watched the sun set over Lake Tana, that vast expanse of water much of which flowed each year into the Nile.

Before leaving Addis Ababa, I gave a party for the student returnees from Britain. A number who had returned from the United States also attended. There were lengthy, good-natured, discussions on the burning issue: whether Britain or the US provided

Siyyum Sebhat, Ethiopian student in England, ca 1950

the best, and most relevant, education for Ethiopian students.

I also travelled to Sudan, on the invitation of my old LSE friend Mohamed Osman Yassein. At that time the most senior Sudanese in the British-run Anglo-Egyptian Sudan Government, he told me that his boss, the Civil Secretary, apparently a somewhat intolerant individual, was aware of *NT&EN*'s anti-colonial stance, as well as, apparently, of my own humble writings in the paper. He had proposed refusing me entry, but had relented as Mohamed had taken personal responsibility for my good conduct.

I spent a happy time as Mohamed's guest in his house in Ondurman. He introduced me to many of the newly emerging Western-educated Sudanese, who, with their country's typical hospitality, introduced me to many of their peers, including several young men, two or three of them Communists, actively working to bring about an end to the British occupation. I also spent some hours driving around the town with Ibrahim Bedri, a well respected intellectual trying to fuse together the interests of Northern and Southern Sudan. Throughout my stay I was not introduced to a single Sudanese woman.

We drove over the flat Sudanese desert to visit the Gezira scheme, to inspect its famous cotton cultivation project, which many then believed the prototype for economic development throughout Africa. In looking at the scheme I recalled my old

Richard's LSE Economics tutor, Jack Fisher, with Mikaél Imru, left, and Habte-ab Bairu and Mrs Barbara Fisher, right, ca 1948

LSE teacher the historian, Jack Fisher's advice that, in evaluating prosperity, one should investigate the contents of peasants' houses.

OPPOSITION TO CONSCRIPTION

When my doctoral studies were completed, I had to face the question of obligatory military service, which had fortunately been postponed during my protracted period of study. The World War had come to an end before I left school, but conscription had dragged on seemingly with no end in sight, and appeared indeed to have become a permanent feature of British life. Conscientious objection was permitted, but only for outright pacifists, who, for religious or other reasons were opposed to any kind of war. For my part I had no such objection, and believed in the principle of a "just war", such as that which Britain and her Allies had only a few years earlier fought against Nazi Germany and Fascist Italy. I was, however, totally opposed to Britain's seemingly endless colonial wars, and the use of British troops in repressing indigenous nationalist movements in Africa and Asia. Refusal of military service seemed moreover one of the few, and perhaps most effective ways, of demonstrating one's opposition to colonial oppression. I therefore rejected my call-up papers. Despite the advice of my lawyer, who advised me to plead conscientious opposition to war in general, I spoke to the Tribunal in an entirely different vein. Taking the Kenya Emergency as an example I pointed out that the number of Africans detained as Mau Mau suspects already exceeded the number of white settlers in whose interests the Kenya Emergency had been proclaimed. I declared that I refused to be a party to such repression as conducted by the British Colonial Secretary, Oliver Lyttleton—but would be quite prepared to participate in detaining the said Minister. The Tribunal, as expected, rejected my contentions, but the authorities, after fining me twice, abandoned their efforts to conscript me, and I was thereafter left free to continue my life and work undisturbed.

NATIONAL INSTITUTE OF ECONOMIC AND SOCIAL RESEARCH; UNIVERSITY EXTRA-MURAL LECTURES

During this period I joined the National Institute of Economic and Social Research, in London. Working under the dynamic American economic historian, Charlotte Erickson, I scanned 19th century British newspapers to collect data of all kinds on the emergence of British industrialists in the iron and textile trades. In the evenings I taught British economic and social history in the University of London's Extra-Mural Department. This was exciting as it entailed travelling northwards as far as Watford and southwards to Woolwich, on several occasions at night by ferry across the River Thames. I also lectured at Toynbee Hall, the renowned adult education establishment in the East End of London. Its Registrar was Frank de Halpert, an Englishman who, prior to the Italian invasion of 1935-6, had served as Hayle-Sillasé's Anti-Slavery adviser. He spoke about the country with admiration.

Toynbee Hall was important to me also, as it was there that I met my future beloved wife Rita Eldon, who also taught there, and whose story follows shortly.

FAREWELL TO BRITAIN

A great change was now about to take place in my life. The Emperor had several times invited my mother, both verbally and in writing, to go to live in Ethiopia. She had always thanked him, but declined. On the last occasion she had written explicitly, saying that she did not want to take up his kind invitation until the British occupation of the Ogaden and the so-called Reserved Area of Eastern Ethiopia (against which she was vigorously campaigning) had come to an end. Much opposed to that occupation, she had pointed out that it was Fascist Italy's attempt to seize that very area little more than a decade earlier that had been the cause of the Italo-Ethiopian war and of world indignation, as well as her own precipitate involvement in things Ethiopian. Soon after this the British Government withdrew from the areas in question.

This withdrawal caused my mother to feel that, after twenty years, her newspaper's *raison d'être* had, at long last, come to an end. *NT&EN* had been founded, as she saw it, to expose the evils of Fascism, and in particular to defend its victim, Ethiopia, against Fascist aggression. She believed that, with the defeat of the Axis Powers in World War II, the threat of Fascism had come to an end—for the time being at least. Nevertheless, she considered that the newspaper had been left with a significant rôle to play in: (1) resisting British colonial attempts to annex parts of the country, or to turn it into some form of Protectorate; (2) opposing Italian efforts to regain the former African colonies; and (3) supporting the unification of the Horn of Africa, in particular the then popular Eritrean demand for reunion with Ethiopia.

With the establishment of Ethio-Eritrean Federation, in 1952, and, now, at last, with the British withdrawal from Eastern Ethiopia, she felt that an entirely different type of publication was needed: an Ethiopia-based journal, which, being produced locally, could publish well-researched information on the country, its history, culture and aspirations.

From this, it followed that my mother had to travel from Woodford, England, to Addis Ababa, Ethiopia, and, at the age of seventy-four, to start a new life, in an entirely new environment. There were other reasons, both personal and public, which weighed in favour of her moving at this time. On the personal level, my father had died in January 1954. He could never have been pried away from the British Museum Reading Room; most of her old Suffragette friends, among them Emmeline Pethick-Lawrence, were also dead; and my University studies in London had come to an end. Moreover, as far as Ethiopia was concerned, the Princess Sehay Memorial Hospital had by then been established, and no longer required extensive fund-raising in Britain.

As far as her new publication was concerned, she decided that it should be monthly, rather than a weekly like *NT&EN*, and be called the *Ethiopian Review*. She bowed, however, to our Kenya friend Mbiyu Koinange, who, impressed by the London *Observer*, and more particularly by its anti-colonialist stance introduced by the South African journalist Colin Legum, proposed that it should be called the *Ethiopia Observer*.

Once the decision to move to Ethiopia had been taken, I spent many days sorting through my parents' books and papers to decide what should be packed in tea chests, and taken to Addis Ababa, and what should be disposed of locally. Though fascinating to go through so many old books and letters, this involved dusty toil which left me with acute hay-fever. Our Charteris Road house had meanwhile been sold, a date for the auction of furniture fixed, and my mother and I were ready to depart.

At last the great day dawned. Early one summer morning we were driven to London Airport. It was an internationally tense time: Nasser had just nationalised the Suez Canal, and the World, and particularly the Middle East, awaited the reactions of the West. It was, however, for me, perhaps even more than for my mother, the opening of a new life, the scope and character of which neither of us could have anticipated.

Sylvia's house in Charteris Road, Woodford, prior to the owner's departure for Ethiopia, 1956

RITA

OXFORD UNIVERSITY

In 1945 the idea of "A gap year" between school and university had not yet taken hold. Having decided to read Modern Languages, it seemed unadventurous to study French and German, two languages which I could already speak, so I opted for French, and one "new" language, namely Russian. To this end I spent much of the summer learning the rudiments of the latter language. I had been accepted at sLady Margaret Hall (LMH) and duly appeared there at the beginning of Michaelmas Term. LMH, founded in 1876, was the oldest of Oxford's women's colleges, and was one of the two with the highest reputation, the other being Somerville. The women's colleges were some distance away from the men's colleges, which were mostly clustered around the two main streets: The Broad and The High.

On my first day, as I wandered around my room, unsure as to what to do, a student on the opposite side of the corridor invited me to tea. There were several girls in the room and conversation was fast and funny, but I did not catch most of the literary or political allusions and felt out of place. I had the impression that they already knew one another and later discovered that they came from distinguished families. Among them was Lois Mitchison, a daughter of one of the famous Mitchison sisters, who became a travel writer. She wore thick glasses, did not care much about her appearance and had a very sharp wit. The girl who invited me had a gentler disposition. She was the sister of a well-known poet and mountaineer. After the first term I exited from this circle and found more congenial company elsewhere.

A young man from Oldham, whose family was acquainted with mine, was also an early contact. Presumably because he did not, at that time, know any other girls, he asked me to a dance. Neither of us enjoyed each other's company and he soon found other women more to his taste to dance with.

My neighbour in the second term, and thereafter, was a South African woman who had been in the Army and obtained a scholarship available to "demobbed" soldiers. Pam Risley was much older and more worldly-wise than I was, and smoked. I liked listening to her wartime experiences and when she returned to South Africa we corresponded regularly until her death. I had obtained a small scholarship from Oldham Education Office, where competition for a scholarship restricted to girls entering Oxford or Cambridge had been negligible. It prompted my father to provide me with a ledger bound in leather in which he asked me to record my income (from the scholarship, and, more meaningfully, from him) and expenditure. He thought it would be good training for the management of my finances in later life. I began dutifully to do as he taught me, but found, gradually that I fell behind with my entries, and, as I could not remember the items exactly, I started improvising instead. Being a businessman, he used to be very proud of my accounting achievements and years passed before I had the courage to let him know that it did not represent a true record of my financial situation.

Among the lectures I attended, I remember best those given by Enid Starkie, on the French poets. She was a Fellow of Somerville and a University Lecturer in French Literature, having first obtained a doctorate from the Sorbonne in Paris. One of her interests was Arthur Rimbaud about whom she had published *Rimbaud en Abyssinie* in 1937. She must have mentioned that, having abandoned poetry at 19, he had become a trader in Ethiopia, but if she did, it had no resonance for me at that time. She would wander into the lecture hall as though by accident, college cap at an angle, starting to mumble even before she reached the podium. Once there, she continued to talk as if to herself, but she nevertheless held one's attention. The study of medieval French did not thrill me and I was glad when it became possible to drop the subject.

I enjoyed Russian studies much more. We were not expected to study the language as much as the literature, which we could read in English translation. I loved the Great Russian novelists, but my favourite author was Chekhov. I was happy to discover that he was not only a fine playwright and short-story writer with an eye for the absurd, but also a physician—a decent and socially active human being. As a graduate I considered making a new translation of some of his short stories, as the Constance Garnett translations had been made more than two decades earlier. However, after working on one or two stories I found that my Russian was not nuanced enough to do them justice.

Rita as an undergraduate at Lady Margaret Hall, Oxford University, 1947

I did not have any contact with the exalted Professor Konovalov, who was the academic in charge of Russian Studies. My tutor for Russian literature was Mrs Gorodetski. I would arrive at her house full of enthusiasm, having spent a part of the previous night writing my essay. She would listen without interrupting, and at the end, putting down her knitting, would pronounce: *Harasho* (Good) and that was the end of it. Finding little rigour in the demands made on me, I found myself taking short cuts. I would go to the college library and read up in the four or five books that had relevant information about the topic assigned to me, and would sometimes paraphrase sentences from them into my own composition. I was never challenged, let alone found out. In this immediate post-war period there may have been a shortage of stimulating women teachers, for contemporary male colleagues fared very well. It is likely also that the older students who had returned from the war were more interesting than we were.

A contributing factor to my situation may also have been my own lack of preparation for university level work. Neither my parents nor any of my other relatives had received a university education.

Among the students of Russian was Donald Swann, who had come up after serving in the forces. He was later to become a popular entertainer, writing the music and playing the piano for "At the Drop of a Hat" while his long-time collaborator, Michael Flanders, wrote the hilarious words that they sang together. Donald got together a few of the students of Russian who liked singing Russian folk songs. He was then already very good at making people laugh, in a humorous, but not malicious way, and was great fun to be with. We were good enough to be asked on one occasion to perform for the BBC. He also taught us Russian dances, including a Circassian round dance that was my favourite.

This choir was not the only one to which I belonged. I sang madrigals with a little group at LMH and was pleased to be admitted to the prestigious Bach Choir. Through it I gained my first experience of singing in works from the classical choral repertory. The choir also performed works by relatively modern composers such as Gustav Holst.

As there were some squash courts near LMH, I joined some colleagues who were interested and we learned to enjoy the game together, improving as we went along. I did not have the figure or the determination to pursue any sport to the point of excellence.

Whereas I made several life-long friends at school, I made only one close friend at University. He was a student of Russian, demobilised from the war. It was a romantic attachment that lasted many years. We shared a love of walking in the countryside around Oxford and would end up in one of those delightful old pubs not far from the town. On one occasion he found a wild orchid and presented it to me ceremoniously, assuring me that it would be the only orchid he would ever have enough money to buy me. He played the guitar and taught me many Russian folksongs. Unfortunately for me, he also liked cricket and I endured watching several games with him before deciding that this pass-time was rather boring. For whatever reason Oxford was not intellectually as important for me as it should have been. I neither joined OUDS, the University Dramatic Society, nor the Oxford Union, the student parliament.

I was awarded an Honours degree Second Class, my French tutor commenting that if I had worked harder I would have got a First. In accordance with Oxford University's regulations, I duly collected an MA seven years later without having done anything to earn it.

As time passed, my Oxford experience faded. When I first arrived in Ethiopia I heard that there was an Addis Ababa Oxford University Club comprising a handful of Oxford graduates. One of these, Stephen Wright, a librarian at the National Library of Ethiopia, who later taught us the rudiments of Amharic, specialised in exposing the fake credentials of persons turning up in the country. One day he telephoned me to ask whether I claimed to have studied at Oxford University. For a moment I wondered whether his suspicions were justified, and I had, indeed, never, been there. However, when I confirmed that I had obtained my degree there he said: "Very strange. You say your name is Rita Eldon but no such person matriculated in the year you say you did." It was then that I remembered that my family was naturalized and changed its name from Einhorn to Eldon during my second year, i.e. after matriculation at the end of the first one. Stephen Wright was thus eventually satisfied with my credentials but, being something of a male chauvinist, never invited me to join the Club.

INTERLUDE IN LONDON

In my last year at Oxford I had read and wept over a harrowing novel *The Twenty-Fifth Hour*, by a Romanian author, Constantin Virgil Gheorghiu. It dealt with an undefined Eastern European exile, who suffered under various oppressive regimes in several other countries during and immediately after the Second World War. While looking for a congenial job I wrote to several publishers offering to translate the novel from Romanian. Heinemann gave me a contract and I translated it, with the help of a French edition that had meanwhile been published. As this was my first translation into English I had the support of a native English speaker who had been my colleague at Oxford. As I proceeded with the translation I became gradually disenchanted with the author's exaggerations and was glad when the work was finished. It was published in 1950, and I was told that it was subsequently made into a film. Later, during a year I spent in Paris, Gheorghiu invited me to Cannes to meet him. As I was about to spend some weeks on holiday in Fréjus, not far from Cannes, I accepted out of curiosity to meet the man. It did not kill the cat, but the visit ended abruptly after a lunch at an expensive hotel, when I declined an invitation to come to his hotel bedroom.

After my parents returned to London from Oldham in 1947, my father, having resided in England for the required minimum seven years, applied for British nationality. We became British citizens on 7 June, and, on 21 August the three of us changed our name by Deed Poll, as my father felt that "Einhorn" was too foreign-sounding. He chose Eldon because it seemed inconspicuous, and was not too well-known—or so he thought. The first time he tried it out, he was asked "Any relation?" He had been unaware that a Lord Eldon existed. My brother, Andrei, had earlier, at the end of the War, joined the British Armed Forces, and had then had to change his name, as ours sounded too German. He chose Edington. My father thought the latter somewhat aristocratic, but Andrei, not wanting to change his name again, opted to join the double-barrelled class by calling himself Eldon-Edington. My own first experience was when taking some shoes to the shoemaker. I gave my name firmly as Eldon, but when he asked me to spell it, it came out as: "E-i-n-h-o-r-n."

My father bought a large house in Wadham Gardens, on the Eton Estate in northwest London, and turned it into three flats. We occupied the spacious ground floor and my uncle, who had arrived with his family from Israel, and was still employed by Shell, lived above us, in a first floor flat. My mother chose the house because it had an extensive garden, which she loved tending, in not very harmonious collaboration with our Welsh gardener, Mr Jones, who had his own ideas. It had a big lawn with a wide herbaceous border at the back and along one side. I noticed that, if I called her when she was working in it, her reply was always rather reluctant—something I remembered in later life when my children called me away from my garden. Her likes and dislikes passed on to me, unnoticed at the time. She was very fond of dahlias, irises, alpines and golden rod. I have tried in vain to grow the latter plant in Addis Ababa, in her memory. We also had a Russian vine that successfully obscured the garden shed, but it, too, refused to grow in our Ethiopian garden. My

Rita's mother with "Omama" Betty after her arrival in London from Romania aged 90, ca 1949

mother would spend a long time creating flower arrangements, often with tiny plants gingerly placed in a small vase. The results were always balanced and beautiful.

After we had installed ourselves in Wadham Gardens my maternal grandmother, Omama Betty, arrived from Romania via Israel. She was ninety years old, erect and neatly dressed as I had remembered her, though she seemed to have shrunk a little since my childhood. An episode from this period stayed in my mind. As we were driving her around London when she first arrived we had to slow down at Marble Arch. She saw a large, elegant black car overtake us. Familiar as she was with the owners of the few cars that could be seen in the streets of Iaşi, she asked who was being driven in it. "It is the Queen's brother" my father replied, unable, on the spur of the moment, to provide a more credible answer. After mulling this over, Omama Betty declared: "If that is the Queen's brother, he must be the King." She was buried in a Jewish Cemetery in North London not long after her arrival.

At this time my father introduced me to office work in London. He was at that time a merchant selling textiles. We would set off together, crossing Primrose Hill, and walking across Regent's Park to Baker Street, from where we could take city trains. His office was very near St Paul's Cathedral and we could hear the choir boys practising in a house next to his office. In writing application letters for jobs he taught me the rudiments of commercial English. He told me that the language should always be as simple as possible. All the flourishes needed to end a letter in other European languages had to be abandoned. "The rules are easy", he told me. "'If you are addressing the person by name, you end the letter *Yours sincerely*. If you have to be more formal, address the person '*Dear Sir or Madam*' and end it *Yours faithfully*'." I followed his useful advice throughout my life.

POSTGRADUATE STUDIES IN PARIS

Despite having spent three years studying French and Russian, I had left Oxford still speaking only French. I could barely make myself understood in Russian, like many of my Oxford colleagues who chose Russian as one of their Modern Languages. My parents and I decided that, if I were to become a translator—and this was a possibility—I would need to improve my Russian and French. We hit upon the idea that I should spend a year living with a Russian-speaking family in France, thus, simultaneously learning to speak Russian and becoming better acquainted with French life and culture.

We found a family who lived in the rue de Passy, near the Bois de Boulogne. They rented two rooms of their flat to students of Russian, and provided meals for them. The husband, Nahum Vermel, a Russian Jew, had been a teacher in Moscow and had moved to Paris with his wife and son, where he worked in the library of the École Nationale des Langues Orientales Vivantes. During the German occupation of Paris, he escaped south with his son, and they survived as agricultural labourers in unoccupied territory. When I came to stay, Vermel was employed by the "Joint"—i.e. the American Joint Distribution Committee. He was a delightful man, intelligent, and with a Jewish sense of humour. His wife, Margarita Vermel, was an Orthodox Christian Armenian from Baku, and, not being Jewish, was able to remain safely in Paris with her sister throughout the occupation. Madame Vermel was an excellent cook and I still remember the Sunday dinners of rabbit and raisins, cooked in rice. At Easter other Armenians came to exchange Easter greetings, proclaiming that Christ had risen. They (and we) then consumed a special Easter cake that much resembled the Italian *panetone*. The Vermels' son, Paul played the piano and wanted to become a professional musician. He later attended the Julliard School of Music in New York wishing to become a conductor, but became a music teacher instead.

My year in Paris (1950-51) was thoroughly enjoyable. I got to know the city, its museums and galleries and soon felt at home there. My French became more fluent as I met more French students. I enrolled at the École Nationale des Langues Orientales Vivantes and, in July 1951 obtained the Diplôme d'Elève breveté (Langue: Russe). More thanks to the Vermels than to the School of Oriental Languages, my Russian also improved considerably.

My fellow lodger was a demobilised American soldier, who worked hard at his Russian and managed on the stipend he received from the Army. He was courteous and shy. The only lurch in our relationship was when he suddenly, and without any provocation on my part, proposed to me. He was some years my senior, and we had little in common other than our intention to get a better grip on the Russian language. We have exchanged Christmas cards and news ever since. In corresponding with him about our year at the Vermels he reminded me that, at that time, my mother thought I might like to improve my appearance—and no doubt my marriage opportunities—by straitening the shape of my nose. I declined.

More to my liking was a Cuban, whom I met through our common interest in madrigals. He was learning the guitar and used to accompany me. No longer a student, he had his own furniture business, as well as glamorous girl friends. He was the only one among my friends who was not only rich but owned a sports car. We would drive out to interesting places. I remember our driving to Chartres, searching the horizon for the cathedral among the wheat standing high in the fields, and seeing it rise above them as we approached. After gazing at its marvellous blue-stained glass

Rita with her school friend Marianne Weil on vacation from Paris, 1951

windows, bright summer light illuminating them from outside, he asked me to look in the Michelin guide and find a restaurant in Chartres with four or five stars. I found a four star one, and ordered *ortolans* with cherries. It was an experimental choice as I did not know what *ortolans* were. Had I known what small, innocent birds they were I would not have chosen to eat them. Decades later, in Addis Ababa, we received a note from my Cuban, introducing his friend, the Princesse de Breuil. I believe he married into the French aristocracy.

My school friend, Marianne Weil, also lived in Paris and we would meet now and again, often reminiscing about our school days and more recently, discussing boy friends. She was aware of the French political scene and gave me an insight into the issues that concerned French socialists at the time. This was almost a decade before the student revolutionary movements of the 1960s.

On returning to England in the summer of 1951, I began seriously looking for a job. My uncle Bruno, who had worked for Shell for many years, suggested I apply for a job with his company. I did so reluctantly and was not sorry that I was unsuccessful in the entrance examinations.

CHATHAM HOUSE PRESS LIBRARY

I then applied for a job in the Press Library of the Royal Institute of International Affairs, then popularly, and now officially, known as Chatham House. It had been founded the year after the Paris Peace Conference of 1919, to promote the dispassionate analysis of international issues. Its library was established in 1921. Chatham House occupied one of the gracious buildings close to Piccadilly Circus overlooking St. James's Square . We had a key to its garden, in which grew an ancient mulberry tree. Each year we picked some of its abundant fruit.

I was successful in my application, no doubt because I could read French, German and Russian. I easily added Italian not long afterwards, the result of knowing Romanian and preparing for, and spending, various holidays in Italy. I opened my first bank account round the corner at 27 Regent Street. As I still bank at the same branch more than half a century later; I have tried several times to derive some benefit from such loyalty, but no, on several occasions when I referred to my probably being their oldest regular customer, I elicited no reaction whatsoever.

In the Press Library, fourteen of us were allocated a part of the world each and were expected to become knowledgeable about it by scrutinising foreign newspapers emanating from "our" countries as well as major British ones, to find out what was happening politically in our area of specialization. Our work had two aspects. The first was identifying articles of importance from the Chatham House perspective. These would be marked and then cut up, folded and pasted on oblong rectangles of paper by the "cutters", a group of part-time retired women. The cuttings were then returned to us, for the second part of our work, namely classifying and cross-referencing them. When a major crisis blew up in a particular area, all the cuttings would be assembled on the desk of our boss, Miss Lois Simpson, and she would decide how to create appropriate sub-headings.

Miss Simpson, though not young, was modern enough to ask us to call her by her Christian name, Lois. I was quite unable to be so bold, and I do not remember anyone else taking advantage of her offer. We shared the canteen with various scholars who came to use the Library. I made the acquaintance of a shy young research worker, Ioan Lewis. By the time I met him again at various Ethiopian Studies conferences, he had become the leading British scholar on Somalia.

At Chatham House I made several friends with whom I would go to the theatre and see galleries and exhibitions. Many of these were close by and could be visited in the lunch hour. I learned to be more sophisticated in my appreciation of contemporary literature and art. With my parents, we went regularly to the Proms, the Wigmore Hall and the newly opened Royal Festival Hall, built on the re-developed South Bank of the Thames for the Festival of Britain in 1951. At home, there was always music, either on records or from the BBC Third Programme, in the days of its glory.

When there was a shortage of staff in the Main Library we were sometimes called upon to help at the library reception desk. One Saturday morning, shortly after my arrival, this happened, and I, as a junior employee, was assigned to this routine task. I was instructed to make sure that every caller wanting to use the library was a member of Chatham House. The first person to appear was a very elderly gentleman who tottered in with the air of someone who knew the place well. Undeterred, I asked him politely whether he was a member. "A Member? A Member?", he exclaimed with some irritation, "I am a Founder Member!" What could I do but apologise. It transpired later that I must have been speaking to Lord Robert Cecil, Viscount of Chelmwood.

To keep my hand in translating, I also translated two further books, not of my own choice, working mainly in the evenings on or at weekends. One was a German novel by Heinz Risse, a gloomy work entitled *Wenn die Erde Bebt*. The translation, entitled, *The Earthquake,* was published by Secker and Warburg in 1953. The other was a history of the Battle of Trafalgar from the French point of view by the naval historian, René Maine. This was more enjoyable as it was co-translated by Basil Robinson, who figures later in this chapter. He was a native English speaker and had some familiarity with the naval vocabulary. The book was published by Thames and Hudson in 1957 under the title: *Trafalgar: Napoleon's Naval Waterloo.*

For holidays, I migrated to southern Europe, usually with my school friend, Laura. She was an expert at finding fine, secluded beaches and good sight-seeing in Greece, Italy, France or Spain. This was not as difficult in the fifties as it became later. Several times, we went to the same beach resort on the Island of Rhodes that had plenty of sand and an inlet with deep blue, calm waters.

TOYNBEE HALL

An unusual situation developed between a graduate student who came to read the Chatham House press cuttings and several of us women in the Press Library. Lawrence Fabunmi, a Nigerian Ph.D. student enrolled at the London School of Economics, came many times to read the files on the modern history of Sudan. He was, I suspect, looking for an English wife to take back to Nigeria, and proposed unexpectedly to several of us in turn. When he would meet with the inevitable refusal, as he was not what any of us had in mind for a husband, he would thrust a chapter of his thesis into our hands and ask us to read and correct it, which we usually agreed to do. Unknowingly, Fabunmi played an important part in my life. When it came to my turn, I went away with my chapter and took it to where I was going that evening. That was Toynbee Hall, where I was teaching French conversation. Also teaching at Toynbee Hall that evening was Richard Pankhurst. As I was signing the register in front of him he caught sight of the envelope with Fabunmi's name on it. Richard had met him at LSE and asked me how I came to know him. The Toynbee Hall Registrar, Frank de Halpert, mentioned above, who was at his desk, then introduced us—and that was the beginning, but by no means the end of my acquaintance with Richard.

My work at Toynbee Hall had come about accidentally. With a view to attempting a translation from Russsian, I had been looking at the Constance Garnett translations of Chekhov in the British Museum Library. Because the main Reading Room was temporarily closed I was working in a room at the far end of the King's Library which ran along one side of the building—a very long, broad corridor lined with beautifully bound books, which later also housed the Meqdela collection of Ethiopian manuscripts. At the end of the day, leaving the room in which I was working, I walked into the King's Library on my way out. So did another person. By the time we were half way down the "corridor" we had made each other's acquaintance and I discovered that I was talking to Herbert Tint, the Head of the French Department at Toynbee Hall. As we reached the end of the long room, he asked me whether I would like to teach French there. I guess that there was, at that moment, a shortage of teachers of French willing to go to the East End of London in the evenings.

One of my students in the French class was an elderly Ceylonese artist, George Claessen, who became a friend. Through him I began to appreciate abstract art. He was a humble draftsman in a government electricity department and spent his free time painting in the proverbial garret. I came to appreciate his paintings, with their swirls of colour, sometimes cheerful and sometimes sombre. When he retired, he devoted many hours to sketching London features that caught his eye. They were never mere copies.

Pen-and-ink sketch of London Bridge by George Claessen, Rita's evening class student and friend, 1971

I treasure a lively sketch of a dancing Eros on his Piccadilly pedestal and another of London Bridge, with St Paul's Cathedral and the slender spire of St Bride's Church in the distance. George never cared about fame and seldom sought the attention of gallery owners, let alone buyers. I appreciated his ability to rise above his circumstances and accept life cheerfully despite a minimal pension. In other respects, too, he had had a difficult life, being left alone in charge of his teenage daughter. He regained his equanimity and positive attitude to life, through his dedication to art and helped by his love of classical music.

JAPANESE PERSPECTIVES

My field at Chatham House had been the Far East, especially Japan, and I developed an interest in Japanese culture and literature. I joined a circle of people who shared this interest. There existed an exalted Japan Society in London, but the likes of me were not knowledgeable enough to seek membership of this august body of scholars. However, we formed a Japan Society of the second order, some of whose members all the same knew a great deal about the country's art and culture. Among these was Basil Robinson, the Keeper of Metalwork at the Victoria and Albert Museum, who, being an expert on many things Japanese, also belonged to the Japan Society proper. He was a leading light of the Catch Club, which I later joined. It comprised a group of Londoners who liked singing. We would meet in one another's houses and sing 17th and 18th century four part catches. The *Shorter Oxford Dictionary* defines these as rounds "in which one singer catches at the words of another, producing ludicrous effects." The words were sometimes bawdy, and always funny. On these occasions the custom was to drink warm beer brought in a barrel. That was the only part of these gatherings that I found difficult. I managed eventually to drink the stuff, but never enjoyed it.

I did, however, enjoy the singing, and the company of Basil Robinson, whom I got to know well as time went on. His wife had died and there were no children, but he had two beautiful Siamese cats. He introduced me to Japanese woodcuts and to jazz. In both areas he had fine collections, and was knowledgeable about many other fields, including every Japanese art form, English silver and much else. He was a typical product of English public schools, confessing to me that he had been beaten three times by a prefect, and, when he reached that stage himself, beat a junior boy

Rita's article in *Asahi Shimbun* reporting on a women's conference in Edinborough, ca 1956

three times. Withal, he was courteous in the old school style, had excellent manners, was immensely learned, and absolutely reliable.

After four years at Chatham House I felt it was time to begin to move on. Continuing part-time there, I obtained another part-time job with the Japanese foreign correspondents of one of the major Japanese newspapers, the *Asahi Shimbun*, on the strength of my knowledge about classifying press cuttings. Their office was in *The Times* building in Blackfriars. One of my duties was to do a one-woman press cuttings service on Japan. I also helped new correspondents find their feet in London, and had to explain aspects of life in Britain that puzzled them. On one occasion they were at a loss to which of them should report on a women's conference that was to be held in Edinburgh. They decided to send me. I still have a cutting of my article about the conference, which duly appeared in Japanese in *Asahi Shimbun*.

The head of the office was Kyozo Mori, Chief of the Editorial Section of the paper in Tokyo. He was elderly, quiet and polite, and had an air of old-fashioned distinction. A man of few words that carried great authority, I never heard him laugh. The other two foreign correspondents were Matsuoka, and Shiino. Matsuoka was Chief of the Economics Department at Osaka. He was young, noisy, joked a lot and was often late in the mornings, having played Majong all night.

I had more dealings with Shiino. He had been Chief of the Research Department in Tokyo, and was interested in learning more about the British way of life, and about European art and culture. I was his guide to art galleries in London and later accompanied him on a visit to the Netherlands and Italy. He wanted me to choose only the most important thing(s) to see in each place. It was a challenge as he had only a few days leave. In Florence I suggested Michelangelo's David. We took a taxi there and spent some two hours looking at it. We followed this procedure elsewhere, and I learnt a great deal about the advantages of concentrating on single works of genius in each place, instead of trying to see everything. It occurred to me at one point that he was rather fond of whiskey. On one occasion he stopped the car to take a swig as, he said, it kept him awake, while on another occasion he came to a halt saying that he would soon be going home and needed some whiskey to help him sleep.

I was, of course, aware of the hostility many people in Britain felt about the Japanese, in view of the savagery that their soldiers displayed during the war. Some of the correspondents had difficulty in finding lodgings when clearly there were vacancies.

It was while working for these journalists that I first became conscious of the strength of anti-Japanese feeling in Britain. On my part, I had come to admire their art, culture and simplicity of living, and I was happy to learn more about Japan through this job. I read some translated classical and modern novels and began to learn something of the manners and customs of Japan through the correspondents. When it came to our going out to lunch I would step back, like a properly brought up Japanese woman, to let the men go first. Unfortunately, about the same time, they would remember that, in the West, women went first, so *they* would step back. A little ballet would ensue, before we passed through the door.

It was while working for the Japanese journalists in London, in October 1954, that I saw Emperor Hayle-Sillasé being driven past in an open horse-drawn carriage. It was an impressive sight which lingered in my mind. I could not have imagined that, within less than three years, I would be summoned into his presence in Addis Ababa, and arranging an exhibition at his Palace.

ENTER RICHARD

When, after our first encounter at Toynbee Hall in 1954, Richard suggested we meet one evening for dinner I had no idea that my life was about to change dramatically. I was at that time on course for marriage to Basil Robinson, then a widower, who was much older than I. We had many interests in common, including Japan and singing in the Catch Club, to which he had introduced me.

Richard and I met, prophetically, at the entrance to Bush House, the Overseas Service of the BBC, later the BBC World Service. It was to play an important part in our lives together. Richard asked me what languages I knew, and when I told him that I had studied Russian, knew German and French, and some Italian, he suggested I learn Romanian. He was delighted to hear that I was originally Romanian and spoke the language. He informed me that he had been to Romania with his parents, as a seven-year old boy, having crossed Germany at the time of the funeral of Hindenburg, the German President, in 1934.

Early in 1956 Richard told me that he and his mother had decided to live in Ethiopia and were leaving London in July. Would I like to come along? I thought about this proposition, but not for long. My interests having centered on Japan, I had little awareness of Ethiopia other than having caught a fleeting glimpse of the Emperor as he passed though a City of London street.

My parents were very unhappy at the idea of my leaving for Ethiopia. They were set on Basil whom they saw as a reliable, courteous gentleman with a good income who lived in London. Shortly before I left he sent me, in his beautiful calligraphic hand, the following composition:

> Hotel rooms smell & food is meagre
> Throughout the province known as Tigre,
> While poison-snakes & scorpions are a

Constant menace in Amhara.
It's true the traffic gets in no jam
On roads as bad a those in Gojam,
But better not be sharp and Snooty
Or say "they're better in Jibuti."—
Remember that the men from Wallo
First cut your throat & then say "Hallo!"
And fierce Somali bandits will
Beset your road in Danakil,
And if you're slightly curvilinear
You're nowhere safe in Abyssinia!
So pause a moment—think of Oldham—
Think of your friends & how you sold 'em—
Think of the many things left undone
In foggy, noisy, friendly London—
Think how we'll miss you when you're gone
Off to the land of Prester John!

"What has Richard done in life?" my parents asked me. Would he be able to keep me? Was I proposing to live in the same house with a mother-in-law, that virago of a woman, well known for fighting with everybody? Did I know what was involved in living in Africa? Did I want to live so far away from them?

Sylvia Pankhurst duly visited my parents and they became resigned to the inevitable. Before my departure I dreamt that I was in a valley with mountains rising steeply on either side. I climbed up one of these and got to the top, only to discover that beyond the top there was a sheer drop, and nothing beyond that, like a mountain on a stage set. However, this did not deter me.

Richard and his mother left in July 1956, and I followed in November. Basil married the year after I left and produced two children as educated and cultured as he was himself.

CHAPTER 3

First Years in Ethiopia

RICHARD

SETTLING IN

As the summer of 1956 advanced my mother and I made final preparations to leave Britain for Ethiopia. At that time it seemed a far greater adventure than it would today. Mass air travel had not yet begun, and few of our British friends had journeyed so far afield. Nevertheless the die was cast. My mother had sold her house in Woodford, after which I packed up the core of my parents' library, and archives, which had been put in tea chests addressed to "Sylvia Pankhurst, c/o H.I.M. the Emperor's Private Secretary, Addis Ababa, Ethiopia." The furniture and the residue of our belongings, which were altogether of little value, were to be auctioned soon after our departure.

When the day dawned the husband of my mother's old friend and assistant, Mrs. Ivy Tims, drove us to London Airport. We could not bring ourselves to leave behind Pitti, our white, half-Persian cat, so we put her in a basket and took it along. We then boarded a British Airlines flight to Athens. There we entered the Ethiopian Airlines plane which took us on its then normal route via Cairo, Khartoum and Asmara to Addis Ababa. In those days, before hi-jacking, it was customary for passengers to alight at each stop and walk to the airport lounge, to have a cup of coffee and look at, or purchase, local tourist items.

We landed in Addis Ababa on 4 July.

Our first impression on landing was of the bright Ethiopian sunshine—much more luminous than a British summer's day—and of the intoxicating smell of the eucalyptus trees. Their aroma was one to which we soon became so accustomed as not to notice it any more.

We were met at the Airport, and whisked through Customs, by several of my mother's old Ethiopian ministerial and other friends dating back from the time of their exile in Britain. From them, we learnt that we had been temporarily assigned to stay in the Gennet Hotel. This establishment formed part of a former Italian workers' housing scheme, in a locality known as *Popolare*, an Amharic rendering of the Italian term for council houses. The place was convenient in that there was a vacant adjacent flat in which my mother's books and papers could be accommodated. It was fortuitous

Sylvia and Richard not long after their arrival in Addis Ababa, 1956

also that a nearby flat was occupied by Habte-ab Bayru and Afewerk Tekle, our ex-student friends from London. I recall how they welcomed us playing recordings of Tchaikovsky's 1812 Overture and his Italian Symphony when we first visited their flat—a happy reunion!

Pitti settled down with ease in Addis Ababa, enjoying the warm weather, though she could never be prevailed upon to enter its travelling basket again. The following year she contracted an ear disease, and gradually declined. Her death in the autumn of 1958 broke a long link with our family life in Woodford.

ETHIOPIAN STUDENT FRIENDS MET IN ENGLAND

We were soon afterwards happy to meet other Ethiopian friends from student days in England, among them Belay Abbay, Mary Taddese, Yeweynishet Beshahwered, Almaz Fasika, Gebre-Kristos Merse-Hazen, the Oxford Group, Siyyum Sebhat, Asrat Welde-Yes, Siyyum Beqqele, and the architect, Gétachew Beqqele. One of the students who brought his intellectual interests from the UK was called Aseffa, a very popular name. To distinguish him from several other Aseffas in our circle, he came to be known as *Aseffa Manchester*, since that city was where he studied. He was once quoted as declaring that he was the unhappiest man in the world if the *New Statesman* did not arrive at Giannopoulos, the Greek bookshop in Addis Ababa, on Monday evenings. Another Aseffa was known as *Aseffa Corrente* as he worked for the Ethiopian Electric Light and Power Authority (EELPA).

The day after our arrival in Addis Ababa we drove to the office of the Emperor's Private Secretary, Ato Teferra-Werq: to pay our respects, to pick up our mail which was then being temporarily addressed care of him, and to hear the news. The latter came as a bombshell. We learnt that, during our journey from Woodford, Nasser's nationalisation of the Suez Canal, with which we were of course familiar, had led to dramatic consequences. Britain, to our amazement, had intervened overnight and the disastrous Suez War had begun.

The conflict led to great public indignation in Britain, comparable to that unleashed by its Government's failure to resist Mussolini's invasion of Ethiopia a generation earlier, and to that resulting from the Iraq war almost half a century later. Ethiopia, however, seemed far away from the struggle, in those times at least, and it was several days before we gained access to a radio to listen to on-going news of Mr. Eden's Egyptian fiasco.

ETHIOPIA OBSERVER

My mother's main concern at this time was the practical one, of launching her new journal *Ethiopia Observer*, to which she was committed. It was conceived as an Ethio-British monthly, to be published simultaneously in Addis Ababa and London. Since the publication was to circulate largely outside Ethiopia my mother decided to speed up circulation and save postage costs by having it printed in Europe. She entrusted the work to the printers, Messrs. Percy Brothers in Manchester. They had produced *NT &*

EN for many years, and their staff were accustomed to reading her articles which were mainly hand-written. Addis Ababa printers, operating in a foreign language, would then have found this virtually impossible.

The journal was thus something of an international enterprise. Mainly written in Ethiopia, the copy was posted to Manchester, where it was set up in linotype. The proofs were then posted to Addis Ababa, where my mother and I read them. We had then to decide how and in what order the articles should appear, and where the illustrations were to be inserted. This entire operation, which required much measurement, was often frustrating, and made both of us tense and irritable. To save postage costs, we cut up the proofs, so as to send back only those with corrections. The proofs were then posted to Manchester, together with the lay-out, after which work on the next issue had to begin again!

Notwithstanding all this posting between two continents, and some interference with transport as a result of the closure of the Suez Canal, the first issue of the *Ethiopia Observer* appeared in December 1956, less than half a year after our departure from England.

A statement in the opening issue recalled the objectives, and history, of *NT & EN*, and, turning to the "Mission" of its successor, declared that it was "to mirror each and every facet of Ethiopia's present renaissance." The journal, which would be under the same editor as *NT & EN*, would have the immense advantage of her living in Addis Ababa and observing events on the spot.

Elaborating on this ambition, the article continued: it "will be the first publication ever published simultaneously in England and Ethiopia. A journal of independent opinion, it will preserve an impartial standpoint, publishing articles on a wide range of topics concerned with Ethiopia past, present and future. It is hoped that each issue will be of immediate and permanent interest. It is anticipated that readers will desire to preserve the monthly editions for binding. Therefore the pages from issue to issue will be numbered consecutively; it is hoped to issue an index and binding case at the completion of every year. In addition to definitive articles on economics, politics, history, culture and the arts each issue will contain a diary of Ethiopian events."

The proposed binding case never materialised, and the indexes appeared irregularly. The promised consecutive pagination was, however, carried out, and each issue tended in fact to focus on a specific topic, with many "definitive articles" as anticipated, on "Ethiopia's past, present and future." The first issue thus dealt with the Ogaden; the second with Addis Ababa; the third with Ethiopian women; the fourth with public health; the fifth with industrial progress; and the sixth with the Queen of Sheba. Each was decorated with cover illustrations by our young artist friend Afewerk Tekle. Other early issues were devoted to Ethiopia's first general election, Pushkin's believed Ethiopian ancestry, and the Battle of Adwa. The advertised "diary", which was mainly written by Rita, was published until my mother's death when the journal, as we shall see, became a quarterly.

One of the formalities in establishing the *Observer* was the renting of an Addis Ababa post-box. We chose the number 1896—the date of the battle of Adwa. That POB number remained unchanged to this day, despite the fact that, in later times, with more of us using it, we could have done with a bigger post box.

UNIVERSITY COLLEGE OF ADDIS ABABA

It had been arranged with the Emperor when my mother accepted his invitation to travel to Ethiopia that I should teach in his country. Having already had several years' teaching experience in London University's Extra-Mural Department, it seemed natural—at least to me—that I should join the country's then only college of higher education: the recently established University College of Addis Ababa (UCAA). This, however, posed a problem.

The College, led by Dr. Lucien Matte, a French-Canadian Jesuit, had been founded in 1950, largely by Jesuit teachers from one of Addis Ababa's secondary schools, the Teferi Mekonnin School. Teachers at the College, like those at the School before it, were largely Jesuits, or, if not, lay Roman Catholics. The employment of foreign staff of other religious persuasions was apparently not favoured, though a number of Orthodox Ethiopian Christians were gradually being appointed.

On arriving in Addis Ababa, I promptly made an appointment to see Dr. Matte. He asked me formally whether I would like to see the College. I readily consented, after which I drove to the Arat Kilo area of the town, where he gave me a tour of the establishment. Though he knew that I had applied to teach at his institution, he made no reference to the matter, and at the end of the tour dismissed me with the polite expression that he hoped that I might again visit the College some day. The idea that I might do as a member of staff, was by implication excluded.

Not long after this the Emperor's Private Secretary, Teferra-Werq (who doubtless knew there would be a problem), phoned me to hear the outcome of the above meeting. He asked me whether there was no other college in which I could teach. I pointed out that I was a historian-cum-economist and social scientist, and as such was not qualified to teach Theology, Engineering or Agriculture, the subjects to which the country's other colleges were then being devoted. I added that failing employment at the UCAA it would be preferable for me to return to London University's Extra-Mural Department, where an appointment still awaited me. He dismissed this suggestion out of hand, declaring that it would "upset the apple cart."

As a result of Teferra-Werq's intervention I was duly appointed to the UCAA staff. I was thereupon given an office, which I shared with three others: Alemayyehu Haylé, an Ethiopian mathematician whom our friend Nerayo Isayas, nicknamed the *Fitawrari*, or Commander of the Advance Guard, perhaps because he seemed to be for ever on the telephone. 2) Thomas Knipp, an American teacher of English literature; and 3) the redoubtable Jacques Godbaut, a Canadian man of letters, who later wrote a novel critical of the College entitled *L'Aquarium*.

University College, new Classroom Building, where Richard lectured, 1957-74

Some years later we moved to a new building nearby, at that time one of the tallest and most modern structures in the town. I shared an office with a young American historian, Harold Marcus, an ebullient and entertaining West-Africanist historian who was just embarking on the study of Ethiopian history, and contributed to a livelier intellectual atmosphere in the College. Knowing that he took an inordinate interest in my visitors, particularly at a time of political tension, I once put a note on my desk stating: "The General will come at 7 p.m." That evening I had occasion to stay late and was amused to see Harold, who usually left early, remain in our office well past 7pm.

On another occasion I was late for the evening class I was giving, and rushed into the building without turning off my car lights. Harold arrived a little later, and seeing the car lights still on, kindly stepped into the vehicle to turn them off. He was immediately confronted by a policeman who asked him whether he was unaware that it was illegal to shine his car lights on the Arat Kilo Liberation Monument in the square below the University College. Harold, unaware of any such regulation, protested that it was not his car, whereupon the policeman, not to be rebuffed, said it was an even greater crime to shine someone else's car light on the monument.

To anticipate: Harold later joined Howard University, and subsequently taught at Michigan State University, East Lansing, becoming a prominent figure in Ethiopian Studies, notably as a historian of the Menilek era. He convened the 12th International Conference of Ethiopian Studies at Michigan State University, in 1994, and supervised a number of Ethiopian history students, several of whom collaborated with him in drafting the English translation of the second volume of Emperor Hayle-Sillasé's autobiography.

The Emperor himself visited our office (unfortunately for Harold during the latter's absence). It was his habit in those days to drive to the University College and other institutions of an evening. Our office door opened while I happened to be taking notes on the history of Harer. After greeting me he asked, in French, what I was doing. I told him that I was studying the five great gates of Harer, and was trying to ascertain what they were called at various historical periods by the local people: during the Egyptian occupation, in the late nineteenth century, and during the time when his father, *Ras* Mekonnin, was Governor, etc. He smiled and asked: "What are they called in *my* time?"

At first, the College rather resembled a strictly regulated boarding school, but succumbed to local pressures on 1 February 1959, when the students were permitted to hold the first dance on college premises. Because of the limited educational background of many of the students, in the immediate post-Liberation period, teaching at the UCAA was based very largely on general survey courses virtually devoid of specialisation. In view of the shortage of staff this meant that many of us were obliged to teach courses about which we knew virtually nothing. I felt qualified to teach both economics and general economic history, both of which I had studied at LSE, and I purchased a copy of the great multi-volume *Encyclopedia of the Social Sciences,* which I had often used there, to add to the UCAA library's meager resources in that area. It was not long, however, before I found myself also lecturing on Egypt of the Pharaohs and succeeded only by keeping a chapter or so ahead of the students. My teaching of ancient Egyptian history was important: I was told that the subject was compulsory, that virtually all the women students had failed it, and that I must pass them as they could not otherwise be promoted to the following year's classes.

I also developed a general course on African history, but this caused some displeasure, as it was said to be "anti-colonialist", and had soon to be abandoned. My relations with the UCAA administration were sometimes tense—perhaps because, as the Dean of Arts, Édouard Trudeau, once complained to me, I did not "think like the College." I, for my part, did not believe that Colleges should "think", but should leave that commendable practice to individual staff members.

Towards the end of November 1959 Rita and I were happy to meet the first two post-war Ethiopians to return from America with doctorates in education: Aklilu Habté and Mengesha Gebre-Hiywet, both of whom were immediately employed at the University College. We invited them to dinner at our house, and were impressed by their academic American English which was sprinkled with long words. Both doctors were full of hopes for improving the state of affairs in Ethiopia. Aklilu's account of America did not tally with the views put forward by the U.S. Information Office. Ethiopians arriving in the US, he told us, were not used to being treated as "coloured" and therefore did not know the places they were not supposed to enter. Consequently they landed themselves in unpleasant incidents, and not only in the South. Another Ethiopian gave us an example of such an incident, when he needed a hair-cut in Chicago. He walked into a barber's shop, unaware of the sensation he had caused, as it was an establishment for Whites only. The barber duly started cutting, but, removing the hair in a circle at the very top of his head, cut the surrounding hair in the normal fashion.

Having long been interested in economic history, the subject in which I had specialised at LSE, I had conceived the plan of devoting myself to the economic history of Ethiopia, about which little had by then been written. Because of the absence or non-availability of basic texts, I saw my task as bringing together primary information, rather than interpreting it: the interpretation, I felt, could come about later. I believed also that I should adopt a wide approach to the subject, to include for example social and medical history. I decided this initially because I had been much fascinated, as a student, by Hans Zinsser's classic work *Rats, Lice and History*. My interest in extending my research into the medical field was, however, later greatly influenced by the writings of several early Ethiopicists, notably the French scholars Marcel Cohen and Marcel Griaule, as well as our Polish friend Stefan Strelcyn. All three had made exciting contributions to the study of Ethiopian medical plants and medical texts, and I felt that their work was worthy of greater attention from historians than it had thus far received.

My studies for the Economic History of Ethiopia would have been virtually impossible, had it not been for the UCAA's Librarian, Stanislaw Chojnacki, who had a remarkable past. A young Polish scholar, who had spent the years of World War II as a prisoner-of-war in Germany, he emigrated to Canada, where he earned a degree in law, and was recruited by Dr Matte as librarian. Knowing little of Ethiopia at that time, as he himself confessed, he asked his prospective employer in which province of Canada was Addis Ababa situated. Duly informed of this strangely little-known geographical fact, he soon mastered virtually every branch of Ethiopian studies and became the world's foremost authority on the history of Ethiopian art.

Chojnacki soon became a close friend—and later an intimate and loyal collaborator. A man of broad culture, he had decided immediately after his arrival at the College, and in the face of some opposition from the survey course teaching staff, that the library should purchase all works available on Ethiopia, without exception. He was successful in his acquisitions policy, for second-hand books on Ethiopia, in those days before the establishment of American and other African Studies programmes, could be obtained relatively easily and cheaply. His library thus contained a good supply of Ethiopica, mainly from Britain, France, Italy and Germany.

Another of Chojnacki's achievements was the establishment of the College's Ethnological Society to interest students to their own culture. The Society began publishing a *Bulletin* in 1953. I was not at that time involved in the society, membership of which was restricted to students, but later wrote an extensive article for it, on the division of labour, and the existence of minority groups in traditional Ethiopia. The publication soon afterwards ceased, but its articles are still highly regarded, and it fell to our son, Alula, long afterwards to organise and edit an indexed reprint of them.

A large part of my time at the UCAA, every available minute in fact, was spent in ploughing systematically through the College library's collection of Ethiopica. I did this chronologically, starting with ancient times, then moving on to the medieval and modern periods. I also read through my mother's by no means insignificant library on Ethiopia—and when going on leave in England in 1959, and subsequently, extending my awareness of the subject, by spending many hours in the British Library, and later the Public Record Office and India Office. I read everything I could lay my hands on in English, French and Italian; Rita, most kindly, translated extensively for me from German; and others did the same for certain passages in Ge'ez, Amharic, Arabic, Tigreñña, Greek, and Portuguese.

The earliest fruit of this research was my first book on Ethiopia: *An Introduction to the Economic History of Ethiopia*, published in London in 1961. That year also witnessed the publication of my earliest work on the country's medical history: an article on the Great Ethiopian Famine of 1889-1892, to which I was later to devote more attention. The country was at that time virtually free from famine, but the subject, sadly, was soon to gain far from expected relevance.

I was surprised when, in November 1962, perhaps as a result of my publications, I was appointed to the five-man [*sic*] College Academic Council.

FIRST FIVE-YEAR PLAN

The Emperor at this time was moving towards a non-aligned stance, and had become good friends with Marshal Tito, perhaps because both leaders had experienced invasion by Fascist Italy. The Emperor visited the Yugoslav Adriatic coast, as well as Belgrade; Tito made his way to Addis Ababa several times, and went hunting in Ethiopia. He offered Ethiopia economic assistance. The two rulers agreed that a Yugoslav team of planners should advise the Ethiopian Government. It was decided that they should draw up sector reviews of all aspects of the Ethiopian economy, with a view to drafting Ethiopia's first Five-Year Plan.

A Yugoslav economist, Professor Borivoje Jelič, duly arrived in Ethiopia in October 1954. His team was put under the supervision of General Mulugéta Buli, formerly Head of the Imperial Bodyguard, and by this time Chief of the General Staff. The Yugoslavs speedily produced a today little known fourteen volume study in French entitled *La Situation et des Possibilitiés de Développement de l'Économie Éthiopienne*, which was issued by the Belgrade publishing house Jugoslavija in 1955.

The project, which entailed the drafting of the country's first Five Year Plan, was entrusted to my friend *Lij* Mikaél Imru, who had read Politics, Philosophy and Economics in Oxford. He was assisted by several other modern-educated Ethiopians headed by our old friend Belay Abbay, who had studied economics in Southampton, England. They needed a native English speaker with some knowledge of economics to edit the final version, and my name was put forward. The Emperor asked Mikaél, as the latter subsequently confessed to me in confidence, whether he was absolutely sure that I could be trusted to keep the project secret. This was because it had been decided to avoid publicity for the Plan, perhaps so as not to offend the susceptibilities of more aligned states. Perhaps, also, it was a manifestation of a more general trait of secrecy in Ethiopian public life.

Be that as it may, Mikaél duly asked me to become involved in the Plan, and introduced me to the Yugoslavs, who briefly outlined it to me. I understood that the document on which I was to work was to be an extended study of the previous sector reviews: a projection as to how the economy could be expected to develop, rather than a policy to be introduced by planners.

The Yugoslavs produced the first draft of the Plan in their native Serbo-Croat and this was translated into both French and English. My responsibility was to go through the English translation with Rita's cooperation, and produce a more polished version. Over the next few months I met a number of the Yugoslav experts and corrected a series of the texts they had prepared. In the course of one of my meetings with Mikaél, the Emperor phoned, and although there was no one else in the room, Mikaél stood up, bowed to the telephone and remained standing throughout the conversation.

My assignment with the Yugoslavs presented few difficulties until Rita and I came to a stumbling block. The English text at one point stated that it was necessary to increase the number of "cattle seedlings" in Ethiopia. We wondered whether this meant small cows, i.e. calves, but this scarcely made sense. I accordingly drove down to the planners' office where one of the Yugoslav economists, also not grasping what "cattle seedlings" signified, consulted the French text, only to find that it merely gave the French equivalent, without shedding any light on what was to be understood by the words in question. We were then obliged to consult the Serbo-Croat original, which revealed that the planners were in fact proposing an increase in the number of *coffee* seedlings.

The Five-Year Plan, though doubtless useful to the Ethiopian Government, was not published for several years. A summary of it, was, however, printed, with *Lij* Mikaél's permission, in *Ethiopia Observer* (Vol. III, No.4). Curiously, though the Plan was confidential, in November 1962, I was given a week's leave to read the final draft before it went to the printers. However, as the Emperor had wished, no mention of the Plan's authorship ever reached the national or international press.

THE END OF UNIVERSITY COLLEGE

The University College of Addis Ababa had succeeded in advancing beyond the level of purely secondary education, but was unable to transform itself, as some had hoped, into a fully-fledged University—and the Emperor was insistent in establishing such an institution in his name.

Ethiopia's increasing involvement in Africa had led him, moreover, to grant two hundred scholarships to students from other parts of the continent—which worked out to be fifty four-year scholarships annually. These African students, with some of whom we had, as we have seen, developed close ties, were more politically conscious than their Ethiopian counterparts, and took unkindly to the College's somewhat autocratic character. They were strongly supported by the then acting Minister of Education, *Lij*

Indalkachew Mekonnin, who wanted his country to play an increasingly dynamic role on the African stage.

Another problem for the then largely Jesuit-run College was that it was considered too parochial to develop effective contacts with the wide world, and in particular with the United States, which by then represented an unparalleled source of both teachers and financial assistance. Many observers also considered that Israel might be a valuable alternative source of technical and other expertise.

All this led to a shift in Ethiopia's higher education policy. It was decided that a Hayle-Sillasé I University should be established independently of the University College, but that the latter should constitute the University's College of Arts. In October 1961 the Emperor donated his residence, the Gennete Li'ul Palace, and its spacious grounds, to the new University. An American University President, Dr. Harold Bentley, a Mormon, was appointed to run it, but he almost immediately left the country. He was replaced by a prominent young Ethiopian civil servant, *Lij* Kassa Welde-Maryam, who was the husband of one of the Emperor's grand-daughters, Princess Seble Desta. He was to prove a dedicated and hard-working administrator, committed to the development of Ethiopian education.

A no less momentous change took place at the UCAA, where the Jesuit, Dr. Lucien Matte, left, and was replaced by an Israeli Dean, Dr. Zvi Yabetz from Tel Aviv University. A Jew of Romanian origin, he had escaped from his native land by jumping from the train in which he was being taken as prisoner to almost certain death.

Dr. Yabetz was a distinguished historian of ancient Rome, whom Ethiopian scholars remember for his article on "The Roman Campaigns in Ethiopia and the Policy of Augustus" which later appeared in *Ethiopia Observer*. He carried out immediate changes in the College. Very critical of the educational value of the old UCAA system of survey courses, he established subject-oriented academic departments—as well as a related research centre: the Institute of Ethiopian Studies. He owed much of his success in the University to the fact that he was, like its then Business Vice-President, Dr Randall Montgomery, a devotee of football, and would discuss the latest game with his boss before handing in his financial requests.

It was at this stage decided that Professor Sven Rubenson, a Swedish scholar of Ethiopian history, and sometime Lutheran missionary in Adwa, should head the newly established Department of History, and that I should become the Director of an even newer Institute of Ethiopian Studies.

RITA

SETTLING IN

I left London on 29 November 1956, boarding a British European Airways twin-engine plane to Athens travelling on from there on an Ethiopian aeroplane. Surprisingly, the second stop, the first in Africa, was Tripoli and the final one was Khartoum. The Suez Crisis had made it unsafe for travel along the normal route to Ethiopia across Egypt, whereas, at that time, there were no difficulties about landing in Libya and Sudan. Gradually I saw hills that turned into huge mountains, cut by deep valleys with small streams at the very bottom. Green, cultivated plateaus at different levels in between were dotted with little settlements with straw roofs resembling brown mushrooms.

Having taken off in brilliant sunshine I arrived, on Friday 30 November, in midmorning expecting the same, but it was raining. The Airport turned out to be a shed with two small public areas. To my regret it has recently been pulled down. It was a historic building. Although erected during the Italian Occupation to serve the airport the Italians had constructed, it was historic because it was the first airport in Addis Ababa to be used by Ethiopian Airlines, preceding the one nowadays known as 'The Old Airport.' The "very old airport" comprised a ticket office and "departure lounge" in one room and an "Arrival Lounge" with a platform for the inspection of in-coming luggage in the other. It was also memorable for us later, when a lion apparently entered it one evening. It was rumoured that the king of beasts had come to buy a ticket, but accounts differed as to its destination.

I arrived two hours ahead of schedule. Neither Richard nor his mother were anywhere to be seen. A kind Ethiopian gentleman, who had worked with Sylvia during the war, lent me money for a telephone call and then, as I found I did not have the appropriate telephone number handy, drove me to the house, where Sylvia was just setting out. She received me, explaining that Richard could not be present as he was giving a lecture to his students at University College, where he had been appointed Assistant Professor. We went back to collect my luggage, and with her help I was let through without paying any customs duty. Richard duly came back to greet me at lunchtime. I learned then that lecture time was sacrosanct, and admired him for it.

The drive to the airport, which was not far from the house, was in the Fiat "Millecento" lent to Sylvia by the Government. It had already passed its prime. Yami, Sylvia's chauffeur drove us. He, too, was not in his first youth. As we shall see, both remained with us for many a year. Yami was quite a character. Although originally paid for through the Government garage, he had become part of our personal staff and could even be coaxed into being our handyman, if correctly approached, i.e., by saying: "Yami, we have a problem with this blind, which is not working properly. What shall we do?"

Several trunks of my "dowry" came by boat. My mother had given me a lot of beautifully embroidered linen from Romanian days, plus tablecloths, embroidered mats and towels. However, some of these things were too fine for everyday use and many are still in drawers, from which they emerge only on special occasions.

The road to our house was a narrow asphalted lane. We owed the asphalt to the fact that it led to the Netherlands Embassy. The asphalt had been cut across at one point to lay a pipe, and the car had had, for many years, to bump over the ditch. It had deepened with every rainy season. We were happy when the Queen of Holland came for a visit and the ditch was filled, but not until 1969.

The eucalyptus grove on one side of the Pankhurst house in Addis Ababa, ca 1956

The house was situated in a eucalyptus grove, and the area that gradually became our garden, was only sporadically fenced. We could go for a walk behind the house towards the stream further down the hill and meet only an occasional farmer with his donkey. When we arrived the lovely smell of eucalyptus trees was everywhere. Today it no longer greets your nostrils as you touch down at the airport.

The mainstay of the domestic staff was our cook, Askale-Mariyam, a gifted linguist who could communicate not only in Amharic and French, but also in Arabic, Greek, Italian and Aderé, the local language of Harer. She had a repertoire derived mainly from French cuisine, to which I gradually added my favourite Romanian dishes, with the help of one of my mother's recipe books. Her husband, a truck driver, was often on the road for days, and was not always sober when he came back. They lived in a two-roomed house on our compound with their two daughters. Her son was born in the same year as our son, Alula, and they remained playmates throughout their childhood. The wedding feast of her daughter was held in our compound. That was the first time

Rita in front of the eucalyptus trees separating the future Pankhurst garden from its only neighbours, ca 1956

I tried my hand at baking the spongy-looking bread called *injera*. The first *injera* had beginner's luck, but unfortunately I tried again, with disastrous results.

It was customary in pre-revolutionary times, for people who could afford it, to employ several servants. We were helped in acquiring ours by Lesley Cramer, a colourful Englishman long resident in East Africa. Invariably wearing a carnation in his botton-hole he had a cockney accent, and an irrepressible sense of humour. He remembered Sylvia's activities in the East End of London with great respect. Loosely attached to the Ethiopian Ministry of Information he collected advertisements for the Press and organised auctions. He had got to know several people from a village near Ambo, west of Addis Ababa, and was for ever finding them jobs.

In the afternoon of the first day I was driven round the town. I was surprised by its extent and pleasant appearance, paved roads, shared by pedestrians, and sundry livestock. I found the food shops unexpectedly well-stocked not unlike the ones in Soho, with Armenians and Greeks selling such specialities as pastrame, salami and olives. Everything else was unexpected, especially the Ethiopian dress, and graceful appearance of the young women with their widely varying hairstyles. Sylvia was a great admirer of the abundant, glossy and healthy-looking hair of Ethiopian girls.

The following days, I observed for the first time the family routine, which was governed by the production of the monthly *Ethiopia Observer*. It did not vary from year to year until Sylvia's death four years later. Sundays were no different from weekdays. The Emperor had invited her to come to live in Ethiopia and continue writing about the country, as she had done for twenty years in England, but, now that independence had been restored, to write about Ethiopia's development. She was thus engaged in collecting material, writing it up, or correcting the proofs, which were produced by her printer in Manchester. Richard, in addition to teaching at the University College, was an unofficial co-editor occupied, not only in writing articles but also in proof-reading, and arranging the lay-out. Sylvia was also engaged in interviewing expatriate staff and procuring equipment for the near-by Princess Sehay Hospital, for which she had energetically raised funds in England.

INTRODUCTION TO COURT CEREMONIAL

I saw the Emperor for the first time at a ceremony prepared for his return from India and Japan, where he had been on a State visit. The streets were be-flagged, two triumphal arches had been erected, and school children lined the route from the airport to the Palace. Ordinary citizens and country folk stood behind the children.

Two rows of dignitaries welcomed the Emperor as he descended the steps from the aircraft, beginning with the Patriarch (the *Abun*) and followed, in strict ceremonial order, by the other dignitaries. These comprised—in addition to the Royal family, often including children and grandchildren of all ages; the bishops of the Orthodox Church and the head of the Muslim community; the Diplomatic Corps; nobles, ministers and other high-ranking officials; representatives of the Armed Forces and Police; regional chiefs and leaders of resident foreign communities. The older ladies of the court astonished me by their pear-shaped bulk, whereas the younger ones were slender, and well-dressed according to the latest European fashion. Many women were in black. I learned later that mourning periods when black had to be worn, could be as long as a year for close relatives, and lasted for months even for more distant ones. As the families were extensive, the noble ladies were very often in mourning.

We were motioned to our seats on the stand that had been erected for the occasion.

Our problem was, and for some time continued to be, that we did not fit any of the categories listed above. This meant that ushers were uncertain where to seat us, though in the end we were usually very courteously and prominently seated. This difficulty was more pronounced when there were receptions at the Palace itself. Especially in the first few years, we were not on any of the various invitation lists, although we were expected to be present. If invitations did come, they often arrived late, or after the event. The most important aspect of the invitation cards was that they specified the correct dress required. Richard suffered most from this, as we were not familiar with the implications of "Morning coat", Black tie", "Tail coat", etc. I discovered that women in European

Rita in ceremonial attire, with hat and long gloves, ca 1958

dress wore gloves and hats for day-time functions, and long dresses and long gloves in the evening. If dresses were sleeveless, gloves, had to be elbow-length.

After the fall of the Emperor we were no longer invited to state receptions and my gloves remained in a cardboard box for years. However, a second life awaited them. When, much later, the Romanian Head of State, Nicolae Ceaucescu, was invited to a banquet at Buckingham Palace, my aunt Gaby and her daughter Ruth were asked to be the translators from Romanian. The problem that immediately arose was that they needed to be in formal evening dress, with long gloves. My box was raided, and thus found a new home.

When they arrived at Buckingham Palace two hours before the time of the banquet, as instructed, so as to dine before the official dinner, Gaby discovered, to her consternation, that she had only one glove. She phoned her husband asking him to look for it, and, if found, to bring it as fast as possible. Uncle Bruno located it at home on the stairs and rushed for a taxi. When the cabbie asked for Bruno's destination he truthfully gave this as Buckingham Palace. The taxi drove off and, after a minute or two the driver said: "Buckingham Palace, very funny, now tell me where you really want to go". Having been persuaded that the address was correct, he duly delivered his passenger to the Palace Gates. No sooner had Bruno begun to explain his mission, than the guard said:" Ah! Mrs Eldon's glove", and, taking it, disappeared into the building. It reached Gaby in time not only for her official work but also to participate in the preceding unofficial dinner.

An additional difficulty in the Emperor's Ethiopia was that our little Fiat came low in the estimation of the Imperial bodyguards who directed the traffic at the Palace, so that our driver was often kept waiting until more impressive cars had been waved in. After depositing us he would be directed to a distant part of the car park.

VISIT TO THE SHASHEMENE LEPROSARIUM

My first experience of the Ethiopian countryside was on the second Sunday after my arrival. It had been arranged that Yami would drive us to Shashemene, in the Rift Valley south of Addis Ababa, so that Sylvia could report on the Leprosarium established there by the missionaries of the Sudan Interior Mission. The three of us got ready to depart early in the morning for the long journey, but Yami failed to turn up. We discovered later that he was always reluctant to drive outside Addis Ababa. As I was the only member of the party with a driving licence it fell to me to take Yami's place. I asked to see the maps. This was met with a smile from Richard who explained that these were unnecessary as there was only one road leading to Shashemene. In the boot there was an ancient jack and a spare tire that had seen better days, but was, mercifully, inflated.

We duly set off on the road to Bishoftu, the Oromo name which had given way to Debre Zeyt, or Mount of Olives, under the Emperor's Christianisation policy. Richard later observed a similar trend at the University College, where notices occasionally appeared announcing that a particular student with a non-Christian name wished to be known by a Christian one. After the Revolution it, and other towns, the names of which had been Christianised, largely reverted to their original designations, and students ceesed to shy away from their given names.

This stretch of road had been paved during the Italian Occupation, but had since developed numerous potholes, only some of which had occasionally been filled after the rains. At Mojjo, further to the East, we saw oranges being unloaded from the train running from Jibuti to Addis Ababa. We then turned into the road that ran down and all along the Rift Valley and up again to Shashamane. Winds had swept the narrow gravel into rills that made the ride very bumpy, unless one had the courage to drive faster over them. This I learned to do, after some trepidation. Fortunately we met very little traffic. The ride between the lakes was unforgettable. The majestic umbrella acacias, alive with birds, spread their canopies over the road from both sides. Beyond them was an uninhabited savannah forest, totally hiding the lakes on either side.

It is sad indeed to travel on that road today. The road has been well asphalted and kept in good repair, but the trees are gone, save an occasional amputated acacia, full of weaver birds' nests that would have had many a tree to choose from in earlier years. The ground is now dry and sandy, the lakes are clearly visible and grass-roofed houses are proof that many families have settled in the area.

In the late afternoon we reached the Leprosarium, situated on a hill just outside the town. We were taken to see the Clinic, the Church, the neat, whitewashed residences of the staff and the thatched huts of the lepers who received their twice-weekly pills after participating in a religious service. In the evening we engaged in prayers. In the morning Richard was asked to say Grace before breakfast, which he did silently, unsure of the correct formula expected of him. One of the missionaries sitting at our table asked me how long I had been in Ethiopia. "Let me see", I replied: "What day is it today?" That I was unaware that the day was the Lord's Day greatly embarrassed my neighbour.

Sylvia having taken copious notes for the article she was preparing, we left for the return journey. I had driven ten hours and 600 km. in two days and felt I had become acclimatised. (*Ethiopia Observer*, Vol. I, No. 4.)

DEATH AND FUNERAL OF THE DUKE OF HARER

During our first year in Ethiopia, I felt that my parents were not too happy that months had passed and Richard and I continued to "live in sin." Sylvia was in favour of our marriage, which had been discussed when she visited my parents in England. We therefore prepared to get married in the spring. However, on 12 May 1957 the Duke of Harer, Mekonnin Hayle-Sillasé, the Emperor's favourite son, died in a car accident, and the court went into mourning. We attended the ceremonies at Christmas Hall in the Palace compound. It was profoundly moving. There was total silence in the spacious hall, interrupted only, now and again, by wailing women.

The death of the Duke of Harer was both a significant public event and one that directly affected us. He was a young man of thirty-three, much loved by his wife and five sons, the youngest of whom was born only a short while before his father's death, and by the Emperor, whose only relaxation seemed to be his children and grandchildren. He had not been told of the accident while he and the family were in Sidamo in the south of the country, so that, at 9 a.m. on Monday when they returned, flags were still flying high.

When we first heard the news, we drove home to put on black clothes. The shutters were going up all over the town and people were flocking to the church. We hastily posted the proofs of *Ethiopia Observer* (Vol. I, No. 8, on the Ethiopian ancestry of Alexander Pushkin), as the Post Office was due to close for three days. Then we went to the Palace where crowds of weeping people were surging forward, into the antechamber itself. The Diplomatic Corps condoled and then we did, with other Europeans (not that Europeans and Ethiopians had been in any way separated during these three days). The Emperor looked so frail and the Empress so pale, it was really terrible to see them having to submit to all this protocol. Then he and all of us walked behind the coffin to the Church—some two km. if not more. The streets were very wide in this area—wider than Whitehall. It looked as though the whole street was moving forward in a slow mass, high-ranking and lowly mingling. I counted a good thirty people in each row moving slowly forward. Included were Ethiopian aristocratic ladies waddling forward heroically though they were not accustomed to move more than a few steps at a time, and even then they would often be supported by servants. It took an hour and a half to get to the church. Luckily, the sun was intermittent, as it was by then midday. In front of the church there was such a crush that we (Afewerk, Habte-ab, Richard and I, plus another Ethiopian) begged asylum in the house of Thomas Knipp, a fellow-lecturer of Richard's at University College. He gave us a longed-for drink of water and coffee. As the Duke was being buried we heard the 21 gun salute.

We joined the procession back to the Palace. The throne was draped in black. We were served a meal: salad, Ethiopian meat dishes and raw meat, the first time I had seen it served at the Palace. There followed dirges and funeral orations until past five in the afternoon.

On the third day there were to be special mourning ceremonies and a church service starting at 6 a.m. When we arrived at 7 a.m. the Church Service had finished. We joined the throngs going to the Palace, to the Great Hall where we had been at Christmas and also on the first day of mourning. The Emperor was on the balcony with his ministers watching the procession of wailing, singing and dancing, women beating their breasts, men with spears, and the Duke's servants leading his horses and carrying his helmet and decorations. We went into the hall where men and women were seated facing one another in long rows, all in black, and again silent and still, except for the occasional woman wailing, or a circle of impromptu dancers chanting improvised verses and bearing aloft a portrait of the Prince. After about two hours, the royal family came in, not in the usual formal order, but as a crowd of miserable black figures. They came up between the rows of men and those of the women. The bereaved royal family sat on their black-draped chairs down among the other people, not as usual, on the platform. The poor young wife was a pitiful sight. One felt sorry for them, having to endure this three-day ordeal of public mourning. It had been amazing, too, to see, on the first day, the spontaneous move of the whole town towards the Palace.

After three days of mourning and weeping, people returned to work and shops reopened. But all Government officials continued wearing dark suits and black ties, the women being clothed in black from head to foot. They would be doing so for a month. Newspapers were framed in black and all Government correspondence had black borders. It was an unforgettable experience to see the spontaneous, deep and uninhibited outpouring of grief by the inhabitants. They flocked to the Palace day after day even after the official three days were over, coming in groups from the countryside. On all the roads leading to Addis Ababa you could see long cavalcades, three or four abreast of Oromo cavalry silently riding to the Palace. The horsemen were not regulars—just peasants who fought in time of war. An Israeli observer told us that it was just the same when British units arrived at the time of the Liberation in 1941: the warriors attached themselves in their thousands and fought with the troops. What was extraordinary was that they came within feet of the Emperor with their spears and rifles and he had scarcely any protection. It was the same throughout the days of mourning: people of all sorts were milling around him, coming and going without any guards in attendance.

As the flow of mourners continued day after day, an order went out instructing people still on the roads to condole with the Governors of their provinces, so as not to continue putting a strain on the bereaved family, particularly on the Emperor, who was once more at work.

In March 1958, the first anniversary of the Battle of Adwa after the death of the Duke of Harer, we were invited to a meeting at the Hayle-Sillasé Theatre to launch a campaign to raise funds for a hospital in his memory. It started almost an hour late, and featured numerous speeches by leading personalities, only the first of which was translated. An hour's delay, we came gradually to realise, was a regular feature of meetings in Ethiopia, being the minimum time that passed between the announced hour of a meeting and its actual start. However, occasions involving the presence of the Emperor started punctually.

The work of raising funds for the hospital began in earnest some time later that year. Sylvia and I attended a Publicity Committee for the Memorial Fund in which ideas for fund-raising were discussed: flag days, pamphlets, stamps, posters, slogans, etc. Sylvia's experience in fund-raising was valuable and the meeting produced many good ideas. Like other major projects some of the money needed was raised by a tax of one month's salary on public employees, who did not welcome this way of showing their grief at the death of the Emperor's favourite son. The Duke of Harer Hospital was duly built. After the Revolution, it was re-named the Black Lion Hospital, in honour of the Patriotic group of fighters who attempted to resist the Italian invaders in the West of the country, following the Emperor's defeat in the North.

Within the first six months I had seen the court ceremonial on a joyous, as well as on a deeply sad occasion; I had savoured the beauty of Rift Valley Ethiopia and caught a glimpse of life outside the capital for missionaries and lepers and ordinary country folk going about their daily lives.

PLANS FOR OUR WEDDING

After a month in Ethiopia I broached the question of our marriage in a letter to my parents, who, I believed, must have been wondering why there had not so far been any mention of a wedding in my letters. I explained that neither of us felt any sense of urgency. I wished to establish my position at the Library as Miss Rita Eldon, and not as a Pankhurst adjunct.

Richard felt, and had convinced me, that, whatever the embarrassments caused by our not yet tying the knot, we should not rush, not till I had become fully aware of the implications of life so far away from them, from my friends, and from my old home. I saw the wisdom of this, as I had by this time learnt much about conditions in Ethiopia, things it was better to know before, rather than after, an irrevocable decision had been made. It was not a matter of disagreements between us, any of us, but rather that Richard thought that I should have proper time to consider Ethiopian life and people, so as not suddenly to say, after we were married, that I wanted to go back to England. For myself I felt more and more certain that I wanted to live with him in Ethiopia, despite the separation from my family, former friends, and earlier way of life.

By February 1957 we were beginning to think seriously about our wedding and I asked my parents to make a provisional note not to be too busy on 5 July 1957. This date had some significance for our family, being my mother's, as well as my own birthday. It would also have been a year and a day since Richard and his mother had arrived in Ethiopia. We planned to get married at the Municipality in the morning and to celebrate with a party in the afternoon or evening. We thus proposed to complete our wedding in one day, which was unheard of by Ethiopians, who normally spent many days getting married. We were considering a honeymoon in Sudan or Uganda, where Richard had a number of ex-LSE friends.

However, there had to be a postponement because of the death of the Duke, and the ensuing period of official mourning. Full mourning extended from 21 May to 21 June— half mourning for a further two months. We were considering whether it would be acceptable for us to get married before the end of the full mourning period, but in the end Sylvia felt it would have been inappropriate.

Sylvia had become a good friend of Princess Tenaññe-Werq, the Emperor's only surviving daughter, at the time of the Ethiopian Liberation Campaign. The Princess had been left behind in Britain with her children. She had limited contact with her family in Addis Ababa, and was subject to British censorship regulation. She had welcomed my mother's' campaign to raise funds for the hospital in Addis Ababa, which was to bear the name of the Princess's deceased younger sister, Princess Sehay. Princess Tenaññe also appreciated my mother's

Princess Tenaññe, eldest daughter of the Emperor, who supported Sylvia's advocacy of Ethiopian independence, as well as her efforts to establish the hospital to be called after the Princess's sister, Sehay, ca 1939

advocacy of Ethiopian independence at a time when various colonialist interests sought to establish some kind of Protectorate control over the country.

The two women met frequently in London, where Sylvia told her much about Italian history, the rise of Fascism, etc.

Selecting a new date was further complicated by the fact that there was no unanimity as to when mourning would in fact end. Some said it would be eighty days from the death of the Duke; others that it would be eighty days after the forty of full mourning. The latter interpretation brought us to the middle of the rainy season, which would have made travel difficult. By the end of June it was established that the mourning period would end only on 15 September. This was better because it was towards the end of the rainy season, but worse as it left little time for a honeymoon before Richard's classes resumed. We did not want a church wedding and the municipal registry office was a dismal outhouse of the Town Hall. We decided for the British Embassy, though, because of his anti-colonialist articles in the Ethiopian press, Richard was not then very popular there.

In July snags erupted with regard to the honeymoon. The idea of a journey down the Nile from Uganda had earlier been abandoned, as there was no longer time for it, and it had also proved expensive. However, a visit to Uganda remained a possibility, especially as Sylvia was feeling much better, and we had made special domestic arrangements to ensure that she would not be alone in the house. This plan, too, had to be abandoned, as Addis-Nairobi flights had been interrupted by a dispute between Ethiopian and Aden Airlines, i.e. between TWA and BOAC. A visit to Mogadishu with Idris, who was going to prepare an exhibition there, also eventually fell through, as he was ordered to fill the plane with airmen, to help set up the displays. A decision was therefore postponed.

We finally decided to get married two days after the end of the mourning period. A fortnight before the selected date, preparations had hardly begun.

RICHARD

SYLVIA WRITES TO RITA'S PARENTS

On 12 September, shortly before the wedding day, Sylvia wrote:

"The two young people will be married in a few days. I hope they will be happy and care for each other. My son has been since his birth more than anything in the world to me and I have therefore naturally observed matters carefully.

"They are certainly good companions and are able to help each other in the work they have chosen here, and that I feel is a great thing which will be to them a lasting asset in their daily lives and a bond between them of the best and most satisfying kind.

"When Rita had to prepare lists of books for the Parliament and Palace. Richard threw himself wholeheartedly into the work of examining with her catalogues and preparing lists of books, just as he does in helping her to choose books for the National Library and in making suggestions regarding persons who might be written to for contributions of books and other publications for the library.

"Similarly Rita has helped Richard in translating from German, which he does not know, and also in knotty phrases from French. Moreover she helped in simplifying some articles he has written to render them suitable for Secondary School textbooks. They have spent many hours working together very pleasantly. This sort of collaboration gives a mutual interest in the daily round and they agree well together in such occupations.

"I have therefore hope that their union will be founded upon a firm and enduring basis of mutual interests and that they will feel that they belong to each other.

"I know it must be sad for you that your daughter has chosen to live so far away from you, but on the other hand I feel sure you will find satisfaction in the fact that she has a companion with whom she shares common interests, and has work of her own which she considers useful and in which she has considerable scope and is appreciated for her ability and diligence."

OUR WEDDING

By 5 August Richard had given the British Embassy the requisite fortnight's notice of his intention of marrying me. He was charged 5 Ethiopian dollars, and jokingly complained that I was not worth it!

Twelve days before the wedding the family began to realise that the occasion was approaching. There was less talk of Ethiopian history, and a little more about invitations, catering, drinks etc. There followed discussions with Princess Tenañ̃e, who offered to—and did—pay the costs of the reception at the Gennet Hotel, then one of the more modern, but far from luxurious hotels in the city.

The day before the wedding we were chasing all over town trying to find some of the guests' homes or offices to deliver invitations. It was not easy for there were, and mostly still are, no street names or numbers in the city. Our address, for example, was "near the Airport, past Princess Sehay Hospital, the Exhibition ground, and the American pilots' compound, on the road to the Dutch Embassy." Richard's ex-student friends, at least, were not so hard to find, as most of them used the old Itégé Hotel as an unofficial club, and could be found there in the evenings, many playing chess.

There were some *faux pas*. Sylvia had sent an invitation to the Crown Prince, forgetting to invite his wife and to preface his name with "'HIH (His Imperial Highness)'". Nevertheless a man arrived in the course of the afternoon with the gift of a carpet from the Crown Prince—a bright red affair—that cheered up our dining room.

In the afternoon Richard and I prepared, for the evening party, a shortened version of a recording of the Old Vic's performance of *Macbeth*. We tape-recorded it, supplying the missing material from scenes we were leaving out, in the form of imaginary announcements and reports in the Ethiopian press of 1000 years ago. It was a wonderful opportunity for parody. Headlines were: "Change of Government in Scotland", "Macbeth regime comes to power", etc.

The evening before the wedding Afewerk and Mengistu, who were to be our witnesses, came to dinner, but we three were feeling tense and depressed. We listened to the conversation and felt apprehensive. Richard had been much against a big party, not believing in ostentation in a country with so much poverty. We therefore cut out the wedding cake for 150 guests and just kept the champagne.

We were eventually married at the British Consulate in the Embassy grounds, on the morning of 17 September 1957. A twelve-page letter to my parents described the events. The day dawned, bright and warm, but there were ominous clouds on the horizon. With a million things to do, we managed to find time to dress—I with white hat and gloves and grey striped silk dress. Richard wore a dark gabardine suit which I managed to wrench from him in time to have it cleaned. Sylvia wore a navy blue outfit. We remembered the camera, by some miracle. Two roses, one pink, one yellow, were in full bloom.

Our *mizé*, or best men, were Afewerk and Mengistu, Richard's closest fiends, both of whom he had known when they were students in England. The occasion was not without drama. First of all Mengistu had not taken seriously our request that he be one of our witnesses and was nowhere to be seen on the day. Fortunately his house was on the way to the Embassy, so that Afewerk, impeccably turned out in national dress, helped to get Mengistu hastily dressed, he, too, in traditional white Ethiopian clothes. All five of us then proceeded to the Embassy in Afewerk's spacious car, whilst our chauffeur was sent to get more eggs for the mayonnaise.

Wedding photo with Sylvia and "best men" Afewerk Tekle and Mengistu Lemma, 1957

A further fly in the ointment resulted from some articles Richard had been writing in support of African, and specifically Kenyan, independence in the weeklies *Ethiopian Herald* and *L'Éthiopie d'Aujourd'hui*. They were translated into Amharic, by Hayle-ab Tedla, and caused something of a stir among the Ethiopian reading public. The articles in English came to the attention of the British Ambassador, Geoffrey Furlonge, who was so incensed that he gave the ridiculous instruction that no member of the Embassy staff should attend our wedding celebrations. Perhaps influenced by this curious edict, the towering Consul, Col. Sandy Curle, with whom we had been on friendly terms, registered our marriage, as quickly as possible, but not before Richard put Omama Betty's ring on my fourth finger.

Afewerk decided that we should go for the traditional wedding drive, which we did in his elegant car. We were invited to his flat for a champagne lunch, which included a toast to absent parents, whereupon both Sylvia and I burst into tears. Princesses Hirut and Seble dropped in for the toast. Afewerk had chosen special paintings from among his works and hung them on his walls for the occasion—one painting was an abstract of "peace." As background music he played, not quite appropriately, a recording of Bach's B Minor Mass.

In the afternoon we tried again to phone my parents from Idris's house, having failed earlier from ours, but to no avail. Princess Hirut and Seble came to help arrange flowers, supplied from the Empress's farm free of charge. You can imagine the chaos, with telephone and doorbells, a temporary, belligerent cook, and the chauffeur, his beard tidied for the occasion, in his haste to run last minute errands, getting caught by the police for speeding. The afternoon flew by, punctuated by Richard telling me that we had soon to go, and was I going to have a rest?

We managed to arrive at the Hotel, at 5:55 p.m., for the party scheduled for 6 p.m. I found I was holding one brown suede glove, having left with the conviction that I had with me two black ones.

When we arrived most of the Emperor's grandchildren, i.e. youngsters of our generation, were there, still in black. They had come early, to congratulate us and go, as they were not fully out of mourning. None of the brothers and sisters of the late Duke came, but *Bitwodded* Andargachew Mesay, Princess Tenañne's husband stayed for a while and we talked about the Library which he visited with the Emperor (see next chapter). In all we had perhaps about 150 people, including the Prime Minister and Ministers of the Pen, Defence, Commerce, Foreign Affairs, Communications and Agriculture. There were so many ministers that Habte-ab quipped that a cabinet meeting could have taken place there and then. There was also a solid contingent of ex-students, friends of Richard's who had studied in England, people from the Library, the University College, and staff of the Sehay Hospital, as well as personal friends of Sylvia's.

The first toast was given by our friend Siniddu Gebru. She said that Sylvia was so beloved by Ethiopians that ours was like an Ethiopian wedding for them. Mengistu, by then a recognised poet, made a short, but entertaining speech commending our marriage ceremony to Ethiopians, many of whom get seriously into debt to lay on a sumptuous wedding. He recommended our type of one-day wedding, contrasting it with the typically more elaborate Ethiopian weddings which continue for a week or so. In *Marriage of Unequals*, a play he wrote subsequently, he has a noblewoman anticipating her daughter's expensive wedding with a cortège including a large number of motorcars "not counting the Volkswagens." Girma Atnafsegged, one of Richard's Ethiopian student friends from England, declared enthusiastically that he hoped we would have many children. I fear we disappointed him.

After the cocktail party, armed with six unopened bottles of champagne we set off for a buffet dinner at home, with thirty or so close friends, all but one being Ethiopians. The foreigner was Eleanor Mansfield. Her husband Philip Mansfield, as a member of the Embassy staff, felt he could not defy his Ambassador's edict, but Eleanor came. She

Wedding photo with Sylvia, Mengistu Lemma and Princesses Hirut, left, Seble right. Photo by Afewerk, 1957

said that, if hauled over the coals, she would claim that she had known me at Oxford (which she had not). After settling in with a glass of red wine we went to the dining room for our fish mayonnaise, salad, and various kinds of *wet*, the traditional spicy stew.

Several people had given us candle sticks, and we sat listening by candle and firelight, on sofas and cushions on the floor. Then, under Afewerk's impeccable

Afewerk and Mengistu drop into the garden, 1958

direction, the evening unfolded. First we had our *Macbeth*, which was greatly appreciated. Mengistu followed and was at his most entertaining. He had prepared a reading from a humorous American poet which brought tears of laughter to our eyes. Then he recited some of his own Amharic poems with witty translations, on the plight of the returned student, and on the clash of values between the older and the younger generations. He had extraordinarily good command of English. I remember particularly one poem in the shape of a Japanese Haiku, about a frog which croaked— and once again he left us all in fits of laughter. Then, spontaneously, people began to stand up and sing or dance Ethiopian style, more parody than genuine. Then we all went for our chocolate mousse and mandarin oranges. Soon it was midnight. We finished off the champagne, Wong, Richard's Chinese statistician friend from LSE days, sang a Chinese opera excerpt, and again we were all helpless with laughter. The guests left. We had another toast and quiet minutes with our delightful witnesses. They left, and we toasted the servants, who had worked splendidly—and the day was over, more successful than we could remotely have hoped. Sylvia had been sitting happily by the fire, just as the youngsters had.

The wedding present from the Emperor, sent by special messenger, was a large silver cigarette box, lined with red velvet, with his monogram in the silver pattern on the lid. The present we liked best was from the widow of the late Duke of Harer: a lovely little silver jug and sugar bowl on a silver tray.

The next day we were at our desks. Were it not for the bunch of presents, which I had stacked together to make sure I acknowledged them, one would never have guessed that a wedding had taken place on the previous day.

To my regret, some three weeks after having Richard put my grandmother's ring on my finger, I found that it had slipped off, probably in the garden, as I was planting nine raspberry canes, five climbing roses and one ordinary rose. I had intended to take the ring to the jewellers, as it was loose, but had unfortunately kept it on in the meantime. We debated whether to dig all the plants up in the hope of finding it, but, in the end, I did not attempt to search for it, nor have I found it since.

RICHARD

HONEYMOON IN HARER

The Harer number of the *Ethiopia Observer* was the fruit of a visit of the three of us to that city via Dire Dawa in September 1957. This enabled my mother to collect material for an issue on contemporary Harer and us to accompany her and learn about the city whilst enjoying our honeymoon. I was to write the historical part later. The Grand Hotel, as the CIAAO, built by the Italians, was called, was then still in relatively good shape and we were given the VIP rooms on the first floor: two double bedrooms with bathrooms, linked by a small sitting room. A number of guests had come up from the French colony in Jibuti to enjoy the fresh air of Harer as was customary since the arrival of the railway from there to nearby Dire Dawa in 1902.

Some of our friends were amused to hear that my mother was with us on this occasion. In fact we did not see much of her. We enjoyed ourselves as tourists, seeing the market and the inevitable evening scene of the man feeding the hyenas by hand outside the gates. We were introduced to Shami, the local amateur historian, archaeologist, geologist, collector of coins and general source of local knowledge. Our guide told us that Shami's mother was a Hareri woman and his father was "a Turkey." We also met the Sandhurst-trained Sikh officers preparing for the opening of the new military Academy, and their wives. A neighbouring green-grocer heard that we were on honeymoon and, as we were

Painting of Harar by Afewerk, 1958

leaving, sent us a present of an armful of large, succulent mangos. We noted that, already at that time, farmers in the area had been turning from coffee to the narcotic *chat* (*catha edulis*) as the latter was more profitable. Sylvia collected the material on present-day Harer that appeared in the issue on the city, Vol. 2, No. 2.

RITA

MY PARENTS' VISIT

My parents could not come for the wedding, but made their first visit to Ethiopia a few months later, in December 1957. I began to store in my memory things of interest to show them. They were astonished and delighted by life in Addis Ababa. My mother was amazed at the variety of the vegetation and greatly enjoyed our garden and Askale's good cooking; my father immediately made friends with our friends. It was a characteristic of his that gave me much pleasure. One morning, asking to be left behind in the Mercato, the city extensive traditional market, he returned on his own by *gari*. We took them to Yeka Mikaél and to Ziqwala. These memorable trips are recounted in Chapter 7. They also met Andreas who observed that her face was fresh like that of a women from a Russian village.

Visit to Mount Ziqwala with Rita's parents, Afewerk and Mengistu 1958

In the evening after my parents had left we were all three working when there was a noise in Sylvia's bedroom. We found that some blankets had been stolen from her bed. We decided to put bars at all windows so that we could keep them open whenever we wished. During the years of the terror after the Revolution, when our house became a Higher *Qebbelé*, or local government office, the bars must have

Afewerk in south of France, preparing stained glass window for Africa Hall in Addis Ababa, 1961

helped to keep prisoners in some of the rooms. One of our friends was imprisoned in the house and, when we returned, would never agree to visit us at home. Another detainee, Yohannis Haylé, told us that, when the worst days had passed, he had been permitted to prune our roses.

Through my weekly letters my parents came to hear about many of our friends, and those that passed through London were always welcomed by them. In August 1960 we sent them a diffident young arts and crafts teacher and amateur artist, Feqadu Gedamu. He came to London on a UNESCO Fellowship to study Museology. Later, after graduating in anthropology at Chicago University, he became one of the first Ethiopian anthropologists at Addis Ababa University and, later still, he rose to be an Ambassador.

In late August 1960 my parents were alerted to the transit visit to London of Princess Hirut, who was off to a teacher training college in the US. She was invited to dinner at their house in Wadham Gardens. In September we informed my parents that Debbebe Habte-Yohannis, who was Deputy Exchange Controller at the Ethiopian State Bank, would be in London on a six-month fellowship to take courses in banking at LSE. He was a good friend of ours, and a kind man. We benefited from his hospitality several times in later life. A genial and jovial soul, when in England he could scarcely bear the idea of being separated from his wife and children for half a year. During the abortive *Coup d'État* of December 1960 my parents spent time with him, urging him not to worry about his family, and indeed nothing happened to them. He returned joyfully to Addis Ababa in April 1961, having finished his course.

The month after Debbebe arrived in London we gave my parents notice that Afewerk would be going to the south of France to supervise the production of stained glass windows for the entrance hall of the Economic Commission for Africa, and would be in England for a week. He arrived on 26 November and made his way to Wadham Gardens, where he was warmly welcomed.

SYLVIA

At home, life à trois had settled into a routine. Sylvia divided her time between collecting material for the next issue of *Ethiopia Observer,* writing it up, reading it in proof form and returning the proofs to the printer in Manchester. In my first few letters home I reported on my encounters with the person my parents thought would be so difficult to cope with. Of course I was in the business of reassuring them, but the letters do sound a genuine note of appreciation. I wrote, of our visit to Shashemene Leprosarium shortly after my arrival, where I shared a bedroom with her. "In the morning, as we dressed, I was given the history of Ethiopia up to Emperor Menilek. I found Sylvia charming. I am quite falling in love with her. We have had an occasional evening alone together, and get along splendidly, even on the subject of Richard. She is remarkably objective about him. Somehow it seems quite normal that we three should form a unit."

Three weeks later I was again commenting on life with Sylvia: "We are usually in bed by midnight and get up between 7:30 and 8 a.m. It is amazing how she keeps up at this pace. She is at breakfast just after eight with us and, if she has no appointments, works on solidly till lunch, all afternoon and after that, often all evening. I try to take her for a stroll at lunch-time or, at weekends, in the afternoon, but work is really her life, though she is far more human, generous and sweet than you or I expected. I can say with complete honesty that we have had no differences" (i.e. disagreements). Again, some weeks later, when Richard was working with colleagues on the First Ethiopian Five Year Plan, Sylvia and I had a *tête-à-tête* dinner, talking about Eminescu, the Romanian poet—some of whose poems she had translated into English with a Romanian's help, and about Dimäncescu, his country's representative in London, who had written a number of articles for her newspaper on the post war world. In truth I had left Romania too young to read Eminescu and had very little knowledge of Sylvia's activities before she left England. However, we were able to discuss where and how to plant some newly acquired roses, and to comment on a newspaper cutting about the Suffragettes which my parents had sent us.

Some weeks later I wrote to them: "You have probably perceived by now, through my letters and Sylvia's, that we really do pull it off remarkably well. She is a most understanding, sincere, and kind-hearted person. She and Richard sometimes shout at each other, and are so rude that it appals me, but it is all superficial, usually about the lay-out of the *Observer,* but I never come into it all, and it is usually sharp and short. Today they are at it again because it is proof day." Sylvia was at times in poor health and occasionally admitted to stomach pains. I found that her energy was incredible. She never complained about the altitude.

Sylvia had another bout of ill health—some bladder trouble and indigestion which she had had before. As it was worse this time, we called Dr Holman, the chief doctor at the Princess Sehay Hospital next door. He gave her some excellent medicine so that she was soon quite well again, though, as usual, she worked far too long hours. Sylvia's health had never been good, ever since the Suffragette hunger strikes. She suffered from swollen ankles, but her spirit remained indomitable. She was seldom discouraged and never complained.

My relations with Sylvia continued to be very good, as I liked to emphasize in my letters home. In one of these I mention that someone had asserted that Sylvia was talkative, but I did not accept this, and wrote: "It may be true that, when we have certain visitors, she talks a lot, but I am never aware of it when we are alone, the three of us. In all honesty I can say that we hit it off very well. At first Richard acted as a kind of mediator, but now we are apt to gang up against him, rather than quarrel about him."

RICHARD

In July 1957, despite the cold weather of the rainy season, my mother, who had great recuperative powers, was feeling a great deal better. She had an audience with the Emperor. He asked her to help him with his Autobiography, the first part of which had already been written, though not published. She recommended the employment of a full-time professional. This work was first translated into English by the British librarian, Stephen Wright, formerly of the Bodleian Library, in Oxford. It was later published by Oxford University Press in a definitive edition by Professor Edward Ullendorff.

Three months later my mother was pleased to see the Emperor coming to Princess Sehay Hospital to lay the Foundation Stone of the Hospital's paediatric wing, funded through Swedish aid, and to witness the graduation of Hospital nurses.

During their stay in 1957/8 my parents noticed with concern that a little girl in the neighbourhood of our house had bow legs. Sylvia went into action, taking her to the Hospital for a consultation with the Director, who said she was improving after having developed rickets. He prescribed rest, milk and cod liver oil which Sylvia provided. A few days later the child contracted pneumonia. Sylvia took her back to the hospital, and when she was cured, arranged with the Handicraft School to make a little chair with a tray in front on which the girl could sit. It had a wooden attachment so that she could play with blocks of wood for building houses. These had been prepared at the school as Christmas presents.

My mother had not been in contact for many years with her sister Christabel, who lived in California, but in the summer of 1957 she wrote to her sister about a book on the Suffragette movement which had then recently been published by Roger Fulford. My mother felt that it slandered their parents. She received a reply in August, sharing my mother's annoyance with the book. She had also informed Christabel of my imminent marriage to a "Romanian graduate of Oxford University" and Christabel had replied, sending congratulations. On her death in 1958 the Emperor condoled with my mother.

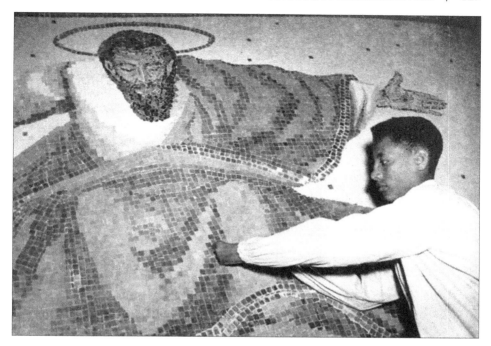

Afewerk installing his mosaics in St George's Cathedral, Addis Ababa, 1965

Before Afewerk went to Asmara for three months in May 1958 to supervise the firing of mosaics for St George's Cathedral, he exchanged paintings with my mother. We thereby acquired his painting of the "Rimbaud" house in Harer, which hangs in our sitting room in London. The painting she gave him, of a forest scene with some little girls, he subsequently gave back to us, and it is in our house in Addis Ababa. After Afewerk's return from Asmara we heard that he had done excellent mosaic work there.

In December of that year, at the age of 76, my mother undertook an extensive visit to Eritrea, flying to Asmara, then on to Massawa, back to Asmara, and then to Assab before returning to Addis Ababa. She remained in excellent health throughout this arduous journey. Seeing the fruits of her campaign for the reunification of Eritrea and Ethiopia, the progress in that province delighted her, and provided material for five issues of *Ethiopia Observer* (Vol. III, Nos 5-9). Her stamina was remarkable. On her return, as a journalist, she attended the ceremonies at the opening of the Economic Commission for Africa, and at the evening reception, had the opportunity to tell the Emperor that her visit had made her feel happy, crowning her work for Ethiopia (which had begun in 1935). As he was walking out he called to her and said: "C'est grâce à vous", which made her even happier. Earlier, after the Liberation, a Sylvia Pankhurst Street had been named in her honour.

RITA

THE SOCIAL SERVICE SOCIETY

The inception of what later became the Social Service Society can be traced to John Barnabas, an Indian social worker, who, upon his arrival in Ethiopia in November 1957, suggested that a voluntary society be formed to rehabilitate Addis Ababa's beggars. He expounded his ideas, as we will see in Chapter 4, at a National Library lecture chaired by *Dejazmach* Zewdé Gebre-Sillasé, the Lord Mayor of Addis Ababa at the time. The *Dejazmach*, a man of progressive views, was much interested in the idea, which also resonated with other educated Ethiopians. It soon became apparent that a Municipality-supported project was needed, to take the following courses of action:

1. Separation and investigation of the different categories of beggars.
2. Cleaning of their existing dwellings.
3. Teaching skills to those able to work
4. Opening of an employment bureau specifically for beggars.

It was expected that once such a citizen's group came into existence it could also study the question of recreation, public parks etc.

Sylvia and I were duly summoned to a meeting convened by the Lord Mayor at the Municipality, which was then located in *Neggadras* Hayle-Giyorgis's imposing old residence opposite Giyorgis Church. Over the years various groups tried to save this fast deteriorating fine example of early Addis Ababa architecture, but thus far without success.

Addis Ababa Municipality, former residence of *Negadras* Hayle Giyorgis, ca 1957

We were called to discuss the Mayor's initiative to provide shelter and training for the capital's numerous beggars. The proceedings were entirely in Amharic, and there was no official or impromptu translator for the two of us. We gathered afterwards that the proposal was to round up, feed and teach a trade to as many able-bodied beggars as possible. Sylvia was enthusiastic.

After several further weekly meetings, we decided, in December 1958, to call the Society the Social Service Society (S.S.S.), with *Dejazmach* Zewdé as President. We were both asked to join the Committee. Richard's sardonic friend Habte-ab Bayru began to call our gatherings the Beggar's Opera.

We heard no more for some months, after which we were invited to visit the compound where the beggars were accommodated. A large walled area had been allocated to the project and big corrugated iron sheds had been built to serve as dining halls, kitchens, and workshops. Sleeping facilities and dormitories were erected because the objective of cleaning the inmates' sheds proved impractical. We were impressed by the speed with which the sheds had been erected, the looms for carpet knotting constructed, and the ovens made fore baking *injera*, the pancake-like bread used for picking up and eating other food. We were less impressed by the facilities provided. The beggars were closely packed together, sleeping on the ground. At that point, there were as yet no *injera* baskets or plates, the *wet*, or stew, was doled out directly into the beggars' hands. The inmates were not permitted to go out to earn their daily bread by begging, and that was their greatest grievance. Sylvia reported on what she saw, but her criticisms were not appreciated, given the energy the municipal employees had devoted to the project.

In February 1959 we had a further meeting at the Municipality at which we divided up the work. Sylvia took charge of publicity and was also to look into conditions at Kolfé, suggesting improvements. I was put on the general policy committee. As we had no secretarial staff we prepared membership forms in my office at the National Library. This was complicated by the fact that our typist was not familiar with the concept of spacing, nor did she have much experience of typing in general. Membership money had not yet been collected and employment centres were yet to be started. One evening Sylvia came into our bedroom obviously not in a good mood, complaining that the Society did not even have a bank account. "It is ridiculous" she said, "who has ever heard of a voluntary society without a bank account!" The Finance Committee had in fact got as far as thinking the Society needed one.

Students from the University College of Addis Ababa had by then almost completed a survey counting the number of children and disabled inmates, their relatives and the occupations of the people at the camp. Children under five were beginning to drink milk supplied through UNICEF and the training and rehabilitation programme was to start the following week. An experienced gardener sent by the United States Point 4 Education Programme was to train the able-bodied in gardening. Meanwhile fresh beggars were appearing in the streets. I realised that we had undertaken a thankless task, but felt that this was no excuse to do nothing. I was introduced to an Ethiopian proverb that says:" "Even those who fear nightmares go to bed to sleep."

The Social Service Society continued to function as a voluntary group of citizens. We pioneered a number of welfare projects, including the establishment of Addis Ababa's first organised playground, and a handicraft training programme for the rehabilitation of the beggars living at Kolfé. Sylvia helped institute sewing machine courses for women, who thus entered a domain in Ethiopia previously monopolised by men. The Society had European and Indian members, as well as a core of Ethiopians, several of whom were social workers. One of them was Dr Yohannis Welde-Gerima, who was educated in America and later taught Sociology at Addis Ababa University. He became the Society's Honorary Secretary.

Another of the Society's stalwarts was Lieutenant Girma Welde-Giyorgis, who, some four decades later, became no less than Ethiopia's Head of State. At presidential receptions thereafter he would call me over by my first name, "Rita, Rita", to the surprise of his ADC and other guests. Another member of the Society, and one with whom I shared an interest in gardening, was Dr Edith Lord, an American educational psychologist who lived with three adopted Ethiopian boys. She was President of the Ethiopian Professional Women's Association, a new venture for Ethiopia, in which professional women of many nationalities cooperated. A useful member of our Executive Committee was Dr Yohann Otto, an elderly German physician, who had settled in Addis Ababa. He had lived in China for most of his life and had become a Buddhist. His little garden was full of plants he had known in China, including many different kinds of bamboo.

The Social Service Society also organised a series of educational film programmes, the first of which was held at the beggars' home. By then the Society was much better organised; clothes had been provided, and the rehabilitation programme had started with training in carpet knotting and sewing for women and gardening for men. My particular job was to look into the employment question. There were good possibilities for gardeners and unskilled labour in newly-opened factories, but there was of course unemployed labour around Addis Ababa.

In February 1960, members were spurred into action again when asked to help organise a fund-rising dance and show. We prepared trifles with loops and canes as fishing rods for 25-cent-a-go in the "Fish pond." We prepared a lucky dip with 30 or so gifts collected from the shops, including a thermos flask, gramophone records, an alarm clock and various ghastly statuettes. For the raffle's main prizes we collected a steam iron and an electric heater. The venue was Gennet Hotel. Dancers volunteered by a Japanese and an Egyptian girl, and as well as students from East and West Africa, were much appreciated. So were various fund-raising gambits Sylvia had used in Woodford at similar events for Ethiopian causes. Foreign and Ethiopian women we knew donated interesting food, enough for a full house. Though the takings, some 3.000 Ethiopian dollars, were not spectacular, and preparations were time-consuming, the event spread awareness and appreciation of the Society's work.

By April 1960 the Executive Committee comprised Yohannis Wolde-Gerima as, Secretary, John Barnabas, Siniddu Gebru, Yeweynishet Beshahwered, two Indian members, H.A. Mehta and P.C., Mukherjee and myself as Chair. In May, at the Annual General Meeting, *Dejazmach* Zewdé was re-elected President and Sylvia became Vice-President.

Before the opening of the Conference of Independent African States in June of the same year there was a series of Government appointments, among them that of *Dejazmach* Zewdé, who was appointed Ambassador. The other members of the Oxford quartet of Ethiopian graduate nobles had already been so appointed. This deprived the Society of an active and supportive President, who had only just been elected for a second term of office. Sylvia replaced him as the Society's President.

In November I reported on limited progress in Kolfé. Men were successfully learning shoemaking and other leather work, and were beginning to learn carpentry, but the training of women in carpet knotting and weaving was not doing well. Oscar Barry, the new and energetic surgeon at the Sehay Hospital was proceeding well with a plan for an Orthopaedic Centre, training Kolfé Rehabilitation Centre inmates as carpenters to make crutches. He was able to extend the limbs of several disabled people who could not previously stretch them out. Our old driver told me, after Sylvia's death, that, on more than one occasion, she had asked him to stop the car, and had arranged to pick up a beggar whose limbs had set in distorted positions, sometimes due to lying for a long time in a cramped position because of polio, and had taken him to Dr. Barry who was able to break and re-set them. He invited the Director of the Polio Research fund who gave us tips about the technique of fund-raising, which we planned to apply to the Social Service Society.

On the eve of the Abortive *Coup d'État*, of December 1960 during a United Nations ECA Conference on women, which I attended, I was invited by USIS to address a meeting for interested women in Addis Ababa. I spoke about "Ways and Means of Social Action", which gave me the opportunity to make Social Service Society better known.

DOMESTIC LIFE

In the first few months after our arrival in Ethiopia our home had resembled a storehouse. Thirteen tea chests of *New Times and Ethiopia News* lay about waiting to go to the National Library archives. There were other tea chests containing Sylvia's papers and books, and Richard's books. There were also two large trunks that held linen, Romanian embroidered mats and my clothes and knickknacks. We therefore wanted first to get settled, deal with urgent problems and become acclimatised. The tea chests holding books and papers remained stacked until floor-to-ceiling shelves designed by a local German carpenter were erected in Sylvia's office. They were very deep and had sliding glass panels to keep out the dust.

In subsequent letters I tried to give my parents some idea of Sundays *chez Pankhurst:* "Today has been a perfect Sunday. Looking out of the window this morning

I saw that the sky was already deep blue and the sun was playing on the bark of the eucalyptus trees. It has been summer-dress weather all day. On Sunday mornings I refuse to cooperate in "higher activities". After hair-washing I attend to domestic matters, including house inspection. We have recently acquired a sort of mop at the end of a very long pole to cope with cobwebs in high corners." Having finally found one in town, I carried it home by holding it out of the car window. It protruded about a yard in front and behind, much to the entertainment of most pedestrians, but to the annoyance of one or two law-minded, probably Swedish, drivers, who, it would appear from their head-shakings as they drove by, thought we were driving not strictly according to the rule of the road.

Richard, meanwhile was preparing a lecture on South Africa and kept interrupting me with information about the difference between the Boer settlers, who came to a country with cheap labour, and the European settlers in America who found practically none, and had, therefore, to develop machinery and higher productivity. I interrupted him to persuade him to wash his hair, or to get approval or comment on my flower arrangement.

There was much to do to create something like a home. We needed tables and chairs, and cover for the cold tiled floors. We used woven Ethiopian carpets and fur rugs. At that time selling animal skins was not considered unacceptable. Richard was an expert bargainer and kept up a running bargaining dialogue with a fur-rug seller whose beat was outside the old Post Office, and whom we therefore met almost every day. He knew that Richard was buying a fair number of rugs, and Richard knew that there was no hurry; they both enjoyed bargaining, and battled away several days running for every rug. On one occasion soon after my arrival, Richard pointed to a rug and asked what it would cost. The reply was 160 Ethiopian dollars. Richard offered ten dollars. I remonstrated with him. "The poor man must have gone into the forest, hunted the monkey, skinned it, sewn it and now you offer him a pittance." Richard smiled and said nothing. The next day the man came all the way to our house gratefully to accept Richard's offer.

We acquired a puppy that grew into a large dog with a roving eye for the neighbourhood bitches. For some bizarre reason we named him Poodlepie. As we were not fenced in for some years, he was at that time able to disappear at will for days at a time, returning with a voracious appetite and a desire to sleep for a very long time. In 1959 he was badly bitten, perhaps by a competitor. As the wound began to swell and both the vets we knew about, were out of town, we took him to Dr Asrat Welde-Yes, then principal surgeon of the Princess Sehay Hospital, who kindly gave him a single injection. It was no doubt the first, and probably the last, animal patient he treated. Poodlepie recovered and soon resumed his profligate life.

Earlier that year, in January 1959, after two years of discussing the pros and cons, we had decided to do what was expected of us, namely to give the house staff a sheep for Ethiopian Christmas. Richard and Andreas mounted an expedition to the sheep market. He gave my parents a graphic description of what happened: "We were assailed by numerous vendors, but counter-attacked vigorously by way of bargaining. Prices fell from 15 Ethiopian dollars to seven without much difficulty, but it was hard going before we agreed on five. The winning sheep was then put in the back of our Volkswagen with Andreas, and *ba ba ba* he bleated all the way back, which was terrible. After each bleat one felt better for a moment as the tension of waiting for the next one temporarily passed; then tension built up for the next ear-splitter. (The animal had by now learnt that the best way was to stand at the back on two feet and place its head just behind one's ear). Then we arrived: Poodlepie was quite charmed with the bleat, and put his head on one side to hear it."

Our first house guest was our life-long Ethiopian artist friend, Afewerk Tekle, at the time when he was building his Gonder-style house, begun in mid-February 1959. He took up residence with us some two weeks later, with his maid which made me think of the old days in Europe when gentlemen travelled with their valet. or maid. The maid was, in the event, a considerable help with household tasks. Afewerk turned out to be a charming, helpful and generous guest. Sometimes in the evening the four of us would listen to a recorded opera from Afewerk's collection. He would be at the table, with drawings and plans for his house, Sylvia would be working at her desk, with the door open, Richard and I following the words from the libretto.

On our return from leave in September 1959 Afewerk welcomed us at the airport and, in the evening, gave us dinner in his by then completed new house. He had a special relationship with Sylvia, who was fond of him, particularly because she appreciated his artistic talent. She was the only one who dared criticise him. However, on one occasion when she felt he was charging too high prices for erecting his stained glass window and sculptures for the new Economic Commission for Africa building, she told him off, adding that he was not Picasso. He did not appear at our house for several weeks, though he continued to invite me to his studio for daily coffee and tea when we were both working at the National Library. At about this time Afewerk was learning fencing, and designed a coat of arms for the sleeve of his fencing outfit, and for his letter head, depicting a fencing sword and a painter's pallette. He liked to do things with a flourish.

RICHARD

Our second house guest was Percy Arnold, an Englishman who had come to assist the Ethiopian Royal Chronicles Department in preparing the Emperor's Autobiography, the production of which was dragging on from year to year. The work involved two distinctly separate tasks: (1) editing the first part of the Autobiography, which covered Hayle-Sillasé's life up to his arrival in Britain in 1936 and (2) continuing the story as a ghost writer, by composing an entirely new text, from the time of the Emperor's exile to his triumphant return, and beyond. In a letter to Rita's parents I described the circumstances surrounding Percy's quasi-secret assignment, and my own involvement, as follows:

"I was called by Ato Kebbede, the Head of the Chronicles Department, who asked me to undertake responsibility for the entire Autobiography, i.e. both the existing text and the continuation still unwritten. This I was unwilling to do, as I felt incapable of entering into the Emperor's mind and writing about events in the first person, as would have been needed in an Autobiography. I did not believe, moreover, that such a work could effectively be supervised by a committee, and was conscious of all the effort I had put into my own attempts to write an economic history of Ethiopia, and the time I would need to complete it.

"*Ato* Kebbede gracefully accepted my rejection of his request—but pressed me hard to find an alternative 'ghost'. When I again hesitated, he told me that he would send me to England with instructions to find an author; but on one condition—that the matter should remain entirely confidential, and should under no circumstances reach the press. When I inquired as to conditions of work, he declared that this would be disclosed later. I accordingly left for England in some trepidation as to what to do— but buoyed by the thought that I would at least have a few days' free to consult some references in the British Library.

"The constraint of not knowing the conditions of work, and Ato Kebbede's insistence on secrecy, made my search for a 'ghost' far from easy."

In due course I came up with two candidates. One was Percy Arnold, a semi-retired journalist who was the Secretary of the Commonwealth Writers' Association in London and had written a popular modern history of Cyprus. The other was John Rosselli, a *Manchester Guardian* journalist, the son of Carlo Rosselli, who, as we have seen in Chapter 1, was founder of the anti-fascist *Giustizia e Libertà* Movement, and had been murdered in France. Kebbede Mikaél chose the former candidate, who had the advantage of asking for a lower remuneration. Percy duly took on the work and stayed with us for the first few weeks.

We took Percy to a famous gorge some 50 km. from Addis Ababa off the road to Debre Birhan. We followed a negotiable track leading to a quarry where we left our car at the beginning of one of the grand canyons which Ethiopian rivers carve into the rocks. It was a colossal rift, wide and cultivated on the shoulders. We walked along the ridge with a sheer drop on one side, looking down on the thatched roofs as though we were in an aeroplane. Andreas was with us, and acted as interpreter so successfully with one of the farmers, who was guarding his wheat stack against baboons, that he asked us into his house and gave us *wet* with delicious dark brown *injera*. Baboons—were a great pest in the area, eating up the grain and annoying the farmers, who hurl stones at them as they scamper down the cliffs. Afterwards we picnicked under a tree from where we had a splendid view.

I soon became aware that Percy's assignment was not a success, as he expected the Committee to do most of the research work, and submitted numerous historical questions for them to answer, whereas *they* expected *him* to find the answers, and provide them with the final text.

The poet and playwright Tsegaye Gebre-Medhin was another regular visitor at our house. He and I had long conversations about everything under the sun, though mainly about Ethiopian history and literature, all the while drinking glass after glass of *qutti*. This is a tea much appreciated by the farmers in Harer, who sold the precious beans as a cash crop, while at home drinking concoctions made from coffee leaves and husks.

Poet and playwright Tsegaye Gebre-Medhin as a young man, ca 1955

RITA

The only armchairs we could find when we first came, were heavy dark brown leather ones, more suitable for the office of a high-ranking government bureaucrat than for our humble home use. They remained indelibly associated in our minds with a visit one morning in 1963 of *Abba* Habte-Mariyam, a prominent cleric, to our friend Mengistu Lemma. The latter was staying with us while looking for a house on his return from India, where he had served as First Secretary in the Ethiopian Embassy—and was still in bed. At that time we had acquired a large and friendly Great Dane called Maximus—Maxie for short, imported from Kenya. As the good *Abba* had sunk peacefully into one of the armchairs, while waiting for Mengistu to rise, in strolled Maxie to greet him. The *Abba*, who had never seen a Great Dane before and was not particularly keen even on normal size dogs, took out his hand-cross and held it in front of him in self-defence. While Maxie contemplated the cross, our other dog Minnie, an equally friendly minuscule dachshund, wriggled under the cross and kissed the *Abba* on the nose. He never came again.

Maxie remained, however something of a local point of reference. The Abba Dina Police College at around this time moved to temporary premises in the nearby former pilot's compound. Richard was asked to give a course of lectures on Ethiopian history there. At the opening class one of the students, knowing that we lived somewhere in the neighbourhood, asked where we dwelt. Richard thereupon inquired if he knew where the big dog lived. On receiving an affirmative response, he modestly replied, "I live there too."

We did not often go out in the evenings, which suited us well. We were particularly glad that there was, for most of this time, a midnight curfew, as this gave us the excuse to leave parties at a reasonable time. We had discovered that classical music records could be purchased in Addis Ababa, and we became the happy possessors of all four Mozart horn concertos. They were often put on during meals and in the evenings, and I got used to them as background music, having at first protested strongly against this practice. I found that a full-time job, the organisation of the house, plus the writing of long weekly letters home kept me very busy.

Gradually I became absorbed in getting to know Ethiopia and the Ethiopians. To maintain minimum contact with the outside world, however, we listened regularly to the 9 p.m. BBC news, and subscribed to the *New Statesman.* Remaining aware of events in distant Europe became more and more difficult. We were soon bound up with Ethiopia, developing interests of a quite different nature from those pursued in England. Richard made occasional attempts to take me to the cinema, but I was not keen. There was too much of interest under our nose. Later, we would go to a restaurant, or meet enthusiasts for classical music sessions. After we had acquired our first Toyota we found that the car, with its Asian background, itself resolved the question where we should eat. It would simply take us to the Chinese Restaurant.

Now and again Richard and I relaxed at the cinema. One evening we went to see *East of Eden.* We penetrated into the National Theatre, the Addis Ababa equivalent of the Festival Hall. I was surprised by the elegance of the place. It was decorated in powder blue and dark strawberry colours. The seats were huge, I supposed, to fit the ample proportions of the upper class Ethiopian ladies. Richard was thoroughly bored, but I was, as usual, taken in by the film's sentimentality, and wept copiously towards the end. It must have been more than two months since either of us went back to the cinema, and I could very easily have gone longer before another visit.

There were four cinemas in the town. Whereas two were not recommended on account of their high insect population; the other two were acceptable. The cinemas drew avid audiences. Mengistu once told us that, at a film performance of *Macbeth*, he heard a woman, who thought she was well-informed, explain to her supposedly less well-informed friend in Amharic, what was happening on the screen. Though a cogent explanation, it bore no relationship whatsoever to Shakespeare's play.

The emergent Ethiopian theatre also had its problems. When Tsegaye Gebre-Medhin's Amharic translation of *Hamlet* was performed, the actor impersonating Iago created such an impressive villain, that an infuriated member of the audience felt impelled to throw a shoe at him.

One of the best films we saw was about Don Quixote, in colour, on a wide screen by an English or American director, with exquisite photography, each picture like a Spanish painting, splendid acting and real poetic truth. We saw it twice, and took Sylvia and Andreas the second time.

Andreas gradually became a part-time member of our household. On several occasions he came to lunch and helped me prune, weed and de-greenfly the roses. He was a most enthusiastic helper, and his conversation was delightful.

However, he was equally at home discussing serious matters. Sharing Richard's view that foreign "experts" on Ethiopia too often tended to pay insufficient attention to

Self-help in Ethiopia

By Dr. Richard Pankhurst and Endreas Eshete

In Ethiopia, as in many other parts of the world, the people have evolved traditional non-governmental methods of self-help which play an important rôle in the struggle of their daily life and are a source of strength to the family at times of birth, disease, marriage, and death. Though almost completely ignored by foreign writers on Ethiopian affairs, these institutions deserve close attention on account of their economic and social significance to contemporary Ethiopia, as well as on account of the possibilities they may afford to those who are planning the present renaissance. They reveal the people's capacity to organise for their own welfare while at the same time emphasising the importance of the Government insurance soon to be instituted. State Action and Voluntary Effort should not be regarded as rivals, but as friendly and co-operating services to the country and people, working together for the general good.

Before examining some of the more important institutions of self-help in present day Ethiopia, it may be useful to discuss the problem historically in the light of foreign experience. Historically, the common people have realized the interdependence of man, not by any scientific study of economics, political theory or personnel management, but through the actualities of their every day life and labour.

Friendly Societies were founded in England for example as early as the sixteenth century. According to

Lord Beveridge, an authority on all matters pertaining to socal security, they sprang from three " seeds ": (1) the desire for security when earning power is interrupted by sickness; (2) the desire to acquire a lump sum of money to spend; (3) the desire to meet the expenses of death, and to avoid a " pauper's funeral." The Ethiopian self-help organisations discussed in this article, as we shall see, are concerned, in part at least, with all three needs, though the most highly evolved societies are mainy concerned with the last two.

Beveridge, discussing English experience divides friendly societies into two categories: those which pay sickness benefit (a weekly sum instead of wages when they are interrupted) and those which do not. He argues that in either case the aid brought to the members of the society in time of want did not involve loss of dignity or undue interference in a man's private affairs. The sick man was happy not to feel overwhelmed with gratitude for services he could not repay, for he knew he had received them by right and not by charity: he had received them in recompense, that is to say for the contributions he had made in the past, and would continue to make in the future. Maintaining his sense of independence, he probably reacted by feeling a kind of missionary zeal to extend the member-

85. Richard Pankhurst and Endreas Eshete "Self-help in Ethiopa", *Ethiopia Observer*, Vol. II, No. 11, 1958

the country's traditional life, Andreas worked with him in studying indigenous self-help associations. This resulted in a joint article on the subject, which appeared in Ethiopia Observer in December 1958, and was notable for being the first scholarly publication, (under the earlier spelling of 'Endrias') of the future Professor Andreas Eshete.

Our cook, Askale, was meanwhile becoming an expert at various Romanian dishes. She had learnt to make first class *vinete* (roasted aubergine salad) from the excellent aubergines available in Addis Ababa, and could produce one of my favourite dishes comprising eggs, hard-boiled, sliced in half, re-filled with egg, onion and spices, and fried. We compromised between Richard's preference for any kind of *pasta* and my interest in salads. Orange juice replaced early morning tea brought to our bedroom.

We rose at about a quarter to eight to try to fit everything into the day. If I delayed, Richard would threaten me with a toothpaste spray. When in a kinder frame of mind he would try Mozart or Beethoven.

In August 1957 Richard passed his Ethiopian driving test. The first time he was examined he drove confidently through red traffic lights, and was whistled by a policeman. The examiner, Alemayyehu, who had been a fellow student of his in England, and had known him since then, was most apologetic for having to fail him. We were, however, happy to see that "cronyism" had not come into play.

Also in August, we were suffering from the absence of our cook, who was on leave. Richard and I resorted to Gorgonzola and Sylvia to Ryvita and honey. She ate very little, and it was difficult to find food that she liked. I discovered that the three of us had widely differing food preferences, and my attempts to introduce a more Romanian cuisine were sometimes resisted. Such was my experience with a quite creditable beetroot *borsch*. Richard: "Whatever is that disgusting stuff?" Sylvia was more polite and suffered a little of it meekly. Richard then had a second helping, assuring me that he did not like it.

For the benefit of my parents I drew up a table of food likes and dislikes. Needless to say we all liked our tea and coffee in different forms and at different times, agreeing only to a lemon tea after the evening meal. I drew up the following table:

Food Type	ESP	RKP	RJP
Aubergines, stuffed or salad	x	x	v
Peppers, salad	x	v	v
Tomatoes	xx	v	v
Cucumber, radishes, cabbage	x	x	v
Artichokes	v	x	v
Berbere (Eth. hot spice mix)	x	vv	x
Curry	x	vv	x
Chips	v	vv	v
Macaroni, other pasta	v	vv	x
Tongue	v	x	v
Brains	v	x	vv
Ham, bacon	x	v	v
Cheese, rice soufflés	v	x	v
Prunes	v	x	v
Cheese	x	v	v
Ice cream	x	vv	x
Rice pudding	v	x	x
Chocolate mousse	v	vv	vv
Orange Cream	v	v	v

v = like   x = dislike
vv = like very much   xx = cannot bear

Having meals tailored to the above table also had some less desirous effects. Richard put on weight, especially after our visit to London in 1959, but did not seem interested in dieting until, one day in October, he read that Colonel Nasser, a man of some size, weighed only 75 kg. Richard decided on the spot to achieve the same weight himself. After several months of a strict, self-imposed diet he succeeded. At the time I commented: "He has, I was surprised to find, a remarkable fund of will-power, perhaps influenced by his mother's ability, while in prison, to endure hunger strikes. In later years, when we were scouring the hills in search of man-made caves, he would go without food or drink, other than a grapefruit, all day long, whereas he proved resistant to going for a walk in the neighbourhood without an approved motive.

Jubilee Palace, ca 1958

After many enquiries we found a seamstress willing to come to the house. A sweet and diligent girl appeared at 8.45 one Saturday morning and promised to come on subsequent Saturdays. She was the recommended product of the Handicraft School and had made curtains for the Visitors' Palace being built for State visitors. It became known as the Jubilee Palace, so-called in reference to the 25th Anniversary in 1955 of the Emperor's Coronation. Communication with the seamstress was by demonstration, as she spoke no foreign languages and I, at that time at least, spoke no Ethiopian. She made blanket and sheet coverings for the ironing board, cushion covers for the sitting room sofa, and turned an old bathing robe of Richard's into squares for hand towels.

The Handicraft School taught woodwork, weaving, knotting rugs and carpets, as well as metalwork and, for women, sewing and embroidery. We ordered rugs, carpets, curtain material, cushions, ironing board and a ladder from the School. Its Director was an ebullient warm personality, Idris Suleiman. He was a very active man, and since he was put in charge of the School, it flourished. I learnt that he was a fine guitarist, and spoke enthusiastically about Sudanese music, to which many Ethiopians love to listen.

If life had appeared busy in our early days in the country it was nothing to the state of affairs that followed. We were becoming an odd job family, and were all three of us being saddled with tasks over and above our regular work. Sylvia was asked to produce a compilation of pictures illustrating Ethiopian buildings, old and new. This led to a special issue of *Ethiopia Observer,* Vol. IV, No. 5. Richard was in the last stages of correcting the English of the First Five-Year Plan, and was having his *History of Africa*

Idris Suleiman, Director of the Handicraft School, showing the Emperor around an exhibition
of items produced by the students, ca 1957

serialised in Amharic in *L'Éthiopie d'Aujourd'hui*, the best local newspaper, and I, as we
will see in the next chapter, was trying to cope with the Palace Exhibition.

Our domestic arrangements were gradually getting sorted out. The household staff
were installed in their own pink-washed, green-shuttered house. It was by no means a
masterpiece of architecture, but was good in comparison with what they were used
to, as it had wooden floors, a ceiling, as well as a roof, electric light and good washing
facilities. Not that we knew exactly who lived there. We discovered that our cook had
an assistant of her own, a buxom lassie whom I sometimes saw at our sink doing the
washing up. We wondered whether she, in turn, employed a domestic.

As it was rather cold indoors, in the first months of 1960, we constructed, with
the help of Yami, our driver-cum-handyman, a cane enclosure in which we lunched.
Situated behind the rock garden, it was open to the sky, and although it warmed us, it
required several fly swats to keep the flies from monopolising our food. The enclosed
sides protected us from the wind and from the inquisitive looks of passers-by. It was
here that, after Sylvia's death, we saw a Volkswagen slowly drive up the hill and heard
some of the opening shots of the attempted *Coup d'État* of December 1960.

At home we had, by this time, three Libraries: four book-shelves in Richard's
study containing his sociology, history and Africana library; two book-shelves in what

became Sylvia's bedroom, containing works on art, literature and music; and four book-shelves in Sylvia's study containing Ethiopian, Italian Fascist and anti-fascist, and Suffragette material.

I myself forgot my first birthday in Ethiopia, on 5 July 1957, until the middle of the afternoon, and so did Richard; he therefore took me off to town there and then and bought me a lovely pair of silver earrings representing a *tukul* (traditional, round thatched house). For Richard's birthday in December of the following year I enlisted Idris's help. He lent me two of his subordinates who bought from the market for the Handicraft School, and were familiar with the shops in the market selling handicrafts Conducted by them I ventured forth into the biggest emporium between Cairo and Johannesburg and bought Richard a walking stick with a carved ivory and ebony handle. Just as some children desire teddy bears, so this big child, it seems, had always desired a walking stick of this kind. It was difficult to persuade him not to take it when we went out for dinner. It accompanied us when we went to Ambo for the week-end.

Richard also had an interest in technical innovations. In 1959 he was much taken with a camera "the size of two fountain pens" that Idris brought back to Ethiopia from a trip abroad in March. Richard did not fail to buy one when we were in London the following summer. He was disappointed not to possess a wind-up Russian shaver, as will be seen later in this chapter. In August 1960 he (and I) gave up our very old watches and bought our first self-winding watch. We found it disconcerting not to have to wind our watches at night and enjoyed the amazing facility only to have to look at our wrists to find what day of the month we had reached.

The tinkling of the glass panels of our book-cases first alerted us to the earthquake that occurred within a year of Sylvia's death and the abortive *Coup d'État*. On the evening of 30 May 1961, as Richard and I were working, I heard rattling, and wondered whether it could have been an earthquake. Richard was not convinced until the next day when there was no denying it. The worst tremors were on the following evening and there was an aftershock the morning after that. Richard, observing it from the front lawn, saw the roof of our house moving up and down, almost like a slow motion dance. The building shook and plaster came down from the ceiling. Our familiar cracks grew wider and uglier, but the house itself withstood the shocks, though we could see the dining room from the library through the largest crack. It was fortunately only a Grade 4 earthquake on the Richter scale. For safety's sake, however, we spent the following two nights in Askale's house, thereby returning the hospitality her family received in our house during the abortive Coup. No modern buildings came down in the city, though walls cracked here and there, especially in the hot springs area near the Jubilee Palace and Giyon Hotel. The traditional houses were of course the safest.

Our house did not crumble any further within the next six months, and so we began slowly to shore it up again, getting going in earnest the following year.

While I was expecting a baby, in spring of 1962, Askale stole a march on me by producing a son, Seggayé. He arrived even before we could get her in the car to go to hospital. I went to see her, and found several efficient-looking old-style Ethiopian midwives boiling kettles over little charcoal stoves and looking as though they knew what they were doing. Askale had been in bed all week, getting fit and was feeling fine, while the baby was yelling heartily. It made me consider why I was proposing to travel thousands of miles to England for a purpose which was being achieved on our doorstep with efficient support. Seggayé remained a constant childhood companion of our son, Alula, who emerged in September.

We spent time during the year preparing for an addition to the family, dividing Sylvia's large room to make bedrooms for the baby and for a baby nurse, and trying to find room for the *Ethiopia Observer* and other papers which were beginning to engulf the house. In the central room and the "Baby wing" we lowered the plaster ceiling, and, mindful of possible earthquakes, replaced it with plasterboard.

As Ethiopian Airlines did not accept women after the seventh month of pregnancy I left for London in the second week of July to have the baby at St. Mary's Hospital, where my parents could be at hand. After some persuasion Alula was born on the evening of 27 September. Richard, who was anxious to get back to Addis Ababa in time for the beginning of classes, tried to visit us the next morning, but Hospital regulations allowed visiting hours only in the afternoons. No amount of pleading that my husband had to be in Addis Ababa for the beginning of term, could persuade the Sister in charge to bend the rules, so he had to miss the plane and travelled later, thus giving him the opportunity to see a little more of his son.

The hospital nurses gave me a few lessons in nursing and feeding, and my parents engaged a retired nurse to teach me more. Nurse Grant was very strict and frightening, pointing, whenever possible, to my incompetence. We came to London again in the summer of 1964 and, as I was by that time a more efficient mother, I had the courage to invite her to see the baby. As my luck would have it, the day before she came, Alula rolled off the couch on which he was playing and his face ended up the next day looking like a bruised apple. Nurse Grant had a "What can you expect" look on her face.

Back in Addis Ababa in mid-November, settling Alula in took much of my time, but once Beqqelech arrived, things became easier as she was a wonderful baby nurse— good-tempered and reliable—and stayed with us for many years.

SOCIAL LIFE

In 1957, our first year in Ethiopia, we were invited to two weddings: one was quite humble, the other, that of the Prime Minister's son, *Lij* Indalkachew Mekonnin, quite the reverse. The Reppi villa, their family's estate on the outskirts of Addis Ababa had a wide semi-circular verandah built out into the rock with a vast view across the valley to another range of wooded hills. For the wedding, we had to be at Reppi at 8:30 a.m. in morning dress for the latter part of the Church Ceremony—and were to appear for dinner in the evening—in evening dress. The ceremony, like all Ethiopian church services, had started long before we were expected, in the very early hours of the morning. We managed to get Richard into morning dress in time. The bride was dressed in white lace with a long train and numerous bridesmaids. I wore a white and grey striped dress—my daytime formal wear—and a white hat. The entire Diplomatic Corps—occasionally and aptly called "corpse"—was invited. We drank champagne and listened to a speech by the outgoing American Ambassador, Joseph Simonson, a devout Nixonite whose *pro forma* resignation was, to his own surprise, accepted.

We had to dress formally again for the evening reception at the couple's town residence. There were several thousand guests and long car queues formed outside their gate. We shook hands with the, by now wilting bride and groom. Eventually it was our turn to fetch our food from a buffet which presented the expected high quality Ethiopian and European delicacies. We sat down at round tables for six people while the band played and we danced. I wore my white piquet dress with red gloves. Richard's evening shirt was adorned with the pearl buttons my parents had given him. The evening continued for so long that we had to abandon the other wedding to which we had been invited, as we risked not finding our car in the throng of departing guests. We reached home, the three of us, at 2:30 a.m.

I was at this time reading Goncharov's *Oblomov*, and appreciated many similarities between the society the 19th century Russian novelist satirises, and the one in which we were then ourselves living.

In June 1957 we were invited to the British Embassy for the Queen's Birthday celebrations, and on the day we drove up through the glorious gardens of the huge Embassy estate. We chatted with the already mentioned Ambassador, Geoffrey Furlonge, and his wife, and with Sandy Curle (Colonel Alexander Curle), who had been Consul for so long that people thought he would never leave Ethiopia. He liked hunting boar and was also the President of the Ethiopian Horticultural Society, which was proudly affiliated to the Royal Horticultural Society in Britain. He sent us a pamphlet he had written on rose-growing in Ethiopia—a courteous and quite sweet gentleman. Then there was the lanky Ronald Peel, head of the British Information Office, and a great horseman; and the delightful Mansfields, Philip, the First Secretary, later Ambassador in Paris, and his wife Eleanor, who came to dinner with us the following evening. Invited guests at the Garden Party included various foreign doctors, teachers and traders—about 200 in all. Dark clothes were worn because of the Duke of Harer's death.

That same week we were invited to dinner by our good friends Major Aseffa Lemma and his energetic wife, Siniddu Gebru. He had acted as Sylvia's guide and interpreter in 1943-44, during her first visit to Ethiopia and was by this time Secretary to the Cabinet as well as Minister of Social Welfare, after having been in charge of the Electricity Authority. He was a Mexican-looking Ethiopian, with a moustache and a brisk, engaging personality. Educated in Switzerland, his wife was Ethiopia's No. 1 woman in public affairs. She was the Director of the Empress Menen Girls' School and introduced many innovations there, taking the girls for picnics on Mount Intoto, which was unheard of. She also made them perform plays she had written in Amharic to give them confidence to speak in public, in their own language.

Empress Menen School for Girls, which Siniddu Gebru directed 1949-1957

Social life was not interrupted during rainy seasons. In 1957, on one occasion we had a delicious Turkish-Ethiopian dinner at Idris's new house. He was a true Muslim in his hospitality and was much liked, especially by me, because he sang and played the guitar. On another occasion we attended a dinner given by the University College Ethnological Society, the first Ethiopian student scientific society, which had grown to a membership of 60 in five years with the encouragement of Professor Chojnacki, who was at that time the College's Librarian. I found him a man of immense charm, with a bird-like, dancing, funny side, and at the same time seriously trying to encourage the students to take a keener interest in their own culture.

On another occasion we invited Afewerk to dinner. He had been painting several canvasses in Harer, and lamented the lack of interest there in the city's historic buildings. We also saw Habte-ab, who had been annoying officials by overstaying his stay abroad in connection with a film being made for the country's first general elections.

RICHARD

In 1958 we were introduced to the renowned church scholar and wit, Alemayyehu Moges. He had learnt Ge'ez, Ethiopia's classical language, and *Qiné*, or traditional Ethiopian church poetry, in Ethiopia before leaving to study theology in Greece. Some of his schoolmates there had attempted to make fun at his expense by asking him whether it was true that his compatriots ate with their hands. Alemayyehu held his own, asking his questioners whether they "ate with their feet"?!

A prolific writer, Alemayyehu was a keen advocate of Ge'ez. A close friend, he used to invite us to his house, together with the occasional lonely visitor to Addis Ababa and one or two cronies, for the Ethiopian festivals of Christmas and Easter. It was a more traditionally Ethiopian experience than being invited by Ethiopians who had studied in the West. Alemayyehu served only traditionally Ethiopian food, his speciality being *annebabero* from his native Gojjam—Ethiopian cottage cheese sprinkled with *awazé* on an *injera* base. The drinks, too, were traditional: *tella,* berr, *tej,* honey wine, and, not for the faint-hearted—*areqi,* spirits.

On one occasion Rita agreed to accept a sip of *areqi.* This emboldened her to ask Alemayyehu to explain to us the differences between the competing Ethiopian doctrines of the nature of Christ. He launched into an elaborate and, as it seemed, perfectly comprehensible explanation. The next morning however the effects of the *areqi* had worn off—and with it, her understanding of that historic controversy.

Alemayyehu's marriage was something of a sensation, for at the end of the ceremony he left the church, bade farewell to his friends—and drove off, in his little Volkswagen, to the University College to give his lecture.

In April 1958 we were drawn in to the preparations for the arrival of Lena, Siyyum Beqqele's fiancée. I was approached by Siyyum, an Ethiopian graduate who had studied pharmacy in Scotland, and whom I scarcely knew when we were students in Britain. When we came to know him in Ethiopia we sometimes made fun of him because, as far as he was concerned, drugs made outside Britain were not to be trusted. While a student in Scotland, he had fallen in love with a young Scottish woman, who had a Diploma in Domestic Science. After a two-year engagement he persuaded her to come to Ethiopia and marry him. To reconcile her to the lack of Western amenities in Ethiopia he painted a highly negative picture of life in Addis Ababa, so that reality would not be as bad as she had been led to expect. He told her, for example, that there was no electricity or running water in the capital. A kind person, he thought she would be reassured to find on arrival that he had, in us, congenial British friends. Siyyum and Lena were duly married in July at the Municipality. Neither her parents, nor his, approved of the marriage. Siyyum's father would have nothing to do with the young couple, but an understanding uncle and aunt held a small party for them at their house. After registering their marriage at the British Embassy, the newly-weds gave a party at their flat.

Siyyum and Lena often came to see us, and we went with them on a number of forays outside Addis Ababa. Their interests, however, differed from Sylvia's and ours. They later had a baby, after which Lena left the country taking their child, Markos, with her.

RITA

Afewerk, meanwhile, was making a mark on the city's social life. I gave my parents advance notice of what was to become the gossip of the town the following week: he had not only had his car re-upholstered and re-painted in black and cream, but had also installed a gramophone. The instrument, which was fitted in the glove compartment, could play

Yilma Deréssa, Ethiopian Minister of Foreign Affairs, 1958-1960

whilst the car was in motion—even on Addis Ababa's rough roads. Whenever the vehicle hit a bump the gramophone's arm conveniently jumped back to the beginning of the record.

Always a trend-setter, in April 1958 he introduced Addis Ababa to the hoolah hoop—a large, ring-shaped slimming aid for rotating round the hips, which was then a craze in Europe. He became an expert with it. Later he had his tailor make a jacket without buttons, held together with magnets.

During the rainy season of 1958, although our cook was on leave, we had Yilma Déressa, the Ethiopian Foreign Minister, and his wife to dinner. She was the daughter of Dr Martin, also known as *Hakim* Werqneh. Yilma had been Ambassador to both the U.N. and the USRR. A product of LSE, he was considered an example of the new generation of modern, able young officials—one of the hopes of the country. Sylvia had met both of them before and thought highly of them.

Still in the mid-rainy season we also entertained at dinner *Dejazmach* Zewdé, then Minister of Public Works and Communications. This was because Sylvia was preparing an issue of the *Observer* on Transport. We not only enjoyed talking to him, but we plied him with questions which he answered most frankly. He was reputed to be the most efficient and keen of the younger Ministers. He was a great source of information on Ethiopian history and culture, did not stand on his dignity and had an unexpected humour.

One of his favourite stories was about a man who forgot his umbrella in a hotel room. On discovering his loss, he went back to the hotel only to learn that the room had been rented to a honeymoon couple. He knocked on the door but there was no reply. Hearing some sounds emerging from within he puts his ear to the key hole to hear the amorous lover declare: "Your hair is mine, your eyes are mine, your cheeks are mine, your lips are mine", whereupon the owner of the umbrella, increasingly frustrated by the seemingly unending inventory, knocks again more loudly, saying: "When you get to the umbrella, it is mine".

At this time we began to notice a change in the type of Soviet diplomats arriving in Addis Ababa. One day in late April we invited Sinitsin, a young Siberian from the Russian Embassy, to dinner. He was an interesting example of the new Russian generation— with a taste for, and knowledge of, jazz and English and American literature.

The change in the attitude of Soviet diplomats was also noticeable in that they freely accepted invitations to other embassies. In November 1958 one such diplomat attended a dinner party at the British Embassy given by Philip and Eleanor Mansfield. Their parties were always entertaining, because Eleanor had a habit of challenging her guests in a rather un-diplomatic manner. Besides us, the Mansfields had invited a South African; William Shack, the first African American anthropologist to devote himself to Ethiopian Studies; and a Second Secretary from the Russian Embassy. We began with a lively controversy about the novelist Boris Pasternak. The Russian diplomat said the author, like all famous Russian writers of the day, had become too rich, and announced that he (the diplomat) did not want to read *Dr Zivago*. Eleanor then suddenly said: "And what do you think of Stalin?" and added: "He was a dictator, wasn't he?" The poor diplomat gave the classic answer about the Great Leader having made mistakes in his old age, trusting Beria, etc. As the Russian was quite merry by this time and had a poor command of English, we were all in fits of laughter.

The more open attitude of Soviet diplomats foreshadowed a greater Russian interest in trade with Ethiopia, and no doubt more widely, with Africa. In May 1960 the Russians opened a trade fair of sizeable proportions in Addis Ababa. For 25 cents Ethiopians could see Russian cars and tractors, radios and TV sets, carpets, shoes, *samovars*, printing presses, spinning machines and the inevitable replica of the nose of the Sputnik—a singularly unimpressive piece of aluminium and wire. A high-ranking official from the Soviet Export Ministry made a long speech on Russian technical development beginning: "Your Imperial Majesty, as the great Lenin said", and pointing out that, only forty years earlier, Russia was at the same level of development as Ethiopia today (1960). Richard's eye was caught by a dry shaver that could be wound up like a clock. He thought it would be ideal for camping trips or during Sunday morning power cuts. However, the two shavers exhibited were defective, and none were scheduled to reach Addis Ababa for another two years. He found this deplorable, "in view of the speed with which one's beard grows."

I was beginning to look at the interior decoration of the Imperial palaces and the houses of the bourgeoisie. Both were furnished in ornate European style. One could tell a foreigner's house because it always contained local handicraft decorations, whereas Ethiopians seldom thought indigenous handicrafts worthy of display.

A new architectural development began to take shape on our doorstep in 1960. It was a so-called low-cost housing project, though it was "low-cost" only for the middle classes. At first, five houses were erected between our home and the Netherlands Embassy. They had well-designed, modern brick structures, each surrounded by its own garden. They had in-built cupboards and double-sink kitchens, under red roofs, with walls white-washed or painted in bright colours. They made a pleasant contribution to our neigbourhood area, though we lost our feeling of living in the countryside. We made friends with our new neighbours, with many of whom we shared common interests, especially when children began to arrive, and a sense of community developed.

Our new friends, who often gathered at their children's birthday parties, included Belay Kasayé, an accountant, and his wife Beyyena Kidané, who are still our neighbours, half a century later. Though their children could never come to such parties, because their parents, as Jehovah's Witnesses, rejected birthdays as "pagan" and refused to participate in them, we had a car pooling arrangement while their children and ours attended the Lycée primary school. Belay and Beyyena kept a cow and several bee hives, the honey from which we received from time to time, in gratitude for the pollen they took from our flowers. Their garden was sheltered from the wind, and well provided with cow manure. Attaching a trellis to one wall Belay also produced excellent grapes, which contrasted with the poor quality ones we grew in our wind-swept garden. On one occasion when they gave us a bunch of their delicious grapes we asked them where their vine had come from, and were amazed to hear that they originated from our garden. At another time we, and other neighbours, were called to help pull out their cow which had fallen into the compost pit.

Mekonnin Feqadu, a veterinarian, came to live nearby. He was attached to the Pasteur Institute in Addis Ababa, where he specialised in the study of rabies. His Danish wife, Lisbet, provided tasty dishes from her home country. Having invited us to dinner one evening, to our surprise she served minced raw meat in the Ethiopian style of *kitfo*. We remonstrated with Mekonnin for eating it at his table, in view of the danger of tape worm from raw meat, but he explained that tape worm eggs could not survive ten days in the refrigerator's ice compartment, where the meat had been kept. We ourselves became *kitfo* addicts, eating it even when we did not know whether it had been made safe according to Mekonnin's prescription. His family later left for America, where he became a distinguished physician. On a visit to Addis Ababa many decades later he told us that Lisbet had remarked that it was only in the United States that she became aware that she had married a black man.

Two university linguists likewise lived in our neighbourhood: Seyfu Mettaferiya, the author of a notable historical study of Ethiopian slave names; and Haylu Fulas, with whom Richard often travelled to Nairobi, in connection with the Ford Foundation-sponsored East African Language Survey. Other neighbours included my sometime secretary and best friend Asmeret Welde-Musé with whom I shared a love of gardening. I much regretted that, as an Eritrean, she decided to leave the country in the aftermath of the Ethio-Eritrean war; yet another keen gardener was Mesfin Fanta, a young official of the Marine Department, who had served in the Ethiopian Embassy in India. Though he left for the US a long time ago the Araucaria he planted in his garden, is now a majestic tree visible from far and near, constantly reminding us of a dear friend.

Another neighbour, Raggasa Gurmu, a pharmaceutical importer, was an equally keener. He took drastic action against our common enemies, the mousebirds, groups of which would descend on our gardens and devour every fruit within sight. The simple solution in his garden was to shoot them. Nearby was the house of Uno Winbladt, a forthright Swedish architect who, when asked what he did, would reply: "I work in shit", meaning that he was experimenting with dry latrines. He had an Israeli wife, as Richard surmised when he noticed that their young daughter was reading a Hebrew children's book. We saw Uno again in 1982 when we attended the 7th International Conference of Ethiopian Studies in Lund. He had invited us to his lake-side home and farm where he kept bees, using a modern electric honey spinning machine.

In early November, 1958 after the rains had ceased, Birhanu Tesemma and his wife Edith, who, were to be our hosts in Kenya, as we shall see in Chapter 6, came to dinner and gave us a graphic account of their ordeal in reaching Addis Ababa from Kenya by land at a time when it was still raining. In many places they had been obliged to build their own road through mud waist-deep. Luckily they had sent their children in advance by air. Birhanu called on us again later, in October 1961, to report on taking a troupe of Ethiopian dancers on a tour of China. They marvelled at a different world and suffered from the cold in Moscow and the heat in Beijing. In 1962 he was appointed Ambassador in Turkey.

We witnessed a double royal wedding in January 1960 of Seble and Sophie, two of Princess Tenañe's daughters. Until 10:30 p.m. on a Saturday we were under the illusion that our first entry on the scene would be on Sunday evening, at the party given by one of the husbands, but just as we were going to bed a telephone call came from Princess Tenañe's husband asking us to attend the service at Holy Trinity Church the following morning at 7:30 a.m. We had to rush to the other end of town, get Yami, our driver, out of bed, and bring him to sleep at our house so that he could be available at 7 a.m. the next morning to drive us to the church. The three of us had been looking forward to rising late, but consoled ourselves with the thought that the service itself would have started at 6 a.m., the usual hour for Ethiopian church services to begin. We managed to arrive in time without too much loss of temper, despite the fact that Richard had to wear morning dress, which he had simplified by wearing a soft collar. All the Imperial family and grandees attended. There was chanting, incense, brides in white, bridesmaids in flying saucer-like azure dresses. One of the bridegrooms, an officer in the Imperial Guard, wore a gala uniform. In keeping with the most binding form of Ethiopian Orthodox church weddings, crowns were placed on each head and velvet cloaks were wrapped round each couple. Some way behind us sat some American tourists who behaved in an usually loud manner.

An ADC then informed us that we were expected at the wedding breakfast at the Palace. It was an intimate and quick affair chiefly for ministers and relatives. The programme for the couples continued with a lunch at the Palace and an evening party to which we had been invited. This was expected to last at least till midnight. For the next few days there was a party every evening. Our next one was at Princess Tenañe's residence, where Richard had to go in black tie straight from his evening lecture. Unfortunately a torrential downpour had erupted in the afternoon. The guests were sent away with the request that they return at 9:30 p.m. It was a spectacular event. Having dug up her lovely roses, the Princess had prepared an enormous tent, fixed with hundreds of coloured lights, carpets, loudspeakers and delicious food. The best was duck à l'orange with a walnut and olive stuffing. No one minded having to wait for it.

Sylvia and Rita at an Ethiopian Airlines celebration, ca 1959

After over three years in Ethiopia, I had had my fill of lavish parties, but felt obliged to attend, as Sylvia felt a need to be present at such gatherings in order to be in contact with important people. I wrote to my parents: "This is the wedding season. We have just returned from a lunch—the usual tented affair. It was rather small and homely (i.e. only about 200 guests!). Tonight there will be one of those mammoth parties for the wedding of one of the Emperor's two grandsons by a previous marriage, to the daughter of Princess Tenañne's husband, also by a previous marriage. About 2,000 guests are invited. There are other parties next week. Last Sunday's was for the step-daughter of the Minister of Information: huge tent, small tables, Ethiopian Orchestra, buffet, cutting of wedding cake, champagne etc. There must have been about 1,000 people. One shudders to think of the cost, merely of food and drink, let alone bridesmaids' outfits, hiring of tables and chairs, orchestra, invitation with gold lettering etc." Subsequently, at the time of the Revolution (and Famine), the lavish life style of such earlier times was to be the subject of considerable critical television exposure.

A ceremony of a different kind awaited the return to Addis Ababa, in September 1960, of Abbebe Bekila, the first Ethiopian athlete to win an Olympic Marathon. He was in fact the No. 2 in the hierarchy of Ethiopian long-distance runners, the first having missed the Olympic Games held

Abbebe Bekila, first African athlete to win, barefoot, an Olympic Marathon, 15 September1960

in Rome in that year. The athletes trained by running down to Dukem—a distance of some 35 km.—and back up to Addis Ababa. On the day Abebe arrived I thought, judging by the masses on the Airport Road, that some foreign monarch was expected. From the Library I could hear the crowd roaring. Staff, who went to look, reported large crowds in the square below the Library. The mascot of the Imperial Guard, a real lion, preceded the crowds in his own truck; the hero, although still only a private, was accompanied by two generals all the way to the Palace, where he was decorated by the Emperor. This gave a great boost to the sport and one could thereafter already notice groups of youths running along the roads, later a familiar sight.

By 1961 I had become thoroughly disenchanted with the endless festivities of the wedding season which always followed immediately after the

Spontaneous crowds in the centre of Addis Ababa welcoming home the Marathon winner.

long period of the Lent fast. It was not unusual to endure three hours in a tent ending in the buffet, wedding cake and champagne. The general result was that one felt tired and sleepy for the rest of the day, the more so as we had become fond of the butter-laden Ethiopian dishes, which required considerable digestion. Young couples were expected to entertain on a lavish scale. At that time it meant a tent on metal scaffolding, neon-lit, with loudspeaker system and band, wedding cake, platform for dancing and the following drinks for a minimum of several hundred people; *tej* and *tella*, imported beer and whiskey, and finally, champagne. Bridesmaids and best men also required new clothes for the occasion. Parents and relatives bore the financial brunt, but I was appalled by this obligatory expenditure.

GARDENING

When we first arrived in Addis Ababa in 1956, our house had next to no garden. As we began to unearth the odd plant and add new ones, I found myself in a dilemma: whether to leave the first flowers *in situ*, or to cut one of the three or four rose blooms, our two daisies and our two irises to make a flower arrangement, thus following in my mother's footsteps. Spurred on by the ease with which plants could be encouraged to grow, our interest in gardening developed.

Many flowers rewarded our attention, and we also began a vegetable garden. However, cattle were still strolling in freely until we put up two rows of barbed wire to save us from having to chase away the cows that would walk calmly and infuriatingly all over our flower beds in search of fodder. On such occasions we found it most effective to march towards them, waving our hands in the air and singing the *Marseillaise* in French at the top of our voices. Surprised by the stirring, unfamiliar sound of the French national anthem, they would look up to identify the source of the attack, and, mooing, beat a retreat.

Richard and I became keen gardeners. After some extraordinarily wet weather everything in the garden began to bloom, especially the roses. We found a rash of marigolds—a legacy from a previous occupier, wild irises growing only four or five inches above ground, small chrysanthemum, nasturtiums and huge white daisies. The few cacti we plucked from the garden of Mrs Cramer, the wife of the afore-mentioned Lesley Cramer, did well. We also brought from the countryside a huge-leaved succulent with thorns which made its presence felt for a week. We planted it in a corner, to remind us that we were in Africa. Richard developed an interest in the lovely local aloes as well as other succulents, which he ordered from South Africa and Madagascar. Exotic cacti that reawakened his interest in such plants, were purchased from growers in Sicily, South Africa and Arizona. He attempted to grow cacti from seed—a complicated business requiring sterilization of the soil, keeping the seeds at a warm temperature under glass, watering once a week by standing the bowl in water until the soil soaked itself through, and then draining it, and, daily, almost hourly, examination by Richard. At long last there were some signs of sprouting, but few survived to adulthood.

In those days, when there were no stringent regulations about cross-border plant exchanges, we also obtained cuttings from my mother and brother, both of whom were keen gardeners.

I began to understand my mother's passion for her garden, wherever she lived. The earth and climate of Addis Ababa responded so easily to attention that we seldom came across foreign residents who remained indifferent to the possibilities their gardens offered them.

Our visits to the countryside often resulted in additions to the garden. We planted rows of a bulb with a fire-ball flower, rather like a mop of red hair, which peasant boys sold on the Ambo Road. I later identified it as *scadoxus* or *Haemanthus multiflorus*, the blood lily.

Within less than two years we were growing plenty of lettuces, good spinach, a few peas, onions, carrots, beetroot, tomatoes and cauliflower, as well as parsley. We reluctantly dismissed one gardener because many of the plants we bought were ruined. His successor was one worthy of the name. Having wondered for weeks how to coax him into the woods behind our house, the pasture ground of innumerable cattle and sheep, I saw him returning from the same fields with a bucket full of manure.

By March 1958 the garden was taking shape. One morning Richard and I sowed the seeds of six varieties of a rock plant he had obtained. So that we should identify them later, the librarian in me decreed that we should sow them in alphabetical order. We also put in the dwarf nasturtiums all round the lily and amaryllis bed. There was already an abundance of pelargoniums and irises at the back and a thick crop of lilies in the foreground.

In those early days in Ethiopia we were full of admiration for the Australian Eucalyptus trees that defined the landscape.

At first, we considered it a great misfortune when the eucalyptus in the pilots' compound bordering our garden were all mercilessly hewn down. (The pilots were at this time from Trans World Airlines. TWA was nurturing Ethiopian Airlines that soon became independent). The old eucalyptus trees lining our access road were cut down at the same time.

However, as we became more knowledgeable about the dire effects of such trees, we decided, reluctantly, to cut and uproot the ones remaining between us and the pilots' compound. This enabled us to grow indigenous trees and bushes in their stead. Our front lawn is a triangle coming to a point at the far end. This is where we planted three *zigba* (*Podocarpus falcatus*), formerly *gracilior*, i.e. "graceful." Two of these trees survive and are a pleasure to contemplate from our veranda. We planted several more *zigba* as time went on—most recently, because, in addition to their beauty, they grow fast, and we expected them to absorb the noise and fumes from the ring-road then under construction. We also planted an indigenous olive tree and the south-American pepper tree. Sylvia nevertheless, mourned the loss of the eucalyptus, and composed several poems about them. One such poem began as follows:

O lofty, lofty Eucalyptus tree
Bowing you dusky crests to every breeze
How upright in your serried ranks you stand
As did your forebears in th'Australian land

In January 1960, in her last letter to my parents, she wrote: "You would see great changes here as all the eucalyptus trees...have been cut down, but we are compensated by seeing the mountains and woods at some distance...[Outside our compound] They are now growing again very fast. Some of them are already 3 or 4 feet high."

At the suggestion of Professor Chojnacki, a prominent member, we joined the Horticultural Society of Ethiopia in December 1958. Throughout our life in Ethiopia we remained supporters of the Society. Having summoned up courage, we took our turn in inviting Society members to visit our garden. As time went on, the Society came largely into the hands of its Honorary Secretary, Elizabeth Asfaw. An Englishwoman married to Colonel Tegeññ Asfaw, an Ethiopian Imperial Bodyguard officer and Sandhurst graduate, she had an inexhaustible fund of energy and enthusiasm. Whenever she met a member, she would immediately accost him or her with a reminder of the Society's next meeting, flower show or open garden. Like other members, we benefited from seeing, and obtaining cuttings of their plants. Elizabeth, on joining the Economic Commission for Africa, later also organised expeditions into the countryside for the Wildlife Society of Ethiopia, thus contributing greatly to the enjoyment as well as, a little, to the scientific knowledge of Addis Ababa residents.

Stash Chojnacki gave generously of his time, teaching us much about gardening and freely giving us cuttings and plants from the various gardens he tended. For one reason or other he had to move residence three times. Undeterred, he each time created an attractive new garden from scratch.

We had built a shelf along our veranda and were sowing all manner of seeds and planting cuttings, including coleus and poinsettia. The rock garden was expanding, and Richard was planning a greenhouse in which to grow tomatoes and tropical plants. However, not all visitors were appreciative: one day we were visited by a little monkey whom we had caught sight of several times. We assumed he might have been someone's escaped pet. He was quite tame and friendly, ate bread and was prepared to play. We all (except Pitti, our cat) liked him—until he became interested in our flowering aloes. As soon as he saw one of us looking at one, he would snatch and break it off in a fit of jealousy. In view of his aggressive attitude to our garden he lost our sympathy. Fortunately for our flowers, he departed as unceremoniously as he had arrived.

I treasure our excitement when we watched the growth of a night-flowering cactus which Richard had ordered from Kenya. We had been watching this plant grow and grow for weeks until, one afternoon in February 1959, it looked ready to bloom. Knowing that it would do so only at night, we went out with a torch and were rewarded with the sight of a large, beautiful white flower, like a large chrysanthemum, though more stiff and waxy-looking, with a yellow crown inside. We heard the rain come down the following night and trembled for it, but the next morning it was still blooming, fading slowly the next evening. I marvelled how so unattractive a plant could produce such an elegant flower.

Andreas often joined us in gardening activities. Shortly after the end of the big rainy season we completed a programme of planting pelargonium cuttings all the way round our defences; we pruned, we moved things, and generally made the most of an important period when the ground was moist and ideal for planting.

One day in June 1960 Afewerk took us to what was certainly the most original and charming garden in Addis Ababa. It comprised an

Gardening with Andreas

intimate series of little well-mown lawns, bushes, creepers, trellises, trees, flowers—some tropical, some from Europe—cacti, succulents and much else. The house was in the middle of town, at the foot of "Corkscrew Hill", the road snaking up to the Old Palace Gates. Nowadays, his former garden is a public park used for wedding parties. It was the first of three gardens its owner had created, driven by the need to move house. He used for decorative purposes the strangest variety of containers, such as car battery boxes and old-fashioned carriage lamp holders from the garage next door—the existence of which one could not even suspect, because of the thick walls of trees, bushes and creepers shutting out the outside world. Sibhatu Gebre-Iyesus, the owner of this remarkable garden, was an official who had become disillusioned with government service and turned to business. He developed a keen interest in creating gardens, and this became his profession. Though he had up to then never been abroad he spoke fluent English, and knew the scientific names of innumerable plants.

On returning home we held an inquest on our own sprawling and meaningless mess of a garden, and attributed it to:

1. The eucalyptus trees, which Sylvia had at first refused to let us cut down because she was so fond of them, although all gardeners in Addis Ababa were agreed that they spelled death to any garden, having numerous water-consuming roots as well as leaves dripping acid on the soil.
2. The absence of a lawn-mower, to which instrument Richard had objected. on the ground that it encouraged unemployment
3. Our lackadaisical approach to manure
4. Our haphazard planting.

On a visit to our garden Sibhatu, who was rapidly becoming a good friend, admired our *coleus* and Richard's rock garden, though he missed our roses, which were not in bloom. His admiration encouraged us, and improvements gradually followed.

A great leap forward, in July 1960, was the eventual acquisition of a lawn mower. The following Saturday afternoon Richard and I—mainly Richard—gave the front "lawn" its first shave. On Sunday morning Habte-ab, who was innocently reading in the hall, was roped in, and, with Richard, dealt with the back "lawn." Richard and I did the remaining areas of grass on Sunday afternoon and felt wonderfully tired, with only a few blisters on our hands. I could not imagine my husband going for it every week, as my father did. I knew that once the new toy ceased to be new, it would become the gardener's chore. The gardener for his part did not see it in that way, and was amazed how quickly and thoroughly the machine worked on such a bumpy surface. I wondered whether, after a century, an English lawn would come into existence in our garden. A less enthusiastic reception for the mower came from Poodlepie. He sat in front of it, cocked one ear and refused to budge.

At the end of November of the following year Richard was beginning to recover from his mother's death, once again taking an interest in the cactus garden and complaining about Andrei: "That brother of yours, whose cactus arrived mouldy, can't he send us a decent cutting of it?"

Our next venture was building a hot house with plastic sheeting on a wooden frame. It extended our range, but not all memories associated with it were pleasant: on one occasion, after my Sunday hair wash, I visited it, but suddenly felt pains in my hair, which was in curlers. A wasp's nest unbeknown to any of us had developed in the hot house, and I could not knock off the fierce attackers, because they had made their way under the curlers.

In November 1962 I participated for the first time in the Horticultural Society's Flower Show, and won an award for a coleus plant in a pot. To my surprise, some people asked me for advice about their gardens!

THE EMPRESS'S FARM

Opposite the end of our bumpy drive began the Empress's farming estate. One day we thought we would drive there to see if we could improve our milk supply. In charge was an Italian, Athos Tagini. We drove into a dream-land of fresh-smelling paths with a series of flowers, palms, acacias, fuchsias as high as a tree, hedges a metre-high draped with pink pelargoniums, arum lilies which grew naturally and very well, petunias, a vast spreading bougainvillea and a great mass of honeysuckle, all possible kinds of roses, some dahlias, a vast array of cinerarias, delphiniums, "love in the mist", some not small grapefruit and orange trees, all sorts of blue and pink border flowers, carnations, poppies, hollyhocks and more. The Italian turned out to be a passionate gardener and gave us cuttings or bulbs which our gardener promptly planted. I wished my mother could have been with us. Tagini was, I discovered later, one of the mainstays of the Horticultural Society of Ethiopia and presented its Rose Cup to the Society. On one occasion it was awarded to me for a particularly beautiful red rose. The great gardener then showed us round the chicken and duck runs and the dairy farm, which was all neatly kept.

RICHARD

The visit to Tagini's farm fuelled my desire to keep geese. Rita managed to dissuade me as she had visions of these ferocious birds attacking cats and dogs and had heard that they were not averse to chasing people. We eventually compromised on ducks rather than the more usual chickens. Ducks did well in Ethiopia, laid more eggs than chickens, and, being taboo to Orthodox Ethiopian Christians, were less likely to disappear, whole or in egg-form. Rita was mainly interested in the duck manure for the garden. We decided, however, to wait until our boundaries were defined and fenced off.

RED SQUARE

Eventually I proceeded to make a moveable duck house out of one of the tea chests in which our books had been shipped from England. A spur was given to these activities by the fact that Rita saw a termite mound in the garden, and, in a moment of inspiration I proclaimed that, with water added, it would be caviare to the ducks. The duck house and frame for the run were duly enclosed with chicken wire but left open underneath, and I painted everything red, including, inadvertently, my clothes and hair. The duck compound became known as Red Square. The enterprise was not a success. We failed to persuade any of the birds to lay eggs, and, in spite of the taboo, one bird disappeared.

RITA

LITERARY WORK

On one occasion, in May 1957, we received by the same post Richard's book, *The Saint Simonians, Mill and Carlyle*, and my co-translation from French of René Maine's book, *Trafalgar: Napoleon's Waterloo*. We had an author's and translator's celebration.

I also began to contribute to the *Ethiopia Observer* which Sylvia and Richard were by then publishing. In July I started putting together for each issue a Report of Public Events. My first published essay was on the National Library (November 1957), and the second, following our honeymoon in Harer, on Arthur Rimbaud's connection with that city, in a special Harer issue. (March 1958).

Richard's articles in the Amharic press, translated from English, by our friend Hayle-ab Tedla, were meanwhile gaining in popularity. Richard also returned to his Ethiopian economic history which had been lying fallow owing to pressure of other work. In mid-August I was helping him with a short history of Africa for schools, which was then being mimeographed. I was interested particularly in the history of Egypt, with Mohamed Ali and the Khedive, and the struggle against the failing power of the Turks.

By the late 1950s Richard was ploughing on with the first volume of the Economic History, which he entitled *An Introduction to the Economic History of Ethiopia*. While we were on our first leave in Britain in 1959 he checked references and filled gaps—on health, on the political background etc—for the first volume, the bulk of which was nearing completion. He managed to obtain microfilms of some books that were not otherwise obtainable, and discussed final arrangements for publishing with Sidgwick and Jackson, who had published Sylvia's mammoth *Ethiopia: A Cultural History*. The *Introduction* was published in 1961 and caused the Emperor to send congratulations. Richard also reported for the London-based journal *West Africa* on conferences held in Addis Ababa. I noted with admiration that he had inherited his mother's a capacity to work on his own for hours and hours, even on Saturdays and Sundays. I certainly did not complain, as his absorption in his work freed me to tidy up the house and my person, and think about all the domestic matters in which my Addis Ababa family was totally disinterested, but nevertheless required attention.

In 1960 Richard began to write articles for various journals based on research he had done for chapters in his *Introduction*. For *Présence Africaine* he wrote on Ethiopian imports of fire-arms in the 19th century. He gave the *Journal of Transport History* a series of articles on the history of transport in Ethiopia which appeared in 1962.

The following year, in November, Richard was given an audience with the Emperor to present the finally published *Introduction*. When Richard informed him that a sequel was on its way, his Imperial Majesty commented: "So this is the father to the coming son."

STRUGGLING WITH AMHARIC

What with my job, organising public lectures, assisting with *Ethiopia Observer*, translating from the works of German travellers for Richard, running the house, tending the garden and, later, having children, I did not give enough attention to learning Amharic. After a month or so I had made only little progress, mainly by learning from the employees in our house and in the library. People told me that my pronunciation was OK, but of course, my vocabulary was pitifully inadequate. By contrast Richard, who had been taught the Amharic alphabet by Zewdé Gebre-Hiywet, a sometime *chargé d'affaires* of the Ethiopian Legation in England, knew many more words, but his pronunciation was poor, and the words I picked up from him came with his pronunciation. At first I had every intention to read the characters and to study in a more systematic way. The snag was that we got along so well without Amharic. Many shopkeepers were, or spoke, Italian, and virtually all western-educated Ethiopians knew English or French. At work many staff members were happy to try out their English on me.

After the first two months we gave up on Amharic evening classes at University College, as our Ethiopian teacher seemed to have little experience in teaching foreigners and neither of us was very diligent. We then tried to learn some Amharic from Stephen Wright, the English librarian who features in the next Chapter. He received us in his house, but we found him an idiosyncratic teacher, more attentive to his numerous and malodorous cats than to our Amharic studies. By this time I had more or less mastered the alphabet and could read like a second year kindergarten child. Richard was streaks ahead of me, being able to write (slowly), as well as read (hesitatingly).

After an interruption of some months in 1959, when we were on leave in England, we somewhat reluctantly resumed our study of the language. We found Wright too advanced and specialised for our needs, and therefore enrolled for weekly evening classes at the University College. The young student teacher had a more palatable approach. One evening, when we were in class, who should walk in but the Emperor on an inspection tour. He was amused to find us there, among a posse of missionaries, and listened with a broad smile as we read—luckily in chorus—a piece on Ethiopian law and justice. These lessons stopped because of some urgent work simplifying Richard's *History of Africa* which Point 4 was in the process of printing.

The disincentive to learn Amharic increased when I moved to University librarianship. Teaching at the University was in English and the book stock was therefore in that language, except for a small collection of locally published books in Amharic. Nevertheless, I deeply regret that I did not put more effort into acquiring a better command of Amharic. I could have done so more easily than Richard, who did not have the advantage of growing up speaking several languages, although he could read and speak a little Italian and French.

CHAPTER 4

The National Library of Ethiopia and the Palace Exhibition

RITA

THE NATIONAL LIBRARY

Soon after my arrival in Ethiopia, I began the process of finding employment. Sylvia had asked me whether I could work in a library, as that had been my experience in England. I replied I thought I could. I was duly assigned to the National Library of Ethiopia, which was administratively under the Ministry of Education. The Canadian Personnel Officer at the Ministry signed my contract, and told me to go and see the Director-General in the Ministry who was also the Director in charge of the National Library. I visited him in his hospital room where he was recovering from a spinal injury. This was Kebbede Mikaél, a much-admired poet, with whom I spoke briefly in French. There was at this time some speculation as to my role. The Emperor referred to me, in talking to Richard, as "your wife." Some people thought I was Richard's fiancée, others that I was Sylvia's secretary. This Sylvia chivalrously denied; "Miss Eldon is an Oxford M.A. and would certainly not be employed to do my shorthand, even supposing she knew it."

I went to work with some trepidation, not being a professional librarian. It was December 11, 1956, eleven days after touching down in Ethiopia, on returning from Shashemene.

The National Library, which was situated in a spacious garden, had been inaugurated by the Emperor on 5 May 1944, with a donation of books in English, French and Amharic, as well as 96 Ethiopic and 18 Amharic manuscripts. The institution also inherited some 15,000 volumes that had formed the nucleus of the Italian Government library, established during the Occupation for Italian state employees. This comprised a small collection of important books on Ethiopia, virtually all in Italian. In the intervening decade the Library had acquired almost 10,000 volumes in Amharic, English and French, mostly simplified texts in English for school children. (*L'Éthiopie d'Aujourd'hui* 15 Feb. 1957). It was not at first clear to me what the functions of the new library were to be.

The manuscripts were kept in a huge safe made in Sweden into which one walked through a heavy door well supplied with locks. There was only one key to the safe, which was kept in the pocket of the employee in charge of the Manuscript Room, in which the safe was located. I did not succeed in getting a duplicate of this key from Sweden as the safe's makers were no longer in business. It was my constant fear that something untoward might befall the attendant and that the key would be lost. Fortunately, it was still there six years later when I left the Library.

Over the years the Library also acquired a small collection of important books and journals on Ethiopia, as well as newspapers and magazines published in the country.

Also in the compound were the National Museum, and later, the Archaeology Department—where French archaeologists had their base and their library—a bindery, with an aged binder using equally antique tools, and a hut in the garden housing a few well-worn young children's books.

The National Museum, a small assemblage of uniforms of officials, costumes of the nobility and other court memorabilia, was housed on the floor above the Library.

The idea of combining the National Library and National Museum in one building and under one administration probably derived from the imperial treasuries of earlier emperors. Eye witnesses of Emperor Tewodros's capital at Meqdela, notably the Anglo-American journalist H.M.Stanley, have described the sheds containing the books Tewodros had collected for the church he intended to build, juxtaposed with hundreds of other objects.

PERSONALITIES

Many remarkable people were, in one way or another, connected with the National Library. To my delight, Afewerk Tekle, Richard's artist friend from student days, had been given a studio on the first floor—and I often had the privilege of being invited upstairs to join him for mid-morning coffee.

The National Library and the Archaeology Department attached to it, seem to have served as places to relegate intellectuals from families considered disloyal. One such scion was Gizaw Hayle-Mariyam Serabiyon, an impressive tower of a man. Gizaw's father, *Basha* Hayle-Mariyam had lived in France and Turkey, where he had obtained his Turkish title. Having supported *Lij* Iyasu in the struggle for the throne that accompanied the terminal illness of Emperor Menilek, Haile-Mariyam fell into disfavour. He sent his son to Switzerland for education. When Gizaw returned with fluent German and French he was not given a grand position in accordance with his expectations, but was attached to the Department as a translator from Ge'ez into Amharic, German and French.

My contract with the Ministry of Education was not accompanied by any detailed terms of reference, but, in their absence, I was able to devise some, in discussions with Hans Lockot, a dour librarian from Riga in Latvia, who had settled in Germany at the beginning of World War II and had come to Ethiopia at the end of hostilities. As he relates in his biography of the Emperor, *The Mission* (1989) when the Emperor visited the Library in 1951, he found Lockot there and had him employed to catalogue the foreign books inherited from the Italian Library. Lockot spent most of his time trying meticulously, and single-handedly, to catalogue these books. He was happier cataloguing than assisting readers. When one of the latter was introduced, or re-introduced, to him, he would click his heels and announce: "Lockot is my name", irrespective of how many times the reader had already met him. Lockot received me with somewhat formal courtesy. We worked smoothly, though not closely, throughout my time at the National Library.

After eventually leaving Ethiopia he produced two monumental, and indispensable, bibliographies: one of books and periodical articles on Ethiopia in German, and a second, completed after his death, by Professor Siegbert Uhlig, of such material in English.

Richard and I remember Lockot every year at Christmas. The reason is that, on a visit to Ethiopia when we were living in London in the early 1980s, we met an acquaintance who mentioned casually that Lockot had died. I was naturally shocked and immediately wrote a condolence letter to his wife, saying, perhaps exaggerating a little, that he had been a wonderful and supportive colleague. To our consternation, a very friendly letter came back from *him* from America, as, in fact, he had not died at all. The woman had mistaken him for another National Library librarian, Stephen Wright, who had indeed passed away. To our further surprise I received a parcel from the States containing a delicious fruit and pecan cake—from him. We liked it so much that, ever since, I have ordered one for us and also, when our children developed families, one for each of these, every Christmas.

At the Library, when I started working, the Director was the francophone Catholic and renowned playwright and poet, Kebbede Mikaél. He was more interested in his creative writing, which was highly regarded, than in the Library. His visits were therefore infrequent. He seldom answered letters and often forgot appointments. On one occasion I heard that he was in his car outside the Library, and dashed out in an attempt to discuss library matters with him, but he already had his foot on the accelerator.

Of the subsequent Directors in charge of the Library, I remember well the French-speaking *Blatténgéta* Sahle-Sedalu, a tall, venerable grey haired gentleman of distinction who had been Minister of Education before the War. I used to ask to see him every now and again, and we used to chat in French about current affairs, before I broached the question of the book budget, or some other Library matter. This Director was often helpful in finding a way through the bureaucracy to enable the library to make some particular purchase. At the time of his appointment I had hoped for a younger man, but consoled myself by the thought that the Director's Office was to be in the National Library, no longer at the Ministry of Education, and would therefore be more accessible.

Blatténgéta Sahle-Sedalu, Pre-War Minister of Education, Director of the National Library, ca 1958

A later Director, Tekle-Sadeq Mekuriya, who was appointed in May 1959, was a hardworking and patriotic historian and diplomat of a younger and far better educated generation. He was the author of a series of Amharic school textbooks on Ethiopian history, and later of three major studies of the country's most important recent emperors. He was particularly interested in the Archaeology Department and moved his office there, but nevertheless kept a closer eye on the Library than had his predecessors. The first time I was summoned to his office I was wearing a bright yellow overall. Almost his first words were: "That was the colour of Ahmed Grañ's flag"—a reference to the early 16th century Muslim conqueror of that name. I declined an offer to become Tekle-Sadeq's secretary, as I had no interest in such a position. Under his direction there was better access to the library budget, more interest in resolving perennial library problems, and less tolerance of the lackadaisical attitude that prevailed in the administration.

I had one disagreement with him about our lending policy. Modelling himself on the French Bibliothèque Nationale in Paris he wished us to stop borrowing facilities,

Abba Jerome Gebre-Medhin Gebre-Musyé, Curator of Manuscripts, National Library of Ethiopia, ca 1970

ignoring the fact that Addis Ababa, unlike the French capital, had no alternative libraries from which students could borrow books. He summoned a committee to study the matter, and, after it had deliberated, borrowing privileges were restored.

In the last week of December 1959 Tekle-Sadiq was appointed Consul-General in Jerusalem. This was a surprise, as he had held the job for only seven months. Although we had had a difference of opinion when he first arrived we had soon developed amicable relations. In later years he became a close personal friend of ours.

The new Director, *Qeññazmach* Zewdé Taddese, had earlier been Secretary to the late Prince Mekonnin, Duke of Harer. All we knew about him was that he spoke English fluently. Above him, Kebbede Mikaél was appointed Vice-Minister in the Emperor's Private Cabinet, also in charge of the Royal Chronicles and the National Library. This was the very man who had been responsible for the Library when I arrived. The new Director was a great contrast to his predecessor, being short and portly.

The most interesting person in the Library was *Abba* Jerome Gebre-Medhen Welde-Musié, a sprightly, bearded Eritrean who was the Keeper of the National Library's Manuscripts. He had become a secular Roman Catholic priest of the Ethiopian rite, but later left the priesthood. Bearing in mind that his name was little known in Ethiopia, he sometimes spoke of himself as *Abba* Joro—or *Abba* "Ear"—*Joro* being a pun on Jerome. A kind and learned man, he was an inexhaustible source of information on all things Ethiopian, especially matters of Ethiopian history and folklore, flora and fauna. In his time he had been an informant to the French anthropologist Michel Leiris. A succession of other European scholars and travellers acknowledged their debt to the *Abba* in their books. He was excellent company and we undertook several journeys with him, with the result that we became good friends. He was often to be found in the Dahab drinking house in Addis Ababa, below St George's Cathedral, reminiscing about former times with his French-educated Shewan crony, Araya Haylé. In his old age *Abba* eventually settled in France under the auspices of Professor Joseph Tubiana and his research centre in Nice.

Another denizen of the Library was Stephen Wright, who, as we have seen, had at one time tried to teach us Amharic. An eccentric English librarian he had taught himself Amharic while employed at the Bodleian Library in Oxford, and subsequently came to Ethiopia under the auspices of the British Council. He was seconded to the National Library to translate Amharic literature into English, and, as we have seen, produced the first English draft of the Emperor's autobiography, as well as some of the writings of Kebbede Mikaél. After a spell working for the British Council he returned to the National Library in October 1959 to work on Amharic books. It was unfortunate that he was an incurable pessimist, grumbling about everything, as he had considerable learning and there were many interesting sides to his character. His transliteration system for Amharic was later adopted by the Institute of Ethiopian Studies and he was responsible for beginning the catalogue of the Institute's Amharic collection, which was purchased from him. Unfortunately, his disparaging remarks about everybody he encountered were apt to give offence.

Among other personalities in some way attached to the National Library, was the amiable and indolent *Qegnazmach* Victor Babichev, a scion of a partly Russian émigré family dating back to Menilek's day. Though not often present, he held a post in the Administration and spoke good French.

Closely working with me, and much appreciated, were Jemaneh Allabsew, a cataloguer and mainstay of the technical processing work, who unfortunately left for a better job in March 1958, and Gebre-Nigus, a tall young assistant from Eritrea who was hard-working and always cheerful. He remained a steadfast worker in the library for many years. A young assistant by the name of Girma Mekonnin joined the staff in 1960. It soon became evident that he combined intelligence with a willingness to learn and work hard. When I noticed that his handwriting was almost illegible, I pointed out to him that it could be improved. He said that not much could be done about it as such was his fate—*iddil* in Amharic. Unhappy with this attitude, when in England, I bought him a special calligraphic pen and board, with instructions as to how to make his own writing more readable. Girma's did improve, though I was not able to ascertain whether my intervention had been responsible. In 1963 he left the National Library for the Library of the UCAA. He eventually became a successful University Librarian of Addis Ababa University, holding the post from 2002 to 2008.

VOLUNTEERS

Two library volunteers were of particular help. One was a small schoolboy called Endriyas Eshete. Influenced by the European forms of the name, which all began with an "A" he adopted the spelling "Andreas". He came with Jemaneh Allabsew, his librarian uncle, on Saturday mornings, and daily during school vacations, to help shelve books, file catalogue cards etc. Although he was already twelve or thirteen he looked younger. He was also of particular help when we received major book gifts from foreign embassies. His *forte*, however, was persuading borrowers to return overdue books. He developed a highly successful technique: he would ring up the delinquent individual and announce solemnly that the borrowed book was "wanted at the Palace" after which it would re-appear in double quick time.

At the end of the morning's work in the Library Rita would often invite Andreas home for lunch, after which we would all three go shopping, inspect exhibitions or visit friends. Sometimes, on Sundays, he would come for breakfast and would arrive while we were still asleep. We would be wakened by the sound of a Beethoven symphony or of our favourite Mozart Horn Concerto when he had switched on our record-player. One thing led to another, and before long he was a regular member, and interpreter, on any expeditions we undertook. In 1960 he won a *New York Herald Tribune* inter-school competition on Ethiopia and the Independent African States, the prize for which was a three month visit to the United States.

On his return, the United States Information Service, USIS, invited him to give an account of his American visit. Asked whether there was freedom of speech in the US, he boldly replied that people were free to speak, but that, in view of the narrow outlook of the media, they for the most part did not have freedom to think. He later joined us on an expedition to Mennagesha Forest, west of Addis Ababa, bubbling with comments of all kinds and told us that he hoped to have arranged a scholarship to Williams College, in the United States. He succeeded, and left Ethiopia in June 1962 when I was expecting our first child. Although Andreas had parents and relatives of his own—his father being a judge—he had also been an integral part of our life for almost six years. We did not treat him as a child, but rather as a companion and friend – as indeed, we did our son and daughter, who, as adolescents, once told us that we did not involve ourselves enough in playing games with them.

Andreas went on to an academic career in the US, and we neither saw him nor corresponded regularly with him for many years. When we did next see him on a visit to the US, not knowing what his tastes were, we brought him a tie. "A tie?", he exclaimed incredulously, "Many thanks. I haven't worn one for at least ten years!" It was strange to find that the self-same little boy, having taught at the Universities of Yale and Pennsylvania, married and had a son, became President of Addis Ababa University and thereby Richard's boss.

The other volunteer at the Library was one of the Emperor's granddaughters, *Immabét* Hirut Desta, also known in English as Princess Hirut. She worked with me in the Library, at first helping to put on the shelves the books which I had ordered five months earlier, and which arrived all at once, causing congestion. I had mentioned to her that, just at that critical moment, two out of our four staff had fallen ill, and she offered to help. She was my age, very obliging, unassuming and helpful. She came every afternoon cataloguing and stamping books with the utmost energy. Half way through the afternoon we used to go upstairs to have tea with Afewerk. She was a practising Ethiopian Orthodox Christian, who later decided to live in semi-retirement in a little house she built for herself in the religious centre of Lalibela, a settlement with many churches carved from the rock, in the centuries after the fall of the Aksumite Empire. A most conscientious worker, she set a much-needed example to the staff by her absolute

Blatténgéta Hiruy Welde-Sillasé with Lorenzo Ti'zaz, right, and Efrem Tewelde-Medhin, left, ca 1937

punctuality and keenness. During the two-week fast of the Assumption in August she drove up every day from Bishoftu, a resort some 50 km. south of the capital where the Emperor and his family were staying. I enjoyed talking with her about English literature and Ethiopian life. She had been to school in England. By her status she also helped to elevate the Library in the eyes of Ethiopian society. On one occasion while she was working in the Library, the Emperor made an impromptu visit (1 July 1957). Apparently because she had not told him of her work at the Library, she was afraid to show herself—and took refuge in my office. Unusually, the Emperor opened the office door and found her there to the amusement of his entourage and our staff. It was my suspicion that he had been informed of her presence in the Library. In any event, there were no untoward consequences. Half a century later, when she was living in London, and I was on my annual visit there, we reminisced about the good times we had had at the Library.

LIBRARY ORGANISATION

When I arrived, it was not fully clear what the functions of the library were supposed to be. Early on, Hans Lockot and I, in consultation with Stephen Wright and Stanislaw Chojnacki, the Librarian of the University College of Addis Ababa, agreed to divide the Library into two divisions, for each of which one of us would be responsible. The nucleus of a future National Library, named the Research Division: a reference library of scholarly volumes, comprising an important collection of books about Ethiopia— would be Lockot's responsibility; mine was to be the Public Division, which served, in effect, as a public reading and lending library comprising material at a more popular level. I soon realised that there was a great deal I could usefully do, even though my experience as a librarian had been limited to working at Chatham House.

My monthly salary of 750 Eth. dollars—exalted because I held an MA (from Oxford)—had to be collected from the Ministry of Education cashier's office. This was a crude procedure, whereby a group of employees, irrespective of rank, at least in the lower echelons, had to come to the counter on the appointed morning near the end of each Ethiopian month. At some point, one's name, together with one's salary was loudly called out. Because of my foreign status and MA, my salary was considerably higher than that of the guards and minor clerks milling around the counter. I found this monthly moment, when all eyes turned towards me, profoundly embarrassing.

The Public Division was used largely by students in search of somewhere with tables and chairs, and reasonable light, where they could do their homework. This they did in a large Reading Hall named after *Blatténgéta* Hiruy Welde-Sillasé, a prominent Ethiopian intellectual and sometime Foreign Minister, who had died in exile in Britain in 1938. The hall was furnished with long tables and decorated at one end with a mural, then recently painted, by Beatrice Playne, a British Council-sponsored artist. It depicted modern Ethiopia and, in front of it, on a plinth, stood a bust of the Emperor. Readers were permitted to borrow two books for up to a month, against a deposit of 10 Ethiopian dollars. The Public Division was open throughout the week and on Sunday afternoons. In 1956 it had registered 28,000 visits. Also in my domain were current periodicals, the small children's library and the bindery.

I discovered that all aspects of library work needed attention. Apart from a few Government newspapers that arrived regularly, all other reading material, whether periodical or monograph, looked dog-eared or simply dusty and out of date. There were no displays. The catalogue was full of errors of all kinds, many books were misclassified, incorrectly cited or misfiled. The poorly paid staff were almost totally untrained and unmotivated. There were no professional librarians among them. The readers were almost all school students. As a result of the absence of professionals my top priority was to give the existing staff at least some basic training. It was not possible, given this situation, to institute any kind of reference service.

The objectives of the Library were not at first well understood. In June 1958 I found myself at loggerheads with an important person. The occasion was the inauguration of the Members' Pavilion at the Addis Ababa Racing Club. One morning a huge uniformed officer breezed into the library. He began peremptorily ordering staff to take down a posse of well-bound books which he felt were needed to fill the empty shelves for the opening ceremony of the new Racing Club pavilion. Unimpressed by his bulk and not knowing that I was facing the Emperor's ADC, Colonel Mekonnin Deneqe, I told him that he could not have the books as they were not lending stock and furthermore he was not a member of the Library. He was taken by surprise and, in his hurry to fill the Racing Club shelves, adopted a more conciliatory tone—and I, too, thought better of confronting him, and let the books go on loan, by "special permission." He went off none too happy, with some 200 respectable-looking books, to populate the empty shelves of the Pavilion, where nobody was going to look at them anyway, because of the races. The following morning we faced the task of trying to retrieve the books. After much fraying of nerves, we managed to get them home undamaged and without loss. It had irritated me to find that the Library had been considered a perambulating exhibition of well-bound books, particularly at a time when exams were in progress and the Library was full. In later years I was never too comfortable when Mekonnin Deneqe was around. Together with many of the Government Ministers he was subsequently arrested toward the end of the abortive *Coup d'État* of December 1960, but escaped the fate of most of these, suffering only injuries from which he recovered. He lost weight and, with it, much of his imposing presence.

GETTING STARTED AND KEEPING GOING

The first phase of my work had to be cleaning, tidying and putting the catalogue in order. I soon discovered that, according to local thinking, nothing, in however poor a condition, could be discarded. The best that could be done was to send such items to the "store." I later found such rooms, piled high with materials discarded for one reason or another, to be a characteristic of libraries throughout the city and indeed the country. Librarians were held responsible for every single item in their care and were liable to be charged for any losses—unlike librarians in the UK where a certain percentage loss was deemed acceptable. In Ethiopia, in one small country library in the post-Revolution period I found one of the only two library rooms occupied by an extensive multiple copy collection of discarded Marxist literature.

Maintaining a decent standard of cleanliness and hygiene in the Library remained a challenge. Help was forthcoming whenever we heard that the Emperor was due, either on an announced visit, or on an "impromptu" one. The whole staff would then go into action. Ladders would be found to reach the top windows, cleaning materials appeared and it was possible on such occasions, not only to clean but even to paint the toilets.

We held our first inventory in September 1958. It revealed a total loss of 152 books out of an estimated 10,000 volumes in the Public Division. Most of the losses were of text books and simplified English readers. This was not a significant loss, but it was enough to worry the library administration. Regrettably we had to introduce a system of locking cupboards containing the coveted books, and obliging readers to fill in slips to obtain them. As the rate of loss did not increase, the matter was not raised again that year.

Another related innovation was annual spring cleaning in which the entire staff participated. All book-shelves were emptied, shelves sponged down, sprinkled with DDT (not repeated!) and waxed, floors scrubbed, windows and lamps washed, toilets scrubbed etc. We had not finished by one Saturday lunch time—so we all came back not only on Saturday afternoon, but also on Sunday morning, to finish the job. The administrator, Cherubel Beqenna, kindly turned up with three bottles of wine and rolls of bread which we devoured at 1:45 p.m. when the work had been completed.

With Rita's parents in London, when Richard and Rita were on leave, 1959

About a year after my arrival I developed a mild form of hepatitis and was out of action for some three weeks. Princess Hirut acted as my deputy, and she and Afewerk called home frequently, as patients are very often visited in this country—it is a tradition. I soon recovered sufficiently to drop into the Library for an hour or so where I was joyously received.

In 1959, as newly ordered books began to flood in, I became acutely aware of the shortage of space in which to house them. A Library extension was proposed, but plans for it moved slowly. In the meantime I asked for the princely sum of 1,000 Ethiopian dollars to increase the shelving in the Reading Hall by building shelves above the Emperor's bust and between the high windows lining one side of the room.

In mid-June I suffered a disappointment: I had gone to the bank to push through a letter of credit for some Library binding equipment, and, when I got back, the Emperor was just leaving after an impromptu visit. As usual, none of the senior personnel from the Administration were there—only Cherubél, who could not be expected to speak up for the Library in front of the Emperor.

The Emperor visited the Library again in 1962 three years later, when he appeared as I was working at my desk. He asked about my Amharic. I managed to make appropriate noises in that language, and, when he asked about the library, I replied in French that it was advancing "petit à petit." He wanted to know why, but I could not go into any details at this point in the conversation. In any case, Hirut could have told him.

We went on leave for the first time in July 1959, staying with my parents. They organised a welcoming garden party on the lawn of their flat at Wadham Gardens, where friends from Richard's circle met friends from mine. Unbeknown to us at the time, several liaisons were formed at these and later parties which my father organised every time we made an appearance in England. Richard spent most of his time reading in the British Museum, later the British Library.

I was much touched, though unprepared, for the joyful reception from Library colleagues on our return. We were met by a large welcoming committee, which laid on a great feast the next evening. There were speeches and dancing. A sheep was roasted and locally made beer, red and white wine and coca cola were liberally supplied. Not all the Muslims present restricted their drinks to coca cola. We left that evening at 9 p.m. but the party went on into the small hours.

There had been both positive and negative developments in my absence. No one had bothered much about cleaning the selves, but the 1959 inventory had been completed and the long-awaited additional shelves were lining the space between the windows as well as above the Emperor's bust. The Hall looked much more like a library than it had done before. Andreas had managed to hold the fort as well as running the inventory. The Director had moved his office into the new small building housing the Archaeology Department. Afewerk was upstairs in a studio with a panoramic view of the town, and Lockot, after long years of service, had acquired an office of his own.

After the unexpected departure of Tekle-Sadiq in December 1959, the new Director, *Qeññazmach* Zewdé, had different ideas. He seemed determined to undo the work of his predecessor, instructing us to shut the newspaper room so that Lockot could gain space for his Division. However, all of us, including Lockot himself, agreed that a public service such as the newspaper room had to be kept open. During the following week a temporary *modus vivendi* was established: We moved the binder into a hut in the garden and Lockot's extension went into the former binding-room. Before long an improvement in relations with the Director took place, at which he showed some interest in the plans for the Library's expansion. I was able to raise with him a delicate matter in a private talk about a member of staff who was regularly drunk. I understood that dismissal was a virtual impossibility, but there was the option of transferring a problem employee to another department. This we were able to achieve. An even more intractable problem was internecine war between employees, so that the interests of the library seemed not always to be the first consideration.

A new challenge then arose, for which a solution was, however, soon found. We discovered that the Library's books were enjoyed not only by students, but also by mice and rats. It was decided in conference to allocate a budget of three Ethiopian dollars a month for the upkeep of a cat. Richard thought this was the first such animal in Ethiopian Government service. He told us that, at the British Museum Library, they kept bitches against rats—bitches in preference to dogs because the latter had certain habits not beneficial to book shelves.

The 1960 inventory was completed in three weeks, though most of the staff were absent with Asian 'flu. There were heavier losses than usual, which was disappointing, after all the trouble it took to get the budget, the books, the cards etc. Added to this my star assistant applied for a better paid job at the University College. I had no chance of getting him the same, let alone a better salary at our Library.

Our reception at the Library, on returning from leave in Britain two years later in September 1961, was even more touching than the one described above. There was the usual party with, in addition, garlands on the table in the shape of R&R. Things had gone smoothly in my absence, except that the lights fused, revealing that there was an urgent need for re-wiring. There could be no service after dark until this work could be carried out.

The subsequent inventory and "spring" cleaning went without a hitch. By the end of the week the idea emerged that we should have a picnic on the following Sunday. A deputation (i.e. myself) was sent to the Minister to request the use of the Archaeology Department's Landrover. He refused, but authorised us to take 100 Ethiopian dollars for the trip—from Library members' cash deposits, assuring us that it would be refunded later. On Saturday another deputation, comprising our chief of ground-floor administration and another personage transferred to the Library from the Museum as a punishment for being frequently, if not permanently, drunk, were sent off to bargain for a bus to hold the thirteen of us. We appointed them because both carried on trading activities on the side, and would have been familiar with any tricks the bus-owners might have used in the negotiations.

Excitement mounted on Saturday morning after the return of the mission to procure the bus when suddenly a scuffle broke out. I turned round to find four staff members trying to prevent Cherubél and Gebre-Nigus punching each other in the face. The cause of the fight, probably initiated by my hard-working assistant, was the proposed intrusion into our picnic of Cherubél's friends and relations. It was by then 12 o'clock, and our hearts fell: a major split among two elders spelled the end of our picnic. We agreed however to meet at the Library on the following morning at 6.45. I was wondering about our two boxers when four people, including the newly arrived Girma Mekonnin, pushed Cherubél's hand out, and four others Gebre-Nigus's, thus obliging them to shake hands. Not satisfied that the tension between the protagonists had passed, they were ordered to kiss, which they did, whereupon all the other members of the staff kissed them both, and we all dispersed merrily.

We almost all arrived on time. Two invited guests came in our car: our driver, Yami, popular for lending a hand at the Library unplugging the sink, mending a fuse etc, and Andreas, considered part of the library family. Our destination was Qoqa. However, it was inconceivable to have a party without a roast sheep, and, as no one would sell us one *en route*, our car was accordingly sent to the Adama market, half an hour's drive away, where one was bought.

At Qoqa we met a friend in charge of the dam and power station who allowed us to camp in the orchard. At first there was some confusion as most of the staff had not been on a picnic before, and were not sure what to expect. A detachment was sent out to collect firewood, others departed to slaughter the sheep and gradually things were organised. It was a joyous occasion long remembered by those who participated.

ACQUISITIONS AND PRESENTATIONS

Other aspects of library work continued in parallel. Top priority was acquiring relevant books. Of the three methods of acquisition practised in libraries, the first—exchange, was not practicable as the Library did not produce any materials that could be offered in exchange. Purchasing, the second method, presented labyrinthine complexities. First of all we had to discover what the book budget was. The Director was privy to this information, as were, probably, the people sitting in administrative offices on the first floor, but the librarians were not in the know. Then we had to get permission to spend any part of the book budget. Obtaining foreign exchange for book purchases proved well nigh impossible. Three *pro forma* invoices were required from three agents. This immediately put second-hand Ethiopica out of reach. The process for purchasing books-in-print was so laborious and slow that little could be acquired in this manner. When, at the end of the financial year, we were told that some remaining funds were available, but had to be spent immediately, it was far too late to complete the formalities.

We were permitted to select books locally, but only from the Saba Bookshop, in which our Director apparently had an interest. Unfortunately most of the stock came from France and was in French, whereas the language of instruction in virtually all Ethiopian schools was English. However, Saba Bookshop kept an eye on current publications about Ethiopia, in English as well as French, and even, on occasion, offered their clients important out-of-print books.

SOLICITING FOREIGN EMBASSY AND OTHER GIFTS

The soliciting of gifts, the third method of acquisition, was an option that was energetically pursued. I discovered soon after I joined the Library that the Indian Embassy had, the year before my arrival, written to the Library offering a gift of 120 books, but had not received a reply. I managed, after a lot of trouble, to phone the Director of the Library, at that time Kebbede Mikaél, to reactivate the gift. The result was that at the end of February 1957 the Indian Ambassador, a huge, turbaned Sikh with a jocund voice, came to the Library to present a really fine collection of 173 books on Indian philosophy, religion, art, finance, education etc, as well as books about Gandhi, Nehru, Tagore and others. To receive them was Kebbede Mikaél. Of small build, with a barely audible voice, he was dressed impeccably in the French style. He and the Ambassador trotted out formalities and left us with the books, which were so good that I decided there and then that they should be exhibited, and arranged for this to be announced forthwith in the media. An additional Indian gift of fifty books followed some months later. Its presentation was again graced by the Ambassador.

Shortly after the second presentation of the Indian books we were informed that the Emperor would be coming that day to see them. The announcement caused great excitement at the Library all day—cleaning up, reappearance of staff that had not recently been seen, etc. The Indian Embassy provided some beautiful woven Indian cloth. We laid it on the tables under the books, and hung round the walls photos of the Emperor's visit to India and photos of Indian temples etc. He arrived in the late afternoon and was shown round by the Director, who successfully prevented anyone else from having access to him. There was no opportunity to ask the Emperor to see that certain urgent things were done for the Library. Feeling sad that the Director had not shown him my pride and joy—the newspaper and periodicals room, I turned to one kindly-looking gentleman and explained about it; he was most sympathetic. While the Emperor was looking at Afewerk's studio, and most notably his painting of the Queen of Sheba, I learned that I had been talking to the Emperor's representative in Eritrea. He was *Bitwedded* Andargachew Mesay, the husband of Princess Tenañ̃e, the Emperor's daughter and a friend of Sylvia's. So I collared him on the way out and asked him to follow up on my request for free copies of all Eritrean papers, which he promised to do. French-educated and a pre-war Ethiopian consul in Jibuti, he was reportedly known to be a cultivated man. The Emperor also inspected the bindery and said, when I told him the total number of our books (about 10,000 in my section and 40,000 in the other) *betam tinnish*, which even I understood as meaning "very few." I think he was pleased with his visit, though I felt frustrated with the Director. Since he was seldom in the library, he did not know what to show him.

Much energy was then devoted to phoning suitable cultural attachés and asking them to visit the Library to see the Indian Exhibition, in the hope that this would goad them into giving books from their respective countries. It spurred on a tall and eager young Yugoslav, who promised cooperation, and a reticent and diplomatic Japanese envoy, who made vague promises. In quest of foreign book gifts Richard and I also began visiting the information centres of the various foreign embassies. The biggest surprise was at the Soviet Information Centre. In its newspaper reading-room there was a huge portrait of Stalin, larger than that of the Emperor. Richard commented that things must have happened since we left Europe, and that Stalin was back! He had in fact died four years earlier, in 1953, and de-Stalinisation was well on its way.

I cajoled Russians, Dutchmen and Greeks to donate periodicals and books, and began negotiating with the Americans for a big gift of basic works. The Library was no longer a quiet, sleepy place, and it had many visitors. Some came to see Afewerk. I met many people in his studio: artists, philologists, the Speaker of Parliament among others. A Russian from the Embassy came to the Library with a splendid collection of pre-Revolutionary classics, and promised some children's books. A man at the British Embassy sent some appetizing British Council publications. Meanwhile *The Times* and the *New Statesman* began to arrive. Our Newspaper Reading Room was beginning to look quite attractive. The Americans had already given us a subscription to the *National Geographic* and continued to supply the *New York Times*. I handed them some booklists of my own, hoping that this might encourage them to make further gifts.

Foreign Embassies were asked for reference material, so that our stock of encyclopaedias, dictionaries and atlases rapidly improved. Anglophone countries were presented with categories of wanted material, as well as lists of desired titles. Periodicals and magazines began further to enliven the Periodicals Reading Room. By February 1957 we were acquiring free newspapers and books from India, Japan, the

Exhibition of books donated to the National Library by the United States Embassy, 1958

USA, and the USSR. Much was made of each presentation, with the encouragement of press coverage, and fierce competition arose among donors for the largest and most appropriate gifts. The American, British and Indian Embassies gave generously. My closest collaborators were the Americans. They sent us a large batch of rejects from their Addis Ababa library which we had re-bound—chiefly American classics in French translation. My contacts with the British Embassy were, however, slow. Whenever I asked for Mr Ronald Peel, the Second Secretary I was told that he was out. Sometimes the operator, in franker mood, would confess that he was "in the Paddock." There was good riding in the Embassy grounds and I found that the paddock was often the best place to find certain people.

Some ambassadors came uninvited to the Library, in preparation for donating books about their countries. The young Yugoslav who had earlier paid us a visit, persuaded his Embassy to donate sixty books and periodicals from his country, mainly about art. Most of them were in English and French, but some illustrated books on medieval art were in Serbo-Croat. After one month we were ready to display them in a special exhibition opened by the Yugoslav Ambassador in April 1957.

In the first week of 1958 the Soviet Ambassador presented a collection of almost 500 volumes, mainly on science and art, donated by the Lenin State Library.

Almost coinciding with the Russian donation, we received a major American book gift of 1300 titles. With Andreas's help during his school holidays we began to come to grips with these books. The photos, enlarged, made a good display in the entrance. Processing the large American collection took a long time.

On 9 February we received from the German Government a gift of a valuable 27-volume German encyclopaedia for the Research Division.

No sooner had we finished identifying books for our last list than we began a book list for the French Embassy who agreed to donate 100,000 francs worth of books, the list to be submitted within a month.

At the beginning of November 1958 Richard and I registered a small triumph. On his suggestion, I had written to the Emperor pointing out the inadequacy of the Library for a country which was to be the seat of the United Nations Economic Commission for Africa (ECA),

Andreas reading one of the books donated by the American Embassy, 1958

due to open in December. He asked me to make a list. We selected 500 titles on economics, politics and sociology which he approved, and were ordered forthwith through the Sudan Interior Mission bookshop. He decided that they would be his personal gift. Six months later they arrived and we spent a hectic few days checking, stamping and labelling before they could be exhibited. We also wrote to the Emperor later that month suggesting that he make a contribution to the initial book stock of the ECA Library. He liked the idea, and asked for a book list of appropriate titles, which we provided.

Some months later, in early May 1959, there arrived from Cairo a new Romanian Ambassador, Constantin Stänescu, to present his letters of credence. He came to our library with his assistant to inquire whether some publications they had sent from Romania had arrived, and what else would interest us. As the envoy's English was not too great I replied in French, showing them the Romanian literature on our shelves—works in translation (Caragiale, Creangă and Sylvia's translation of the poems of Eminescu). Stänescu said that of course he would be happy to send more books, but the snag was that nobody in Addis Ababa could read Romanian. I could not resist the temptation to tell them that I did. They were very pleased and left after much hand-shaking.

After a few days the assistant appeared saying that Mr. Stänescu was about to depart and had left a small gift for me; would I accompany him to the car to fetch it. It crossed my mind that he might wish to kidnap me, but I rejected the idea, fortunately, for he presented me with a brown paper parcel which emitted enticing gurgles. Inside I found a bottle of Romanian Riesling, one of țuică, the national brandy, and an embroidered Romanian blouse! I wrote a letter of thanks in Romanian.

In mid-June 1959 the Emperor visited the Library again, to see the book donation he had made, and all went well. It was not an official ceremony, and he asked me what progress had been made since his last visit, to which there was enough to reply.

In April 1960 it was the turn of the British to assist the library. A big donation of books from Britain descended on us, thanks to the efforts of Philip Mansfield, the dynamic First Secretary at the Embassy, so that yet another ceremony loomed. The presentation took place in December, shortly before the abortive *Coup d'État*, in the presence of the Crown Prince. He spoke on behalf of his father, who was out of the country, but, as we shall see, quickly returned.

A further British contribution came later from the British Council, which purchased Stephen Wright's unique personal Ethiopica library. It was divided into two parts: books about Ethiopia in foreign languages—an area in which the National Library was weak—were presented to the Library in May 1961, while books in Ethiopian languages, at that time mainly in Amharic—went to the newly established Institute of Ethiopian Studies Library. The National Library presentation was the occasion of a farewell party for Stephen Wright (who, having resigned, returned a few months later). The books were received by the then Director, Kebbede Mikaél, some of whose poems Stephen Wright had translated into English. One of these was read out at the ceremony by young Girma Mekonnin.

As a result of a gift from the British National Library for the Blind we introduced a service for the visually impaired. It proved popular.

Although many appropriate books were thus acquired, both for our school clientele and for the educated adults—who were becoming members of the Library in increasing numbers, but this method of acquiring stock made for uneven and haphazard growth. Further evidence of unplanned, though sometimes felicitous, acquisition, came when a Customs official wanted to know whether the Library would be interested in unclaimed books that had accumulated. Several days' sorting provided us with useful titles.

Asked, decades later, to survey higher education libraries in Ethiopia I found them to contain archaeological-like strata reflecting periods when particular donors were active, and others when the book stock stagnated, and few periodicals were received.

QUEST FOR A LAW OF DEPOSIT

I discovered in 1957 that Ethiopia possessed an embryonic "Law of Deposit." It took the form of a letter from the Ministry of the Pen, i.e. the Emperor's Secretariat, to the five printers at that time in existence in Addis Ababa, instructing them to deposit at the National Library free of charge, three copies of every book they printed. I do not think any of them complied automatically. We therefore prepared boxes for each printer, and instituted monthly visits to collect their publications. It was uphill work.

I first spoke to the Emperor about the need for a Law of Deposit while I was working on the Palace Exhibition described below. He agreed with a grin, but said he feared that I would regret it, as a librarian he had spoken to in the Cambridge University Library had complained of being flooded with material. I did not think that danger would arise in Ethiopia for some time. A draft proclamation was drawn up in 1959, with the help of his legal adviser, Sir Charles Mathew, but no action followed. I took the matter up again with *Lij* Indelkachew Mekonnin in April 1959 when he was Vice-Minister of Education. He agreed to put forward a Proclamation to publishers in Ethiopia making it compulsory for them to send to the National Library three copies of every book they published. Had this Proclamation been issued it would have been invaluable, particularly in Ethiopia where many books were privately printed, in small runs, often not reaching the bookshops. Later again, after the establishment of the Institute of Ethiopian Studies, librarians and scholars attached to it, especially Richard and the University College Librarian, Professor Chojnacki, tried repeatedly to extend the deposit requirement to the Institute Library, so that the national collections should not be housed only in one place, but to no avail. Such a law, which, to the distress of the Institute, applied only to the National Library, came into force after the Revolution, thanks to the efforts of Dr Aklilu Habté when he was Minister of Culture. A Proclamation gave the force of law to the requirement that printers deposit printed books and periodicals at the National Library.

STAFF DEVELOPMENT

Two initiatives in staff development were later launched in the Library. The first was in August 1958, by persuading Lockot, an expert cataloguer, to hold a short course teaching the elements of cataloguing to some of the Library staff. It was not a total success. Lockot's version of English was difficult enough for me to understand, let alone for some of the library assistants who had only a smattering of the language. Furthermore he would indulge in an esoteric sense of humour which tended to retard comprehension.

We then started a more coordinated elementary library training programme for assistants from all the capital's libraries. We were able to involve the best-qualified person in Addis Ababa, the Librarian of the newly established UN Economic Commission for Africa, Surjit Singh, and a few other people with library qualifications. Despite Singh's busy life setting up a Library and Documentation Centre to meet the needs of the Commission, he was willing to help, as were a few other professional librarians temporarily in the capital. The weekly classes were held at the National Library. Assistants from several libraries were initiated into the elements of cataloguing, classification and filing. Few of the trainees had completed secondary school, but a beginning was made, especially in demonstrating that librarianship was a profession.

I decided to obtain formal library qualifications, by becoming an Associate of the [British] Library Association (A.L.A.). In those days the Association of Assistant Librarians provided correspondence courses that led to examinations that could be taken at British Council offices. My one local tutor was Surjit Singh, the only librarian in Addis Ababa with modern professional qualifications and years of experience, who kindly agreed to supervise my work, though I saw little of him. A few other professional librarians temporarily in the capital also came on occasion to my rescue. I started the course in November 1959. It was not easy to acquire the necessary books, nor to work in isolation, and no one in those days had yet heard of e-mail. However, I was determined to have a try. By February 1960 my correspondence work was making good progress. I enjoyed the first course and learnt much that was directly applicable to the Ethiopian library situation. Bearing two children delayed my progress. However, I soon mastered the elements of librarianship even though the actual qualification, the ALA, had to wait until I sat the fourth and final exam in 1964. Almost thirty years later the Library Association awarded me an Honorary Fellowship of the Library Association (FLA) for my services to librarianship.

In early April 1959 I was asked by a UNESCO representative to organise the selection of Ethiopian candidates for a library science fellowship. It involved preparing a test and interviews. The short cataloguing test took place two weeks later and eight candidates were selected for interview by a committee comprising the UNESCO Director and Deputy in Ethiopia, Lockot, Chojnacki, Stephen Wright, and Mary Taddese then the UNESCO Representative. None of the three candidates from our library obtained the scholarship, but they were satisfied that the selection had been fair. Our recommendations were then passed on to the Scholarship Committee.

The next initiative took place in May and June 1959. We decided to organise a summer evening course in librarianship four times a week during July, August and September. Richard and I were then due for our first overseas leave, and I was therefore unable to participate. The course was intended for the various Ethiopians who worked as Assistant Librarians in schools and ministries, at the YMCA, the United States Information Service, the British Council and several other libraries in the town. Chojnacki was not going to be in Addis Ababa either, but Lockot, Stephen Wright and Mrs Martinson from USIS agreed to give their services voluntarily. The Director of the Library gave his approval for the course in early June. The preparations entailed a considerable amount of work and it was gratifying to find that the project was received with great interest by students and working people from all sorts of places.

The summer course had done well. The exams were due at the beginning of October, after my return from leave. On the first Sunday of that month it was my job to invigilate while 35 examinees sat busily writing their second hour's exam. It had taken a week to get papers set, dates fixed, and to arrange for the marking of papers. There followed the preparation of certificates for the students who passed, getting the prizes (books in Amharic) and obtaining the signature of the Director. We were pleased that 38 out of an enrolment of 63 finally took the exam and 21 passed with over 50%. We had a prize-giving ceremony with Director and Press, followed by local Vermouth plus peanuts. The course seemed to have been a great success, and we hoped to take it all a step forward the following summer.

In April 1960 we had a meeting of all the Addis Ababa librarians (Lockot, Chojnacki, Wright, Singh and I) to prepare the coming summer's evening course and to consider library science training in teacher training programmes. Whereas the summer course continued—Lockot, Wright and Singh agreeing to give one lecture each a week—some years passed before there was again a move to provide library training for future teachers.

In early July *Lij* Indelkachew came to inaugurate the second summer course. Fifteen of the twenty-two people who passed the first year's exam wished to continue, which was encouraging. However, as there were not enough newcomers for a second elementary course we restricted ourselves to teaching at the next level. I undertook to teach classification. Approaching the subject from a severely practical viewpoint I handed out book jackets to the students and asked them to classify the books from their introductions, tables of contents and blurbs. We then discussed the problems involved. I greatly enjoyed teaching, and indeed, believe I might have been happy as a full-time teacher. By the third year the summer course took place routinely, though it still required much preparation. The fourth was the last one with which I was involved.

In the autumn I started teaching classification to our own library staff twice a week in the early mornings.

In February 1961 several members of the staff thought we should start a Library Club, for more informal get-togethers of people working in Addis Ababa libraries. When Dorothy Obi arrived to become a librarian at ECA, she breathed life into the club. An American, she was married to a Nigerian economist and named her baby girl, Almaz, an Ethiopian name. By May 1961 the club was flourishing. Some twenty Ethiopians and five or six foreigners met in different libraries each month and discussed library problems. When it came to our turn at the National Library we served, in addition to *qollo*, the roasted local grains, *injera* sandwiches—an unheard of innovation.

PUBLIC LECTURES AND THE GROWTH OF AFRICAN CONSCIOUSNESS

Already in December 1956, as soon as it emerged where I would be working, Richard suggested that we start a public lecture programme. We were thinking in terms of regular lectures, with supporting book exhibitions in specific subjects. A programme of lectures had been started in Addis Ababa on a small scale already in the early 1930s, by Georges Pecoul, a French teacher of philosophy who was an advisor at the Ministry of Education. These were attended by a few prominent intellectuals, but came to an end when he died in 1934. After the Liberation of Ethiopia in 1941, very occasional lectures were given at the University College and regular ones at the YMCA and the USIS. We felt there was, however, room for lectures at a higher level, touching on contemporary issues. The Post-Liberation public lectures were launched in mid-October 1957. They were held in English at the National Library, and were open to one and all. From the beginning they attracted a wide range of listeners and proved most successful.

The first speaker was a South African sociology professor from Chicago, Leo Silberman, who had come to study the elections in Ethiopia and Sudan. It was quite

Postage stamp commemorating the First Conference of Independent African States, Accra, 1958,
designed by Afewerk Tekle

a feat of organisation finding the people we knew and spreading the news of the lectures. We went to the Itégé Hotel, where most of the returnee students were apt to congregate; we managed to trace many to their ministries or other offices. There was an audience of about seventy Ethiopians, mostly students, who asked pertinent questions. Our verdict on Silberman, however, was that he had been "a little too cautious."

The lecture series, as it progressed, provided the Ethiopian public with a hitherto almost unknown opportunity to hear—and question—ministers, scholars and other prominent figures of the day. By the end of the year the lectures were beginning to take shape. We aimed at a fortnightly event, each chaired by a different Ethiopian. Early on we found an Indian woman physicist to talk, topically, about sputniks. We tried next for a lecture on the thorny question of the Aims and Problems of Ethiopian Education.

As from 1958 the lectures were attracting considerable attention. For a talk on the penal code the room was full of listeners standing crowded together everywhere. The speaker, Justice Grabowski, was excellent. He had been Minister of Justice in Poland from 1936 to the outbreak of World War II, when he fled to Romania where he was interned. Ethiopians have a passion for things legal and listened with great attention. The new Penal Code, which came into force shortly afterwards, attempted to define punishable offences more clearly and was regarded as liberal—though both capital punishment and the lash were retained.

In February there was an entertaining lecture on the Ethiopian Church by a traditional scholar, Alemayyehu Moges, who later became a family friend. His talk was good, but his English left something to be desired. He talked, for example, of Christ being born "in a manager among cattles."

Another lecture billed for the end of that month was on "Popular Wisdom in Ethiopian Proverbs" to be given by Professor Soloduhin, a Russian geographer teaching at the UCAA. It was eventually cancelled because the would-be speaker, a trusting fellow, lent his lecture notes to a friend, who promptly lost them.

At the beginning of March 1958 the Prime Minister's son, *Lij* Indelkachew Mekonnin, though Vice-Minister of Education, chose to speak about Ethiopia's Foreign Policy on the occasion of the impending conference of Independent African States, convened in Accra, Ghana, the following month. Extracts of the speech, entitled "Ethiopia's Role in Africa and the World" were published in a special, locally printed supplement to *Ethiopia Observer*, with a cover by Afewerk. Richard was in the chair. This was the first of a series of lectures which highlighted growing Ethiopian interest in the African freedom movements. The lecture was so well received that it was given again the following week in Amharic, with *Lij* Amha Aberra Kasa, a fellow Oxford graduate, and grandson of *Ras* Kasa, in the chair.

One much appreciated evening was devoted to Shakespeare. Our American friend, the poet Lynn Martin, who was teaching secondary school English, talked about *Julius Caesar* and *Macbeth*.

Harry E. Shore, an English employee of the Addis Ababa Post Office who had studied Ethiopian philately, interested the audience with a talk on the history of Ethiopian postage stamps.

In early April Richard followed with a lecture on the historical background to the Ghana Conference. Despite his quiet voice, he was perfectly audible and knew how to make himself easily understood by the younger students who were less familiar with English.

A lecture by Dr Jan Szuldrzynski of the UCAA, on the Ethiopian Constitution was badly attended on account of that day's announcement of Cabinet changes. It was a long-established custom, which continues to this day, to visit new Government appointees in their homes to congratulate them, on which occasion they are expected to provide drinks for the callers.

Geoffrey Last, Richard's LSE friend, who had become an expert on Ethiopian geography, gave a lecture on that subject. He helped many of his students through school, and with his extended family, decamped annually for the long vacation to the wilder shores of Lake Langano, in the Rift Valley.

In the third week of May 1958 there was a crowded audience of about 150 for Abbebe Retta, Minister of Commerce, who gave a report on the Ghana Conference. A man much respected in Ethiopia, with a sophisticated, scholarly turn of mind, he had studied in Scotland before the war, and had written in Sylvia's *NT&EN*. Owing to the unavoidable absence at the last minute of the proposed Chair—another delegate—I took the Chair myself. As usual there was a crop of penetrating questions. Abbebe rose excellently to the occasion and altogether the evening was a great success.

Professor Wolf Leslau of the University of California, Los Angeles, authority on the
Semitic languages of Ethiopia, ca 1985

Professor Wolf Leslau, the prolific Semitist at the University of California at
Los Angeles—and compiler of several dictionaries of Ethiopian languages—gave an
impressive talk on his work. He was greeted by several Ethiopian academics whom he
had launched on their careers.

Returning from a field expedition, the French archaeologist, Henri de Contenson,
reported, in French, on the latest discoveries at Aksum. I tried to act as interpreter, but
much of the regular audience, fearing that the lecture would be given in French, stayed away.

Another archaeologist, L.P. Kirwan, a British specialist in medieval Sudan, spoke
about recent finds in Christian Nubia.

In August Lynn Martin gave a second lecture on modern English poetry. It was
difficult to understand, especially by the Ethiopian youths in the audience. As a result,
the hall was not unlike a railway station, with a constant coming and going of people,
who either could not stand another minute of it, or had recovered enough to come in
for a second round.

More comprehensible, by all accounts, was a lecture by Sean Kelly on "The Here and Now of Jazz."

At the beginning of October 1958 we learned from the Kenya African leader, Tom Mboya, whom we had met in Nairobi two months earlier, that he was visiting Addis Ababa. We immediately invited him to address a meeting about the political situation in his country. Bereket-ab Habte-Sillasé, an Ethiopian lawyer who had studied in England, was in the chair. I had borrowed loudspeaker equipment from the US Information Service so that the speaker was plainly audible, even in the entrance hall. Mboya made a great impression on the young people because of his firm, calm voice and his humanitarian and un-embittered attitude. The meeting was scheduled to start at 7pm, and the hall was packed twenty minutes before that. We finished at 9.30pm, and then had dinner at home with Bereket-ab, Miliyon Neqneq of the Ministry of Education and Befeqadu Taddese from the Ethiopian Ministry of Foreign Affairs.

Later in October we had an excellent lecture from *Dejazmach* Zewdé Gebre-Sillasé. Then Mayor of Addis Ababa, he talked about plans and problems of the Municipality. One of the Quartet who had studied in Oxford, he had previously been Minister of Public Works, and had done a splendid job in a thorny position.

Some three weeks later, in November 1958 John Barnabas, an Indian welfare adviser who was, as we have seen, soon to assist in the launching of Ethiopia's Social Service Society, followed with a talk on ways of helping the rehabilitation of beggars. *Dejazmach* Zewdé, was in the chair.

Lectures continued to the very end of December when the Ethiopian delegates to the Accra Conference of Independent African Countries, made an enthusiastic report at the Library on their return. There was a record crowd.

The first lecture in 1959 was from a Russian ethnologist, Maria Rait, who gave an almost incomprehensible lecture on Ethiopian Studies in the USSR, in a thick Russian accent. Maria, who became a close friend of ours, later carried out ethnographic research in Ethiopia. We met her again in her own country and at several later International Conferences of Ethiopian Studies, which she attended with patriotic enthusiasm. She was to emerge as the doyenne of Soviet Ethiopicists.

Tom Mboya gave a second lecture in early January 1959, at which there was a record attendance of 670, a large number of whom stood in the entrance-hall and on the outside steps where they could hear perfectly because of the loudspeaker. Mikaél Imru was in the chair. The subject was "Pan-Africa." Tom spoke in his usual quiet manner, with a mixture of common sense and fearless adhesion to democratic principles. No question could provoke from him the slightest hint of extremism. Many students from other parts of Africa attended and the audience was enthusiastic.

One week later, the lecture was by Dr Felix Moumie, a young French-educated surgeon and politician from Cameroon, President of the French Cameroons Nationalist Party, who had been sentenced to 57 years' imprisonment. He was expected to become Prime Minister when his country gained independence in 1960, but was assassinated, allegedly by the French secret service, later that year.

Further lectures by many other African leaders followed, notably by Oliver Tambo, Vice-President of the National Union of South Africa, then in exile, as well as speakers from South-West Africa, Ruanda-Urundi and other African territories struggling for independence. Commenting on this at the time I wrote: "You can't imagine the crowds that pressed to hear these speakers. We introduced a system of tickets to be collected in the afternoon, and arranged loud-speakers for overflow listeners in the corridors and outside the Library. Certainly more than 500 people turn up each time. This makes the point quite clearly that Ethiopia considers herself part and parcel of Africa."

In connection with a visit to Ethiopia by Marshal Tito in February 1959 Afewerk gave an exciting talk on artistic life in Zagreb, where he had been working on putting the finishing touches to his statue of *Ras* Mekonnin, the Emperor's father. Afewerk had met many Yugoslav sculptors and painters, and came away impressed by the vigour of their cultural life, and apparent absence of political constraints. He showed slides of his statue and of the works of artists he had met.

At about this time a young assistant of Tom Mboya's by the name of Oyange visited Addis Ababa and was roped in for a lecture. We also had him to tea one Saturday afternoon to meet African scholarship students then studying in Addis Ababa, and Ethiopian friends. Though Oyange was not as mature as Mboya, he had the same seriousness of purpose. The Library was full. It was evident from the crowds attending lectures on Africa, that Ethiopians, especially the young, had become fully aware that they were Africans. I wrote to my parents: "Let no one say that Ethiopians do not feel African." I should have qualified the remark by "Ethiopians of the younger generation".

Many older Ethiopians were supremely uninterested in such developments which took place, as they saw it, in a distant part of Africa still remembered for the slave trade. When Nkrumah left Addis Ababa, at the end of an official State Visit in June 1958, an elderly Ethiopian official asked me at the National Library, perhaps in jest, whether "the King of the Slaves" had departed.

Younger Ethiopians, many of them our friends, and the educated in general, were on the other hand imbued with very different ideas. A number who had studied abroad had joined, and played a leading role, in university Africa societies, and felt a strong sense of identity with colonial Africans struggling for independence. Not a few such Ethiopians recalled that Africans from other parts of the continent had displayed solidarity with their country during the Italian Fascist invasion, and felt an almost sacred duty to reciprocate by supporting freedom-fighters in other territories. It was in this atmosphere that, in 1959, unbeknown to the powers that be, an Africa Society was founded in Addis Ababa, as noted in Chapter 6.

In connection with Adwa Day, the national holiday commemorating the Battle, Professor Sven Rubenson, the Swedish historian of 19th century Ethiopia who had written a history of that period, gave a talk entitled "The Battle of Adwa," which probed into the background of the battle as revealed in diplomatic archives.

On the introduction of an "Africa Day" in Ethiopia, (15 April 1959) Sylvia gave her first and only lecture at the Library, speaking on "Africa today." She was an excellent speaker, as we knew she would be, frail and small though she now looked. As usual when the subject was Africa, the hall was full.

At the end of May 1959 the annual archaeological work at Aksum had come to an end and a lecture was arranged to report on results of the year's expedition. The team spoke on recent important finds: two statues one with braided hair African style, and an interesting large throne with bass-relief work. They were deposited in the National Museum.

Tekle-Sadiq Mekuriya, while in charge of the National Library in December 1959, gave a lecture in French on Aksumite civilization. It was perhaps pitched too low for the rather educated, mainly French audience.

This lecture was followed a week later by Professor Yuri Potekhin, of Moscow, on African Studies in the Soviet Union. His visit will be reported later in this chapter.

Statue excavated at Asbi-Dera, Tigray, 1953, deposited at the National Museum, Addis Ababa

One of the early post-war returnees from the US, Dr Mengesha Gebre-Hiywet, spoke on a subject which he considered relevant to Ethiopia: John Dewey's ideas on education.

Early in June 1960 there were feverish preparations in the city for the forthcoming Second Conference of Independent African States. Last minute efforts were made to improve the roads in the town centre; gaping holes in the tarmac and cracks in pavements were mended. Near the National Theatre some of the streets were dug up and drain pipes and paving stones littered the area. Our own stretch from the main road to our neighbourhood was miraculously repaired, it turned out because visitors might have been interested in the newly constructed low cost houses, the roofs of which were painted red for the occasion. We seized the opportunity to have the Ethiopian Foreign Minister, Yilma Déressa, give a lecture about the conference. Concentrating our attention more on the lectures than on the Conference, we succeeded, after strenuous efforts, to obtain money to raise the platform of our lecture pulpit so that the lecturer no longer appeared to be speaking from a pit. We had a lectern built, with light for the lecturer's notes, and had connections installed for sundry tape-recorders, microphones, etc. The audience was packed to a previously unheard of degree, and there were numerous interesting questions about the meaning of independence, Ethiopia's policy towards South Africa, etc.

With a view to expanding the lecture programme we established a small committee. In addition to the Secretary Ayyele Wubayyehu, appointed by the Library, it included Habte-ab, Afewerk, Hirut, and Belay Abbay, as well as Stephen Wright and me. We hoped to use our friends' contacts to persuade some of the more lofty personages to speak. However, like many committees, attendance proved poor: one member never attended, another came only once, another twice and the remainder gradually resigned. The Secretary soon lost interest altogether. I was not sorry, as the formality of a committee caused more trouble than it was worth. I found that contacts could just as easily be made without it.

We developed a series of lectures in honour of the Conference: a first evening dealt with Central and South Africa; and a second with East Africa, with Julius Nyerere, soon to be elected Tanganyika's first Prime-Minister, and Mbiyu Koinange. On the last evening, there was a report by delegates from already independent states. The first event was a moving speech by Oliver Tambo. Other speakers included a South-West African graduate of an American university, who looked strangely like an Ethiopian, and a nationalist from Ruanda-Urundi, who had studied in Rome. He spoke in French and I did (almost) simultaneous translation.

The next evening we had hoped to hear from countries whose independence was in the offing. Unfortunately Nyerere was ill, but Koinange managed to hold the audience by himself. The last occasion was to be a report from the delegates of the already Independent African countries. Unfortunately again, the Conference decided on a last-minute plenary session, so only two delegates—from Liberia and Libya—were able to come. Crowds of people pressed forward to hear these speakers. We arranged for loud-speakers for overflow listeners in the corridors and outside. Undoubtedly more than 500 people turned up each time.

In February 1961 I arranged a symposium on West African Economic development to be given at the Library by the West African delegates to the Conference. Alas, after accepting, they preferred to attend the numerous cocktail parties competing with our event. In the end I had to rush to the Sudanese Embassy party and haul out the necessary speakers to keep my important audience satisfied.

Later in 1961, Yohannis Welde-Gerima, Secretary of the Social Service Society, gave a lecture on Problems of Urbanisation, based on his experience in the Society, which was described in the previous chapter.

Also in that year, Bernhard Lindahl, a Swedish academic and long-time resident in Addis Ababa attached to the Swedish-supported University's Building College, gave a lecture on Architecture in Ethiopia.

Mbiyu Koinange came again from Nairobi with the Kenya African leader, Jomo Kenyatta, in November of the same year, and also to see his sons who were then at school in Ethiopia. We seized the opportunity and he obliged us with a lucid lecture on the situation in Kenya, held at the National Theatre. He was at that time standing for the Kenya Parliament and hoped to become a Minister. His jovial manner and knowledge of Ethiopian history made him very popular. The lecture was due to start a 6.30pm. At 5.15 when we arrived, the hall was filling rapidly and was full to overflowing well before 6pm. Several windows were broken by persons who could not be accommodated in the crowded hall.

The last lecture of the year was given by a Caribbean speaker, Victor Stafford Reid, on the emerging West Indies.

In January 1962, a visiting scholar, Constantin Grous, gave the only lecture on traditional Ethiopian music in the series. It was on the country's five-tone scale. There followed an interruption in the lecture series, caused by a break-down in the Library's electrical system, which had not been repaired by the time I left the Library later that year.

GROWING REPUTATION OF THE LIBRARY

The Library continued to be heavily used by school students. There were 65,000 recorded visits in 1960/61. The lending service, for which students did not have to pay a deposit, attracted over 1,000 registrations in the following year. More educated readers began to use the library as a result of the lecture programme and the influx of relevant books, though only some 200 remained active readers after paying a deposit.

A lending service of Braille books for the Blind came into operation in 1961 as a result of a gift of books from the British National Library for the Blind. These were much appreciated by sightless students.

Library lectures, many of which were delivered, as we have seen, by African political figures from Kenya and other African countries, proved popular, and brought many members of the public into the Library. These gatherings reflected, and helped to form, the then current and expanding Ethiopian interest in African affairs.

Gradually, as the collections of books on the social sciences began to provide reading material of interest, a small, but growing number of professional Ethiopian civil servants, doctors, lawyers etc joined the Library to borrow books. Alas, few of them took the loan periods seriously. Only *Dejazmach* Zewdé returned books on time—and gained my life-long admiration for being so considerate to his fellow readers.

Important visitors to Addis Ababa also made their way to the Library. In January and February 1959 two church leaders visited the Library. They were keen to see our early Ge'ez manuscripts. First came Cardinal Eugène Tisserand, a learned scholar who, in 1935-6 had published, together with Sylvain Grébaut, a two volume catalogue of Ethiopian Manuscripts in the Vatican Library. I described him at the time as a kind of sub-Pope, in vivid scarlet cloak and cap, of moiré silk. He was accompanied by two less eminent clerics, both clad in very bright purple, one of them the Papal Nuncio in Addis Ababa. When the three of them walked together, one's eyes tended to blur. I shook the Cardinal's hand, and the other library staff followed suit.

By contrast we were visited by an Archimandrite from Moscow. He was as rubicund and sparkling as the Cardinal had been learned and reserved. The Ethiopian who accompanied him translated my explanatory remarks into Greek, the only language the interpreter and the Archimandrite had in common. The latter then translated the Greek into Russian for his companion, a professor from a Theological College in Leningrad. My Russian, though adequate for understanding, was entirely absent when I wanted to speak it.

Professor Yuri Potekhin, of the Soviet Institute of African Studies, on a visit to Ethiopia sponsored by the Ethiopian National Library, 1959

In connection with the 1960 Independent African States Conference the National Library was expected to participate in an exhibition showing Ethiopia's progress in education, health etc so charts had to be planned, boards painted, artists (not of course Maestro Afewerk) enlisted to arrange it etc. We exhibited the 15th century illuminated manuscript of the Four Gospels—one of the finest MSS in the Library, as well as a copy of the earliest printed book in Ge'ez. Published in 1513 by Yohannes Potken it contained the Psalter, Canticles and some Old and New Testament hymns.

VISIT OF PROFESSOR YURI POTEKHIN

While Tekle-Sadiq was Director of the Library, he had invited the colourful Professor Yuri Potekhin, Director of the newly created Soviet Institute of African Studies in Moscow, to be the guest of the Library for one week. This was in return for a visit of Ethiopian librarians to Moscow some years earlier. After Christmas, in December 1959, the Soviet Cultural Attaché rang up to say that Potekhin was at the Airport—which showed us that, although the Russians could photograph all aspects of the moon, they were not as adept at giving us advance information about prospective visitors. A social anthropologist, specialising in Africa, Potekhin, as we have seen, duly gave a lecture on African Studies in the Soviet Union.

We showed him around Addis Ababa, and then on the Sunday, went in a big Landrover of the Archaeology Department, on the northern road over Intoto towards the Blue Nile and as far as the medieval monastery of Debre Libanos. It was a jolly 80 km. trip in which several members of the Library staff and Andreas participated. We were joined by the Cultural Attaché with a Russian biologist and a botanist in tow. They were dreary companions, but redeemed themselves by bringing some wine and caviare, which we consumed in a picnic lunch on the slopes of the ravine leading down to the bridge popularly ascribed to the Portuguese, though in fact constructed by Menilek's uncle, *Ras* Dargé. Naturally we sang Russian songs, especially after some circulation of whiskey—which terrified us non-drinkers lest our guests step incautiously over the edge and drop down some hundreds of feet. However there were no mishaps.

On the return journey Potekhin, a Communist of the old school, announced that he would like to see an Ethiopian "peasant." The vehicle was accordingly brought to a halt and the driver went off in the dark to meet the visitor's request. The "peasant" found, Professor Potekhin requested the interpreter, in a thick Russian accent, to tell the "peasant" "I am Social Anthropologist." That done, he asked the "peasant", how much of his crop he gave to his landlord. On hearing the fraction, he instructed the interpreter to enquire: "Is that just?" The "peasant" laughed!

There was later a farewell cocktail given for Potekhin by the Library and a caviare-and-vodka lunch at the Embassy for senior Library staff and other Ethiopians. Before his departure Potekhin invited Richard to the Congress of Orientalists, due to be held in Moscow in 1960. He suggested that, if Richard sent him an article on Ethiopian economic history it could be published in one of their learned periodicals, and that the fee would be enough to cover both our journeys to Moscow and our accommodation in university dormitories, but not our food. Richard duly wrote the article, but no more was heard until May 1960, when Potekhin wrote to inform us that the article had been accepted in *Problemi Vostoka* (Problems of the East) and would soon be published.

BUILDING OTHER LIBRARIES

My brief by now extended well beyond the National Library. One afternoon in early 1957 I was informed that the Emperor wished to see me to prepare a book list for the Library of the new Jubilee Palace. I had just settled down to this when I was suddenly summoned to the Palace. I went thinking it was in connection with the Exhibition mentioned below, but the Emperor, instead, asked me to help him draw up a list of books for the Library of Ethiopia's new post-war Parliament. Richard and I then went through dozens of catalogues and book reviews, making three piles of paper slips with titles, publisher, author and price: one for Parliament—mainly Constitutional, Economic, Historical and Legal—the second for the Jubilee Palace— the third for additions to our library. The Jubilee Palace library, intended for State guests, was allocated basic books on Religion, Ethics, Philosophy, Literature, the Arts, and Reference Books—a few of them in French—and all in hardback high quality bindings. This was a task we both enjoyed—the selection of distinguished authors and the dilemmas caused by the need to select only about £700 worth of books, at least for the Jubilee Library. We were not informed of any financial limits for the other library.

The book lists for the Jubilee and Parliament libraries were duly handed in. The Parliament one was immediately approved and the books were ordered directly from London. As soon as they arrived I discovered with concern, that I was expected to "see the Parliament Library in", i.e. prepare the room and get the necessary furniture, as well as classify and catalogue the books. I sent an SOS to my parents in London to send library furniture catalogues. The following month I went to the Parliament building in search of space for the library. I was met by a gentleman who was introduced as the *Wag Shum*, or Ruler of Wag, who bore the only hereditary title in Ethiopia. *Wag Shum* Wessen was President of the Chamber of Deputies, a short, French-speaking, lively man inhabiting a huge, well lit office which I greatly coveted for the library. His son Teferi Wessen and the latter's wife, Tabotu Welde-Mikaél, later became good friends of ours.

By October the books for the Parliament and Jubilee Libraries had arrived and I had a word with the Emperor about them. He had decided on a room in the Jubilee Palace and had ordered shelves to be made.

In my first year at the Library Richard's close friend, Mengistu Lemma, came to ask advice on setting up a small library for the Civil Aviation Department where he then worked. After we had discussed this I found that our little Fiat car had not turned up to take me home—there had been a break-down. Mengistu kindly took me home on his scooter. It was a bumpy ride all the way. We were observed by pedestrians *en route*, apparently causing a small sensation.

In November 1961 a call came from the Air Force, asking for help in setting up the library at their base in Bishoftu. It was a small library, about a couple of thousand volumes, intended for the cadets. In the course of several visits assisted by Girma Mekonnin, we catalogued the books and I gave the Lieutenant in charge some basic instruction. He introduced us to the starchy Swedish commandant of the base, who rendered official thanks for our cooperation. He paid for our petrol, and provided us with a free lunch at the Ras Hotel.

NEW NATIONAL LIBRARY PLANNED

In 1958 we began to work towards a new Library building. A young Norwegian architect at the Ministry of Works had been asked to look into such a project, and he and I met a number of times. Through Princess Hirut I also obtained an interview with the Minister of Public Works, *Ras* Mengesha Siyyum (her brother-in-law) to tell him what I believed we needed.

My colleague Lockot and I devised a preliminary plan: we would add a large storeroom to the existing Library and let the Scientific Division take over the whole existing building. We would build an entirely new Public Library several storeys high on the lower lawn, adding a larger historical and ethnological museum. We were ambitious, thinking in terms of a Reading Room to seat 500; a lecture hall-cum-theatre also for 500; plenty of store-rooms, wash-rooms, a large canteen, club-rooms, periodicals room, a microfilm viewing room, a room for listening to gramophone records, and a children's library. The architect was enthusiastic and the Director went along with our ideas. It was an era of construction in Addis Ababa, and we saw no reason why the Library should not also benefit.

In December of that year the UNESCO man kept a promise, given during a dinner, that he would visit the Library. I showed him the new plans and pleaded for scholarships for Ethiopians so that we could work towards a pool of professional librarians.

The new library did not materialise, but a building on the lower lawn was erected to house the National Archives, which, in 1967, merged with the National Library into a single department later known as the Ethiopian National Archives and Library Agency (NALA). It was placed under the Ministry of Culture and Sports.

CALL FROM THE EMPEROR AND THE PALACE EXHIBITION

In parallel with my work at the National Library I found myself involved in a quite different project. On the last Saturday of February 1957 our Director, Kebbede Mikaél, called me to say the Emperor wanted to see me. I hastened to the Ministry and we went together to the Palace. We were ushered into the Audience Waiting Room. Through the window, under the trees, groups of Ministers and aspirants were talking quietly, waiting to be seen. After about an hour in which I prepared what I wished to raise with the Emperor, should I be asked (need for a Law of Deposit, book-binding equipment, new linoleum for the Reading Room floor, a Library car and a bicycle for the messenger etc.) I was ushered in, past various Ministers, Chamberlains and the ADC, etc. I bowed at the door. We shook hands no doubt because I was there on business, not on a ceremonial occasion. It was a largish room in which the Emperor generally transacted business. He stood at the far end, in his usual beige jacket, smiling like a benevolent grandfather with many wrinkles on his forehead. In halting, but good French he told me he had been given many presents in the course of his visits abroad and wished to exhibit them for selected visitors in a hall in the palace. He wondered whether I could identify and display the various works of art: in short prepare an exhibition.

As I could not very well tell him that I lacked the qualifications and experience for the task, I merely asked to see the room and hoped he would consider giving some of the things to form part of the permanent museum which was housed in the National Library building. He said he had not yet decided what to give to the University College, what to keep in his own library, etc. He also promised to come to the Library the following afternoon unofficially to see the books donated (as we have seen above) by the Indian Embassy. He thought the Palace exhibition could be held in about three weeks. This seemed most unlikely. I foresaw that the main difficulty would be identifying the art objects as I presumed the donors would not have been obliging enough to enclose an exact description with every gift.

My second visit to the Emperor's proposed exhibition took place in the following week. I worked with his young private librarian, Seggayé, who was formerly at the National Library, and the Emperor's second valet, who was with him on his visits and helped identify unlabelled objects. As Seggayé and I were walking from a side gate towards the Palace, I heard the clanking of a chain behind me. I looked round and saw a lion, some ten yards behind us, ambling in our direction, the chain dangling on the ground behind him. A further ten yards behind the end of the chain, two men were also walking in our direction, deep in conversation. I assumed that one of these was the keeper of the animal. I whispered to Seggayé not to look round, but that a lion was not far behind us. "Oh, that old lion", he said, "don't worry about him." I must confess that I felt safer when we got inside the building and shut the door.

We were in the huge semi-basement underneath the Throne Room. There were windows on three sides and six heavy, square pillars supporting the ceiling. It seemed sensible to surround each of these with enclosed display cases, and this is what was done. I did not see the objects to be displayed until it came to arranging them, months later. Many of the finest were crafted in Japan, Burma and India, but there were also elaborate gifts from many other parts of the world, in gold, silver, precious stones and carved wood, many not identified. There was an assortment of gifts from Europe and the USA, including doctorate gowns, signed photographs and books.

Towards the end of March 1958 I was working almost daily at the Exhibition, shuttling to and from the Palace in an un-palatial Landrover, deciding about a carpet, having conferences with craftsmen, including an Italian carpenter who worked on the showcases and the repair of broken frames, mirrors, etc.

On 28 March I requested another interview with the Emperor, to obtain his approval of my plans for the Exhibition. This he granted, so that we were able to move forward, albeit slowly. I took the opportunity to ask for the two most important things the Library needed, namely a Law of Deposit, as mentioned earlier in this chapter, and the need to separate the Public Lending Division, and moving it to the centre of the town and re-naming it the Municipal Library of Addis Ababa. He agreed to this too— but it took a long time to be enacted.

At the interview there were also present the Minister of the Pen, *Sehafe-ti'izaz* Teferra-Werq, through whom I had applied for the interview, and the Emperor's two tiny Chihuahua dogs that yapped at my arrival and departure, but listened to our conversation without comment. This took place in mid-morning in the main Palace building, in the Emperor's book-lined study. Richard usually asked me ("usually" meant on both occasions when I was given an audience) what the Emperor was wearing, but I could not remember. His face interested me more, so that there was no time to observe other matters. I remembered vaguely that he was in uniform.

In April I was glad to have the help of the wife of the Japanese Chargé d'Affaires in identifying some of the Japanese gifts. She was one of the stars of the diplomatic world here, impeccably dressed in Parisian style, a trim figure, well made up, with pretty hats and a vivacious manner.

Work on the Exhibition continued steadily in June.

On my birthday (5 July 1957) I was still working on the American and European gifts. There were some interesting scrap albums made by supporters of Abyssinia as they called it, during the 1935-6 war; lovely Steuben glass, a gift from the US, an American Indian feather headdress, and hundreds of plaques, medals and scrolls. There was a layer of dust covering most of the objects.

Having arranged the exhibits in showcases it remained only to prepare the labelling. The idea of hanging signed photographs of world personalities in a frieze all round the wall had to be abandoned as it would have entailed too much plaster work. I was glad when my responsibilities for the exhibition came to an end.

In the first week of May 1958 I had a further private interview with the Emperor at the Palace Exhibition Hall which was nearing completion. I put to him my fear that the collection was unbalanced as many of the gifts he had received were dispersed, but he said that all that could be arranged when distinguished visitors from a particular country made their appearance. It was evident that he intended the room to have flexibility for future exhibits, and we made plans accordingly.

An unexpected development in the same month was a call from Mammo Widdneh, Chief of Press and Information, announcing a last minute decision to arrange an exhibition of Amharic and Ge'ez books at the Press and Information Ministry. We had a great rush of work preparing labels. This exhibition was duly opened by the Emperor shortly afterwards.

In June of the following year I saw the Palace Exhibition again. I was whisked off to the Palace as the Emperor was inspecting the Exhibition Hall, about which I had almost forgotten. He toured it with the Prime Minister and the Empress, who asked me how my Amharic was. It was quite an intimate affair, in which the Emperor kindly said he wanted to thank me for all I had done which, though time-consuming, was really not so very difficult.

LEAVING THE NATIONAL LIBRARY

By the beginning of 1961 I was finding my work at the National Library frustrating. Wages were low and increments virtually non-existent. The better employees were leaving to obtain higher salaries elsewhere and those who remained were increasingly demoralised. Furthermore, in the spring of 1962 I learned that, because there was a need to economise, the entire book budget for that year had been cut, while less essential budgets, such as for new furniture, were apparently untouched.

By this time I felt I had gained enough experience and confidence to look for a new and more challenging job. Just then, I was asked if I would be interested in a position in the UCAA Library, involving classification. I knew that I would find working in an academic atmosphere more congenial, and the prospect of learning from Stash Chojnacki, the highly educated College Librarian, appealed to me, and so I applied.

In March the UCAA students went on strike because of a new library regulation, introduced by Chojnacki, that only fourth year students were to have access to the library shelves, others having to fill in forms using the catalogue—a lengthier and more onerous process than merely picking the books off the shelves. Chojnacki's decision was based mainly on increasing book losses and the difficulty of patrolling an ever-growing number of students. He was much criticised by some members of staff, including, vociferously, by Harold Marcus, Richard's flamboyant American room-mate. Chojnacki, who was suffering from a gland infection, asked me to approach John Macfarlane, the then acting head of UCAA, and to explain the reasons for the change in library policy. It was my impression that the students were less resentful of the decision itself than of the authoritarian manner in which is was announced, without prior consultation or explanation—a Jesuit legacy. I explained this to Macfarlane, and also to Princess Hirut, who asked me for, and received, a report on this UCAA Library problem, no doubt for the Emperor. I took the opportunity to tell her of my application for the college position as she was on the University Board of Governors, and I did not want the matter to come to her as a surprise.

After some months, I had an interview with Macfarlane in the course of which he threw out the possibility of amalgamating the National Library and a projected University Library. I declared that the idea seemed to be probably premature. I was duly appointed Head of the College Library's Classification and Cataloguing Department, with a hypothetical starting date of September 1962, the month in which my first baby was expected. Having decided to have it in London, near my parents, I left the library in July. The baby arrived on 27 September and I returned to Addis Ababa with our 45-day old son, Alula, on 12 November.

Since I was still nursing him, I asked whether I could work part-time. The University accommodated me by giving me a two month cataloguing assignment in the Engineering College Library. It was, conveniently, near our house, so that I could feed him at lunchtime, and also, in the afternoon, look in at the National Library, where I had not yet been replaced. I had heard about Be'imnet Gebre-Amlak, an Ethiopian graduate who had worked in the National Library some time before I arrived. He had qualified as a librarian in Australia, there was the possibility of his returning to the Library. This was heartening news and I hoped he would take over from me. In the event, he joined the University instead.

CHAPTER 5

Notable Visitors, Festivals and Other Events

NOTABLE VISITORS

In the early years of our stay in Ethiopia we described the reception in Addis Ababa of several prominent foreign figures. These visits, which may serve to recall the spirit of the time, were an indication of the country's growing diplomatic importance on the world stage.

RITA

VICE-PRESIDENT NIXON

The first of these visitors to arrive in our time was Vice-President Richard Nixon, who came to Ethiopia in March 1957. In one of my letters to my parents I wrote: "Addis Ababa is breathing normally again after the excitement of Vice-President Richard Nixon's visit. A day or two before his arrival there was frantic tidying of the streets and painting of corrugated iron fencing along the main roads. Critics, local and foreign, deprecate this pretence that things are in fact what they aren't; friends felt, however, that a tidy-up never did any city any harm. What was wrong in making a little effort to receive an important guest?

At five o'clock in the afternoon Nixon touched down, welcomed officially and unofficially, despite a heavy downpour. The next day was the first day in weeks that the morning started off with a deep blue sky and no clouds developed. While he dined at the Palace, the thirty-four journalists who accompanied him were entertained by the Press and Information Ministry at the Gennet Hotel.

The local press included, besides the Amharic papers, one English weekly newspaper, *Ethiopian Herald*, run by two politically-committed Afro-Carribeans: Homer Smith and the more prosaically named David Talbot. Another weekly, *L'Éthiopie d'Aujourd'hui*, half of which appeared in French and the other half in Amharic. The editor was Gingold Duprey, a long-time French friend of Ethiopia. Then there was a daily called *Voice of Ethiopia* which had no official Government connection, but was edited by a Canadian, Percy Richards, on behalf of the prominent Minister of Finance, Mekonnin Habte-Weld, President of the Ethiopian Patriotic Association.

After a reception for visiting journalists we went to a night club in the basement of the modern Hayle-Sillasé Theatre. The decorations were on a Press theme against a background of strips of black and white crepe woven in a domino pattern, designed for the occasion by the Imbreys, who were American diplomats. The wife, who was attending Richard's lectures on Africa, had adorned the night club in tandem with a dynamic figure called Habte-Sillasé Taffese. An artist in his own way, and one of the most hard-working people in Addis Ababa, he produced a daily bulletin for the Ministry of Foreign Affairs. He had been a refugee during the Italian Occupation, and, according to report, had at one time been obliged to earn his upkeep as a shoe-shine boy in Cairo, before travelling widely in Europe. He was so quick on his feet that Richard and I likened him to a the speeding car in a Shell petrol advertisement, then widely displayed, which depicted the vehicle disappearing into the distance with the caption: "That's SHELL— that was!" He was subsequently imprisoned by the *Derg*, and several years later was released, and told to report for work at his office the next morning.

We found Afewerk in the night club. He had been invited in, having intended to go to the cinema. He asked me to dance and I was able to confirm that he was an artist in this field, too. In fact he went in for dancing championships in one phase of his adolescence in England. Richard and I also danced for the first time, with some success.

On the following day there was a press conference, followed by a cocktail at the Giyon Hotel—the newly finished luxury hotel. Its swimming pool was fed with warm water from the nearby hot springs. Here again were many familiar faces and opportunities to meet younger Ethiopians, in addition to diplomats, many of whom had been to the National Library to see the major Indian book exhibition (described in the previous chapter). Everybody was introduced to Nixon who was as bulky and youthful as he was reported to be. There were all types of snacks, cocktails and champagne.

A third function in Nixon's honour was a party given at the Patriotic Association Theatre by Mekonnin Habte-Weld, a man with a strong personality, who dressed in an old-fashioned manner. He preferred to work in a small hut in the grounds of his Ministry rather than in its imposing building.

We saw a performance of Ethiopian folk dancing and singing which I found quite delightful. The orchestra consisted of a kind of harp, the *begena,* which sounded sweet, rather like a lute. The singing was in one or two phrases often repeated and the dancing contained movements of the shoulder, neck and eyebrows, somewhat in the Indian tradition. There was also a warrior dance and a ballad which was so like *Kabuki* that even the sounds they uttered sounded Japanese to me. The women wore their usual white dresses gathered at the waist and ending in a border woven with coloured silk thread in varied designs. The whole was by no means polished but had the charm of the not too often rehearsed. This troupe performed every Sunday night and I decided to go again to get a closer look at the dancing and instrument playing.

In the interval we were offered a first class buffet, even better than that provided at the Government-owned Gennet Hotel. There was excellent red and black caviare, plus the usual ham, chicken, mortadella, meat balls, salads and sponges with cream. I met Richard's friend, Bereket-ab Habte-Sillasé, a law graduate who held a position in the Ministry of Justice, and found him very witty. Zewdé Hayle-Mariyam, another of Richard's friends from London days, was also there. Zewdé was the first Ethiopian I ever met. Richard had arranged for us to get together at an Indian restaurant in Soho (London). Zewdé assured me that I would enjoy Ethiopia, where chickens could be bought for six pence.

PRIME MINISTER NKRUMAH

The visit of Kwame Nkrumah, the Prime Minister of Ghana, in early June 1958, created a stir among Addis Ababa's educated citizens. The daily newspaper, the *Ethiopian Herald,* came out in sepia ink in his honour, with a welcoming biography by Richard. He was not introduced to Nkrumah when the latter visited University College and gave a short laudatory speech from the staircase of the imposing new building. However, Richard met him later during the visit, when Nkrumah exclaimed: "So this is he, at last!" Sylvia was asked to a cocktail party in his honour, given by Teferra-Werq, the Minister of the Pen, at the Giyon Hotel. Although she had not remembered Nkrumah, he remembered her, and asked her how things were at "the Village" (i.e. Woodford).

We later had tea with George Padmore, the prolific Afro-Carribean author and PanAfricanist, who was Nkrumah's friend and a member of his delegation. The next day Nkrumah visited the Princess Sehay Hospital. Sylvia was present as Hon. Secretary of the Hospital Committee, and I was with her. Nkrumah asked me what I was doing in Ethiopia. I told him about the National Library, and regretted that he had no time to visit it. He was then whisked off to Gonder, returning in the late afternoon. That evening the Mayor gave a reception for him in the Hayle-Sillasé Theatre, with an excellent performance of Ethiopian folk dances and songs.

TOM MBOYA

In the first week of October 1958 there was great excitement in Addis Ababa about the arrival of Tom Mboya, the young Kenya African leader whom we had earlier met privately in Nairobi. We heard a lot about his activities in the trade union and cooperative movements. He came to ascertain the Ethiopian government's attitude to trade unions, and suggested that some Ethiopians should be sent to the new Labour College in Kampala, Uganda, to study trade union leadership. He was well received and was invited by the Emperor to attend the opening of the Harer Military Academy. On this occasion he gave his first lecture at the National Library. (reported in Chapter 4).

Mboya also had discussions with the daughters of Princess Tenañ ñe, who wanted to start a cooperative settlement on some unused land.

The Emperor welcoming African scholarship student Robert Ouko, subsequently Prime Minister of Kenya Ketema Yifru in attendance, ca 1959

We had a tea party for him at our house. With Andreas's help, and valiant teamwork, we placed two sofas along one wall, and managed more or less to find accommodation for some fifty Ethiopians and a dozen students newly arrived from British East Africa. They had come to study at UCAA on scholarships from the Emperor, offered at the First Conference of Independent African States in Accra. Tom made a short speech, and the invitees asked questions, with Sylvia "in the chair." An excellent speaker, humorous, informative and with good English, he impressed the students, as well as our Ethiopian friends. On this occasion, as we have seen, he gave a further lecture at the National Library.

In a letter to my parents I wrote: "The better one gets to know him the more one realises his outstanding intelligence, his dynamism and his objectivity in assessing a given situation." Many foreign observers thought that he was potentially a great leader, but others pointed out that, as a Luo, he was not popular with the Kikuyu.

RICHARD

SEFTON DELMER

Later, in October 1958, we met Sefton Delmer, the famous *Daily Express* journalist. We first bumped into him at the preview of a Russian exhibition of Children's Art. Later, he was in the audience at the National Library lecture by Tom Mboya, where Sefton was introduced to us. He was a mountain of a man, slightly old-fashioned in dress and manner, which was surprising for an *Express* journalist. He was in his fifties, very large, multilingual, having been brought up in Germany with excellent French and some

Russian. He had been a foreign correspondent for over thirty years. When he invited us to dinner we became aware of his pungent wit, quick intelligence and excellent turn of phrase. He told us that his employer, Lord Beaverbrook, still took an active interest in the paper, measuring articles by the inch, and complaining if they were too long. When Sefton invited us to dinner, he ordered wine; the waiter attempted to pour out some for him to taste, but our host declined, saying he knew that wine well, and there was no need for him to taste it.

I was much entertained by him, but listed three of his failings when describing his visit to Rita's parents:

1. His conception of the world was limited to the all-dominating struggle of the Kremlin and "its pawn, Nasser", to rule the world.
2. His main interest in Ethiopia was to prove correct Beaverbrook's thesis that the British Council, soon to open up here, was "no good."
3. He thought it humorous to list names of people, by implication, Jewish, with the word "gold" in their names, i.e. Goldberg, Goldstein, Goldman, etc.—and then, being in Ethiopia, added: "Teferra-Werq", the last word, *werq*, being the Amharic term for "gold."

Sefton managed to get an interview with the Emperor despite the British Embassy's attempts to prevent it, because he was so strongly anti-British Council. Sefton's thesis was that the work of the Council could be done as efficiently, and much more cheaply, by adding a few clerks to the British Information Services—and there was something to it, except that the Embassy probably would not have welcomed the idea. The Emperor, if we could believe the good journalist, agreed that it would be more useful for Ethiopia to be given a British-run school than a branch of the British Council.

RITA

DUKE OF GLOUCESTER

Duke Henry and Duchess Alice of Gloucester were welcomed in November 1958, in bright sunshine, which must have been a change from dark and cold Britain. There was a banquet for them at the Palace. The imperial cook asked me, through the British Information Officer, whether I could find the coat of arms of the Gloucesters—presumably for some cake decoration, but I was unable to oblige on the spur of the moment. We met the Duke and Duchess at a Garden Party for the British community on the Embassy's wonderful lawns. The gardens and trees were so beautiful in the sunshine that one put up with the chunky, stale sandwiches containing unripe and unsalted tomatoes, and with the fact that the cakes disappeared in the first few minutes. We had only these sandwiches and lukewarm tea.

The Duchess turned out to be a trim and friendly figure with plenty of conversation and a sweet manner. I had seen them both before at a party given by Chatham House in London. She wore a wide pink skirt and white hat and so did our less elegant ambassadress. Eleanor Mansfield and other people who had been away on leave, looked ravishing in ballooning sacks, but, these were the exceptions. They still looked out of place in a society where the latest fashions take their time to arrive. I preferred Addis Ababa with its two freedoms—from domesticity and from fashion.

The day before, the Duchess had visited the Sehay Hospital and had had a talk with Sylvia about its problems. The visit was screened on British television, where it was seen with delight by Ivy Tims, Sylvia's long-time dedicated voluntary assistant in Woodford.

RICHARD

PRESIDENT TITO

A special guest who arrived on 3 February 1959, on one of several visits to Ethiopia, was Marshal Josip Tito of Yugoslavia, who came with his wife Jovanka for a two week visit, staying at the Jubilee Palace. He was prominent among the leaders of the Non-Aligned States and was reportedly close to the Emperor. That day I wrote in one of my letters:

"Tito arrived this morning and was greeted by the whole town, or so it seemed, as nobody was left in any government office. The streets were decked with Ethiopian and Yugoslav flags, and we are in for a week of celebration."

Our Yugoslav visitor brought the Emperor a yacht called Brioni, the name of an island off the Adriatic coast where Tito had a residence; and was given an Addis Ababa

mansion for a Yugoslav Embassy. It is now the Serbian Embassy, popularly referred to as the Tito House. Tito thanked the Emperor for the gift and the Yugoslav Government provided a building for an Ethiopian Embassy in Belgrade.

A trip was arranged for him into the countryside, as he was known to enjoy hunting. As a result he was scarcely seen in the capital, though Jovanka duly inspected the Handicraft School, under Idris's guidance, and visited Gonder. As we were lunching at the Airport on the day of their departure, we saw them at close range, he in Air Force grey uniform with a red stripe down the trousers, she in deep blue to tone in with his clothes. The Emperor and Empress saw them off to the aeroplane.

President Tito of Yugoslavia and his wife Jovanka on the state visit to Ethiopia with the Emperor, February 1959

Tito's first visit to Addis Ababa, had been in 1955, when he stayed in a specially extended wing of the Gennete Li'ul Palace, ever since known as the Tito suite. On that occasion he visited the University College. Security had been tight on account of the presence in the capital of Yugoslav refugees. Disliking air travel, he came to Ethiopia by ship to Massawa, proceeding to Addis Ababa via Asmara. He stayed for three weeks, mostly hunting in the south of the country.

As a precaution Yugoslav refugees resident in Addis Ababa were, on at least one occasion, generously quartered free of charge at a government-run hotel and holiday spa outside the town.

Tito came again on short visits in 1968, and in 1972, when the University awarded him an Honorary Doctorate. Relations between the Emperor and Tito remained cordial, Hayle-Sillasé visiting Yugoslavia no less than eight times. On such visits the two leaders celebrated the fact that they were born in the same year, i.e.1882.

KING PAUL OF GREECE

Also at the beginning of March 1958 it was announced that King Paul and Queen Frederika of Greece were coming. This royal visit was of great interest to us. Not only was the road from the Airport to Jubilee Palace thoroughly mended. It was also widened. For such reasons we always welcomed foreign potentates. This contrasted starkly with the situation half a century later when important visitors elicited only groans because of the inevitable traffic jams which ensued.

In preparation for the Greek King's visit the hideous corrugated iron sheets in the Piazza were removed, and disclosed to view a row of six semi-basement shops leading to what Afewerk would call a "Superscrumptious" W.C. In the end the Greek King's visit was postponed to the following year, which meant that a bridge near the Giyon Hotel was built of stone. Had he come as scheduled there would have been time only for a wooden one.

When the royal couple eventually arrived in March 1959 the procession was a grand one, with cavalry escorting the open cars. Triumphal arches were put up for the occasion on the Airport Road, and at Jubilee Palace where the guests were staying. This was an imposing new building very different in style from Gennete Li'ul, the Emperor's Palace, built in 1935, immediately prior to the Italian Occupation. There was a plethora of flags. The Palace reception was at 10 p.m. and was the usual arrangement of diplomats and Ethiopian dignitaries in two rows, with minor stars like ourselves behind them. The two royal couples then appeared in full evening dress, the diplomats and their wives paid their respects, and cocktails were served. We escaped this ordeal, but, to our surprise, were ushered upstairs where a sumptuous dinner followed. It was at small tables in three connected halls, with gorgeous liveried servants, scarlet and green for the food waiters, and purple and scarlet for the wine ones. Having been on a long walking expedition that day, we were too tired to do justice to the food, but recovered enough towards the end to appreciate the strawberries, meringues and cream.

King Husein of Jordan visiting the Princess Sehay Hospital, in the presence of Abbebe Retta, Minister of Health, Colonel Bayam, Director of the Hospital, and Hospital staff, including doctors Reginald and Katherine Hamlyn, later founders of the Addis Ababa Fistula Hospital, May 1959

RITA

KING HUSEIN OF JORDAN

In mid-May it was the turn of King Husein Ibn Talal to visit Addis Ababa. There were as usual flags to welcome the royal visitor, plus military parades and celebrations, in three of which we had to participate. First there was a reception at 10 p.m. in the throne room. Foreigners and Ethiopian dignitaries faced each other in rows on either side of the long hall while Emperor, King and retinues proceeded solemnly towards the throne at the far end. There they conversed, and were filmed and photographed. Eventually there was a move upstairs to the dining halls where the usual first class food was accompanied by wine and champagne. Richard's latest fad was a taste for the latter drink. He would make sure that Sylvia and I did not refuse the glasses offered to us and would then methodically empty them, and his own. This he did with such an air of innocence that one could imagine it was fizzy lemonade. He has long since lost a taste for alcoholic drinks. We reached home at 1:30 p.m.

The next evening we, like the dignitaries we had seen the previous evening, were guests of King Husein at a shorter reception in the Jubilee Palace. Sylvia was whisked off to the table of one of the princesses and we escaped to a further room, which happened to be the library. Of course, on the shelves were the very well bound books we had earlier ordered.

Going out we all shook hands, the women curtseying to our royal host. He came over as a rather stronger personality than we had imagined, though he seemed taken aback by the extent of the ceremonial to which he was subjected. At the time, we could not help wondering for how long he would hold out. Little did we imagine that he would maintain his throne for very much longer than the Emperor.

The very next evening we were invited again, this time to a performance of Ethiopian folk dances in the King's honour, from which Sylvia sensibly abstained.

RICHARD

COLIN LEGUM

Colin Legum, the South African journalist, who wrote for the London *Observer,* came on a number or occasions. A friend of several of the Ethiopian students who had studied in England, he was much preoccupied with Ethiopian politics. When he visited Addis Ababa in connection with the Second Conference of Independent African States, six months before the *Coup d'État* of December 1960, we drove him around the town; he kept on pressing us to tell him which general would make "the Coup." For his part, he thought it would be General Mulugéta Buli. We did not then take our journalist friend seriously, but later at times found him a useful and well-informed observer.

CROWN PRINCE AKIHITO AND PRINCESS MICHIKO OF JAPAN

Towards the end of November, 1960, flags went up for the visit of Crown Prince Akihito and Crown Princess Michiko of Japan. A roundabout which, by 1960 standards, was considered "huge" had been constructed near the lion statue by the National Theatre. The impressive stone image of the lion was seen in rather a different light by a little girl who referred to it as " the lion who looks like a chicken"—the effect of its jagged mane.

We feared that we would have to attend a number of receptions in the Japanese couple's honour, but we were involved in only two. The arrangements were slightly less formal than usual, which enabled us to move about and talk to people. Akihito and his consort became Emperor and Empress of Japan in 1989.

JOMO KENYATTA

Addis Ababa was excited by the visit of Jomo Kenyatta in mid-November 1961. His party included our old friend Mbiyu Koinange and Kenyatta's private secretary Achang Oneko. The latter was well known to Mehr Fardoonji, my old LSE friend and colleague. Oneko had been tried with Kenyatta, and was later acquitted, but on leaving the Kenya court was, like other freedom-fighters, promptly re-arrested.

The Ethiopian Prime Minister, Aklilu Habte-Weld, gave a reception for Kenyatta who was enthusiastically welcomed. He was at that time President of the dominant Kenya African National Union Party (KANU) and a member of the Kenya Parliament. Already in his seventies he gave the impression of a man physically in good condition. Only three years later he would become Kenya's first President.

As I had to give a lecture that evening, Rita went instead to present Kenyatta with my last remaining copy of *Kenya: The History of Two Nations,* which I had always kept back to present to Kenyatta one day. He remembered Sylvia well, also her house in Woodford, which he had several times visited. He was very pleased with the book.

ANNUAL FESTIVALS AND CELEBRATIONS

Annual festivals played an important part in Ethiopian religious and social life. They were, incidentally, sometimes useful in providing us with opportunities to meet people and discuss issues and projects of mutual interest. We learned that the eve of major religious celebrations was as important as the day itself.

RITA

GENNA, OR CHRISTMAS

The first festival in which we participated, not long after our arrival in 1956, was *Genna*, or Christmas, celebrated on 7 January. I wrote to my parents the following Sunday that the festivities had been some of the most memorable that I had ever witnessed. The croaky voice of the Finance Minister, Mekonnin Habte-Weld, the most powerful person in the Cabinet, informed us on the telephone the previous evening that we should attend the morning celebrations at the Palace. We duly drove there in our little Fiat and were shown in, Sylvia and I hatted and gloved (I wore the white floral dress from Fenwicks) past the assembled crowd to the side of the throne. The Emperor and Empress were listening to children's carols and receiving Christmas presents. Sylvia was one of the few to be offered a seat. When this part of the ceremony was over we went to pay our respects. The day before I had practised a curtsey or two with Richard's friends Afewerk and Habte-ab. Sylvia did not believe in that sort of thing and just bowed. She could get away with it, but it seemed more becoming for me to curtsey. So up we went, Sylvia leading, bowing and shaking hands. The Emperor asked me in French how I thought I would like it here, and I made a suitable reply. He had a warm, benign smile, but, I was told, an iron will.

The next morning we rose at six, stood through a church ceremony and then through a further Marathon in a tent on the grounds of the Palace. (In later years this annual event took place in a large "hangar" known as Christmas Hall). Streams of school children, boy scouts, college students, nurses and police cadets filed by to collect their presents. They received a shirt or blouse, and cloth for trousers or skirt, an orange, and a parcel, brightly wrapped, probably containing cake. Each member of the Emperor's family did some handing out—Emperor, Empress, Crown Prince, Prince Sahle-Sillasé, and the Princesses. It was a colourful occasion and all of them were in National Dress: the *Shemma*—a woven white cloth draped over the shoulders with a woven coloured border, each one done to order and different from every other one.

In the afternoon we were asked to attend a Christmas performance at the Empress's orphanage. Re-hatted and re-gloved we set off leaving Richard behind to work. The school, run by Canadian missionaries, was under the Empress's personal supervision—a beautiful airy building in a park full of old trees. Evidently she had lavished much care on it. We saw lovely white cots and healthy-looking uninhibited children. Many of them had been begging in the streets, and several were blind. Both Emperor and Empress were there. I talked mainly to Princess Hirut, who had recently accompanied her grandfather to India and Japan, and to her sister Seble who was at Lady Margaret Hall, which had been my college in Oxford; I also spoke to their brother, Iskinder Desta who was an officer in the Imperial Navy, which he later commanded.

Coming, as I did, from rather drab London, I was much impressed by the two-day colourful event. The sunshine, the trees and the cool interiors set off the ceremonies perfectly. I hoped, all the same, that there would not be too many such occasions to keep me from work in the Library.

TEMQET, OR EPIPHANY

Temqet or Epiphany, as in other parts of the world, falls twelve days after Christmas. In Ethiopia *Temqet* thus comes in the second half of January, and is one the most colorful events of the year.

We missed the 1957 celebrations on the eve and the next morning. In the afternoon, however, we did go to the scene of the morning's events at *Jan Hoy Méda*, the "Emperor's Meadow", which is also a race track. All around, we could catch sight of the mountains, enveloping Addis Ababa at a discrete distance. We watched the tail end of the festivities. There were still a few groups dancing in small circles and many people happily milling about, as well as boys selling sweets and cold drinks. It felt not unlike the end of an August Bank Holiday in Britain, but without the litter and sordid food remains.

In 1959 on *Temqet* afternoon, we took Edith, Birhanu Tessema's wife, to witness the festivities, at *Jan Méda*, Birhanu having gone hunting for the week-end. There were circles of Amhara, Oromo, Gurage, Tegray and other groups of dancers, each performing in their own ethnic style. We watched a polo match between the Imperial Bodyguard and the police. They were playing the European version of the game, not *gugs*, the less regulated, traditional form, played in Ethiopia on such festivals from time immemorial. In anticipation of the annual festival of Mikaél the following day, women were selling home-made yellow wax tapers, dried raisins and incense which the faithful bought as gifts for the church.

Temqet celebrations are particularly dramatic in Gonder. The congregations of the city's thirteen churches gather round them, awaiting the emergence of the *Tabot*—the symbolic representation of the biblical Ark of the Covenant, which sanctifies an Ethiopian church.Fully wrapped in richly coloured velvets the *Tabot* is carried on the head of a specially designated member of the clergy, followed by the faithful, singing and jubilating. After being paraded three times around their church they take the *Tabot* to a nearby river, pool or other source of water, where it spends the night (in the case of certain churches, two nights). *Temqet* in Gonder was a sight etched in my memory. The followers of the town's churches, with their *tabots*, gradually came together in a vast procession, moving like tributaries joining a larger, slow-moving river, singing and

Emperor Fasiledes's pavillion set in a pool, used for Timqet celebrations

dancing until they reached their destination: the field in front of the pool, attributed to the 17th century Emperor, Fasiledes. On three sides of it, majestic age-old trees provide shade, while their roots enlace the papapet encircling it. The pool had been filled with water by damming two rivers a few weeks before the festival. The *tabots* were assembled in a little pavilion within the pool, where priests prayed and chanted through the night—and, handing us sistra, invited us to join them, at least briefly.

When dawn came, crowds were already assembling around the pool to await the morning. When the chief priest arrived he blessed a cross formed by two sticks, on which stood a lighted candle, and launched it to float on the water, symbolising the baptism of Christ. At this point in the ritual some of the excited children, who had been sitting expectantly round the pool's edge, jumped into the shallow water, and a general splashing, shouting and collection of blessed water took place. Sometimes some of the children, anticipating the proceedings, jumped in too soon and thereby extinguished the candle. They then had to be ordered out of the water, to wait, shivering, until, a candle having been re-lit, they jumped in again.

Thereafter the joyful congregations returned, singing and clapping, to their respective churches. I was amazed that so many people could squeeze through the small gate closing off the compound, without there ever being any jostling or ill word.

Festivals such as the above, though with local variations, take place in Ethiopia every year.

RICHARD

BATTLE OF ADWA ANNIVERSARY

This is an Ethiopian public holiday on 2 March, commemorating the Battle of Adwa, when Emperor Menilek and his chiefs mobilised an army that defeated an Italian one in 1896. Surprisingly there is still no monument to the Adwa victory in Addis Ababa. Some survivors of the Adwa Battle were however still alive in the early years of our stay in the country, and would participate in the ceremony held at Arat Kilo where wreaths are placed beside the obelisk commemorating the country's Liberation in 1941. Gradually, fewer and fewer Adwa veterans remained, but Patriots from the more recent struggle were still there, some wearing old uniforms, with their hair uncut in Afro-style as it used to be, when, during the Italian Occupation, they were partisans in the mountains.

RITA

FASIKA, OR EASTER

Another important holiday in the Ethiopian Christian calendar marks the end of Lent, as elsewhere in Christendom, though the fasting season in Ethiopia is longer than in the West. Many devout Ethiopians throughout Lent fast until the afternoon, and barely eat during the last three days. The day before the holiday is one of feverish excitement and, as before all major Christian festivals, there are long church services on the eve.

I described that week what I saw at *Fasika* in 1958. All over town sheep and chickens were being sold in various corners, and fattened cattle were brought to market. Practically the entire library staff borrowed money to meet the additional expenses incurred by the celebration. On Easter morning I saw groups of friends sitting around a freshly killed cow, sharing the meat, while elsewhere abandoned carcasses were visible. Countrymen with newly slaughtered sheepskins slung around their necks, searched for purchasers. I was told that, on the first day after the end of the fast, when people can once again relish meat, the unwise may fall ill by passing too quickly from fasting to gorging. However, not all members of the Orthodox Christian community kept the fast, and in particular some young foreign-educated people, had got into non-fasting habits abroad. On this particular Good Friday morning, we saw the car of an artist friend of ours near an Italian restaurant. Inside there was no trace of him. Undaunted, Richard made a further search and caught sight of a sleeve—and there, in a corner, we discovered the culprit with a companion, having a double portion of egg and bacon.

In later decades many of the "emancipated" young people, shaken by the experience of Revolution and Civil War, returned more strictly to the security of their age-old faith.

RICHARD

LIBERATION DAY

Liberation Day ceremonies on 5 May, witnessed by us for the first time in 1957, commemorate Ethiopia's liberation from Italian Fascist Occupation—the day the Italians marched into Addis Ababa, in 1936, as well as the day the Emperor chose to re-enter the city in 1941—and it was also Sylvia's birthday. We received a huge invitation card asking us to attend the ceremonies at the Old Gibbi (Gibbi = Palace) built by Emperor Menilek, and reserved for big functions requiring formal evening dress with decorations. By now we had learnt how to get smartly into our evening clothes. As a result we arrived on schedule. We waited in procession to be ushered into the reception hall, in order of rank. Sylvia wearing her Patriots' and Queen of Sheba decorations, was way ahead of us, entering just after the judges. We were at the bottom of the queue, below the diplomats and the directors of hospitals, but in front of the press. We advanced in single file up the long room with huge painted portraits of Ethiopian royalty on the walls. The Emperor was on his throne at the far end, without the Empress, who was unwell. Our names were called out: "Dr. Richard Pankhurst, Miss Rita Eldon." (The last time this happened was at Toynbee Hall, the educational establishment in London's East End, at an annual day, which we both attended.) Rita managed to curtsey, having advanced without tripping past the long row of Ethiopian notables on the right and diplomats to the left, most of them plastered with decorations.

This ordeal over, we spent a delightful evening. First there were fireworks, then chats with the many people we knew. We talked so long, the two of us, that we were the last in the food queue. Refreshments were spectacular. We threaded our way through the crowded tables to the end of a long gallery from which we could see, but scarcely be seen. We had a table to ourselves and before we knew where we were the motor cycle escort had started up, the Emperor had left and it was time to go home. In the course of time we found that getting home would take longer than expected, because the impressive limousines were given precedence over our inferior-looking Fiat.

On the same day the statue to commemorate the Patriots who fought during the Italian Occupation was unveiled at the Holleta Military Academy. It was the work of Antun Augustinčić, the Yugoslav sculptor who had made the beautiful obelisk-like memorial to the Graziani massacre of 1937 erected in Siddist Kilo Square in memory of the thousands of innocent Ethiopians who were killed in retaliation for an attempt on the life of the Italian Fascist Viceroy of that name.

The next year's Liberation Day reception followed the same pattern, but there were also fireworks that could be seen all over Addis Ababa.

In May 1961 the Liberation Day reception at the old palace was enlivened by a chorus of school children singing the *Alleluyah* chorus from Handel's *Messiah*. The words had been translated into Amharic by the young Ethiopian musician, Efrem Yisak, who had returned from music studies at Harvard University. It was touching to see the amount of work and enthusiasm that had been put into it. The Emperor, who had heard of the presentation at the National Theatre, requested a repeat performance, and rewarded the singers with a Palace banquet.

Many decades later, Rita proposed that Efrem, who had become a renowned scholar of Semitic Studies at Princeton University, be invited by her choir, the Motley Singers, to come back to Addis Ababa from the US to conduct the Motleys for the same *Alleluyah* chorus. He agreed with enthusiasm, and, the performance took place in May 2004. In the audience at the City Hall were grey-haired gentlemen who, as schoolboys, had sung in Ephraim's choir and remembered their performance in front of the Emperor. It was an emotional occasion.

EMPEROR'S BIRTHDAY

During our first summer in Addis Ababa, in 1957, we observed the celebrations of the Emperor's birthday on 23 July. My mother presented him with a bound volume of *Ethiopia Observer* Vol. I, which the Emperor seems to have appreciated. We went to the Palace at 9:30 a.m., the time Ethiopian officials went, and were shown in after the Ethiopian women had paid their respects. He was in a genial mood, smiled broadly at our little gift and shook hands. We were still looked upon rather as an oddity, by the Palace ushers, being considered neither fish nor fowl, i.e. something between Ethiopians and foreigners.

RITA

The following evening there was a party in the foyer of the Hayle-Sillasé Theatre in honour of the birthday, given by the Mayor of Addis Ababa. The food had to be carried down a flight of steps. By this time I had become adept at negotiating stairs in a long dress. Afterwards there was dancing, which the two of us were beginning to enjoy. Many of our Ethiopian friends were there, and, had we not had to take Sylvia home, we might well have stayed till morning and, like Afewerk, regretted it the next day. He managed to teach us the rumba—at which we were both hopeless. It occurred to me that, if we could really enjoy dancing, besides being good for our health, it would greatly reduce what we were beginning to view as the tedium of these social obligations.

ENQUTATASH, OR NEW YEAR

There were the usual ceremonies at the Genete Li'ul Palace annually on 12 September, Ethiopian New Year. In 1960 the Emperor received visitors in the large main hall, which had been redecorated in cream and gold. He and the Empress were in white and remained almost immobile, while at their feet all around the throne, the now considerable throng of royal grandchildren were behaving like other young things.

Since Eritrea's Federation with Ethiopia the occasion also celebrated the Anniversary of that event, so that there were a number of congratulatory speeches.

We went in with the Ethiopians who were all in Ethiopian dress. Some of the Ministers looked rather odd in combinations of Western and Ethiopian costume: a waistcoat from a suit under the *shemma*, pullovers, white Ethiopian trousers but black shoes, etc. This was the tradition on New Year's Day. It was a constant surprise to me, at the end of the rains, to see townspeople emerging in brilliant white from a still muddy capital.

We were becoming expert at negotiating the formal dress required for different occasions. On Ethiopian New Year's Day 1960 Richard donned his Morning Coat without losing his temper and we arrived at the correct gate of the correct palace at the correct time. The Emperor's chihuahuas took a dislike to some players from the Ethiopian Patriotic Theatre who came clad in garish colours to represent Spring, Ethiopia, etc. But there was only some inappropriate barking. It was to be the last time that the New Year celebrations were held at this Palace, which, after the abortive Coup d'État of December 1960, became the University.

MESQEL, OR FEAST OF THE CROSS

After our honeymoon in Harer in 1957, described in Chapter 3, we returned to Addis Ababa on 28 September, *Mesqel*—the day commemorating the "discovery of the True Cross" by St. Helena, Empress of the Eastern Roman Empire—as well as of a piece of the Cross that was believed to have reached Ethiopia. As we were landing in Addis Ababa we saw fields covered in the bright yellow of the *Mesqel* daisy (*Coreopsis boraniana*)—an indigenous plant that grows up to a height of over two feet, and, as if by magic, regularly flowers at this time. The hamlets were alive with figures in the white of the national dress. Everybody seemed in excellent spirits. Children were going round from house to house clapping and singing, to the accompaniment of a drum— in the style of carol singers in England at Christmas, and with the same ulterior motive.

We had witnessed the eve of the holiday in Harer. People brought long, thin branches of eucalyptus, tied bunches of *Mesqel* flowers to the upper end of each branch, and festooned them around a thicker, taller Eucalyptus pole. Then everyone walked round it three times, led by a procession of priests and dignitaries, and, amid singing and dancing at night, the pole was set alight and burned till it crashed to the ground. People would at times make predictions based on the direction in which the pole fell.

RICHARD

EMPEROR'S CORONATION ANNIVERSARY

The Emperor's Coronation Anniversary on 2 November was often chosen for other public events, notably the opening of Parliament. On this occasion in 1958, for example, the United Nations decision to hold the Economic Commission for Africa in Addis Ababa was welcomed by the Dean of the Diplomatic Corps—the Indian Ambassador—and by the Emperor. Both speeches were significant in emphasising African developments during the year.

Scarcely had we returned home for lunch than we had to start preparing for an invitation from the Vice-Prime Minister to attend a reception at the Giyon Hotel. This again required formal dress. We were by now aware that such occasions could be put to good use. Rita, for example, was thus able to (1) press Princess Hirut and Prince Sahle-Sillasé to help us obtain a microphone and loudspeaker for the Library lectures; (2) ask the Minister of Commerce, Abbebe Retta, to arrange a series of lectures on the new Five-year Plan; and (3) persuade a young man, a friend of ours, to take the chair at the following day's lecture, which was to be in Amharic—on the History of Aksum.

Another event which we attended was the opening by the Emperor of the Archaeology Museum in a windowless building below the National Library. It was a modern structure with a large central hall in which the small exhibits looked even smaller.

The 29th Anniversary of the Coronation in 1959 was marked by an exhibition of paintings by Ethiopian artists at the National Theatre, opened by the Emperor. Afewerk had the end wall to himself and appeared in a spectacular national costume designed by himself. There were interesting paintings by other artists of a higher level than what we had seen the previous year. A few months later Afewerk was elected President of an Ethiopian Artists' Association, but shortly withdrew, to devote himself exclusively to his art.

OTHER EVENTS

ETHIOPIA'S FIRST POST-WAR ELECTIONS

In 1957 the forthcoming direct elections—the first in Ethiopian history—created a small stir. Several of our friends were in one way or another involved, among them Oxford-educated *Dejazmach* Amha, and my LSE friend, Habte-ab Bayru. Five million people registered—about a quarter of the population. There were six women candidates, but, according to my mother, two of them were wasting their time standing against each other.

After the election had taken place Rita wrote: "Little activity could be noted by the foreign observer. Many people that I have asked were waiting to vote next time as they felt that as members of an educated class they were a mere drop in the ocean." Siniddu Gebru was one of only two women to be elected to the Chamber of Deputies and had to give up her directorship of the Empress Menen Girls' School. She was an active parliamentarian and spoke eloquently in defence of women's rights. She was subsequently chosen as Vice-President of the Chamber, and was so forceful that a fellow-Parliamentarian, a male chauvinist, referred in the Chambe to her as *Ato* Siniddu, i.e. "Mister Siniddu." Her instant response was to give him a good slap in the face.

The total number of votes cast in the Election—just over three million out of a total estimated population of 20 million—was disappointingly low. Those expecting to use the voters' register as a census gave up the idea. Many people we talked to nevertheless seemed pleased that a start had been made.

SHUM-SHIR

A high point in the social round, as well as an important feature in traditional Ethiopian political life, was the announcement of government appointments, or *Shum-Shir*, literally "appoint-demote." The appointee was expected to keep open house for the next several days to receive congratulations and offer refreshments, generally including whiskey or other strong drinks. Interest revolved round the political significance of the appointment: was it a promotion, demotion or a "sideways shunt"? The *Shum-Shir*, according to some

Siniddu Gebru, elected vice-President of the Ethiopian Chamber of Deputies, one of only two women who won a seat in the Chamber at the 1957 elections.

Mengistu Lemma in India at an international conference, ca 1959

political scientists, was devised to achieve the appointee's dependency on the ruler but had the disadvantage of weakening continuity and hence government efficiency.

Good personal relations of the monarch with his subjects were traditionally regarded as of the utmost importance. Courtiers waiting in the Palace compound in the vicinity of the Emperor's office were at one time popularly referred to as members of "the "Sunshine Club". Great attention was paid by them to the direction in which the monarch was looking, and the expression on his face, whether favourable or unfavourable.

We became more closely conscious of the *Shum-Shir* process when, in February 1958 we were surprised to hear that our good friend Mengistu Lemma was called to the Palace and asked by the Emperor what he wanted to do with his life. He told us that he replied "To serve your Majesty and to write." H.I.M. then asked him if he had any objection to being appointed First Secretary to the Embassy in India. There was no question of a negative reply. Mengistu accordingly left in April. We knew we would miss him, but were well aware that he would find India most interesting. His Ambassador, *Ras* Imru, cousin of the Emperor, was himself a distinguished writer, and may well have intimated that he would be happy to have Mengistu, a fellow-writer and son of a distinguished church scholar, as First Secretary. Mengistu would meet an ancient Eastern civilisation, an as yet undeveloped country, facing its economic difficulties squarely, and a focal point of neutrality. In addition he would be well paid and would have time to write, as the Emperor had pointed out to him.

A *Shum Shir* in December 1959 affected the National Library directly. In early December *Lij* Indalkachew Mekonnin was appointed Ambassador in London and, some two weeks later Tekle-Sadiq Mekuriya, was sent to Jerusalem as Consul-General.

THE ALL-AFRICA FOOTBALL CUP

There was great excitement in the town on 21 January 1961, the one and only time when Ethiopia won the All-Africa Football Cup. The Emperor attended, of course, and everyone who managed to get hold of tickets. Not being football fans, we did not attend, though we heard the commentary on Addis Ababa radio, which at one point proclaimed that the Ethiopians were truer sons of Africa than their opponents, the Egyptians, who held the cup in the previous two years. The crowds in the town were jubilant and the bus carrying the winning team sped into the town, wildly acclaimed, through a number of red lights, with the traffic police on duty clapping them on.

The popularisation of football in Ethiopia owed much to an Ethiopian sports enthusiast, Yidneqachew Tesemma, whose father, *Negadras* Tesemma Isheté, Menilek had been sent to Germany in the early 1900's to become a mechanic and learn to drive the Imperial car, one of the first to reach Ethiopia. Tesemma, however, made his name there as a musician, and recorded the first ever gramophone records of Ethiopian music.

CHAPTER 6

African Perspectives

RICHARD

AFRICA AFTER MAU MAU

Rita and I arrived in Ethiopia as believers in the Rights of Man, and the Freedom of the Individual. At home and at LSE I had been exposed to Anti-Colonialist ideas, and had many friends from colonial territories then struggling for political and social emancipation. They included Africans and persons of African descent, many inspired by the ideals of Pan-Africanism.

The late 1950s, when we began our joint life in Ethiopia, was a time of crisis for Africa, where the "winds of change" were only just beginning to blow. However, the situation on the continent, from the point of view of colonial emancipation, seemed dire. The South African *apartheid* regime, which appeared irremovable, was taking increasing control over South-West Africa. Developments in Anglophone Africa were likewise far from satisfactory. The Central African Federation was consolidating White minority rule in a wide stretch of territory. In Rhodesia Ian Smith's pro-Settler rebellion seemed to have succeeded. In Kenya the White Settlers appeared likely to edge their way to power.

The position elsewhere on the continent was equally unsatisfactory. The French settlers seemed irremovable in Algeria. The Belgians were in virtually total control of the Congo, and the Portuguese of Angola and Mozambique. And, nearer to Ethiopia, the Italians had returned to Somalia, albeit officially for only a ten-year United Nations Trusteeship.

Ethiopia, when we arrived in 1956, was one of only three independent African States, the others being Egypt and Liberia. However, in the following year the British colony of the Gold Coast became independent as Kwame Nkrumah's Ghana.

In April 1958 at the First Conference of Independent African States in Accra it was announced that the Emperor had granted 50 secondary school students from other parts of Africa four-year scholarships at Ethiopian institutions of higher learning.

Mikaél Imru and his sisters photographed on their return from exile in Jerusalem, 1942

Students came in due course from Kenya, Tanganyika, later Tanzania, Uganda, Zanzibar, Nigeria, Ghana, Sudan, Egypt and Somalia. These students, though few in number, made a notable impact on young Ethiopians, and helped to break down the country's traditional isolation. I invited some of those who attended my lectures to write articles on their countries.

The resultant students' issue of *Ethiopia Observer* (Vol. III, No. 3), featured a number of remarkably fine essays. Some dealt with important or original subjects, such as "Kenya Education and the African District Councils", by Robert Ouko, a future Foreign Minister of Kenya (who was to be assassinated in 1990), and two others by Kenya students: "A Short Note on the Kenya Land Problem" by Leonard Otieno, and "The Political Development of Kenya" by Omogi Calleb. Other articles were more personal and/or autobiographical, among them "From Tanganyika to Ethiopia", by George Magombe, of Tanganyika, and "My First Two Months in Addis Ababa", by Henry Botchway, of Ghana.

During this period Rita and I invited many visiting African leaders and students to our house, and asked them to give informal talks to as many of our Ethiopian friends as we could pack into our central room. My mother, until her death, invariably served as chair-person for such gatherings. A frequent visitor to these meetings was the Eritrean Unionist leader Tedla Bayru, who had become a family friend.

Guests at such meetings from other parts of Africa who attended included Sheikh Anton Diop of Senegal, Kenneth Kaunda and Simon Kapepwe of Zambia, as well as James Gichuru, Chairman of the Kenya African Union, Odinga Odinga, our old friend Mbiyu Koinange, young Tom Mboya, and Mwai Kibaki, the five latter, all from Kenya.

Though I was mainly concerned with Ethiopian history, I gave a number of lectures on African issues, and wrote articles on the subject in the *Ethiopian Herald* and other Ethiopian newspapers. We also befriended students from other parts of Africa then studying in Addis Ababa. Most came to our house for lunch, tea or dinner.

AFRICA SOCIETY

In January 1959, Yodit and Hirut Imru, two of Mikaél Imru's sisters—daughters of the Emperor's "progressive" cousin, *Ras* Imru—decided to form an unofficial Africa Society. It was convened by Judith, then the only woman Director-General in the Ethiopian Government, and Hirut, a teacher of Social Work and one of the Ethiopian delegates to the first Conference of Independent African States held in Accra in 1958. Its objectives were to: sensitise the Ethiopian public to African issues; publicise and rally support for African independence struggles; and popularise Pan-African ideals. Members of the Society sought also to interest themselves in students from other parts of Africa, who were coming on scholarships granted by the Emperor, but were often lonely. By this time there were some 34 students, mainly from Kenya and Tanganyika, but also from British and Italian Somaliland, Zanzibar, Uganda, Ghana, Nigeria, Sudan and Egypt. We wanted to make them feel at home in Ethiopia, and on several occasions chartered a bus to take them for picnics in the Ethiopian countryside. As a result of the presence of such students in the capital, a more cosmopolitan atmosphere reached the Ethiopian student body, who developed a more international outlook.

The leading light of the Africa Society, about which few people ever knew, was Seyfu Felleqe, a dedicated educator, who was the first Director of Addis Ababa's Commercial School. A man of dry humour he had studied in India, where he had imbibed Anti-Colonialist ideas, and it was in his office that the Society met. There were also several other politically conscious Ethiopians, including Mary Taddese's husband, Befeqadu Taddese, a conscientious official responsible for Africa in the Ethiopian Ministry of Foreign Affairs, as well as Rita and myself. We all, in our different ways, did what we could to foster the Society's objectives and ideals.

Rita, who had started a popular Public Lecture programme at the National Library of Ethiopia, as was seen in Chapter 4, used it to publicise African freedom movements which were springing up throughout much of the Continent. These lectures, given mainly in English by nationalist leaders from colonial or ex-colonial territories, created considerable interest in the city.

AMAN ANDOM AND ASEFFA DULA

One of two prominent figures attending my evening lectures on Ethiopian economic history in the University's Extension Department at that time was Major-General Aman Andom. A distinguished military officer of Eritrean origin, nick-named the Lion of the Ogaden for his successful defeat of a Somali military incursion, he took a keen interest in Ethiopian military history. When I had spoken for an hour, and it was time for a break, he and the other student would take over the class, summarising what I had said, and trying to draw out conclusions. Hearing that I was in contact with several Mau Mau refugees in Addis Ababa, (who had been secretly given asylum in Ethiopia) Aman asked to meet them. The upshot was that the two of us, and two Mau Mau veterans, had dinner together, after the following class, at Addis Ababa's Buffet de la Gare, where, over a hearty meal, they discussed guerrilla tactics—and the three military men arranged to meet again a week later.

Aman was then one of the most popular stars in the Ethiopian military firmament, and, at a time of growing student radicalism, it was put to him that it would be unwise for him to be seen consorting with the students. He accordingly withdrew at the end of the first semester and I seldom saw him again.

After the 1974 Revolution he was elected Chairman of the *Derg*, or ruling Military Committee, and was always most friendly on the few occasions when we met. He subsequently ran into difficulties with prominent members of the Committee and was summoned to the *Derg* Headquarters. Rumour had it that he was somehow in detention. Shortly after this, we saw him driving from his house, which was near our own, and waved to him. Later that day we saw a tank drawn up pointing towards his house. That evening we heard the boom of heavy gunfire, and it was announced that he died resisting arrest.

The other prominent Extension student of that time was the remarkable Aseffa Dula, who had earlier worked in the Emperor's Private Secretariat. We first became friends soon after our arrival in Ethiopia, when, realising that we were without transport, he volunteered to drive us for the day to Bishoftu. It was a rough ride, along a road then full of pot holes that I remembered for some time owing to the bumps on my head. In December 1958, when Addis Ababa was sprucing itself up to receive its first international organisation, the United Nations Economic Commission for Africa, Aseffa, who then held a position in the Addis Ababa Municipality, phoned me out of the blue one afternoon, and told me he was producing a guide to the city. He asked whether we would help him with the text, which was in English.

Rita and I accordingly at once drove up to the Municipality, where we spent the evening drafting a brochure on Addis Ababa and its amenities. When we had finished, Aseffa informed us that we were going, there and then, to spend the night at the Ambo resort, which, in the dark, in those days, would take about three hours. He then drove us to his house to pick up his girl-friend, we had a leisurely dinner and only after this did we leave for Ambo in his Opel—at 11 p.m. It was a rapid and pleasant trip although on the way we almost ran over a leopard.

On arriving in the middle of the night we found the government hotel closed and no amount of knocking roused anybody. Undeterred, Aseffa took us to a small nearby private hotel, of which he knew the lady owner, and had no compunction in waking the establishment. We were warmly welcomed by her in person, no doubt roused from her sleep. He then took out of the car his night's reading which comprised some half a dozen text-books on law, a subject which he was then studying with a view to becoming a trained lawyer. Always a great reader he told us that he had formerly patronised the British Council Library, but had been so frustrated by its pedantic librarian, Stephen Wright, that he had once thrown a book at him. Later, to anticipate events, Aseffa involved himself in the Abortive *Coup d'État* of December 1960, and was duly imprisoned. Some months after this he nevertheless called on me at my office in the University College. When I asked him what he was doing there when he was supposed to be in detention he told me he had been given permission to visit a hospital for medical purposes, but, not liking to be seen with his jailer, had bribed him to keep out of the way.

Aseffa was eventually freed, after which we had dinner together in the company of Professor Norman Singer, of the Faculty of Law one evening in 1967. In the course of the meal I suggested that since little was then known about the Abortive Coup, he should try to write his memoirs. He replied that he would do so willingly—but "not until after the next Coup." This he never did. One night, only a few weeks later, he was involved in a duel with pistols outside the Ethiopia Hotel. He and his opponent, Jarra Mesfin, son of the nobleman *Ras* Mesfin Sileshi, and a also mutual friend who had studied in England, had both been drinking excessively. Jarra addressed Aseffa as "you, son of a slave", whereupon the latter challenged his friend to come with him outside the hotel to see who was a slave. In the ensuing encounter Aseffa shot Jarra dead, but was himself mortally wounded, and bled to death while being driven around to find a hospital open at that time of night.

Aseffa, a man of scholarly as well as impetuous inclination, came from Chercher, a province in the east of the country. He wrote me an informative essay on that territory which we published in *Ethiopia Observer* (Vol. XII, No. 2). It remains the only testament to his sad and prematurely ended life.

KENYA

Our colonial contacts were for the most part with Kenya. This was in part because Jomo Kenyatta had been one of my mother's closest African collaborators at the time of the Italian invasion of Ethiopia; in part because, while still in England, I had written my book *Kenya: The History of Two Nations*; and in part because we had subsequently befriended the Kikuyu leader, Mbiyu Koinange. Though older than Rita's father he delighted in saying that the latter was, in Kikuyu fashion, *his* father.

There was, however, one no less compelling reason for our Kenya contacts: we had become close friends of Birhanu Tesemma, an Ethiopian who, as a refugee in Kenya during the Fascist Occupation of his country, had been in contact with my mother. He was later appointed Ethiopian Consul in Nairobi, where he invited the three of us to stay with him and his German wife, Edith, in early August 1958—and introduced us to the principal African and several Asian leaders. As an exile in Kenya during the Italian Occupation he had provided my mother with information about Ethiopian patriot activity for *New Times and Ethiopia News*. He was later a diplomat in the Ethiopian Embassy in the Soviet Union, Counsellor in London and Ambassador, successively in Liberia and Turkey.

We accepted with alacrity Birhanu's invitation to stay with him and Edith. It was the beginning of a life-long friendship which continued with each of them separately after their divorce. They turned out to be delightful hosts, Birhanu being very interested, and knowledgeable about East Africa.

We stayed for almost a week enjoying their hospitality. In her letters home, Rita observed that the house was tastefully arranged, with polished parquet floors and Persian carpets; that they lived in a beautifully designed old-style house, small only by Kenya's palatial standards for Europeans, similar, but more luxurious than the mansions in Bishop's Avenue, London; that each house nearby was in a different style, some Spanish-looking and others like the London mansions, and that they all had spacious and beautiful gardens.

Rita went on: "As we arrived at the beginning of the week-end, Birhanu, having a single additional hunting permit, invited Richard to join him on a day's expedition in the Masai Reserve. Sylvia and I were thankful to be left out. Although Richard had, as a London school boy, been shown how to operate an anti-aircraft gun, he had never held a rifle, so this was his first and only experience of this kind of weapon. Fortunately, Birhanu did not expect him to do any shooting. We learned much later, when we visited him and his family at their summer house at Bishoftu, on Lake Babogaya, that he was a very good shot, and also a keen bird-watcher and conservationist.

"Nairobi itself we did not find particularly interesting, though Rita thought it tidier and more "English" than Addis Ababa. All the roundabouts were carefully tended, some with bougainvillea stretched on wires to make a carpet of different colours. On the Monday we visited the main Nairobi Library, endowed by Lady Macmillan, and opened to non-Europeans a month earlier. In the afternoon Birhanu took us in his huge old car to the Limburu Hills where one could see the stark contrast in the living standards of Africans and white settlers. We were interested to see Kenya in the period after the end of the Mau Mau rebellion. Unlike Richard, who had written a book about the recent history of Kenya, I had no exposure to the country's history and independence struggle, and understood little of the politics of that time.

"The first evening we were invited to a party by Ismaili Indians connected with a new-multiracial hospital endowed by the Agha Khan. My most abiding impression was meeting the young and energetic Tom Mboya, a prominent Kenya Trades Union leader, who became General Secretary of the Kenya Federation of Labour. He showed us round a new housing estate built by the Nairobi Municipality. His enthusiasm and dedication made us feel hopeful about Kenya's future." As we have seen in Chapter 4, he later came to Ethiopia and lectured most interestingly at the National Library. Little did we know that, less than ten years later, in 1969, he was to be assassinated.

At another party, given by a prominent member of the Indian community, we met Hari Chhabra, a post-graduate Indian student from Delhi University completing a thesis on Indian-African relations. He was a voluble Punjabi who, under a jolly façade, had a deep commitment to African independence.

Commenting on the situation in Kenya Rita wrote: "A mighty struggle is in progress and they [the Africans] are alert and ready to win their freedom. Kenya has capable leaders, and the country has taken a great step forward as a direct result of Mau Mau. There is no longer any discrimination in hotels, lavatories, restaurants. There has been much progress in education, though on the land the Kikuyu are still confined in their reserves and living at a subsistence level, while next door huge areas of land are empty, reserved for future white settlers."

I later reported on our visit in a polemical article, which appeared in the October-November 1958 issue of the Addis Ababa *Menen Magazine*. Writing for the Ethiopian reader, and having the Italian Occupation largely in mind, I wrote:

"Mau Mau lost the recent war in Kenya, but the cause for which it fought is not defeated. The British Commander-in-Chief, Sir George Erskine, admitted as much on

28 October 1953 at the height of the Emergency, when he declared that basically the Kenya problem was not a military one and that there was no military solution to it.

"There was no negotiation with Mau Mau for a peaceful solution; instead African resistance was destroyed by the heaviest possible bombing in which thousands of animals were also killed or wounded.

"Peace has now returned to Kenya. With it one can see the truth of Sir George Erskine's prophesy, for the African people are united in their determination to achieve their historical aims: self-government in an African State, and an end to the European monopoly of the colony's best lands. These were the aims of the Kikuyu Central Association before the war [i.e. World War II], of the Kenya African Union after the war, of Mau Mau, and of all present-day African leaders. They must be accepted by all lovers of Justice.

"As a result of the Emergency almost all the African patriotic leaders are either in prison or in exile. Jomo Kenyatta is serving the last few years of his sentence for 'managing Mau Mau'. Letters smuggled out of the prison by his colleagues suggest that conditions are awful, but the Government has so far refused to allow impartial observers to inspect. Instead, the Governor, Sir Evelyn Baring, took the opportunity to declare that even when his sentence expires in 1960, Kenyatta will still not be allowed to live among the Kikuyu.

"Kenyatta remains, however, an internationally famous African leader. In 1936 he founded the 'International African Friends of Abyssinia' and presented an address of welcome to H.I.M. the Emperor Hayle-Sillasé on his arrival in Britain. Ten years later he assisted Dr. Kwame Nkrumah (now Prime Minister of Ghana) in organising the Pan-African Congress which was held in Manchester in 1945. Mr. Odinga, one of the African elected members of the Legislative Council, in a speech in the Council recently, declared that he [Kenyatta] was still the leader of the Kenya African people, and his portrait can still be seen on the walls of African patriots of Kenya."

HEADING FOR UGANDA

After a whirlwind visit to Kenya, my mother, wishing to return to Addis Ababa, we decided on the spur of the moment to make an even shorter visit to Uganda.

When I went to purchase the train tickets for Kampala the European saleswoman declared: "You will be travelling First Class, of course". "Why of course?" I asked. "Because you are European," she replied, "Europeans travel First Class, Asians Second Class, and Africans, Third Class."

RITA

UGANDA

One of those travelling Second Class was Hari Chhabra, an Indian friend of Mengistu Lemma's whom, as we have seen, we had met in Nairobi a week or two earlier (He became our friend, too, and was later to be our guest in Addis Ababa). Since he could not visit us in our First Class compartment, we broke the rules and spent a good part of the journey in his Second Class section of the train, though we had to retire to our First Class sleeping compartment for the night. In the daytime and evening we enjoyed many hours of serious talk and much laughter with Hari.

After climbing over 2,700 m. past a station on the Equator we descended to 1,200 m. to reach Kampala—lying in a much greener, more tropical landscape than Nairobi, let alone Addis Ababa.

In Kampala we made a brief stop at Makerere College, the centre of higher education in East Africa. The College was more like a University than the University College of Addis Ababa, but that was not surprising, since Makerere had been founded much earlier, in 1922. We admired its library, noting that there was a collection of works on microcard. Several former LSE colleagues of Richard's took us to lunch and we were invited to dine at High Table, just as though we were in Oxford, but, not having planned to go to Uganda, we were able to see only a few Makerere scholars interested in African history or current affairs. However, we were introduced to Ugandan political leaders at a cocktail given in our honour by the Sudanese Consul, to whom Birhanu had recommended us.

We met several of Hari's cheerful Indian friends who lavishly entertained us. Among them was young Rajat Neogy, a local Indian enthusiast, founder and editor of *Transition*—the first cultural journal to be produced in British East Africa, for which Richard later wrote an article on the history of 19th century Ethiopia's acquisition of fire-arms, a subject with which he was then much fascinated.

Rajat visited us in Addis Ababa not long after the birth of Alula, our first child. I shall always remember that, when we set out for a drive into town, he insisted that we should take the baby with us, explaining that babies like movement and activity, but got bored in their cots.

Decades later we visited Hari in New Delhi. Much older, and not in good health, he was nevertheless as ebullient as he had been in his youth.

Richard produced a booklet in April 1958 to commemorate the First Conference of Independent African States, which was to open in Ghana in December. It was issued as a Supplement to *Ethiopia Observer*. Rita commented that the impeding Conference was "arousing quite a lot of interest here", but added: "it surprises us how little attention is being paid to it on the BBC."

It became evident, when lectures at the National Library were connected with Africa, that Ethiopian interest in African affairs was at this time escalating, especially among young educated professionals.

ECONOMIC COMMISSION FOR AFRICA

In December 1958 the finishing touches were being put to preparations for a United Nations Economic Commission for Africa. The Emperor had given it a large and beautiful new building, named Africa House. It was, and is, situated opposite the main gates of the Jubilee Palace, where important guests were at that time accommodated.

Africa House, donated by the Emperor, later named Africa Hall, headquarters of the United Nations Economic Commission for Africa

Our friend Idris Soleiman was on the Reception Committee, every evening working on preparations for the Conference. Roads were repaired and some, near the Commission headquarters, were widened. There was a general cleaning up of the town, several restaurants and cinemas being threatened with closure if they failed to improve their facilities.

Sylvia and I hoped that the Social Service Society would be able to take on, and eventually rehabilitate, at least some of the beggars then being removed from the streets. However, after the Conference they, or others, were soon back.

Mekki Abbas, the Sudanese Secretary-General of the Commission, arrived in advance, along roads festooned to receive him. Just as all hotels were full to bursting point, there landed a four-engine plane, full of Swiss tourists who had not announced their arrival ahead of time. We heard no more as to where the hapless tourists were accommodated. Another sign of the times was that in honor of the occasion two Ethiopian weekly newspapers, *Addis Zemen* and *The Ethiopian Herald,* were transformed into dailies.

The Emperor opened the proceedings with a long address which evoked echoing speeches from all the delegation heads, welcoming his presence and praising both him and what he had said. There were also speeches from Dag Hammarskjöld, the United Nations Secretary-General, and from Mekki Abbas.

Sessions took place in the Ethiopian Parliament building, suitably adorned with the flags of participating states. The Commission's Chair was Abbebe Retta, who had led the Ethiopian delegation to the First Conference of Independent African States and had earlier been Ethiopian Ambassador in London. Delegates and the Press, which included Sylvia and Richard, were, for the first time in Ethiopia, equipped with headphones that offered simultaneous translation into English and French. Richard, reporting on the Conference to my parents, observed that the Arab powers had not been able to address the Conference in translation, though a few of their delegates insisted on speaking in Arabic, getting a fellow delegate to follow in English or French. The claim of the Arabs was, in his view, mainly one of prestige and precedent, as the delegates were, he believed, all able to speak either English or French. Delegates of the Arabic-speaking countries, for their part, pointed out that the South Americans could use Spanish in similar conferences, and that, out of 65 million people represented directly at the Commission, about 40 million in five states used Arabic as the language of instruction. Richard found the formal speeches rather boring. He wrote: "To listen [to all of them] is time consuming, but to read them is delightful as one just puts the verbatim reports in the waste paper basket."

Richard continued: "The Conference has been captured by the independent states, who have the Secretary-General (Sudanese, elected by the UN), the Chair (Ethiopian) and two Vice-Chairs (Liberian and Tunisian), elected at the first session. The colonial powers tried, contrary to the Constitution, to elect a third Vice-Chair, suggesting that he should be one of them, but the Ghana Delegation insisted that there should be no departure from the Constitution. Ethiopia, Sudan, Egypt, Libya, Morocco, Tunisia, Ghana, Guinea and Liberia outnumber Britain, France, Belgium, Italy and Portugal, so that the independent states dominate. This may regrettably result in a withdrawal of interest in the Commission on the part of the colonial powers. Tom Mboya, whose speech we went to hear, spoke as a non-governmental representative, a delegate of the International Confederation of Free Trade Unions. It was a well-reasoned speech. Incidentally, it underlined the importance the UN attached to trade unions, which, however, receive less respect in some parts of the African continent."

Sylvia, Richard and I were invited to the reception the Emperor gave for the Commission delegates and observers. It was at the new Jubilee Palace, tastefully decorated in muted colours. Richard and I sat with Tom Mboya and his colleagues from the East Africa Labour College and heard about their work in training trade union leaders, though we were mainly in a lighter mood, induced by the wonderful food served by Japanese house-keepers in kimonos. Mboya, who had settled the Mombasa dock dispute when barely out of his teens, moved about the Imperial Palace, with its mirrors and fine cutlery, as though he had been born with knives and forks—fish and ordinary—as well as golden spoons, in his mouth. The title role went to the Emperor, who was obviously happy, walking to the buffet and talking with many of his guests. Not a few observers contrasted his position that day, and the day less than a decade earlier when he spoke at the League of Nations in Geneva, booed by Fascist journalists.

SECOND CONFERENCE OF INDEPENDENT AFRICAN STATES

There was much enthusiasm in Addis Ababa for the Second Conference of Independent African States, held in the Ethiopian capital in June 1960. I wrote to my parents: "Something must have happened to the time-table for the Conference, as the whole of the area near the theatre is still dug up, with drain-pipes and paving stones everywhere. Even during the Conference Addis Ababa was not at its best, as the road works increased the mud which the regular rainy season was letting loose. We met the plane bringing Koinange from Ghana where he had been adviser to Nkrumah on Kenyan affairs". He told Richard several times how well he remembered the party my parents had given at their house in honour of our visit to England the previous summer. The Conference achieved considerable unanimity on many subjects, especially, of course, on South Africa. A Libyan statistician explained that, from an economic point of view, Africans in South Africa were likely to suffer more if the *status quo* were maintained than from the hardships that might befall them through a boycott. Richard's first article, on the Conference, appeared in *West Africa* on 2 July.

At the National Library several participants gave lectures to packed audiences (See Chapter 4). Julius Nyerere spoke to Tanganyika students at University College. He launched the idea that an East African Federation should be formed before any of the countries concerned reached independence, arguing that, once a country had achieved independence, it would be less willing to abdicate it again, as was the case with Nigeria. He struck me as a real teacher and leader, with a ready laugh and even temperament. To one student, who started making a highly political speech—as far as I can remember, denouncing colonialism—he replied that the most important thing was to think about providing milk for their country's children.

Richard at this time gave a number of lectures on African political issues. One of these was an opening address to an East, West and Central Africa student seminar on Imperialism and Colonialism held at the UCAA in January 1960.

In February 1962, through Koinange, we met Jean Jenkins, a musicologist interested in African folk music. She travelled widely in Ethiopia and made unusual recordings of ethnic music. Jean introduced us to a number of African personalities passing through Addis Ababa, including Kaunda and Kapepwe, who were then friends working for the independence of Northern Rhodesia. They came to a gathering at our house, and sang independence songs, with Simon playing the guitar. We were most impressed with Kaunda and were not surprised when, two years later he became the founding President of what was re-named Zambia, nor that he remained President for twenty-two years.

***

In the period covered by this volume, the idea of an African Union permeated the thinking of our Africa Society, of the National Library lectures, and of freedom fighters throughout the continent, no less than of the great conferences of African Heads of State. That idea, despite much opposition, took root, as witnessed by later generations—and remains on the agenda of history.

CHAPTER 7

Travels in the Land of Prester John

RICHARD

Like previous foreign residents in Ethiopia—the renowned Land of Prester John—we undertook a number of journeys to various parts of this far-flung and very varied country. Our travels differed from those of historic travellers of the past in that ours were mainly conducted by car, rather than by camel or mule—and although some journeys took us to historic antiquities, others, especially while my mother was alive, were to development sites—for Ethiopia by our day was entering a state of post-World War II modernisation.

We were accompanied on many of these expeditions by Andreas Eshete , who was then a student at Menilek School and a volunteer in the National Library, as seen in Chapter 4. He was with us in 1960, when we travelled in our Volkswagen all the way to Massawa, and to Assab on the return journey.

Italian roads at the time under consideration were much in evidence, but were extremely narrow by present-day standards. Traffic was likewise sparse, so that it was not unusual to drive for an hour or more without encountering a vehicle travelling in the opposite direction.

On one occasion, preparing for our journey, Andreas and I went to a baker's shop to buy fresh bread, while Rita stayed in the car. The salesman urged us to purchase some of his cakes, declaring they were "good with coffee." When we finally came to eat them—without coffee—we found them distinctly mediocre, after which the phrase "good with coffee" entered our private language for anything that was not much good!

TRAVELS IN THE ENVIRONS OF ADDIS ABABA

HAYLE-SILLASÉ SECONDARY SCHOOL AND THE EMPEROR'S GIFT

Several of our trips in the environs of Addis Ababa took us to visit modern schools. The most prestigious at this time was the Hayle-Sillasé Secondary School, situated at

Kotebé on the road to Asmara. This school was called after the Emperor, who often visited it, bringing fruit, clothes and other gifts. Many of its alumni, who were our friends, went on to study abroad.

Shortly after Rita's arrival Afewerk took the three of us on an excursion into the plain below Kotebé. At that time it was lined on both sides with huge, elegant eucalyptus trees, planted in Emperor Menilek's time, but later cut down for road widening. We went for a short walk away from the road, as Afewerk wanted us to see a little known, natural pool where he and other schoolboys used to bathe.

Graduates of the school, to this day remember a curious incident which resulted from the Emperor's habit of bringing gifts of food to the school. One day, the students, seeing some food they did not recognise, presumed that His Imperial Majesty had come with a gift of pork, which was, of course, forbidden by the Ethiopian Orthodox Church. What to do? A vigorous debate ensued. Some students concluded that the royal visitor was testing their faith, and that they, therefore, should not touch the gift, while others believed that he was testing their loyalty to *him* and that they should accordingly eat it with fortitude. Our friend Mengistu Lemma, the son of a prominent priest, staunchly refused to touch it, while our friend Habte-ab, a Protestant, facing no dilemma, thoroughly relished it.

We think that it is impossible that any Ethiopian Palace cook would not have been aware of the religious prohibition on eating pork. However, the Emperor usually had a highly recommended foreign house-keeper. She may have prepared a dish which the students, who had never seen pork, may have thought it to be that forbidden meat, and which caused them to react in the manner described. History does not relate what in fact the Emperor brought.

MULU FARM

At the beginning of February 1957 we paid our first of several trips to Mulu Farm, then a two and a half hours' drive north of Addis Ababa. With Andreas we visited Brigadier Daniel Sandford and his wife Christine, who lived there, far away from the capital, and had done so for countless years. The Brigadier had farmed in Ethiopia already before the Second World War. After Mussolini's declaration of war on Britain and France in June 1940, the British Government sent him on a mission to the Patriots of Gojjam. Richard once described the Sandfords as the northernmost of the Kenya settlers, and indeed their way of life had something in common with European immigrants in Africa further south. Rita wrote: "The Brigadier is in his seventies and runs the farm. He looks a mere fifty, with a huge protruding stomach, a large frame and plenty of energy."

Mrs. Sandford was the author of *Ethiopia under Hailé Selassié* (1946) and a biography of the Emperor, *The Lion of Judah Hath Prevailed* (1955). The mother of several by now adult, and socially conscious, children, she used to run the Sandford School in Addis Ababa. Later she helped with the farm and ran a large household, baking her own bread, making cheese, butter, jam and cakes, as well as organising a clinic and being very jolly, large and healthy. We drove over Intoto along a chain of mountains and golden plains on which a multitude of cattle were grazing. The Sandfords' house and farm was an oasis of pine and acacia at the head of the gorge of the Muger River, a tributary of the Blue Nile. We were given the traditional English tea and sandwiches on the lawn. Mrs Sandford presided in her famous wide-brimmed straw hat decorated with dried flowers. Rita wrote: "The scenery is spectacular, with flat mountain tops, waterfalls and a difference of 500 m. (meters) between their upper and lower farms. On the upper one grow most of the English herbaceous border flowers: pink honeysuckle, six colour combinations of fuchsia, spirea, sunflowers, lilies, salvia, lobelia, eschscholzia and myriads of roses. The Sandfords are successful with plums—and with strawberries, which they alone produce for the Addis Ababa market. In the lower farm they are experimenting with bananas, oranges, grapefruit, figs etc. It is amazing what the earth will produce here, with proper irrigation and care."

With my mother and Andreas, who was on holiday from school, we visited Mulu Farm again a year later. The Sandfords, Rita wrote, "are doing community development—building a school and clinic and doing some social work, as well as running their strawberry etc. farm and garden. They are hospitable and hardworking and doing an important job in the area. Andreas was a great help as interpreter and asker-of-the-way, and enjoyed himself enormously. Alas, on Monday he goes back to school and I don't have him at the library any more, except Saturday mornings."

AMBO SWIMMING POOL

Shortly after our first visit to Mulu, we went to Ambo, some 230 km. west of Addis Ababa, a spa with a warm water swimming pool fed by natural springs, and the source of the much appreciated Ambo Mineral Water. Mikaél Imru, Belay Abbay and Richard came to work there on editing Ethiopia's first Five Year Plan. Mikaél Imru had gradu-ated in Philosophy, Politics and Economics at Oxford. He was popular and hard-

Idris Suleiman and Belay Abbay beside the Ambo Swimming Pool, 1957

working and looked like a don, with a thin, long neck and a mass of burly hair. He was the descendant of a distinguished family with a resis-tance record and a reputation for liberalism. Belay was an economist who had studied at Southampton University. His father, *Fitawrari* Abbay, was a Tigray Patriot. Others who joined the party included Idris Suleiman, Head of the Handicraft School, who brought his guitar, but not his wife, which was surprising for someone as modern in all other ways, and Habte-ab Bayru who wore a comic straw hat. Afewerk did not come because he was finishing his Queen of Sheba painting for St. George's Cathedral.

On arrival at 8 p.m. we all went straight into the pool. Rita was happy to be swimming again, particularly in warm water. Then we adjourned to the empty Ambo house of the Imru family. People brought in their air mattresses, blankets and cushions. An entirely Ethi-

Miliyon Neqneq and Rita swimming in the Ambo Swimming Pool, 1957

opian meal had been prepared, with *injera* and the chicken-and-hard-boiled-eggs in a goulash-like very peppery stew called *wet*, which you pick up between bits of "bread." We enjoyed it thoroughly. Then we all sat back and listened to Idris on the guitar. Various people danced, and drank *tella*—the Ethiopian beer. We had discovered the perfect week-end resort, which we were often to visit again in later years.

Model of a Landrover made by local children, and sold along the Ambo Road.

On one visit in August 1960 we were intrigued by some cleverly made model churches, aeroplanes and cars that young boys tried to sell us along the Ambo Road. We could not find out from which plants they had extracted the white pith they used to construct these realistic, but fragile structures. On subsequent visits we were always in a hurry to arrive—or depart, so that we are still in the dark, as no one, as far as we know, has investigated the matter.

WENJI SUGAR ESTATE

With the Fiat we joined Sylvia on a visit to the Wenji Sugar Estate, near Nazaret (which reverted to its Oromo name of Adama in later years), some 115 km. south-east of Addis Ababa. It was a beautiful drive. A Dutch company formerly operating in Indonesia had established a sugar plantation with Indonesian cane, the stated aim being to produce enough sugar for all Ethiopian needs. This proved unrealistic, in view of the expansion of demand, fuelled by the steep population growth, and the increasing national addiction to highly sweetened tea and coffee.

When we visited, the factory was only four years old. It reminded Rita dimly of some family sugar concern in Romania—only at Wenji the sugar was less refined, and not cut into neat white squares. We visited the school built by the company for employees' children aged 3-8 and run by the government. The cane was not ready to be processed. We were told that, when the time came for cutting it, migrant labourers would arrive from different parts of the country. In the past, seasonal workers had been known only in Addis Ababa. The Wenji area had been malaria-infested, but recent plantations of eucalyptus, by drying the land, had reduced the mosquito population.

RITA

QOQA DAM WITH MAJOR ASEFFA AND WEYZERO SINIDDU GEBRU

Also in our first year we accompanied Sylvia to the Qoqa Dam and Reservoir, financed out of Italian War Reparations funds. We were taken by Major Aseffa Lemma, Sylvia's guide on her first visit to Ethiopia, and his wife Siniddu Gebru in their comfortable Chevrolet to see the progress on the Dam. It was to flood a reservoir area of 26 km. and completion was expected in time for the 1959 flood waters. The work force was composed of Ethiopian labourers, Ethiopian and Italian technicians, and Norwegians supervisors. There was great enthusiasm for the project on the spot, and no apparent inter-racial tension. Major Aseffa was chief of the Electric Power Authority. He was a young energetic person, like his wife, newly elected to the Ethiopian Parliament. We much appreciated the trip, also because the Italian engineer who came with his wife to live at Qoqa 16 years earlier to run a very small power station, had started an orchard which was an oasis of green in the dust. It was our first sight of many fruit trees. He grew oranges, lemons, grapefruit, tangerines, mangos, avocados, papayas, bananas, guavas, raspberries, and more. He and his wife lived there in solitude for many years and found themselves suddenly in the middle of a whirlwind of activity, with dynamite and dust.

WHERE WAS MOUNT BORARA?

Major Aseffa Lemma, showing the Emperor the construction site for the Hydro-electric Dam at Qoqa, about to be built from Italian Reparations funds, ca 1955

For some time Richard had been wondering whether we could identify a place discussed by O.G.S. Crawford in *Ethiopian Itineraries* as having existed in medieval times in an area not too distant from today's Addis Ababa, when the Ethiopian court was situated in that vicinity. One Sunday in early June 1958 we set out with Andreas on an unusual errand: to find the location of a place called Mount Borara, the capital of Ethiopia in the sixteenth century. One theory was that the old capital was on Mount Borara, south-east of Bishoftu, and so we headed in that direction. Rita was driving the Fiat used by Sylvia, as our Volkswagen was in the garage. This was unfortunate as the Fiat was old and not strong; beyond Bishoftu, Richard directed me off the road, towards Mount Yerer. We had to reverse several times, once because of a river we could not cross, another time because of the steep railway embankment. We drove on a number of tracks, Andreas asking local shepherds whether they had heard of Borara. No one had, nor did we come across any imposing ruins.

As the sun was setting we had to turn back. The expedition failed, although the Fiat proved its worth. On the return journey we played various word games and were surprised by the extent of Andreas's general knowledge. He was, of course top of his class.

YEKA MIKAÉL ROCK CHURCH

The following year, in December 1958, continuing our visits to places of historic interest, we introduced my parents, who came on a visit, to the concept of a rock church. The expedition, on foot, was undertaken with Philip Mansfield and Andreas to see the Yeka Mikaél rock church at the eastern end of the Intoto range, behind the British Embassy. The roof of the church had caved in, but there were pillars, a doorway and several windows still clearly visible. It was in the style of the Lalibela churches except that the architecture was somewhat cruder. It was in a bad state of preservation, with trees growing through the walls. Unfortunately the authorities were at that time uninterested in preserving historic monuments. All we could do was to trust that there would be something to salvage when interest was awakened.

Half a century later, an American artist, Bruce Strachan, made a study of the church ruins and, in the Ethiopian archaeological journal, *Annales d'Éthiopie*, urged the need for immediate preservation. Action to shore up the walls of the church and clear the bushes growing within them was finally being taken in 2011.

ZIQWALA WITH RITA'S PARENTS

With a group of friends, including Afewerk and Mengistu, we took my parents for a picnic on Mount Ziqwala. Already a place of pilgrimage in medieval times, as indicated in the 1460 map of the Venetian cartographer Fra Mauro, it is a convent, as well as a monastery, Ethiopian style, made up of two separate clusters of small huts, and a modest church. The mountain, an extinct volcano, is a landmark visible from a great distance from most directions, and can be seen on a clear day from Addis Ababa. The crater had formed a lake, the water of which is considered holy and therefore out of bounds for swimmers, though the faithful carry it away in bottles. The road was as rocky after the rains as it is today, but, unlike today, the mountain was densely forested and almost uninhabited. The only vehicle we could obtain was a pick-up with a tarpaulin cover. Our most vivid memory of this trip was our appearance, when we returned: the dust had lined our faces and turned our hair white, so that we were given a glimpse of what we might be expected to look like in old age.

We visited Ziqwala again to see the *Temqet* , or Epiphany, celebrations, in which the waters of the lake play an important role. On this occasion, in January 1961, we went with *Abba* Jerome, whose company and knowledge of all things Ethiopian we came to appreciate more and more. Though there were fewer aged trees on the mountain, nothing had changed up there except that the view by this time included the new reservoir produced by the Qoqa Dam. Through the good offices of *Abba* we were given some *injera* prepared for the worshipers of the church by some Eritrean nuns.

On a subsequent visit, during the annual festival of Gebre-Menfes-Qeddus, popularly known as Abbo, the Egyptian saint closely associated with the monastery, we followed the Christian procession round the lake. Half way, we heard drumming. Following these sounds we came upon a celebration by followers of traditional religious beliefs, dancing and singing. The two very different forms of worship co-existed in harmony.

DEBRE BIRHAN AND POINT 4

On a Sunday towards the end of February 1959 we accompanied Sylvia on a visit to Debre Birhan, North-East of Addis Ababa, then three hours' journey on the Asmara road. It was the Ethiopian capital in the fifteenth century and was named "Mount of Light" by Emperor Zera-Yaqob because he saw it illuminated (by Haley's comet) in 1466. We drove there in order to visit an American Point 4 Community Project, a teacher training facility about which Sylvia was writing, for *Ethiopia Observer* Vol. III, No. 1. The town is at an altitude of about 3,500 m., considerably higher than Addis Ababa. It felt cool, as the sky was overcast. Furthermore we were in the middle of the small rains and there was only the occasional hour of sunshine.

A Point 4 expert took us to the school, which was still being built. It offered a two-year further training course for teachers who then went out into the country as inspectors or community leaders. They were instructed in all sorts of subjects: weaving, carpentry, agriculture, sports, and sewing for women. It was a residential school with separate quarters for families and bachelors, built out of stone, quarried a few dozen yards away. The staff was entirely Ethiopian and the trainees were partly recruits from secondary schools, and partly teachers, some with long experience.

The countryside was much bleaker than around Addis Ababa but did not look forbidding, as the fields were brightened by flowering red and yellow aloe. In this area houses, though round, were not made of wattle and daub as in other parts of Shewa, probably because here wood was scarce. Instead they were built of stone, rather like Yorkshire walls between fields. There were barely any eucalyptus trees at this altitude but many herds of cattle and numerous horses grazed on vast plains.

CAMPING BELOW QOQA DAM

In November 1959 we chose to camp for the weekend with Andreas beside one of the small lakes scheduled to be submerged by the waters which the dam would be holding back. We were pleasantly surprised to find the Bishoftu-Mojjo stretch of road paved, which considerably reduced the length of our journey to the little Lake Sombay, which was due to disappear in the reservoir. The countryside was already partly under water. The next morning we drove on to Lake Iléni, which would also disappear from the map. The hippos that used to patronise the area were evidently late risers as there was no sign of them. We lunched beside the main road which the flooding was approaching and saw with regret, trees submerged up to their branches. On our way back we passed an Oromo shrine, in the shape of a huge tree draped in cloth and hung with bells, leather straps and all kinds of pieces of iron.

LAKE WENCHI

For the five day holiday around *Timqat* in January 1960, we gladly accepted an invitation from Gebre-Kristos, a friendly mining engineer, to go with him into Kefa Province, but, as his Landrover was fully booked, we needed to come in our own transport, necessarily a Landrover—the only four-wheel drive vehicles in Ethiopia at the time. Aseffa Lemma kindly found us one, but he and his wife arrived on our doorstep with it at 9 a.m., whereas Gebre-Kristos's party had left at 5 a.m. We had to change our plan and decided to go on our own, to see the Jibat forest, westwards beyond the vineyards of Guder. We would take Sylvia with us, overnighting at Ambo. Having packed up the Landrover, we collected Andreas, and drove to Ambo on a Friday afternoon. The government hotel was full, as there was a ten-day gambling season in progress, but we stayed in medium comfort in a small hotel to which Aseffa Dula had taken us earlier. The hostess was famous for her cooking, though its somewhat fatty nature had bad consequences for Sylvia and me.

The next morning we set out for the forest, but after following the track towards it through woods, fields and streams for a good hour, the starter suddenly refused to obey. We pushed the vehicle down a hill with the aid of some local inhabitants, for, as so often happens in Ethiopia, there were people nearby. We could not get the engine going, although the battery seemed to be charged. Andreas volunteered to get on a horse lent by a neighbouring chief. It was a three-hour ride to the main road, where we hoped he would be able to hitch a car ride to Ambo. There two of *Ras* Imru's daughters were in charge of restoring their father's house and looking after their vineyard.

The two of us had acquired sleeping bags. Sylvia was ready to wrap up snugly in the thick fur Siberian rug that Rita's parents had brought from Romania and she had purloined for camping trips in Ethiopia, plus the eiderdown and pillow which Sylvia always had with her. One of the farmers offered us his house to sleep in and some milk to drink. At this juncture, Richard and Sylvia, the optimists of the party, decided that we should try once more to start the car. Richard driving, we pushed it down another slope, when I heard the engine roar. We hastily packed up and rushed away, found Andreas on the road and drove safely back to Ambo. A mechanic there played about with the Landrover, which was far from new, but found nothing wrong.

The next day we decided to make an attempt to reach Lake Wenchi, a crater lake only 30 km. from the town, but high up in the mountains. Not being entirely confident of the Landrover we persuaded Sylvia to remain in the Ambo residence of the Imru family, in case we had to make the final ascent to the edge of the crater on foot. We deposited Sylvia, picked up Hirut and Mamie Imru, and set off, up and up along narrow tracks, into a country of juniper and pine. As Rita was driving on a crest between steep drops on either side, she noted that it was difficult to put the car into first gear but we managed to reach the high point of the mountain where, when we got out, we were rewarded with the view towards and across the lake. We clambered down to the water's edge and looked across the deep blue water to a small island on which the thatched roof of the church was visible.

We were at such a high elevation that even at midday in the sun, a sweater was needed. We found a sheltered spot and inaugurated our gas stove—actually a small cylinder with a ring, which enabled us to brew some hot tea to drink with our picnic.

In the afternoon we drove back uneventfully, dropped the Imrus, picked up Sylvia and were driven back to Addis Ababa by Richard, who specialised in starting defective cars and driving by night. We arrived at midnight, two days before the end of the holiday. We were thus able to look forward to working on our projects for two days whilst many people were still on the road, eating the dust of other people's cars. We were very lucky: as Yami was taking the car back to the Ministry from which it had been borrowed, in the Piazza one wheel fell off! This event was not reported to Rita's parents.

MENILEK'S INTOTO

One Saturday afternoon in March 1961 we drove up to Menilek's capital with *Abba* Jerome, Odette Lovelace and some of her students from the Hayle-Sillasé Secondary School. We inspected the ruins of Menilek's Palace, subsequently restored. It was on the steps of the Palace that, almost half a century later, in February 2007, we saw an impressive performance of *Macbeth* by the local drama society, *Addis Stage*.

We visited the two churches: Raguél, built with the help of an Indian craftsman, Haji Kwass from Peshawar—an unusual, two-storey octagonal edifice with a balcony, around which Menilek walked on occasion; and Mariyam, completed by Empress Taytu, at which she and Menilek were crowned in 1890. The *Abba* was most helpful in persuading the truculent gate-keepers to let us in. His ripe old age was not at all evident as he skipped about agilely, but we got an inkling of it, when Richard mentioned the Great Ethiopian Famine of 1890-93, and *Abba* promptly told us all the details, since, as a boy, he had walked with his father to the Red Sea Coast near Massawa in search of grain.

NATIONAL PARK AT MENNAGESHA FOREST

In April 1961 with Andreas recently returned form the US and full of things to tell us, we visited the newly laid out National Park in the ancient Mennagesha Forest which clothed a good part of Wechacha Mountain south-west of Addis Ababa. We were enchanted by this magnificent forest with its huge indigenous trees, including juniper, *podocarpus*, and the beautiful *hagenia abyssinica*—the *koso* tree, which provides the traditional cure for tape-worm. The natural environment was further enhanced by the statuesque presence of the black and white Gureza monkeys and the cries of numerous colourful birds. A picnic site had been levelled, a water tap installed, and paths leading further up the mountain opened.

We were so delighted with the forest that we were back there the following month, this time with *Dejazmach* Tedla and Dorothy Obi, a librarian at ECA, who was also a poet and painter. She read us a poem about Ziqwala which we published in the *Observer* (Vol. V, No. 3). Later that year she and her husband invited us to dinner. On the walls were her poems and paintings—inspired mainly by Afewerk, with whom she fell in love. Though unrequited, this passion stimulated her artistic talents. A gifted woman, full of life, we were sorry when she and her much more sedate economist husband returned to Nigeria.

TRAVELS FURTHER AFIELD

RITA

JIMMA AGRICULTURAL SCHOOL

In late May 1957 we journeyed in a south-westerly direction, to Jimma, centre of the coffee-growing area, to visit the Agricultural Secondary School that Sylvia wanted to describe. Her account appeared in *Ethiopia Observer* Vol. I, No. 10. The town is a couple of thousand feet lower than Addis Ababa, in very pleasant country with luxuriant green vegetation against deep red soil. We travelled in a transport plane together with chickens and assorted agricultural produce, over spectacular scenery, and were met by Hugh Rouk, the Director of the School. It was staffed by some ten families from Oklahoma in a friendly, efficient manner. Their aim was to train boys in simple methods of improved agriculture, particularly coffee growing.

In the evening the boys arranged an interview for Sylvia, complete with microphone. It was the first time I had heard her speak in public. She was a born speaker, clear, to the point. They asked about Ethiopia and her place among the independent African countries, but also about London and women. Both of us were also unexpectedly called upon to talk about the University College of Addis Ababa and the National Library respectively. We had to do the same the next morning at classes to which we were sent separately. The students did class-work in the mornings and practical work in the afternoons. We had our meals with a different family each time and were subjected to American breakfast with jam, scones, egg and bacon on the same plate, eaten together. We stayed in the house of the Director, a young and quiet Oklahoman, and were much impressed by their work and enthusiasm.

We also were introduced to the Governor of Jimma Province, Colonel Tamrat Yiggezu, who was a quiet, well-educated and popular, youngish man, and his wife, a sister of Mikaél Imru's. We also saw one of Sylvia's wards, an Ethiopian nurse trained in London, who was fighting against odds to train others and to improve conditions in the Jimma Hospital. She was much to be admired, as she was from a rich and respected family and could easily have remained in Addis Ababa, leading a life of ease.

At lunch-time the next day we were to fly back. However, the plane was unexpectedly so full of mourners for the Duke of Harer's funeral that we could not get on: panic, as Richard had a lecture to give the next morning at 9 a.m. There was no alternative but to go by road. The School kindly lent us a Landrover and a driver, and we set off, leaving Sylvia behind to take the plane the next day. As the road unfolded in its mountain sweeps we did not regret it at all. Gradually we came to the huge chasm of the Gibé River, a gorge so deep and wide that one was left breathless. Odd mountains kept springing up out of the blue as it were. It was getting dark as we descended, and down at the bottom we saw the river only in flashes of eerie lightning, as owls peered at our headlights from the middle of the road.

This was the country of the Gurage, an industrious people. At a point on the road called "Banana Bend" by the Oklahomans, the vendors swarmed around the car—lovely girls with finely platted hair and huge eyes, offering us bananas and limes in banana leaf and straw baskets, as well as the three legged stools, for which the area was famous. We piled several of the stools and baskets of fruit up into the back of the Landrover after Richard had had his fill of bargaining.

When Sylvia returned, she brought a small pale blue plaster-cast plaque, presented to her by the school students, on which there was, in relief, the single word "Others." We thought it was the most appropriate present they could have given her. It summed up perfectly her way of life and philosophy.

MAJITTÉ COMMUNITY DEVELOPMENT CENTRE

Some months later we accompanied Sylvia in quest of information on community projects for the *Ethiopia Observer*, which, appeared in Vol. II, No. 10. We went to Majitté, some 300 km. in the Asmara direction, to visit the UNESCO Community Development Training Centre. The night before we set out Sylvia had been unwell and we worked hard to persuade her to abandon the journey. Not likely! "Does this mean that I have come to the end of my working life?", quoth she (aged 76). We tried to explain to her that there was a happy medium between spending the rest of her life in an armchair and going on an eight hour drive on an exceedingly rough road, on two consecutive days. Nothing doing!

We eventually set out by car with Idris and duly reached Debra Birhan, where we spent the night.

Early the next morning we were off in a Landrover up the long winding roads and through a tunnel with Mussolini's name still painted on it, before descending steeply down to Debre Sina. We stopped for tea at a lorry drivers' pull-up. There were quite a number of these along the route, catering mainly for the Italian drivers who brought huge trucks at a snail's pace up from Asmara.

Hirut Imru at Majitté Community Centre, 1957

After the refreshing breeze of the mountains at 3,500 m. we drove gradually towards a wide river valley—but there was only parched sand in the river bed. We rattled on through bushy country past Karakoré—an important market town which we visited on our return journey. It was later the site of a major earthquake. We then branched off for the last 10 km. westwards, crossing this dry river bed. The "road" was almost impassable in the rainy season and, at this time, was a bumpy track caused by irrigation channels through which our Landrover bull-dozed its way with various degrees of success. The area, being irrigated, had bananas and beautiful 1.5 m. high maize. By this time it was two o'clock and the heat was blistering. At last we saw Majitté, a market town perched on the steep slope of a mountain—a cluster of downy looking round roofs in brown thatch, and below: the training centre—designed in a square and whitewashed, with neat corrugated iron roofs.

We were welcomed by Hirut Imru, who was stationed there, teaching the trainees and village women fundamental hygiene, literacy etc. She was full of enthusiasm for the work being done there. The staff and trainees lived simply in houses built of compressed mud bricks and with rather rudimentary sanitary arrangements ("Turkish" WCs) but this, we thought all to the good: if the trainees lived at a luxury standard they were likely to be much more unhappy when they were finally sent out to work by themselves in the villages.

We visited a lively, cramped market there and admired the two-storey houses in the village. In the evening, to Idris's strumming, we danced and sang in honour of one popular member of staff, by entoning her name: *Yeshimabét Teferi*". Much enthusiasm was generated by M. Garraud, the French chief of the project, a sturdy, energetic, and wise person ideally suited for the job. His assistant was a Dutchman whose wife strummed on a banjo to the extent of Loch Lomond and Tipperary. Sylvia, as fresh as a cucumber and fresher than the rest of the party, was of course busy gathering information and visiting the establishment.

At night some slept in the rudimentary guest house while others were billeted on members of staff. The spirit of the staff and trainees seemed excellent. On our way back we stopped to admire the crescent-shaped metal ear-rings and bright beads of the women at Karakoré market. Sylvia was really amazing throughout. Only two days later did she admit that she'd had a headache!

ENCOUNTER WITH CROCODILES ON LAKE ABBAYYA

In marked contrast to the above social-research-oriented expeditions was a 500 km. excursion to the then fairly remote Lake Abbayya, formerly referred to as Margherita, in the south of the country. The five-day journey was undertaken at the beginning of May 1959, during a long week-end, combining Easter with the Liberation Day holiday on 5 May.

We travelled on that occasion with an English teaching couple, Mr and Mrs. Lovelace, and their friend, Colette Cunningham, all three of whom were employed teaching English at the Hayle-Sillasé Secondary School. Neither of us remember calling the Lovelaces by their Christian names. He and his wife were inveterate travellers, who loved adventure and found these expeditions a change from teaching in a secondary school. They inspired us with the confidence to undertake our first ever camping experience, both of us having lived entirely urban lives. We grew gradually more confident, and acquired our own tent in 1960. However, on our first camping occasion, and with some trepidation, I enquired whether there were snakes near the lake where we were proposing to camp.

Mr Lovelace wistfully replied: "Unfortunately not."

The Lovelaces believed in comfortable camping and brought with them in their Landrover, folding chairs, a table, a portable gas cooker which was very easy to use, and a lamp which worked on the car battery.

Driving southwards towards the town of Dilla the countryside was truly beautiful: deep green grass and mountains, often red earth, majestic *zigba* trees, and women with intricately platted and buttered hair.

We then branched off to negotiate the 65 km. to Lake Abbayya.

The track was easy enough to start with, until we came to the first river—one of five without bridges. It would have been simple in dry weather; however, the rain had turned the slope into a muddy track. The Landrover slithered but forded the river well, but we, in a Volkswagen beetle, got stuck in the water. By this time Mr Lovelace was beginning to enjoy life. The trip had so far lacked adventure. As soon as we got stuck, his face brightened, he got his camera out of his car and, estimating the distance, took several photographs. Meanwhile the river was rapidly rising, as well as the water in our Volkswagen so that we appeared to be having a footbath. We scanned the river apprehensively in case a crocodile or two made an appearance, but luckily none did. The Lovelaces tied the two vehicles to each other by a nylon tow rope and then the dance began up to the far slope, which was very steep. Eventually they succeeded in pulling us up. On the flat land at the top we took some refreshment among the laughing shepherds who considered it all great entertainment.

On the following day we set off in the Lovelaces' little boat, to which he had attached an outboard engine. Cruising across the calm water to the main island, we heard about an ethnic group that lived only there. We found the entrance to their "harbour" through reeds in which the occasional crocodile lay sleeping on the shore at some distance away. The inhabitants greeted us in a friendly manner. One of them

Boat from Lake Abbayya, ca 1958

spoke Amharic well, and through him, Andreas discovered that they were by no means isolated: they transported the cotton they grew from one shore to the other in exchange for coffee, in boats of balsa-like, very light wood, shaped like a gondola and propelled by means of long poles. Their only request was for medicine, particularly against malaria.

As we left the island, Mr Lovelace, disappointed at not seeing any crocodiles at close quarters, decided to turn off the engine, which he thought, might be keeping them away. Immediately, one croc knocked forcefully on the bottom of our little boat while two or three others appeared in the vicinity, opening their mouths. One of them seemed to be eyeing Andreas, the smallest member of our party, as a possible *hors d'euvre*. We all screamed, urging Mr Lovelace to waste no time in re-starting the engine. He duly put his hand in the water to start it, whereupon, as he reported in the *Ethiopian Herald*, May, 1959, "another great mouth, full of pink tongue and fearsome yellow white teeth rose only a foot from my hand". He was able to retract his hand in time to start the boat. Frightened by the noise of the motor, the crocs slowly swam off to quieter waters.

Needless to say, the encounter with the crocs was not included in the letter to my parents describing this expedition.

For this journey to Lake Abbayya we had taken with us a hoolah-hoop, to which Afewerk had introduced us. We hoolah-hooped in front of astonished but silent shepherds. At a certain moment Richard demonstrated a neck technique and behold, they burst into merry laughter. He offered it to them to try. They accordingly laid aside their spears, which were purely decorative, and were soon hoolah-hooping with gusto.

A boat from Lake Abbayya which was some years later transported by truck to the Institute of Ethiopian Studies Museum, Rita in the foreground

BRIEF VISIT TO SUDAN

Returning, at the end of September 1959, from our first leave in Britain, we paid a brief but memorable visit to Sudan. Rita wrote:

"How can I begin to describe this land: flat with few trees except majestic big ones near the two Niles, hot of course, but not unbearably so, as the rainy season has only just ended. The fun of it was meeting so many Sudanese, some old friends of Richard's, such as Mohamed Osman Yassein, now Permanent Under-Secretary for Foreign Affairs, who was our host and treated us like royalty. Yasein is in his fifties, full of energy, very capable, and probably Sudan's most experienced administrator, as well as excellent company. There have been a number of tea parties (6:30 p.m.) and dinners (10:30 p.m.) at various houses, a breakfast with the grandson of the Mahdi in a luxurious palace—he is now the leader of the Mahdi's sect and a shrewd, educated man, talks with ministers, judges, civil servants, doctors. We were taken by Landrover up along the White Nile to the Jebel Aulia dam, 65 km. away…to see a new threat to navigation in the form of a type of water hyacinth which grows and grows, choking the whole width of the Nile. The dam receives water for Egypt and is run by Egyptians. We took a short trip by motor launch to Khartoum North, and visited the market at Omdurman—in fact tried to get an idea of the country and its problems."

Elaborating on this account in a subsequent letter I described the Sudan as "in so many ways a contrast to Ethiopia, culturally, economically, climatically, administratively, religiously", and added: "the countryside is quite flat and was only mildly green just after the rains. Normally it is just a desert of dust interrupted by brown squares of baked clay which make up the houses of a village."

WAITING FOR A FAN-BELT IN LEMMA'S LANDROVER

During the Easter holidays, in April 1960, we gladly accepted an invitation from Lemma Fire-Hiywet, who was Secretary of the Ethiopian Coffee Board, to accompany him on a journey into the Sidamo coffee country, one of the most fertile and beautiful areas of Ethiopia. Lemma was an economist educated in the US whom we first met on our journey back from Kenya. One of the ablest returnees, he had a delightful, slow sense of humour. As he was on duty, he was taking his driver with him, which made the journey easier. Neither Sylvia nor Andreas were able to come with us, but we were joined by Siyyum Beqqele, Lena and her minuscule dog. We arrived at Lake Awasa in the late afternoon and managed to pitch our new tent without Andreas's help. As night fell we could see the fires of other campers on either side, but not across the lake, which was vast. In a letter to my parents Richard described our dinner on the lake shore. "A sheep was slaughtered, and much local fish consumed—particularly by Siyyum's cook, who had just ended the long fast preceding Ethiopian Easter. Lena's pocket dog behaved most excellently. It took no notice when the sheep was done in and skinned; it refrained from leaving the camp, where it might have provided a snack for a hyena by night or for a vulture by day. One of the vultures had its eye on it, however."

The journey to Dilla was uneventful and all went well until, on the return journey, at a hamlet called Bulbula, the Landrover's all-important fan-belt snapped, and there was no spare in the car. Since by then the holiday was over, no car with the correct size fan-belt passed, so we had to send Lemma's driver to Addis Ababa for a new one—a delay of almost 24 hours. Lena, Siyyum and I put up in the two "rooms" at a simple local inn, while Lemma and Richard shared the Landrover, hoping to hail one with the desired spare fan-belt. There was no food on sale at the inn, but we soon found a kind woman who scrambled some eggs for us. Beside a river at the end of the settlement some papaya were being cultivated, but they were unripe. The next day in the afternoon the owner of a passing Landrover provided us with a spare fan-belt, and we set off, Lemma's driver arriving from Addis Ababa with a fan-belt half an hour later!

Bulbula is firmly etched in our memories.

RICHARD & RITA

TOUR OF NORTHERN ETHIOPIA

Very different was a journey to Eritrea, Gonder, the ports of Massawa and Assab, and other parts of the north, taken during the summer of 1960. It is described in three of Rita's letters to her parents.

We drove in our orange-coloured Volkswagen, in the company of K.C. Wang, a Chinese friend of Richard's from LSE. student days, and, of course, Andreas. Early on in the tour we found democratic decision-making too time-consuming and appointed

Wang our dictator. We left Addis Ababa on a Saturday in late July and returned exactly a fortnight later.

Our tour is described in three of Rita's letters to her parents:

The journey northwards was one of getting into the rhythm of daily travelling for about 300 km., leaving in the early morning and arriving at our destinations in the afternoon. This plan allowed for possible mishaps and gave us time to stretch our legs and visit places before dark. After three days with overnight stops at Desé and Qwiha, we had our last lunch in Adigrat, before crossing into Eritrea. At Adigrat, we tasted our first *qwulqwual*, or prickly pear, the fruit of a cactus imported long ago and now growing wild all over the hills in this part of the country. We then made for Asmara.

Rita described it in diary fashion:

"26 July: Here we are in Asmara. The car behaved wonderfully as we took it over the mountain passes—three of which were formidable. As it was the rainy season many fantastic views were behind clouds, but even what we did see, was breathtaking. The roads were dust-free and the lower lands pleasantly green instead of the more usual dusty brown. We saw monkeys and partridges, a fox, and an infinite variety of bright blue, yellow and red birds. Above Dessie we visited the palace of Negus Mikaél, King of Wello—a stone, solid structure, vaguely Turkish in design; and at Meqele we saw the palace of Emperor Yohannis IV with its banqueting hall, and imposing throne, as well as manuscripts and guns. There we paid a courtesy call on the present Governor, *Ras* Siyyum Mengesha, himself a descendant of Emperor Yohannis. While in Addis Ababa, he had invited us, to one of his banquets in honour of the wedding of Princess Aida to his son Mengesha. The *Ras* was sitting on the great throne, emulating Emperor Hayle-Sillasé, even to the point of having two chihuahuas at his feet. Neither he nor his ample wife had a clue who we were, as our name had been badly mauled by the translator—so we exchanged courtesies and he told us, thinking no doubt that we were a British mission, how much he believed in friendly relations between Ethiopia and Great Britain. He did not venture to express similar feelings toward Wong's country, perhaps because he was not sure what country it was.

"From Asmara, where we found a number of friends and had no time for shopping, we dropped down to Massawa, arriving in the late afternoon to view port lights and sample the excellent sea food at a restaurant. Although everyone warned us that Massawa in July was hotter than Hell, it was by no means unbearable, except during the night when we did not sleep too well, as we were unwilling to pay the exorbitant price of air-conditioned rooms.

"The next morning, duly revived, we swam in the hotel pool and were rowed to the Green Island of green trees which was remarkable in the otherwise brown desert of rock and shrub. Shortly before noon we departed, all of us having left behind a fraction of our weight but otherwise in good shape, especially Wong who liked the relaxation of really hot weather after the cool temperature of rainy-season Addis Ababa. Throughout the journey he had been wearing a thick woollen waistcoat and, to our surprise, kept it on even when we were in Massawa. Our stay proved that, even at midday in July, it is

Andreas in Gonder, 1960

possible to enjoy life at 33 degrees Centigrade in the shade. (If, of course, one is not working and can have frequent glasses of lemonade or tea).

"Returning to Asmara we took the road to Aksum, passing within sight of the Adwa Battlefield, site of Menilek's victory over the Italians in 1896. Aksum, though historically the centre of the Ethiopian Orthodox Church, turned out to be little more than a sleepy village. The magnificent towering obelisk and its smaller neighbours lie among overgrown weeds in a neglected square.

"The dramatic road from Aksum to Gonder—a ten hour journey—was one of the most memorable experiences of our tour. Though clouds often obscured distant views of the Simén mountain range leading up to the height of Mount Dashen (4,542 m.), we had our fill of ever-changing views as we wound our way up and down mountain sides, finally getting a glimpse of the Gonder castles from a distance.

Rita's diary continues:

"29 July: The sun is shining on the castles, which we can see out of the hotel window. A reddish brown, they are spread out below, overgrown with greenery, and set in a huge walled compound. Constructed by the early seventeenth century Emperor

Fasiladas and his successors, each building in a different style and gradually more elaborate, they bear testimony to a culturally important period of Ethiopian history.

"We knew the Mayor, Dr. Siyyum Gebre-Egziabher; he had been a teacher at the University College. Highly energetic, he introduced many innovations, including the publication of a local newspaper.

"Wong is staying with Dr. Han, a Chinese doctor and his wife, who had been in Gonder for nine years. Han is an employee of the World Health Organisation and Acting Head of the Gondar Health Training College which prepares sanitarians for preventive health in the villages. Under Chinese leadership teachers of eight nationalities are doing the training. In the evening we had a real 100% proper Chinese meal served by Dr. Han's wife in Chinese dress, in a house with furniture from Singapore, Chinese scrolls on the wall and dim lighting. There we were, with Ethiopian guests from the Health College, eating "instant veal" cooked in front of us on the table, and consumed with chopsticks operated with varying degrees of expertise.

"In Gondar we also saw Dr Otto Jäger, a learned German physician who was to publish a valuable guide book entitled *Antiquities of North Ethiopia* in 1965. He had been living in the city with his family for many years. When I entered, I found his house furnished in the best European tradition and a Beethoven piano concerto emanating from the gramophone. His Ethiopian assistant was in the process of copying the Jäger family tree onto parchment.

"The next day we saw the elegant pavilion of Emperor Fasiladas, an ingenious building in the middle of a basin which is still flooded at Epiphany with water from a nearby river through pipes installed centuries ago. We also visited the famous painted church of Debre Birhan Selassie up on a hill above the town, and surrounded by protective walls, like the castles. The often reproduced ceiling of large-eyed angels' heads is truly spectacular. From there we drove to the outskirts of the town, where we walked among, and saw the ruins of the great Queen Mentewab's church and palace."

At a later date, when again looking at the palace, Rita caught sight of a couple of tiny furry animals climbing in and out of the ruin. Never having seen any before she inquired as to their identity and was informed that they were hyraxes, who were related to elephants. She thought my informant was pulling her leg until someone else confirmed the bizarre relationship.

The diary continues:

"Next day we drove down to Gorgora on the northern side of Lake Tana, but did not venture into a *tanqwa*, or local reed boat, having been forewarned of the risk of bilharzia, endemic along the shore.

"Here we saw one of Ethiopia's greatest treasures: a pre-Gonder (i.e. pre-1636) Church, Debre Sina, round, of course, with thick wooden pillars held on a square roof frame. It was beautifully painted, but in a state of dilapidation and neglect. In another church an acolyte coolly told us that birds came in to eat the paintings; in this one the sanitarians had sprayed the church with DDT so efficiently that one whole wall of paintings had disappeared together with the bugs."

It has since been restored.

"With renewed pleasure, we drove back from Gondar along the Simén Mountain road, to Aksum, where we again spent the night at the comfortable government hotel. The next morning we set out for Adwa, this time visiting nearby Yeha. We had to wade across a marsh in gum boots, having taken the precaution to pack them, to see the ancient pre-Aksumite stone temple, the oldest standing structure in Ethiopia. There we marvelled at the precision with which the stone slabs had been cut and erected, so that the walls were still standing, well over twenty centuries later.

"Just beyond Adwa we took a secondary road to Adigrat to join the Asmara-Addis Ababa highway. This part of the journey was memorable for the stark Tigray mountain ranges and a swarm of locusts which banged against the car like hail. We saw farmers attempting hopelessly to limit their incursions by waving blankets at them. This was traditionally locust country and a locust control agency had been established in the area. Because of national and international initiatives locusts seem no longer to pose such a terrible threat to crops as in the past.

"Stopping at Inticho, we crossed a river, shoes in hand, to visit a famous painted rock church now called Cherqos. It was allegedly founded by Ezana, the fourth century king, believed to be the first Ethiopian monarch to accept Christianity. We held long negotiations with the monk in charge, before the key was produced, and our five Ethiopian dollar entrance fee was accepted. Like some Lalibela churches, Cherkos was hewn from the living rock, but was still attached to the mountain at the back.

"Driving south along the highway we reached Kwiha in the evening, greeting again the pleasant half-Italian manageress who had looked after us when we had spent the night there on our way north; she kept her promise to give us some plants we had not seen before.

"The next day we drove over formidable mountain ranges to Kombolcha, in the plain below Desé in readiness for the 500 km. spurt to Assab the next day. We crossed desert plains, following pleasant savannah country with umbrella acacias, monkeys, gazelles and partridges. In the low-lands, as we went down and down into the Danakil desert, we saw camels and even the odd ostrich. How people exist in that arid land is inexplicable.

"The villagers lived in poor shacks near rivers which were almost dry, though it was the rainy season. Luckily we did not suffer from the heat as the sky was overcast we arrived not completely roasted, for although this was the hottest season some wind made it feel cooler. Assab was visible first by the steel of the petrol storage tanks. We went directly to the beach and bathed, jumping over the waves. It was Andreas's first acquaintance with this sport.

"'We managed to sleep with the aid of electric fans, spurning the air-conditioned rooms costing an exorbitant 24 Ethiopian dollars each. After breakfast we visited the port, escorted by a local port official, a jolly cauliflower-eared Englishman from Bahrain who seemed perfectly happy with the local climate of over 90 degrees Farenheit. The port is being expanded by 90 Farenheit Yugoslav technicians, two of whom we watched inspecting the foundations of the new quay. The port official claimed that trade has not increased since, some years ago, the Ethiopian government accepted 50% interest in the railway to Jibuti. Freight rates consequently dropped and undercut the Assab-Addis Ababa route.

"On the way back we had the sun as companion, but, with a good supply of mineral water, we all survived, arriving in Kombolcha by moonlight. The last lap from there to Addis Ababa was uneventful except for the discovery of a first class lorry drivers' restaurant with excellent spaghetti for Richard, and the sighting of a baby leopard crossing the road in front of the car.

"We arrived in Addis Ababa on a Saturday afternoon, having set out on a Saturday morning fourteen days earlier. The city was rain-soaked, as it had been when we left, whereas on the journey we had had excellent weather, with only one convenient hailstorm which washed the dust off our car. Our companions were congenial— both Andreas, our interpreter, and Wong, our "dictator", and good humour prevailed throughout.

"We had covered 4,500 km. in our car, an average of 300 km. a day and returned without as much as a flat tire. We skipped over vast mountain ranges of over 3,000 m. and descended into the salt plains of the Danakil desert 12m below sea level; we went through a hail storm, where we needed our thick sweaters and warm slacks; and lost pounds at a temperature of 95 Farenheit or more in the shade. We climbed mountains, crossed rivers barefoot, swam, boated, and above all, drove; collected cacti, wild flowers, and Simén hats. We saw monuments of ancient and modern Ethiopia, obelisks, tombs, a rock church, castles, the field of the battle of Adwa and the sea port of Massawa." Our only misfortune was losing our new minicamera and thus a visual record of this journey.

Although driving in our own car reduced our opportunity to meet local people, it gave us an appreciation of the beauty and variety of Northern Ethiopia which none of us will forget. We visited Massawa again in June 1961, driving in a local bus to the old port of Adulis on the southern side of the bay. Iskinder Desta, brother of Hirut, and Commander of the Ethiopian Navy, invited us to lunch in the middle of preparations for the arrival of the Emperor, who was expected for the graduation of some naval cadets. We travelled back to Asmara by the Littorino, the famous Italian-built railway that groans slowly up to Asmara through hills and mountains—12 km. in four hours! Before leaving for Addis Ababa we renewed contact with the government librarian Ato Gebre Mikaél, and also took a local bus in a westerly direction to Ad Teklesan, to see more of the northwestern Eritrean countryside.

RICHARD

LALIBELA BY PLANE AND MULE

Our visit to Lalibela was a great experience and gave us a taste for going right off the main roads. It was an incongruous spectacle to land in an aeroplane, but on a strip of grass, find our bags in the "airport"—a small thorn tree—and mount the saddled mules waiting for us. As we had seen during shorter excursions into the countryside, people in remote areas were extremely kind and welcoming to strangers.

The party was cosmopolitan. It included an Irish peer with no conversation, Sir Harry Luke, an ex-colonial administrator, a few Greeks, Armenians and Italians, a Maltese judge, an Egyptian, and several Norwegians from the Economic Commission for Africa.

Rita found the three-hour mule ride not as painful, as we had been told to expect, perhaps because she walked part of the way up and the next day, down the mountain. However she was inconvenienced because she was unable to get her feet into the very narrow stirrups. We discovered later that, in former times, stirrups were held in place with the big toe, since shoes were not worn until the nineteenth century. Looking more carefully at earlier paintings we found that, indeed, riders had bare feet and toe stirrups. When we were in London in the nineteen eighties we learned that our neighbour, a prominent surgeon, collected stirrups. We were surprised to hear that he had never heard of toe stirrups, and so we promised to bring him a pair. To our consternation we could not find any, neither at shops selling ironware objects, nor in the market. When we were in Debre Birhan we thought we would surely be able to buy a pair, but none were to be had, and, furthermore, the blacksmith claimed he had never seen any. He kindly made some, following our instructions, and we brought them to our London neighbour. We realised that in Ethiopia, a mere twenty years later, people who could afford to ride mules or horses, had shoes.

We had come with Italian style food and tents for, at that time, there were no hotels for tourists in Lalibela. Since then at least a dozen have sprung up in a town which, like many other urban settlements, and especially tourist centres, has vastly expanded.

Rita wrote to her parents: "The churches are truly remarkable and very different one from another—some interesting for their paintings, others for their shape". I commented that the visit was memorable from the point of view of architecture, of the rock churches, melody of the priests' singing, and benevolence of the mules concerned.

ANKOBER, THE OLD CAPITAL OF SHEWA

In order to have more time in Ankober, we set off one Friday evening in March 1961 to cover the three hours to Debre Birhan. After a night in a simple inn there we set off for the six-hour journey to Ankober—6 hours to cover 58 km.—which gives an idea of the state of the road at that time. Several years had passed since it had last been repaired.

We arrived at three in the afternoon in new Ankober, which the Italians had built on the high plateau onto which we crawled with our Landrover, to descend a good 1500 feet to Sahle-Sillasé's—and later Menilek's—old capital. The view from the plateau over the huge Awash valley and mountains, many dark green with juniper forests, was impressive, even by Ethiopian standards. We much enjoyed the descent on foot (though the ascent at dusk was less easy going) to the various churches full of fine manuscripts, paintings and relics—and up again to the ruins of his palace on a steep hill of its own.

The traditions of former times were still alive and the school teachers took a keen interest in local history. They kindly offered us a school room to sleep in, which was doubly welcome because of the cold at that altitude (about 2815 metres). We were busy preparing our meal when in came a procession of servers with *injera* and *wet*, eggs, pancakes and all sorts of things, sent along by the Governor, who had been a Patriot during the Italian Occupation. We had a jolly evening with him and the school teachers. The next day we drove back at leisure, stopping to walk to the edge of the plateau whenever there was a view across the ranges of mountains in the distance. We got back in mid-afternoon, before a thunderstorm, which gave us a marvelous panorama of clouds, and luckily, the brunt of it missed us altogether.

On that, or perhaps another occasion, we were walking in the high mountains near Ankober, which were at times above the clouds, when I was accosted by a young Ethiopian schoolboy, who addressed me in quaint, but perfect English, saying, "My Lord, give me a sweet".

RITA

DEBRE MARKOS WITH ABBA JEROME

Later again, in March 1961, we journeyed north-westwards with Wong, who drove us in his car to visit the Blue Nile Gorge and Debre Markos. We invited the renowned octogenarian scholar, *Abba* Jerome to join us. "Octogenarian" gives completely the wrong idea, for he was as robust and active in mind and body as a man of fifty or less.

We duly took the Northern route over Intoto and the fertile plains interrupted by the gorges of the Blue Nile tributaries which stretch to the edge of Shewa province. After refreshments (of a somewhat alcoholic nature in the case of *Abba*) by a village called Goha Seyon (Dawn of Zion, or Jerusalem, as it was called) the great descent began along a rocky and tortuous road.

It was hard to imagine the magnitude of the gorge—its width, its different layers and colours of rock, its marble veins, its red and yellow sandstone cliffs, its granite blocks jutting out like tables, flat topped and rectangular. Leaving the area of eucalyptus and wild olive we passed on to a steppe of umbrella acacias and thorny bushes, down and down, the heat increasing all the time to a point where there were no more people— the haunt of lions only. Finally here was the last deep cut and there, in front of us was the Blue Nile—very muddy with no more blue in it than the Danube—spanned by a single bridge. It was the only one linking Shewa to the massifs of Gojjam, a province that had had its own kings and has shown traditionally a dislike for being ruled by any but their own people. We took a brief rest near the bridge, which was at about sea level. We had descended from 1,300 m. (not feet) to 400 m. Then, on the far side the climb began—an hour and a half of it to pull the Volksie up the 15 km. to the top. At times we had to get out and push her. Once we reached the level plains on the plateau nothing remained to remind us of the depths we had just crossed, with their totally different climate and vegetation.

We hurried through the Gojjam plains to reach the capital Debre Markos, before nightfall. The "Hotel" could not by any stretch of imagination be put in any classification of a guide-book but we had DDT, and our own sleeping bags and fell into the beds provided for us. It was Good Friday, the beginning of the very severe fast which the Ethiopians keep till the early hours of Sunday morning, but *Abba* coaxed some food out of them, as we did not have the energy to organise a meal out of the provisions we had brought with us. The innkeeper came from Tigray, so that *Abba* was able to speak to him in Tigriñā, and this made things much easier.

"Next morning we had a demonstration of *Abba's* charm as well as his mastery of public relations, when he took us to the great Markos Church, constructed in the 1880s on the orders of King Tekle-Haymanot of Gojjam. On arriving, we asked to speak with the chief priest. The latter officiously asked our permission (which we did not have) to enter the church. We did not come equipped with one, but *Abba*, not to be defeated, thereupon asked who but the priest himself could grant such permission. The priest, thus flattered, was fully mollified—and duly wrote out the required permission himself!

We admired the remarkable paintings of angels playing the drum and sistra sistrum which were echoed by the priests below, making exactly the same gestures as they sang, beating the drum and keeping time with the sistrum. Owing to *Abba's* charm we were even permitted to take photos. Both of us desisted but Wong who had become an intrepid and somewhat tiresome photographer, was very happy.

The town of Debre Markos stood inside a eucalyptus forest, like Addis Ababa, though when *Abba* had last been there in Italian times, in the 1930s, there had scarcely been any trees.

"We then paid our respects to the Governor, a youngish man who spoke good French. He and the local bishop were receiving deputations from the different churches, each group of priests colourfully robed under velvet and gold umbrellas. Fortunately for us he was called away urgently, and we were able to set out on a more leisurely return trip as we intended that day to go only as far as Goha Seyon, on the far side of the gorge. This time, with more experience of the road conditions, Richard did not have to push, though we had all fed him well beforehand to make him stronger. When we reached near the top we decided that the car should be stopped artificially so that Richard should not be deprived of the pleasure of pushing.

We spent the night at another "Hotel" where the lady of the house produced tolerable spaghetti on a charcoal brazier which warmed us well while the heavens poured down, mainly on the gorge which lay behind us. It was for fear of the rainy season that we had decided not to camp.

"DISCOVERY" OF LAKE LANGANO

Our 1961 European Christmas was spent, with Wong and Andreas, on one of the best camping trips ever. After a traditional egg and bacon breakfast by Lake Awasa, we met up with Belay Abbay. He and his new young wife, Nigist, were much in love with one another. Belay had just returned from an ECA mission to Ruanda Urundi.

We drove over to Lake Langano, which we had heard about but never visited. An expanse of sand coloured water stretched before us, as far as the eye could see. Peace and quiet reigned. There were no other visitors, let alone buildings, in sight. At that time Langano was not yet the pleasure ground of well-to-do Addis Ababa residents. There were no hotels, and camping was not yet fashionable. We walked along the shore, making pebbles skip over the calm surface of the Lake, while Belay spoke about Africa, where the winds of change were beginning to blow.

Driving through the Rift Valley on our way home we did not realise the extent to which Ethiopia was involved in a great transformation which was, by then, irreversible.

CHAPTER 8

Sylvia's Death

RICHARD & RITA

Sylvia's health was often of concern to us. She suffered from different pains at different times, including backaches and headaches, and we had a doctor from the Princess Sehay Hospital in several times, but she had great recuperative powers and recovered quickly. We would sometimes drive down to Bishoftu at the week-end, where the lower altitude and warmer climate was good for her. It was pointless to urge her not to work so hard, as work at all hours was, and remained, essential to her life. In April 1960 an x-ray revealed that she had developed a duodenal ulcer. The doctor prescribed a milky diet, which she in any case preferred. He informed us that the ulcer presented no great difficulties and could be healed with careful dieting. The main problem was that she ate too little. By April she felt slightly better and in May she was keeping to her diet and feeling well enough to consider, but decide against, joining us on a visit by Landrover to the south of Ethiopia.

That same month the BBC asked her to take part in a programme on George Lansbury, the British Labour politician who had supported the Suffragettes. She agreed, and, at the end of June we recorded her, and sent the tape to London by air mail. It was broadcast on 17 July of that year.

In mid-August she was quite well. We nevertheless connected an emergency alarm bell from her bed to our cook's quarters. She looked frail, but carried on relentlessly as usual.

On the Saturday of the long *Mesqel* week-end, of 1960, towards the end of September we were thinking of camping somewhere in the Rift Valley. Sylvia was feeling well—so much so that we suggested that she come with us, as she had often expressed the wish to go camping. We received an invitation from Lena and Siyyum Beqqele to travel with them in their new Opel Caravan car. Siyyum, the Ethiopian pharmacist educated in Scotland, had brought Lena to Ethiopia in 1958, and married her. Their new car could easily have accommodated five of us for the journey; at night, the two

Portrait of Sylvia, ca 1957

of them and Sylvia could have slept in it and the two of us were proposing to use our little tent.

At first Sylvia was inclined to accept, but then she remembered that she had two important appointments: one with Dr Ghose, the Indian anaesthetist at the Princess Sehay Hospital, on Monday for dinner to discuss the establishment of a Blood Bank and a supporting voluntary blood transfusion service, so that blood plasma would be available in all hospitals whenever needed; the other with Siniddu Gebru, the Ethiopian woman Parliamentarian, on Tuesday, to discuss the position of Ethiopian women in the new Civil Code. She was worried that the rights of women were not well safeguarded in this Code, which, being based on Swiss law, departed from the more liberal aspects of traditional Ethiopian law. However, she urged us to go.

We left early on Sunday morning. On Monday evening she used the bell we had installed to summon Askale, our cook. She called one of the Hospital doctors, who came immediately. Sylvia complained of pains in both arms and near the heart, but refused his advice to go to the Hospital. He stayed with her for two hours after which she said she felt better, but promised to come into Hospital the next morning. On Tuesday morning she rang the matron and told her that she felt better and did not need to go to Hospital, but at 1:30 p.m. she sent a note to say she was not well again. Another doctor came and diagnosed coronary thrombosis (which she had had before, severely, some eight years earlier). He gave her morphine in the presence of Princess Tenañ-ñe who had just arrived. Sylvia did not recognise her, and died peacefully at 4 p.m. on Tuesday, 27 September 1960. We arrived two hours later.

The news spread quickly. The Minister of the Pen, *Sehafe-Ti'izaz* Teferra-Werq, came with condolences from the Emperor, and asked where she should be interred. Richard thought that the best place would be with the Ethiopian Patriots, with whom she identified herself and who considered her one of themselves. Teferra-Werq, later informed us that the Emperor, agreeing to Richard's suggestion, had ordered that she be buried at the Sillasé, or Holy Trinity, Cathedral. Teferra-Werq asked for a list of our friends and said he would do the rest. By this time Afewerk, Habte-ab, and Lena and Siyyum had arrived in dark clothes, and other people followed.

Sylvia's coffin in the entrance to Trinity Cathedral, Addis Ababa, 28 September 1960

THE FUNERAL

The cortège set off from our house at 3:15 p.m. the next afternoon, and passed through the Princess Sehay Hospital compound, where nurses and doctors lined the way. It was a terrible moment, the sun shining on the white uniforms of the staff, the coffin on its last journey through the Hospital and the town.

The Emperor, Princess Tenañne and other members of the Imperial family, as well as innumerable old Ethiopian friends from the time of their exile, and many people who knew of her only by reputation, came for the service, which was quite brief, with the various priests intoning church chants. *Ras* Andargachew Mesay, the former Ethiopian Consul in Jibuti, who was mentioned earlier in this text, gave the Funeral Oration. He declared: "when a person or country is in trouble, friends become scarce", but "she came forward as a friend to the suffering and friendless people of Ethiopia during the dark period of the Italian Occupation. We consider her as Ethiopian." Though scarcely a believer she was duly buried at the Sillasé Cathedral. The name Sylvia being unknown to the Ethiopian Orthodox Church she was given that of Welette-Kristos, or Daughter of Christ. The place selected for the grave was immediately in front of the Cathedral. *Ras* Imru was subsequently buried nearby.

Wreaths were laid by the Emperor and Empress, the Crown Prince and Princess, Princess Tenañne and family, the Lord Mayor of Addis Ababa, Zewdé Gebre-Hiywot, with whom she had worked in England, Amdé-Mikaél Dessaleñ, Minister of Information, as well as the Ethiopian Patriots' Association, the Women's Welfare Work Association, the Ethiopia and Eritrea Unionist Association, the Social Service Society, the Ethiopian Red Cross Society, the Princess Sehay Memorial Hospital, the National Library, whose staff came to the funeral *en masse*, the Hayle-Sillasé Hospital, the Ethio-British Society, the four principal Ethiopian newspapers, the Tedla Bayru family, Afewerk Tekle, Siyyum and Lena Beqqele, Dr Ghose, the Doctors Reginald and Catherine Hamlyn, who later founded the Fistula Hospital, and finally, ourselves.

The Emperor laying a wreath at her grave

Shortly after the funeral the British Embassy's Chancery in Addis Ababa wrote to the Africa Department of the Foreign Office on 30 September reporting on the event. Recalling that the deceased had opposed British Government policy over Eritrea and Somaliland, the letter recorded that "a very large crowd, mostly Ethiopian, but also members of the European community was present at the Cathedral". The British Ambassador and the Consul were among the diplomats who attended. The text added that "as far as we know, no other foreigner had been similarly honoured".

In May 1961 Afewerk produced an elaborate design for a monument on Sylvia's grave, embodying scenes from her life. This was approved by the Emperor, but never executed. The grave-stone selected took the form of an open book with a stone bench on either side.

CONDOLENCES

Letters and telegrams of condolence meanwhile poured in from men and women who had known and worked with Sylvia over the years. Some of the oldest included Lord Pethick-Lawrence, the former Treasurer of the Women's Social and Political Union, who had, in 1946, been Secretary of State for India in 1946, at the time of Indian Independence; Norah Smyth, Sylvia's principal aide in the East End of London, and Frida Laski, Professor Laski's widow, who had also worked with her there; Charlotte Marsh and Grace Roe, two prominent Suffragettes, who had been in prison and forcibly fed; and Henry D. Harben, Treasurer of the First Suffrage Committee of 1913.

Other messages came from friends, who, like Sylvia, had supported Ethiopia at the time of the Fascist invasion. Among these were Philip Noel Baker, MP, who defended Ethiopia in the British House of Commons; Francis Beaufort-Palmer, a strong opponent of Appeasement; Gingold Dupré, a French friend of Ethiopia, who later became editor of the Addis Ababa newspaper, *L'Éthiopie d'Aujourd'hui*, and Dr J. B. Th. Hugenholtz, of the Dutch Reformed Church, a supporter of Ethiopia in the Netherlands; the African American, Mignon Ford, who later founded the Zennebe-Werq School in Addis Ababa, and the dedicated author Morris Mattavous.

Others long connected with Ethiopia, who sent letters of condolence, included Frank de Halpert, the Emperor's pre-war adviser on the abolition of slavery (who introduced us to each other at Toynbee Hall), and Clarissa Burgoyne, whose husband, Major Gerald Burgoyne, a Red Cross volunteer, was killed during the Italian invasion. Scholars interested in Ethiopia sending condolences included the veteran African American, W.E. Du Bois, one of the founders of Pan-Africanism, as well as Professor Marcel Cohen, Professor and Mrs Eward Ullendorff and Dr Otto Jäger.

Condolences from other parts of Africa included letters from Mohamed Osman Yassein, Permanent Under-Secretary in the Sudanese Ministry of Foreign Affairs, Mbiyu Koinange, Joseph Murumbi and Tom Mboya, all three Kenya African Union leaders, and the Ugandan nationalist, Semakula Mulumba. Letters also came from African students who had studied in Ethiopia: Omogi Calleb and G.H. Mwangi from Kenya, J.M. Kessi from Tanganyika, and Dennis Ejindu from Nigeria. From India came condolences from our journalist friend, Hari Chhabra, of the Indian Council for Africa, who had earlier told us much about Kenya and Uganda.

Further messages came from persons connected with the Princess Sehay Hospital: from its Director, Professor J. Le Fleming Burrow; from Princess Rosalie Viazemsky, Gordon Selfridge's daughter who had taken over from Sylvia as Hon. Secretary of its Hospital Council in London; from Mrs Ivy Tims, her devoted Secretary, who always helped in every way, and Elsa Fraenkel, an artist who organised an Exhibition of Sylvia's art at the French Institute in London. The Social Service Society was represented by the venerable German physician, Dr Yohann Otto, a member of its Executive Committee, and long-time resident in China, who had told us about Chiang Kai-shek, Mao Tse-tung and other leaders of that country whom he had known personally.

The largest number of messages came, however, from Ethiopians. In addition to members of the Imperial family, they included the following diplomats: *Lij* Indalkachew Mekonnin, Ethiopian Ambassador, and Efrem Tewolde-Medhen, former Ambassador, in Britain; and Ethiopian ambassadors in Germany: Girmachew Tekle Hawariat, France: Akale-Werq Habte-Weld, Yugoslavia: *Lij* Amha Aberra Kassa, Egypt: Engida Abbebe, Japan: Yohannis Redda-Igzy, and Pétros Sahlu, both Ministers in Mexico.

Messages also came from General Abiy Abbebe, the Emperor's Representative in Eritrea, Colonel Tamrat Yiggezu, Governor of Jimma, Kebbede Abosen, Mayor of Gonder, Idris M. Suleiman, former Director of the Handicraft School, Arefe-Ayné Abraham, Chairman, Ethio-British Society, Almaz Ayyele, President, International Women's Club of Addis Ababa, Hayle-ab Tedla, who had translated Richard's newspaper articles into Amharic; Gétachew Beqqele, a British-trained architect in Asmara, and Be'imnet Gebre-Amlak, both of the Marine Department.

Among her other friends there were innumerable messages from Ethiopians abroad. They included Mengistu Lemma, who happened to be in India, Tekle-Sadiq Mekuriya, and Tamrat Amanuél, in Jerusalem, and Zewdé Hayle-Mariyam, in the U.S.; and State Bank of Ethiopia officials Debbebe Habte-Yohannis and Mesfin Bellete, the one studying in London and the other managing a branch in Khartoum.

There was a letter from Sylvia's only surviving sister, Adela Pankhurst Walsh, from her home in Australia, and telegrams from Rita's parents and brother in London.

Richard's old time friends also sent messages. These included a sweet, odd letter from Louis Haber—in which he wrote that if more people in Britain had been like Sylvia, Britain "would have been a great country and would have had the affection of people like me" and Mehr Fardoonji, from India, who recalled her country's age-old saying, that "once born, death is inevitable", and added: "We, too, often forget this." There were also calls from many friends in England, including Richard's school friend, Basil Taylor, and his long-time Egyptian friend from university days, Salah Serafy. (*Ethiopia Observer,* Vol. V, No. 1)

COINCIDENCES AND REFLECTIONS

The date of Sylvia's death was the feast of *Mesqel*, or the Cross, and, by coincidence, the day when, exactly twelve years later, our son Alula, her first grandchild was born. This was not the only Ethiopian coincidence in her life; she was born in 1882, on 5 May— the day of the year on which Badoglio's Fascist armies occupied Addis Ababa in 1936, and the day, too, when the Emperor re-entered the capital in 1941. He, like Sylvia, was born in the year 1882.

Richard reflected as follows on Sylvia's death as it affected our future: "My mother's death was naturally a great blow, from which it took months, if not years, to recover. She had been our original link with Ethiopia. It was on her account that Rita and I originally came to the country, and it was largely her Ethiopian friends—and their children—who had become our first Ethiopian friends. It was, however, perhaps significant, looking back on it, that after her death, neither Rita nor I ever thought for a moment of leaving the country, even though we did not yet have a family, and neither of us had yet assumed positions of any prominence. Our involvement and loyalty to Ethiopia was beyond question."

However, the afore-mentioned British Chancery letter of 30 September complained that Richard taught "history of a strong anti-colonialist variety" which had "proved somewhat of an embarrassment to the Canadian Jesuits who run the [University] College, but attempts to have him removed have invariably been frustrated" by his mother.

The letter concluded optimistically: "It will be interesting to see whether Dr Pankhurst will survive now that his mother's protection has gone".

Richard wrote to Rita's father, her mother being in Switzerland at the time: "Our life here has been happy, though in retrospect one feels there is so much one could have done, and said, if one had realised that these were our last months, hours, with her. But

I suppose this is always so. In the hour of grief Rita and I feel the only thing is to push on as fast as possible: to complete what can be finished, to abandon what cannot be continued."

There followed a stream of visitors, mainly close friends. In between, we managed to wade through the sea of papers on her desk and despatch current business. It was amazing to find how many plans and projects were in her mind.

Richard sent a letter to the Emperor thanking him for coming to Sylvia's funeral, and expressing our desire to continue serving Ethiopia as she had done. He also mentioned Sylvia's idea to turn *Ras* Haylu's garden and swimming pool on the Ambo Road into a public recreation centre, as well as her hope that responsible Ethiopians could be persuaded to take an interest in refugees and students from other parts of Africa, by inviting them to their homes, to make them feel fully integrated in Ethiopian life.

RITA

The following Saturday we attended one of the Committees of the Social Service Society dealing with the Kolfé Rehabilitation Centre which Sylvia usually attended, to push on with her various plans there.

On Sunday, Richard was beginning to feel the loss at a deeper level and needed a lot of support. The following day we both resumed work, which made things easier. However he was still badly shaken, sleeping and eating little and working too hard. Occupying himself on a memorial issue of the *Observer* helped. Richard remained in a rather depressed state throughout October, a kind of second shock. It took him much longer to recover his spirits and normal high level of energy.

We noted that the obituaries in the British papers tended to concentrate on her political activities, at the expense of her humanitarian ones, which were the mainspring of her actions. I reflected that my father's tailor and my brother's barber both remembered her with devotion and affection, whereas the papers seemed rather cool. I wrote to my parents: "Why did she want votes for women or independence for Ethiopia? For reasons of justice and humanity, to improve the lot of the East End working women and the life of the Ethiopian peasantry."

Meanwhile Richard had come to the decision that he would continue the *Ethiopia Observer*, but as a quarterly, with longer, more scholarly articles. This proposal was welcomed by the Ethiopian Government.

We knew of a number of initiatives in which Sylvia was engaged, but was unable to complete. Among the plans for the Social Service Society was the establishment of a chain of playgrounds in different parts of the city to keep the children off the streets. Though the Society established one playground, it was not until the 1974 Revolution that such a plan was implemented, but was unfortunately thereafter abandoned.

Sylvia was also writing letters to raise funds for a new Maternity Wing of the Hospital in connection with its Maternity School and the training of district midwives. She hoped that a pilot home service by midwives could be started in one district of

Addis Ababa, to provide aid when serious cases developed. With the help of the British Ambassador, she was attempting to form a Hospital Fund-raising Committee in Addis Ababa and tried to establish one in London, with the participation of the Ethiopian Ambassador there.

ARCHIVES

Only three weeks after Sylvia's death the Institute for Social History in the Netherlands, which had earlier published an article of Richard's on early 19th century Socialist thought in its *Bulletin,* wrote, at the suggestion of his old LSE teacher, H.L. Beales, to ask Richard to donate Sylvia's papers to the Institute, in order to form a Sylvia Pankhurst archive. We were informed that the Dutch Embassy, conveniently located close to our house, was willing to transport the documents at its expense. This offer was particularly attractive in view of the abortive *Coup d'État* which had taken place in December, scarcely three months later, (see the next chapter) and seemed to threaten a period of instability. Richard accordingly gave the Institute his mother's papers dealing with questions prior to the Italo-Ethiopian war and the Appeasement Period—which he knew he would never use. He retained the post-1934 documents for use in a book he was planning. This material was subsequently taken to England, and provided much of the data for his book *Sylvia Pankhurst, Counsel for Ethiopia.* (Tsehai Publishers, 2003). The papers were deposited at the British Library later that year.

MEMORIALS

In 1999, the Library of Wortley Hall, the British Trade Union centre, outside Sheffield, was named after Sylvia, and a Sylvia Pankhurst lecture was inaugurated as an annual event held in that library. The lectures, sponsored by the National Assembly of Women, are organised by the Sylvia Pankhurst Memorial Committee, which has also been campaigning for a statue of Sylvia, designed by Ian Walters, to be erected in London. A plaque was placed on the site of her house in Charteris Road, Woodford, an earlier one having been unveiled at 120 Cheyne Walk, Chelsea, where she had lived when she first arrived in London. A garden in Woodford was named Pankhurst Green. A portrait of Sylvia, placed in the Mayor's Parlour of the London Borough of Redbridge, was unveiled by Rita. The 50th anniversary of Sylivia's death was commemorated by services in front of the Cathedral, where she was buried, as well as in Ethiopian Churches in the US, UK and elsewhere.

CHAPTER 9

The Abortive *Coup d'État*

RICHARD

THE CONTEXT

Looking back on those days immediately before my mother's death I recall that one sunny Sunday morning she received a friendly telephone call from Girmamé Niway, the American-educated intellectual who three months later was to be the driving spirit behind the abortive *Coup d'État* of 14-17 December 1960, in which he met his death. Rita and I at the time of that telephone call were somewhat exasperated that it went on and on, inordinately delaying lunch. Failing to eavesdrop, we have however to this day no idea what was the topic of conversation between the aging Englishwoman and the young Ethiopian returnee, both of whom had only a few more months to live.

Life in Ethiopia in those days before the Coup had been seemingly slow-moving. Progress had not been as fast as most of our friends hoped, but it was generally orderly, and by no means negligible. One has only to look at Ethiopian newspaper files for the years between 1941 and 1974 to see that new institutions were constantly being founded, and reforms promulgated. Listening to the proclamation issued by the leaders of the Coup, and the propaganda broadcast with it on the radio, we nevertheless felt that a challenging new era of Ethiopian history was underway, and that we would have to work even harder for the country's on-going renaissance.

TUESDAY 13 DECEMBER

We heard subsequently the next day, that, on the night of Tuesday, 13 December, when the Emperor was on a State visit to Brazil, officers of his Imperial Bodyguard had occupied the radio station, central bank, and the Ministry of Finance, and had also taken over other key points in the city. This move was opposed by the leadership of the Army, the Air Force and the Police, as well as the Church hierarchy.

WEDNESDAY 14 DECEMBER

I myself learnt of the Coup only on Wednesday morning, after Rita had gone to the Women's Conference mentioned below, and I had arrived at the University College to teach. Just inside the front gate, I was hailed by Édouard Trudeau, the Dean of Arts, a Canadian Jesuit. He told me with surprise, mixed, I believe, with a touch of admiration, that there had been a Coup, and that the UCAA students were going to demonstrate in its support—but that classes would be continuing as usual.

When I entered the lecture-room in the New Classroom Building, at about 9 a.m. I found, however, that the students were in no mood to study—given that armed members of the Imperial Bodyguard could be seen surrounding the campus. As I was reluctant to waste students' time, we agreed that I would give my lecture as usual, but that one of the students would take his notes while glancing out of the window—and that if he saw any movement on the part of the Bodyguard he would immediately tell us—so that we could watch too.

My class proceeded as usual that morning, but we heard that, at about midday, a prerecorded Proclamation by the Crown Prince was broadcast over the radio announcing that he had taken over the Government. In the afternoon groups of students met with the Coup leaders and gave them their support. In the evening there was a meeting of the University College Ethiopian student body who endorsed the support given earlier by some students, when approached by Colonel Mengistu Niway, Head of the Imperial Bodyguard. The scholarship students from other African countries met and decided, however, that these events were "the internal affairs of Ethiopia" and that they should take no part in them.

One story we were told at that time was that the young American social anthropologist Donald Levine was driving in the town on the first morning of the Coup, when he chanced to see a fellow graduate of Chicago University and mutual Ethiopian friend, Lemma Fré-Hiywet, whose cousins, the brothers Mengistu and Girmamé Niway, had organized the Coup. Lemma allegedly asked Donald what had happened, to which Levine replied, "Your cousin has just seized power."

THURSDAY 15 DECEMBER

The next morning, feeling that our house was far away from both the University College and the centre of the town, I insisted on driving in, much against Rita's advice, to assess the situation. Returning home, to her relief, I reported that everything seemed quiet. All the same, she went to stock up with candles and emergency food.

I was told that intense negotiations and mediation efforts were in progress. Meanwhile the students of the various colleges decided to organise a public demonstration the next day in support of the Coup and spent the evening and night preparing for it.

The British Embassy in Addis Ababa, like other diplomatic missions, had a system of district wardens to help them look after their nationals in times of emergency. Our warden duly phoned to inform us that we could take refuge in the Embassy but we declined to take advantage of the offer.

We were in our back garden, eating our lunch that afternoon, when we saw a small Volkswagen "beetle" slowly driving up the road, apparently heavily laden, towards a radio station some half a kilometre behind our house. Suddenly there was a small explosion, followed by machine-gun fire. We hastily ended our lunch, and retreated into the house. After a while the shooting stopped, but later that day fighting broke out between the Bodyguards, attacking from the North of Addis Ababa, and the Army established at its Headquarters near the railway to the south.

The previous day, an American woman with long experience in the Third World, had advised us that, whenever unrest threatened, the first thing to do was to rush to the bathroom and fill the bath with water. Rita did just that.

We found refuge at home in the long corridor between kitchen and sitting room, where we were protected by thick walls. Remembering World War II, we stuck scotch tape across the one window which overlooked the corridor, to prevent glass splinters flying in our direction, and placed sacks filled with earth outside nearby windows.

The shooting flared up again at dusk. We decided that we should prepare for a night in the corridor and assembled mattresses, cushions, blankets, food and water. We invited Askale and her family to join us. Soon afterwards shooting broke out in earnest. We did not get much sleep that night. The noise was so loud that we imagined that the capital must have been seriously damaged.

FRIDAY 16 DECEMBER

Driving into town in the morning I saw some evidence of destruction, though not as much as I expected. The University College's New Classroom Building has been hit by a shell, the signs of which were shortly afterwards removed.

A large UCAA student demonstration set out behind the national flag, processing round the sports field, carrying leaflets and banners and singing songs in support of the Coup. The students then moved through the centre of the town and southwards towards the First Army Division, but were dispersed peacefully, persuaded by their teachers not to confront well-armed soldiers. Last minute attempts to mediate among different military units continued, but by the evening it was clear that the coup supporters were losing ground.

SATURDAY 17 DECEMBER

The Coup collapsed on the Saturday. Eighteen of the Ministers and other important persons taken hostage at the beginning of the plot, and kept in the Green Salon of the Genete Li'ul Palace, were shot as the coup leaders retreated. That evening, the Emperor, having cut short his visit to Brazil, returned via Asmara to Addis Ababa, to find that many of his trusted officials had been killed. Among them were Mekonnin Habte-Weld, the Minister of Finance, and *Ras* Siyyum Mengasha, Governor of Tigray, both of whom figure in this memoir.

SUNDAY 18 DECEMBER

This day witnessed the funerals of the dignitaries killed in the Green Salon. Large numbers of people attended the mourning ceremonies at the homes of the deceased Ministers.

RITA

INTERNATIONAL LEAGUE OF THE RIGHTS OF MAN

I happened to have been asked by the International League of the Rights of Man *(sic)*—a women's organisation in the US, later known as the League for Human Rights—to represent them at the United Nations Economic Commission for Africa Conference on African Women and Economic Development. It opened on 12 December at the National Theatre—shortly before the Coup—and continued right through the momentous events referred to above. It was a colourful and significant gathering of each African country's most prominent women. Richard and I entertained a number of them to lunch before the Coup started. Some had met Sylvia in London in the old days, and we ourselves had met the chief delegate from Uganda, Mrs Kisosonkole, at an artist's house in Kampala. There came a judge from Madagascar, a newspaper editor from Tunisia, a lawyer from Ghana, a welfare officer from Zanzibar, a headmistress from Sierra Leone and many others, some highly educated and sophisticated, especially the North African women from the French territories, who looked like *Parisiennes*. Others looked more homely in local dress, particularly some ample mammies prominent in politics from West Africa. I learnt much about the economic situation of women in different parts of the continent, and the means by which improvements could be brought about.

On 14 December, the day the Proclamation about a *Coup d'État* was broadcast, the poor women struggled on valiantly with the Conference in a truly "manly" spirit and continued to do so throughout the following tumultuous days, though the Conference venue moved to the Hotel in which they were staying. I, too, attended most sessions despite the military presence in the streets.

The Conference ended on Saturday, 17 December. In the morning of the following day delegates were invited to the Jubilee Palace to pay their respects to the Emperor and take their leave. I was there as one of the participants, and when it came to my turn to shake hands, the Emperor, speaking, unusually for him, in English, asked, "Where is your husband?" When I told him that Richard was working at home, as was his wont, the Emperor asked whether it would be "convenient" for Richard to come to visit him on a specified day in the following week.

This caused us to wonder—in a society prone to gossip—whether by any chance Richard had been accused of having been somehow implicated in the Coup. Such fears were, however, groundless. When Richard duly visited the Emperor by appointment at the Jubilee Palace, it transpired that he had called Richard because, on account of the

Emperor's travels abroad, he had not seen Richard since Sylvia's death—and he wished to renew the condolences he had earlier expressed at the Cathedral.

THE AFTERMATH

On the way to the Palace Richard saw our friend Lemma, one hand chained to the ground. He seemed remarkably relaxed. We had heard that he was on the run and, without mentioning it to each other, we had both considered where he could be hidden, if need arose.

The time had come, after days of being *incommunicado*, to re-connect with our old friends. One of our first visits was to *Ras* Imru, who had been detained during the Coup, to congratulate him on his safe release. He responded by giving us an unexpectedly detailed—and objective—account of the events. Another early visit was to Sibhatu, our gardener friend, whose house had been in the area of fighting. We were glad to find him and his family unharmed.

After the Coup there was a forty-day period of mourning for the Ministers and others killed in the Green Salon. The Emperor made a speech on Christmas Eve urging people to work hard and promising to continue his policy of educational and other advancement. There was no Christmas reception at the Palace and there were no immediate appointments to replace those shot.

Philip Mansfield of the British Embassy, reflecting on the Coup, observed that the Embassy's contacts had previously been so limited to the Ethiopian aristocracy that, had the Coup succeeded, Embassy diplomats would have known no-one in the country's new Government.

After the end of the mourning period, on 26 February, trials of the Coup leaders opened, ending with "guilty" verdicts on 28 March. Mengistu was sentenced to execution and was hung beside the body of his brother Girmamé, who had killed himself in the fighting. We were shocked to see their hanging bodies publicly displayed.

A week before the verdict was announced the armed forces received substantial salary increases, that of a simple soldier rising form 26 Ethiopian dollars per month to about 40.

While the trial was in progress we had lunch with Professor Edward Hambro, sent by the International Commission of Jurists, as an observer. He was favouraby impressed with the fairness of the proceedings. Colin Legum had written to us to get in touch with "my friend Hambro" whom he had met at the Johannesburg Treason Trials. When we introduced ourselves, it turned out that he did not have the faintest recollection of Colin, but swore us to secrecy on this point. Colin, we assumed, wanted to put Hambro in touch with us, and to that end, invented the story of his "friendship" with him.

Less than two years after the Coup the Emperor suffered the loss of his wife, Empress Menen, and, two months later, his youngest son, Prince Sahle-Sillasé. He had been ill for some time and died 15 February 1962. It was pathetic to see the Emperor, Crown Prince, Princess Tenañne, her daughters, and other members of the family on foot, behind the gold and black hearse to Sillasé Cathedral, followed by a throng of officials and ladies, all on foot, and flanked by a troop of cavalry in scarlet and white uniforms on grey and white horses. The splendour and dignity of the occasion befitted the death of an empress who had held this title for over thirty years.

Although the Emperor died only twelve years after her, his coffin did not lie in the Cathedral alongside hers for almost forty years. Prince Sahle-Sillasé, the Emperor's youngest son, died some two months after his mother. A rather private person, he did not relish the ceremonial of the Imperial Court.

The Emperor had already lost his daughter, Princess Sehay, who had been educated in England and qualified as a nurse. While he was in exile in Britain, she interpreted for him on important occasions, and, with her eloquent turn of speech, acted as spokesperson in defence of Ethiopia on many occasions. Her death was a great blow to him. A further blow had been the unexpected death, in an accident, of his second and favourite son, Prince Mekonnin, in 1957.

With these deaths Hayle-Sillasé lost valued informal channels of communication with Ethiopian society and the world at large.

CHAPTER 10

Later Years

Our lives changed dramatically in the years which followed—as we hope to show in an ensuing volume. Both of us were inducted almost overnight into the fledgling administration of Hayle-Sillasé I, later Addis Ababa, University, and became members of the University Senate, where, to the general entertainment, we on occasion voted on opposite sides.

Richard, by this time Director of the newly established Institute of Ethiopian Studies, enjoyed the close collaboration of the Librarian and Museum Curator, Professor Chojnacki, whose earlier life has been touched upon in this volume. They were together responsible for developing the country's foremost Ethiopian research library and the internationally renowned ethnological-cum-art museum, both situated in the Emperor's former palace. They also jointly launched a number of publications, most notably the University-based *Journal of Ethiopian Studies,* of which they were the principal editors. All this had to be done on a minimal budget, and necessitated constant improvisation.

In 1963 the Institute organised the first International Conference of Ethiopian Studies ever to be held in the country. This gathering set the stage for an on-going series of international and inter-disciplinary conferences which continue to be held usually every three years to the present day. Though successful in bringing together the few handful of Ethiopicists scattered throughout the world, the Conference involved the Institute in now forgotten political and personal confrontations. These were also reflected in the operations of the Hayle-Sillasé I Prize Trust, which was instituted by the Emperor to recognize the achievements of Ethiopian and foreign scholars.

Rita, by then University Librarian and head of the Kennedy Library, the main University Library, was involved in gradually pulling together into a single system the previously disparate college and institute libraries. Until then each of these had been operating on a shoestring, in isolation, and without professional assistance. In view of the virtual absence of qualified Ethiopian librarians, she succeeded in using a generous grant from the Ford Foundation to employ several foreign professional cataloguers, while gradually wheedling from the University administration a number of scholarships to train Ethiopian graduates in library science. At the same time she taught in Library Science courses leading to an Education Faculty Diploma intended for teacher-librarians.

During this period she also published a notable article on the Ethiopian Emperor Tewodros's library of manuscripts at Maqdala, which appeared in 1974 in the *Bulletin of the School of Oriental and African Studies* of London University. This revealed the size of his collection and the extent of the loot seized by Robert Napier's forces in 1868.

***

Two years after the outbreak of the Ethiopian Revolution of 1974 Richard and Rita, for different reasons revealed in the sequel to this work, decided to return to Britain with their two children, Alula (twelve) and Helen (ten). Neither parent had resided in Europe for several decades. They had never used a washing machine or a dishwasher, nor were they familiar with the modern meaning of Mouse, let alone Apple.

Richard, whose office was now near London's Bond Street, and Rita, who worked in the East End of the city, found these localities very different from Addis Ababa's Siddist Kilo. They soon learnt that life in England had, in their absence, undergone a great transformation. To survive, they had to study the habits and customs of the British "natives"—and the way they maltreated the Queen's English as we knew it.

On returning to Britain, Richard was appointed a Research Fellow at both LSE and SOAS. In this period with an Ethiopian friend, Girma-Sillasé Asfaw, he edited Emperor Tewodros's tax documents, which had been looted from Maqdala in 1868. The resultant monograph was published by SOAS.

Richard later became Librarian of the venerable Royal Asiatic Society, established in the early 19th century to study the continent of Asia, which was considered to extend to the North-Eastern "Semitic" periphery of Africa. His presence at the Society led to an unexpected measure of Ethiopianization. Finding in the basement a large traditional Ethiopian painting of the Battle of Adwa he elevated it to adorn his office. The picture evoked varied interest among visitors, and was followed by the production of a video on paintings of the battle. Ethiopianization also found expression in the appointment of a scholarly Ethiopian care-taker, Haylé Larebo, then at an interval in his career.

While continuing to write for the Ethiopian Airlines magazine *Selamta* Richard completed his *Medical History of Ethiopia* and his *Social History of Ethiopia* and later wrote a two-volume *History of Ethiopian Towns.*

Rita meanwhile had been appointed Librarian of the City of London Polytechnic, subsequently elevated to university status, the first woman to head one of the 32 polytechnic libraries in Britain. She played a crucial role in persuading the reluctant Polytechnic to offer accommodation to the Fawcett Library, which was for various reasons unable to continue in existence. Ironically, this library had originally been assembled by the Fawcett Society, an organization which advocated a constitutional approach to women's suffrage, as opposed to that of the militant Suffragette group led by the Pankhurst family. This library in the course of time became internationally known as the Women's Library, the foremost library on women in the United Kingdom.

Richard and Rita's car sticker during the campaign for the return from Rome of the obelisk on Mussolini's orders, ca 1991

Through contact with Fawcett Society women Rita, to the bemused surprise of her husband, became a feminist and wrote occasional articles for women's publications. Gaining increasing interest in Ethiopian studies, she began to present papers to the International Conferences to which Richard had long contributed regularly. She also had the idea of holding a series of Conferences on the History of Ethiopian Art. The first of these still on-going gatherings was organized in London by the Royal Asiatic Society at the Warburg Institute, in 1986.

***

Richard returned to Addis Ababa in the autumn of 1987 and Rita, who took longer to disengage from her post at the Polytechnic followed several months later.

It was then that Richard conceived and launched the agitation for the return from Rome of the Aksum obelisk looted from Ethiopia in 1937. This resulted in the drawing up of petitions, committee meetings in an Addis Ababa tailor's shop, a procession round the Addis Ababa stadium, and colourful protests with Rastafarians outside the Italian Embassy in London, in which Rita was enthusiastically involved.

Richard and Rita, in the 80s, 90s and beyond, participated in the evolution of Ethiopian civil society. One or other of them was, and often were both, involved in the formation of a number of non-governmental organisations and were elected to their executive committees. Below we list these bodies and some of their achievements:

- SOFIES, the Society of Friends of the Institute of Ethiopian Studies, purchased what was to become the world's finest collection of Ethiopian icons, and began the successful campaign to build a new IES library.

Members of the Society of Friends of the Institute of Ethiopian Studies (SOFIES) and IES officials. Front row (right to left) Demeke, Debebe Habte-Yohannes, David Shin (former U.S. Ambassador to Ethiopia), his wife Judy, Yewoinshet Beshahwured, and Ahmed Zakaria. Others are: Ian Campell, Rita Pankhurst, Richard Pankhurst, Abdussamad Ahmad, Birhanu Gizzaw, Tekalign Gedamu, and Fikre-Mariam.

- AFROMET, the Association for the Return of Ethiopian Maqdala Treasures, repatriated looted Ethiopian artifacts, including Emperor Tewodros's amulet, and erected a monument of a canon in Addis Ababa's Tewodros Square to commemorate that monarch's commitment to technical innovation, albeit only in the military field.

- EHT, the Ethiopian Heritage Trust, advocated the preservation of Addis Ababa's historic buildings, and started the process of returning Intoto Forest, overgrown with imported eucalyptus, to its indigenous trees.

- The UWC (United World Colleges) Ethiopia National Committee, on which Rita was active and one-time chair, selected Ethiopian students from all parts of the country and prepared them for scholarships in other parts of the world.

- EGT, the Ethiopian Gemini Trust, later Foundation, of which Rita was a Board member, helped poor Ethiopian families with twins, by providing employment, education and health services.

Such were the some of our interests and concerns in which we continued to be involved for the rest of our lives.

Glossary

Abba	Father, used in reference to a priest, or churchman
Abun	Bishop, or archbishop
Annebabero	Layers of *Injera* spread with hot butter and *Awazé*
Awazé	Spicy paste containing *berberé*
Areqi	A distilled alcoholic spirit
Ato	Equivalent of Mr
Basha	Military title, derived from the Arabic *Pasha*, formerly given to the chief of the riflemen
Berberé	Mixture of spices, the main ingredient being dried red pepper.
Betam tinnish	"very small"
Begena	Large stringed musical instrument resembling a Lyre
Birr	Silver, and by extension, money, or a coin of that name
Bitwedded	"Beloved", a high government title, awarded to the "beloved" of the monarch
Blatténgéta	Title given to a scholarly or highly respected court official
Chat	*Catha edulis*, the narcotic known in Arabic as *qat*
Dejazmach	Government title, often held by a provincial ruler
Derg	Committee, a term used for the Military Government of the 1970s & 1980s
Fasika	Easter
Fitawrari	Title, originally given to a commander of the Advance Guard, but later to a Minister of War
Gari	Cart, Hindi loanword
Hakim	Doctor

Iddil	Fate, destiny
Immabét	Princess
Injera	Pancake-like bread
Inqutatash	New Year
Jan Hoy Méda	The King's Field
Joro	Ear
Kitfo	Raw meat, minced
Lij	Literally, "boy", a title usually given to a young man of high lineage
Mesqel	"Cross"; annual festival commemorating the discovery of the True Cross by Emperor Constantine's mother, Helena.
Neggadras	"Chief merchant"; head of customs; Minister of Trade
Nigus	King
Qebbelé	Local authority
Qiné	Poetry, usually religious
Qeññazmach	Governmental title, originally given to the army commander of the right wing
Qollo	Roasted grain, eaten as a snack
Qwulqwal	Prickly pear
Qutti	Tea made from dried coffee leaves, widely drunk in Harer
Ras	Head; highest government or military title after king
Sehafe-ti'izaz	Title given to a court secretary or chronicler
Shemma	Light cotton toga traditionally worn by many Ethiopians
Shum-shir	"Appoint-demote": process of allocating political office
Tabot	Holy Ark; altar slab
Tejj	Mead, or honey wine, traditionally drunk only by the nobility
Tella	Barley beer, traditionally drunk by persons of lower class
Timqet	Baptism; Epiphany
Tukul	Loan word for traditional hut, originally in Sudan
Wagshum	Title of the *Shum*, or ruler, of Wag and Lasta
Werq	Gold
Wet	Vegetable or meat stew eaten with *Injera*
Weyzero	Originally title of a noblewoman; now the equivalent of Mrs.
Zeyt	Oil

Index

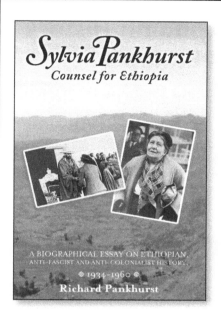

Sylvia Pankhurst
Counsel for Ethiopia

Richard Pankhurst

Book Information

ISBN: 0-9723172-3-6
Format: Paperback, 6" x 9", 228 pages, illustrations
Price: $19.95
Publication date: May 2003

About the Book:

Sylvia Pankhurst, the British Suffragette, devoted the last forty years of her life to fighting anti-fascism and supporting Ethiopia. She responded to Mussolini's invasion of the country in 1935 by founding a weekly newspaper called the New Times and Ethiopia News, which she edited for twenty years. Her paper condemned Britain's "appeasement" of the Axis Dictators, and supported the Republican Government in the Spanish Civil War. Ever against colonialism, she clashed with the British Government in demanding the full restoration of Ethiopian independence and advocated the "reunion" of the former Italian colony of Eritrea with Ethiopia.

Reviews:

"Based on unpublished correspondence from the last 25 years of Sylvia Pankhurst's life, this fascinating work offers unique insights into the final campaign of a great campaigning journalist."
—*Nicholas Rankin, author of Telegram from Guernica: the extraordinary life of George Steer, war correspondent.*

"A truly extraordinary and remarkable individual, the story of Sylvia Pankhurst stands as a human monument to the ideals of freedom and justice and fearlessness."
—*Robert A. Hill, Professor of History & Editor-in-Chief, The Marcus Garvey & UNIA Papers at UCLA*

About the Author:

Professor Richard Pankhurst, is Sylvia Pankhurst's only child, and was an adult throughout much of the period covered by this book. Using largely unpublished materials he traces his mother's opposition to Italian Fascism and advocacy of Ethiopian independence. The author, who bore witness to his mother's political activities on behalf of Ethiopia, and other victims of Fascism, is a historian of the country, in which he resides with his wife Rita.

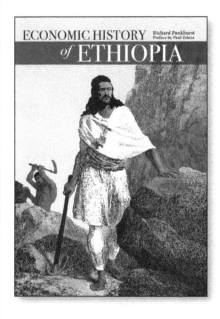

Economic History of Ethiopia

Richard Pankhurst
Preface by Paul Zeleza Ph.D.

Book Information
ISBN 13: 978-1-59907-055-1
Format: Paperback, 794 pages
Price: $54.95
Publication date: January 2013

About the Book:
The original pioneering text in African economic history holds its value with the second edition of *Economic History of Ethiopia* by Richard Pankhurst. This comprehensive title beams with intricate details and enlightening insights about the economic structures and practices in Ethiopian society in the nineteenth century, and provides a compelling platform for theories and conclusions to be drawn from. This second edition – the first printed in 1968 when African economic history was in it's inception – retains its value despite the dramatic changes and struggles over the past four decades. Pankhurst's novel is booming with data but also rich in description, and brought to life with beautiful illustrations. It is a competitive force in the field of African economic history and presents the key questions pressing today's writers of African economy.

Reviews:
"Unencumbered by faddish theorizing, [*Economic History of Ethiopia*] gives us a vast and intricate portrait of the Ethiopian economy and society, the political system that undergirded it, the prosaic activities that characterized it, the episodic watershed developments that transformed it, and the structures that sustained it."
—*Paul Zeleza, Ph.D., Dean of the Bellarmine College of Liberal Arts, LMU*

"Nothing remotely comparable has yet to appear for the equally important 1935-1975 period. Economic History remains a standard reference for those who wish to take a stab at such puzzles and conundrums as Ethiopia's continuing inability to produce a robust fiscal system that undergirds political order and economic security[...]"
—*Berhanu Abegaz, Professor of Economics, College of William and Mary*

Ethiopian Royal Chronicles

Edited by Richard Pankhurst

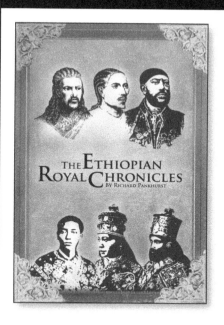

Book Information
ISBN 10: 1-59907-040-5
ISBN 13: 978-1-59907-040-7
Format: Paperback, 6"x 9," Index, 186 pages
Price: $24.95
Publication date: Fall 2011

About the Book:
Ethiopia's long established written language has given the country a unique position in Africa. Most importantly, it has provided modern readers with the opportunity to explore what life was like during the two thousand years of Ethiopia's recorded history. From the Aksumite Kingdom to the eventful reign of Haile Selassie, this compilation of first-hand chronicles offers an inside look at the life of an Ethiopian monarch. These excerpts also help to illuminate some of the more unchanging aspects of traditional Ethiopian life.

The Ethiopian Royal Chronicles serves a useful purpose by introducing the reader to the chronicles of Ethiopia, many of which have not been available in English before. Readers new to Ethiopian history will acquire an in-depth understanding of the changing character of the different dynasties as well as an appreciation for the cultural innovations that allowed for that history to be recorded and preserved.

Contents:

$\mathscr{T}sehai's$

Sharf-Pankhurst Series

Editors:
Frederic A. Sharf and Richard Pankhurst

Expedition from Abyssinia to Somaliland (1901)
ISBN: 978-1-59907-045-2

Expedition From The Sudan to Abyssinia (1899 – 1900)
ISBN: 978-1-59907-006-3

Expedition From Uganda to Abyssinia (1898)
ISBN: 1599070073

Ethiopia in Wartime (1941-1942) A Memoir by Brian F. Macdona
ISBN: 0974819824

Letters from Abyssinia: 1916 and 1917 by Major Hugh D. Pearson
ISBN: 0974819808

Abyssinia, 1867 - 1868: Artists on Campaign
ISBN: 0972317244

and MORE...

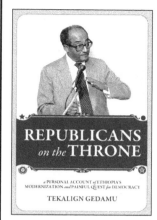
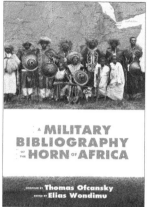
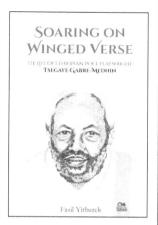

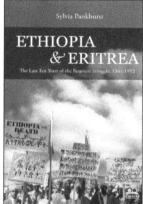

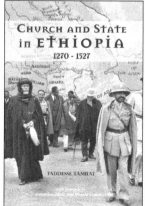